The Business of
Radio Broadcasting

by Edd Routt

Instructor in Station Administration at Southern Methodist
University; former executive assistant to the president,
McLendon Corporation; General Manager, KNOE, Monroe,
La., KIXZ, Amarillo, Texas, CKWW, Windsor, Ont.

TAB BOOKS
Blue Ridge Summit, Pa. 17214

Foreword

I have known Edd Routt for a very long time; he and I started off together in the radio business. That was in Palestine, Texas, in 1946. During the past twenty-five years, the business drew us apart at times; but, the mortal skein being what it is, we seem to always wind up together. And, as Winston Churchill said in his memorable speech to Congress during World War II, "England and America," like Edd and I, "have gone through a lot together." However much it pains me to acknowledge human indebtedness, I must admit that I am richer for my association with Edd.

He probably will not say it in this book...out of reservation and modesty...but I will say it. Edd loves radio, and he works hard at the business. Now, that may not seem like much for one man to say about another, but I believe it is a great deal. It is seldom these days that we find a man who loves something so much that he really works at it, really puts his heart and soul into it.

I realize that I am leaving out many of his other virtues, such as an innate kindness, a deep interest in other human beings of any race or belief, and a sense of unremitting loyalty; but if I go into all of these things, this introduction will sound more like a eulogy. I don't want it to because Edd is very much alive...I would prefer to say vibrant...and I believe we should deal with this book as the best living instrument on radio broadcasting that has been written. Edd is a great teacher. Now, about this book:

Unlike most of the very few good books on the business of broadcasting, this one does not hopelessly enmesh itself in theory and high generality. It is far more concerned with the practical aspects both of operating a radio station, as well as, with the advancement of an employee who may wish ultimately to become either a manager or licensee.

I have emphasized the word practical because, in the end, there is nothing very theoretical about an operating radio station, be it commercial, educational or eleemosynary in objective. All must assiduously seek their required funding for operational purposes, whether that money comes from advertisers, the state, or public-spirited citizens. No amount of theorizing will provide that operational capital. It comes only through action.

In our corporation, we have always believed that the very first part of that action must be in the field of programing. This book's grasp of that fact is evident on almost every page. Time and again--without exception--sucessful broadcast operators have proved that in order to survive and prosper financially, any radio station must provide a programing service of utility to a meaningful segment of the potential listening audience. Neither sales nor general administration nor engineering comes first. Programing does. The station failing to provide some service of unique programing utility to one or another reasonably large demographic element of the population is doomed.

The author's abiding belief in that fundamental principle of broadcasting is not surprising in view of his heterogeneous background in the industry: licensee, general manager, sales manager, sales executive, news director, newsman, announcer--your name it. In fact, I know of no man who has ever written a book on the subject of broadcasting who has had such a totally rounded foundation in the field. Through long and sometimes painful experience, he has learned and utilized, toward his own success, the fact that radio has undergone a complete metamorphosis since those halcyon days of the thirties and forties when it was merely enough to have a facility capable of transmitting a signal carrying almost any odd form of program fare.

But the book first leads its readers into the practicality of this programing theory with both thoroughness and gentleness. It recognizes, for many pages, that in order to seize an audience of any financially viable size, one must first recognize the practical limitations placed upon the programer by the frequency and power of the facility, by the Federal Communications Commission, by advertisers and their agencies, by the size of one's market and the radio dollars available therein, by the availability of qualified personnel,

The author deals with the 5- and 15-minute newscasts, with the technique of effectively communication, both with MOR formats versus contemporary, with program rates versus spot, with the duties of every station employee, and with virtually every operational phase of a radio station with which a serious student should find concern.

I have been in love with radio broadcasting since the dim days of the nineteen thirties when I used to spend Saturday afternoons listening to the great sports broadcasts of my boyhood idol, Ted Husing, and then spend the rest of the week driving around in my car attempting to emulate him. The romance that was radio in those days of Husing, Graham NcNamee, the Atwater Kent Hour, the Happiness Boys, Myrt and Marge, Stoopnagle and Budd, Jolson, Cantor, Jessel Benny and Allen--it has never left me. I am much too old now to fight the romance any longer.

Nonetheless, it was left to me and to others of my era to learn the business in the school of hard knocks. Many times, during those years, I wondered if there was a book somewhere, that would tell me something. But there was not. Radio was a jeolous industry.

Now here, finally, is the book. I wish I had written it.

Gordon McLendon

Acknowledgments

In the preparation of this text, the author drew mainly from his own experiences, observations, and studies over a period of 25 years in radio stations billing from $30,00 to $3,000,000 a year. The following publications, however, were used to background or bring the author up to date:

Kahn, Frank J. **Documents of American Broadcasting**. New York: Appleton-Century-Crofts, 1968.

Editors of BM-E Magazine. **Interpreting FCC Broadcast Rules & Regulations**. Blue Ridge Summit, Pa.: TAB BOOKS, 1968.

Etkin, Harry A. **AM-FM Broadcast Station Planning Guide**. Blue Ridge Summit, Pa.: TAB BOOKS, 1970.

Settel, Irving. **A Pictorial History of Radio**. New York: Grosset & Dunlap, 1960, 1967.

Broadcasting Yearbook, 1970, 1971, Washington, D.C.

Volumes I and III, **Rules & Regulations**, Federal Communications Commission.

In addition, counsel and guidance was kindly given by Glenn Callison, National Director of Engineering, McLendon Corporation; Rick Nease, Chief Engineer, KLIF; John Wheeler Barger, Station Manager, KRLD; Nathan Reeder, CPA, former Secretary-Treasurer, McLendon Corporation; Blair Radio, Radio Rep Firm with headquarters in New York and The National Association of Broadcasters. Mrs. Kitty Ruth Norwood, former instructor of English at Southern Methodist University, provided tremendous and indispensable help in editing and organization of the text. Dozens of other professional broadcasters, lawyers, and friends contributed material, ideas, and encouragement.

Contents

Preface

Radio broadcasting as a business has gradually evolved into a combination of management principles, pub relations, policies, legal interpretations, and federal politics. The purpose of this book is to integrate these concepts and to interpret the everyday operating problems of commercial radio stations for practical application in commercial radio stations of every class, regardless of operational or programing format, regardless of market size or appeal.

The student of radio broadcasting must recognize initially that the federal government holds considerable control over the day-to-day operations of radio stations. The degree of this control is a subject of controversy. Justin Miller, president of the National Association of Broadcasters in 1947, said, "The FCC's control over broadcasting climaxes a long series of steps toward star chamber government. The phrase, 'public interest,' is used by administrative crusaders as a hook upon which to hang many strange and devious notions."

Senator Wallace H. White, on the other hand, commented, "I never had supposed that there was the slightest question as to the right of the federal government to grant or refuse a license."

For the station owner, manager, program or news director, the controversial questions are academic. His problems are immediate. How does he solve them? How can he comply with government regulations, fulfill his obligation to serve the public interest, and also make of his station a profitable business?

James A. Noe, former Governor of Louisiana and licensee of five broadcast facilities in the state, declared waggishly that he should hire lawyers rather than broadcasters to manage his stations. Such drastic action, of course, was not taken; but the governor's remark does illustrate the industry's need for personnel who have, in addition to a professional understanding of station operations, a thorough knowlege of the permeating and overriding rules, regulations, and guidelines of the Federal Communications Commission.

The FCC derives its authority from the Communications Act of 1934, and most broadcasters agree that the Act itself is fairly clear. The Commision is authorized to control power and frequencies, as well it must. Many broadcasters, however, feel that this should be the limit of its influence over stations. But government officials, both elected and appointed, as well as some pioneer leaders of the industry, have felt that the radio spectrum belongs to the public and that the federal government has not only a right but an obligation to police station operations. Those sections of the Communications Act which refer to "public convenience, interest and necessity" lend themselves to broad and varied interpretation and, therefore, provide most of the debate ammunition.

Strong sentiment on both sides of the control issue was expressed in public hearings on the White-Wolverton Bill (S1333) in June, 1947. It was during these hearings that Senator White and Mr. Miller stated their contradicory arguments. Many other arguments developed at those hearings and are still quoted.

Any serious student of commercial broadcasting will recognize the necessity for early legislation regulating power and frequency. The first effort of Congress to control the country's new "miracle" communications medium was in the Wireless Ship Act of 1910. This measure was so weak that Secretary of Commerce Herbert Hoover found that he had virtually no control over licensees and their stations. Since then, broadcasters have been forced to study regulations, laws, amendments to laws, FCC guidelines, The Radio Act of 1927, the Federal Communications Act of 1934, the Blue Book, the 1960 Programming Policy Statement, the Mayflower Decision, the Fairness Doctrine, the Section 315 Primer, the Policy Statement of Comparative Broadcast Hearings, the Red Lion Case, the WHDH decision, questions on multiple ownership, the rise in strike applications, additional involvement of the FCC in daily programing, and literally hundreds of other miscellaneous court decisions and questions regarding newspaper ownership of broadcast properties.

A problem for today's broadcaster? Yes! He cannot operate his station for the sole purpose of making a profit on his investment. He hopes to improve the quality of his programing and thereby gain larger audiences; yet he cannot exercise uncontrolled creativity in programing. Both the commercial and program aspects of his operation must be in the public interest and must conform to all other FCC rules, regulations, and guidelines.

These restrictions make it vital, then, that the broadcaster find and train personnel in all departments to a high degree of skill. The integrity of every staffer must be beyond question. One improper remark on the air, one unscrupulous or legally naive manager, salesman, announcer, clerk, or engineer can cost the owner a heavy fine or the license to operate his station.

For years, station managers and owners have searched for young personnel trained in one or more of the station skills. Staff members traditionally are educated on the job or "pirated" from other stations. Neither method is entirely satisfactory. It is encouraging to note that more and more colleges and universities are developing staffs, campus stations, and curricula capable of producing professional broadcasters. Effective broadcasters must be professionals But the Communications Arts departments and colleges are hampered in their efforts because existing textbooks discuss inadequately, if at all, the day-to-day management problems of the average station. Most books on broadasting regard modern radio as a pure art form. The truth is that radio as an art form is dead.

There are many excellent textbooks on radio and television writing, direction, producing, newscasting, and other on-the-air techniques. Few of them, however, attempt to relate routine operations to the routine yet extraordinary requirements of the FCC.

This book was prepared from the point of view of the licensee or general manager because he is the broadcaster who must understand all the radio station management problems and their relationships to each other. All areas of station operations are discussed here, but major emphasis is placed upon the role of the FCC in daily operations, sales, administration, traffic, promotion, community relations, and the individual staff members. These problem areas often mean the difference between the success or failure of a station.

A detailed policy book written for use by the McLendon Stations, based upon the author's experience during twenty-five years in the business of radio broadcasting, provided the nucleus for this text. The earnest desire to pass this experience on to a new generation of broadcasting professionals led to the development of this book.

Edd Routt

CHAPTER 1
The Station
in the
Community

Like many of the world's orphans, radio broadcasting has been fostered by a multitude of parents. It issued from the creative genius and curiosity of scientists, inventors, tinkerers, politicians, promoters, and profit minded businessmen. Like Topsie, it just grew and ultimately was adopted by the Federal Government and put to work for the mutual benefit of producer and listener.

To those whose political bent favors a strong, central authority, the federal government does an inadequate job of controlling broadcast stations. Hard-line regulators have argued for many years that government must protect every aspect of **public ownership** of the airwaves. But to the softline regulator and the free entrepreneur who believe "that government is best that governs least," any government control of **our** radio station is offensive and often oppressive.

Such is the climate in which the Federal Communications Commission attempts to do its job of promoting broadcasting for the public's interest, convenience, and necessity, and of providing for the orderly development of all communication services.

DEVELOPMENT OF THE PUBLIC OWNERSHIP CONCEPT

The concept of **public ownership** of the airwaves was probably first established in 1922 at the first National Radio Conference, which was attended by electronics gear manufacturers, interested government officials, including Secretary of Commerce Herbert Hoover, and others concerned with the new wireless communications medium.
The first conference:

1. Established federal authority to control all transmitting stations except amateur and experimental.

2. Established that radio communication was to be considered a **public utility** and, as such, should be regulated by the federal government in the public interest.

Measures taken and resolutions passed at the conference

were based upon earlier thinking by broadcast pioneers that the new medium should belong to everyone. Secretary Hoover had declared that the country was on the threshhold of a new means of widespread communication which would have profound importance from the "point of view of public education and welfare." He felt that broadcasting should be supported by industry and **not by advertising.**

David Sarnoff, then vice-president and General Manager of RCA, felt radio contributed to the happiness of mankind and deserved to be rated with libraries, museums, and educational institutions. He advocated outright endowment of radio broadcasting by government. In 1916, Sarnoff, then working for the American Marconi Company in New York, wrote to his supervisors, "I have in mind a plan of development which would make radio a household utility."

Government's first official move into the new medium was in 1910 when the Wireless Ship Act was passed. This Act required simply that all ships carrying fifty or more persons must install equipment capable of sending and receiving messages over a distance of at least one hundred miles. At this point, there were no controls over land experimental stations, and frequencies belonged to the experimenter who was first and had the greatest signal strength. In August, 1912, Congress entered interstate communications by radio with an amendment to the Ship Act which provided that:

1. Every station be licensed.
2. Every operator be licensed.
3. Frequencies be more than 500 or less than 187.5 kilocycles.
4. Private stations not engaged in the communications business use a frequency of 1500 kilocycles.

The Secretary of Commerce had the responsibility of enforcing the Act which, it developed, was not enforceable. It was not until 1927 that the Federal Radio Commission was established to ride herd on the country's growing radio station population.

The greatest controversy during Congressional debates over what to do about the FRC and the Radio Act of 1927 was the so-called Wagner-Hatfield Amendment, offered on May 15, 1934, which required that 25 percent of facilities be allocated for religious, cultural, agricultural, cooperative, labor, and similar non-profit organizations. The amendment was rejected but not without a fight. Broadcasters were furious. They marshalled all available forces, declaring that the amendment would destroy the entire structure of American broadcasting.

President Franklin D. Roosevelt, in 1934, finally pushed through a new Communications Act which established the Federal Communications Commission. The Act gave broad powers to the Commission. However, like the Radio Act of 1927, it went no further toward providing the Commission with a standard to follow than to state that broadcasting should serve the "public interest, convenience, and necessity." This phrase conferred an almost unlimited area for administrative judgment and discretion. From the very beginning, the radio industry has been torn between the desires of government, the dreams of idealists, and the hopes of financiers. Clearly, the Congress has **wanted** to increase government control over broadcasters but has been held back by the First Amendment which guarantees freedom of speech. The FCC has **wanted** to increase control of broadcasters but has been unable to get Congressional authority for such action. And whenever Congress or the Commission made moves toward greater control, the hue and cry set up by broadcasters and their associations blocked all efforts.

But controls **have** grown since the days when the government could not even refuse an application for a broadcast license. Now, a license can be denied, for example, if a broadcaster is caught cheating in an audience contest. While **public ownership** of the airwaves was long in coming, not many modern licensees will seriously defend their operations as unadulterated parts of the free enterprise system. And any broadcaster who bows his neck and declares, "This is **my** station, and I'll run it as I please," is likely to find himself looking for a new investment.

Several volumes are required to contain the mass of FCC Rules and Regulations. In addition to these rules, usually clearly stated, there are so-called **guidelines** which indicate current Commission desires. Along with the rules, statutory requirements, the regulations, and the guidelines, there is what has come to be known as the "rule of the raised eyebrow," which usually is transmitted to the licensee by his Washington attorney who is adept at reading and understanding the official and unofficial meanings of spoken and written communications by Commissioners and staff members.

Example:

LICENSEE: What did the FCC say when you told them I don't want to provide free time to the Northern Association of Freedom Lovers to rebut the President's speech?

ATTORNEY: Well, I never did get a clear answer. But I talked to a young lawyer in the Secretary's office, and he raised his left eyebrow when I said you probably would not provide the group with free time.

LICENSEE: Then what did you say?

ATTORNEY: Nothing. I smiled, thanked him, and told him we had really just been kicking the thing around and that you would probably run the rebuttal and would, in fact, supply him with a copy of it.

LICENSEE: And what did he say then?

ATTORNEY: Nothing. He just smiled and said that would be nice. Now, my advice to you is to run the rebuttal and forward transcripts of the broadcast to me for the Commission's and my files.

Criteria of Evaluation

The licensee, then, is essentially a custodian of the frequency on which he operates his transmitter and once every three years the FCC takes a close look at his trusteeship. Has the licensee surveyed the service area to identify community problems? Has he paid particular attention to the needs, interests, and desires of minority groups in the area? Has he operated the station as a public trust? During the last year of a 3-year license period, the Commission issues a composite week upon which performance judgments will be made. A composite week is composed of a Monday in January, a Tuesday in March, a Wednesday in November, etc., until a seven-day week has been designated. The licensee, upon receipt of the composite week dates, must collect the indicated program logs for those dates and prepare an analysis of them. When a license is sought, the licensee promises to broadcast a certain number of hours and minutes of news, public affairs, and other kinds of programing. The Commission issues the license on the basis of the licensee's **proposed** programing. At renewal time, the Commission compares, through study of the logs of the composite week, the station's **performance** with its promises or proposals. Suppose, for example, that in his last application, the applicant proposed to broadcast:

News: 14 hours, 30 minutes
Public Affairs: 5 hours, 30 minutes
Other: 41 hours, 30 minutes

Then, after studying the program logs of the composite week, the licensee discovers:

1. He broadcast only 10 hours, 40 minutes of news.
2. He broadcast only 3 hours, 0 minutes of Public Affairs.
3. He broadcast only 1 hour of "Other" programing.

The broadcaster has a problem. He **must** explain, through various exhibits and to the complete satisfaction of the Commission, why he was short in all three of these non-entertainment categories. If he cannot explain the shortages, he is subject to a hearing which could result in (1) a short-term renewal while the Commission watches his performance closely or continues to study his activity during the current license period, or (2) the Commission's refusing to renew his license and declaring the frequency vacant.

The Commission has no specific rules for how much news a station must carry. It does not specify how much religious, agricultural, or public affairs programing a station must broadcast. Staff members may **suggest** to the licensee that he carry fourteen hours of news per week, but nowhere is it written that a station must carry some or no news. Therefore, a station must carry only what it **proposes** to carry when the licensee applies for a new facility or applies for a license renewal.

Example:

PROPOSED LICENSEE:
Mr. Washington Attorney, I want to operate my station with **no** news, **no** public affairs programing, and **no** religious programing. It is my opinion that what our town wants is a station that plays music twenty-four hours a day. Our people aren't interested in editorials, newscasts, long-winded forums, and round table discussions. What do you think?

WASHINGTON ATTORNEY:
You'll never get the license. The Commission doesn't specify how much non-entertainment programing you must carry, but **I know those guys.** A fellow in Scranton tried the same thing and was lucky to get his application acknowledged, much less processed. And don't argue that your community wants wall-to-wall music unless you've got an exhaustive, totally substantiated community survey to back you up. It's my opinion that, even with such a survey, you won't get the license.

If you had a unique programing idea, such as broadcasting nothing but classified ads, the Commission might give you a short-term license to try it. But the idea of music twenty-four hours a day is not unique, and my advice is for you to forget it.

Remember, the Commission looks at your radio station...even though you own the building, grounds, and equipment, as operating on **public airwaves**. You **must** operate according to what the Commission calls in the "public interest, convenience, and necessity." You **must** meet what the Commission regards as "public needs, tastes, and desires." You might have a chance if you decided to broadcast only classical music, but you'll never get away with your proposal to broadcast only rock-and-roll music.

NON-ENTERTAINMENT PROGRAMING

The Commission has evidenced relatively little concern over a licensee's entertainment programing. It is in the area of non-entertainment that extraordinary performance is expected. Commission rules specify eight program categories: Agriculture, Entertainment, News, Public Affairs, Religion, Instruction, Sports, and Other. The total of these eight categories must equal 100 percent of the programing.

The Commission also has three additional sub-categories: Editorial, Political, and Educational Institution Programs. These are supplemental classifications for specific programs. All programs must first fall into one of the eight categories. In addition, some also have the secondary classification in one or more of the three sub-categories.

Non-Entertainment programing excludes the categories, Entertainment and Sports, and includes **only** News, Public Affairs, Agriculture, Religion, and Instruction, and the sub-categories, Editorial, Political, and Educational Institution programs.

News includes reports dealing with current local, national, and international events. It also includes weather and stock market reports. If commentary and analysis or sports news are an integral part of a news program, they should be classified as News. Therefore, unless they constitute separate programs, commentary, analysis and sports are combined with hard news; and the entire program is classified as News. Separate sports news broadcasts are **not** classified as News. Separate news commentaries and analysis programs are classified as Public Affairs. A mobile news report from the scene of an accident may also be classified as News if it is properly logged. Stations which emphasize local news provide not only a greater actual public service, but also find that the Commission staff has a special interest in the programing. The ideal news staff includes newscasters and outside mobile reporters. The use of mobile two-way radio-equipped vehicles is desirable in many markets, but certainly is not necessary for effective coverage of the daily news.

Public Affairs includes talks, commentaries, discussions, speeches, editorials, political programs, documentaries, forums, panels, round tables, and similar programs concerning local, national, and international affairs. No distinction between "discussion" and "talk" programs is required. The Public Affairs category is limited to local, national, and international public affairs. Safety messages, school openings and closings, and "community calendar" programs provide a public service, but they are not Public Affairs, according to the FCC definition.

When a Senator or other government official broadcasts a report of his activities, the program is clearly Public Affairs unless he is campaigning for re-election. A telephone talk program which permits public discussion of current events is clearly a Public Affairs Program. A problem arises, however, when a minister devotes his entire religious program to a discussion of local politics. The licensee must then decide whether the program is Public Affairs or Religion. Regardless of how the program is classified, if the minister attacks anyone during his broadcast, the Fairness Doctrine requires that the "victim" be notified and offered equal air time to reply.

Although some Washington attorneys are reluctant to classify a **one minute** editorial as a Public Affairs program, there have been cases where the Commission accepted such classification. Some attorneys argue that a one-minute editorial is not a program, that nothing under two or three minutes should be so classified. Others argue that a strong one-minute editorial is a better Public Affairs Program than a weak five-minute discussion of the U.S. Foreign Policy. It has not been established by the Commission that a one-minute editorial is not a one-minute Public Affairs Program. It depends, apparently, upon a particular attorney's interpretation of a particular member of the Commission staff.

There are two occasions when the broadcaster must deal with other types of programing. The first is on the daily program log. After he has indicated every type, from News (N) and Public Affairs (PA) to Religion (R) and Agriculture (A), those programs that do not fall under a specific category are typed as "other." For example, a station might have an elaborate "sign on" and "sign off" where a full five minutes are used to identify the station and open or close the day's programing with music. Another example of "other" type programing is a monologue on women's fashions or, perhaps, a horoscope program.

The other case is when the broadcaster is completing Section IV-A of the FCC's license renewal application (Form 303) or the application for a Construction Permit (Form 301). Then, the Commission requires that all non-entertainment programing be classified as News, Public Affairs, or "other" types of material. In this case, "other" types means everything in the non-entertainment category except News and Public Affairs. For example, in determining total "other" types of programing for a license renewal application, the operator combines Agriculture, Religion, Educational, Instructional, and "other."

When a station licensee has proposed to run certain non-enterainment programs, it is critically important that the programs be aired consistently. If the County Agent's weekly five-minute broadcast is cancelled because the Agent decides he doesn't have time to prepare the material, the licensee should take immediate steps to replace the program with one of a similar type. He might, for example, offer the time to the director of the local office of Future Farmers of America.

In establishing a schedule of non-entertainment programing, the licensee should be very careful to show that his community needs the kind of material he plans to broadcast; and he should be prepared to support his proposed programing with extensive community surveys.

PUBLIC SERVICE ANNOUNCEMENTS

There are several ways to satisfy the PSA (Public Service Announcement) commitment, some of which enhance the station's position in the community, while others help, or at least do not hurt, the total station sound. The FCC requires that the applicant indicate the number of PSA units to be broadcast. The length of the announcements and the time periods in which they will be run are not indicated. Therefore, the announcements may be tailored to any length.

One of the oldest and best known techniques for handling a multitude of PSA's is the Community Bulletin Board. This may be a three- or five-minute program containing one or many Public Service Announcements. With this format, credit may be taken for five Public Service Announcements in each single program.

COMMUNITY BULLETIN BOARD

Boy Scout Encampment
Red Cross Board Meeting
P.T.A. Picnic
Boys' Baseball Tryouts
Veterans Administration

It is essential that stations appoint a Public Service Director. In most cases, particularly in small stations, the PS Director is assigned other duties. In larger stations, he may occupy a full-time slot. The Public Service Director may also be known as the Director of Public Affairs, Director of Community Relations, or some other title; but regardless of title, regardless of whether the position is full-time or part-time, the responsibility is basically the same.

In the past, most stations have assumed a passive attitude toward development of Public Service Announcements. For example, when the president of the P.T.A. called and wanted free time, the part-time Public Service Director talked with her and arranged to get the material on the air. In recent years, in an effort to set up greater protection for the license, stations have taken affirmative steps to conduct Public Service campaigns. The newer procedure calls for the Public Service Director, full or part-time, to go after PSA's much as the sales department goes after commercial spot units. It is not uncommon for the PS Director to call or visit Mrs. Jones, president of the local P.T.A., and ask for information to put on the air. Not only does this draw greater interest from the FCC, but it also builds friends for the station.

The McLendon stations, one of the largest independent chains in the country, have, in most cases, full-time or part-time Public Service Directors although this specific title is not necessarily used. The technique is to concentrate on twenty- and thirty-second announcements delivered by someone representing the receiving agency. Mrs. Jones, president of the local P.T.A., is contacted, for instance, and asked to come to the station to personally record the PS message. In most cases, although the voices certainly are not professional, the total sound is enhanced by the "different" and often more believable voice. Even when the voice is unpleasant, most broadcasters will agree that the brevity of the message precludes the possibility of serious format damage.

Many stations use canned PSA's sent in by agencies which employ professional production companies, or the station

PUBLIC SERVICE CAMPAIGN RESUME

Station(s) ___KXXX___   City: _Ourtown_

Client/Organization: ___Ourtown Lions Club___

Address: ___1718 Main St.___

City: ___Ourtown___

Phone: _239-7766_   Contact: _Bill Williams, Pub. Chm._

Start Date: _July 5_   Stop Date: _July 12_   Number of Spots: _40_

OBJECTIVE OF CAMPAIGN: _To raise $1000 to purchase eyeglasses for indigent children in North Side Slums through sale of tickets to Spaghetti Supper_

Spots voiced by (Give position within campaign and local business affilation, if any):

John Astor, Campaign Chairman

COMMENTS: _Station KXXX provided most of the media support for Campaign, - over 600 persons purchased meals @ $3.00, Campaign very successful._

_William A. _____
Public Service Director

Fig. 1. Public Service Campaign Resume.

production department prepares and records local material for airing. One effective technique is the combination of a national PSA production spot with the voice of the local representative. For example, the Post Office Department might provide the station with a quality jingle that includes a thirty-second musical "bed" suitable for the insertion of a local voice. The local Postmaster may voice the insert, identifying himself and the station.

Example:

Jingle Open

POSTMASTER: This is Jim Smith, Ourtown Postmaster, reminding you to mail Christmas packages early this year.

Jingle Close

Through this plan, the benefits of a professional, well produced jingle, combined with the voice of the Postmaster, give the announcement a local flavor. When non-professional voices are used to record PSA's, the announcements should be as brief as possible. Nothing damages station sound more than a sixty-second PSA voiced by a rank, and often boresome, amateur.

Some stations find it beneficial to prepare regular billing invoices on PSA's and mail them to the receiving agency marked "paid." This is an acceptable method of keeping track of PSA's, and it identifies the service performed, not only in terms of units run, but also in terms of the dollar value of the time donated. It is more meaningful to the Commission to receive an identification of Public Service **campaigns,** in which a schedule of announcements is run to accomplish a specific goal, than to note a random schedule of miscellaneous PSA's. Although the renewal form itself does not require details of PSA's which have been aired, there is ample room to expand on the Public Service effort in one or more of the exhibits which must accompany the application for license renewal. A resume record of significant campaigns is helpful at license renewal time. Fig. 1 is a sample format.

PUBLIC SERVICE IN SINGLE AND MULTI-STATION MARKETS

There are a great many format differences between the Public Service effort of the number one station in Chicago and the only station in Rayville, Louisiana. The Chicago station must provide a specified amount of Public Service, including the airing of PSA's; but to retain its number one position in the market and protect its financial flanks, it must beware of amateur production and poor placement of programs or of PSA's. If the station included a fifteen-minute report from the Mayor every week, it would be imprudent to place the program at 8:15 A.M. on Wednesday. It would be better, for example, to run the program on Sunday afternoon where it would do less damage to the important weekday audience ratings.

Historically, America's radio listeners would rather be entertained than informed. Fifteen minutes of talk from any government official (except perhaps the President) on Station A invariably causes a mass switching of dials to Station B which provides entertainment. Most advertisers buy Monday through Friday commercial schedules, and many of the buys are based upon weekday ratings. Any programing that tends to weaken ratings, Public Service or otherwise, is commercially destructive.

It is possible to produce Public Service Announcements and Public Affairs programing that do a public service and also enhance rather than damage a station's audience ratings. The telephone talk show is one of the more notable examples. These programs are broadcast in virtually every major market in the country; and some of them outrate, in total audience, solid contemporary music. These programs give listeners a chance to express themselves and to, in fact, argue a point of view. The Commission accepts these as Public Affairs programing because, in most cases, the subjects discussed are of general public interest. Most such shows use a delay-tape cartidge system to avoid the risk of profanity being aired.

In a major market (a trade area of one million or more population), the quantity of Public Service and Public Affairs programing is less important than how well the programing is done and how it is scheduled during the broadcast day. Regardless of what the licensee and the Commission want, some consideration must be given to the station's competitive position in the market. Even the Commission does not like to see a licensee fail financially.

In the single station or non-competitive market, the licensee is freer to program Public Service and Public Affairs material and, indeed, must program more of it if he happens to operate the only information medium in the market. In markets where the only newspaper is a weekly, usually with no wire service, and in one where the market will support only one radio station, the station occupies an unusually important position. The citizens depend upon the local radio station for timely news, market and weather reports, and other non-entertainment or informational programing.

It is simple for the licensee to determine the needs of a small market. In a farm community with a population of only three or four thousand, the program might include a variety of music as well as programs from the County Agent, a Future Farmer of America, Home Demonstration Agent, and a solid 6:00 A.M. to 12:00 noon "block" of religious material on Sunday. The 6:00 to 9:00 A.M. Monday through Friday block might contain a five-minute devotional, a ten-minute program furnished by the Home Demonstration Agent, Standard Pop Music, several Community Bulletin Boards, a Woman's News program, and the usual hourly or half-hourly news reports.

In small markets, station personnel are more intimately known by local citizens and, because they are "with our radio station," are expected to participate in or furnish leadership for community affairs. There is no rule relating to the degree of participation in community life by the station or station staff members. Competition and economics, more often than FCC guidelines or raised eyebrows, determine a station's community activity.

If the manager of the leading local department store asks the manager of the local radio station to join and become active in the Lions Club, the manager's sales instinct, if not his interest in the community, compels him to join and participate enthusiastically. When there are two or more stations in the community, the manager or licensee has virtually no choice but to participate deeply in community affairs, assuming that one of his motives is to make profits.

In the small market, management can afford to sacrifice program quality in order to program to public needs, tastes, and interests. The licensee can afford to train local high school teenagers as disc jockeys for the afternoon 3:00 to 6:00 Rock 'n Roll Show. The manager of the number one station in Chicago, San Francisco, or Detroit would be insane to hire beginners for air shows. Audience, ratings, revenue, and, consequently, the station's ability to perform any service for anyone would be sacrificed.

KNOWING THE COMMUNITY

The Commission requires that broadcasters conduct frequent surveys of community problems and then develop programing that will meet, aid in meeting, be responsive to, or stimulate the solution of those problems. In the early and mid-50s, broadcasters knew about community surveys but made no more than a token effort to make them. In a classic case, McLendon made what was considered a routine and acceptable survey in an effort to purchase WCAM in Camden, New Jersey. The Commission ordered a hearing on the application to determine (1) whether McLendon had trafficked in radio stations and (2) whether he had, indeed, surveyed the market. McLendon's Washington attorneys believed that the main issue dealt with the charge of trafficking. McLendon, a devoted, life-long, and professional broadcaster, was astonished at the accusation and proceeded to deal promptly with the charge, of which he was later cleared. However, at the hearing, the attorney for the Commission paid unexpected attention to the routine survey that had been conducted in the Camden and Philadelphia markets and charged that McLendon had made no significant effort to actually determine the needs of the market of license, Camden. Subsequently, McLendon's application to buy the station was denied by the Commission.

Shortly thereafter, the Commission began to spell out in considerable detail what it wanted in community surveys. Licensees and Washington attorneys received massive interpretatives of the Commission's policies, guidelines, and raised eyebrows.

After the Camden affair, McLendon established new corporate policies dealing with community surveys. When he applied for a power increase for KNUS (FM) Dallas, he sent station executives and other personnel into Dallas and several surrounding communities to interview three hundred persons. The objective was to talk with as many different echelons of human life as possible. A certain percentage were Blacks, another Latin American. Of these, certain percentages were teenagers, the remainder between 20 and 60 years old. He was careful to see that people on the street were interviewed, as well as those persons classified as community leaders, such as the Mayor, city councilmen, club presidents, and bankers. Housewives, salesmen, file clerks, typists, nurses, and law students were interviewed.

In the days when no one paid much attention to the surveys, the interviewer simply asked the interviewee what he believed the community needed in the way of a new or changed radio station.

Example: Don't you think 5-minute newscasts are better than those long, dreary 15-minute newscasts?

                  Yes, of course, I hate those long, dreary 15-minute newscasts.

In the new directives, the approach was completely changed and McLendon was among the first to admit that the change was for the good. The new idea was not to ask a citizen how to program the station. The citizen survey could be useful, it was determined, only by helping the broadcaster understand community needs. Under the new plan, the licensee is expected to determine, through exhaustive surveys, community problems. Then, the Commission wants the licensee to show precisely and in detail exactly what he did or proposes to do to solve those problems.

If KXXX determined through its survey that grade school children were not getting hot lunches at school, the station might launch an editorial campaign demanding that the school board solve the problem. In this way, the station actually uses its facilities to help solve a community problem.

If KXXX learned that a group of parents were irate over the design of a proposed new school building, the station could set up a round table discussion between adversaries. It could editorially join one side or the other, making certain that the other side was given equal time.

In essence, the Commission has said, FIND OUT WHAT COMMUNITY PROBLEMS EXIST AND SEE WHAT YOU CAN DO TO HELP SOLVE THEM. And the broadcaster who doesn't do this will surely be subject to a strike application or a hearing the next time he applies for license renewal.

The Commission wants the licensee to be commercially successful, but it demands a high degree of public service. Some licensees have felt they could not succeed financially if they did everything the Commission asked. But under the constant threat of license revocation, most have learned they can perform a public service and at the same time maintain a sound business operation.

Students might consider conducting a meaningful general public survey and present results of it to community broadcasters. A class of 15 or 20 students, with a viable plan, could easily interview 500 persons in all walks of life.

After the survey is completed, the students might suggest ways in which the licensee could help solve the problems ascertained in the survey. This kind of field work can give the student a real head start in broadcasting because he will know how to perform a valuable task. (See Survey Forms, Chapter VI).

Continuing Community Survey

The licensee should, during the three-year license period, conduct at least two major surveys. Some stations require two surveys per year to determine whether the station is keeping abreast of community developments. But in the periods between surveys, the station staff should conduct a continuing public survey. This may be handled by all members of the station staff who have contact with the public.

For example, the switchboard operator, or person regularly answering the station's telephones, frequently receives complaints and praise on station programing and on conditions in the community. Members of the sales staff, of course, are acquainted with the business community and are, therefore, the richest source of information on community leader thinking. Each person on the staff should be given a supply of forms on which to report his converstions.

In another case, a time buyer might remark that bus service in the city is inefficient. A salesman would record this report and place it in the Continuing Community Survey File, which should be reviewed periodically by management. An appliance store clerk might suggest that the city doesn't have enough parks. Other citizens may complain about garbage pickup, inadequate city power, excessive utility rates, too many or too few laws dealing with everything from lease laws to control of fireworks. Each year, a station receives dozens of valid complaints from competent citizens about city problems. The progressive licensee should be able to report to the Commission that he is continually interested in community problems and development and that he has helped to solve some of the problems.

Some Washington attorneys argue that the Commission merely insists that only broadcast facilities be used to help with community development. Others contend that station management and staff involvement in community life are essential to the licensees' understanding of, and interest in, the community.

The station whose staffers belong to the Lions Club, work with the Red Cross, function as auxiliary firemen and policemen, and attend church regularly, is sometimes said to be "in tune with the community." Certainly this is true. Such participation not only indicates that the station is performing its proposed public service, but also tends to ingratiate the station in the business community and therefore improve sales.

Example:

SALESMAN:	Morning, Bill. Boy, that was a great Jaycee meeting last night. That clean-up campaign on the North side of town will really be something.
BUYER:	Right, Joe. By the way, what's the station going to do on this? Sure hope you can get behind it.
SALESMAN:	No problem. I talked with the manager this morning and he's agreed to support us editorially as well as with Public Service Announcements asking for the extra manpower we'll need.
BUYER:	Great! Knew we could count on you. By the way, I spoke to my manager this morning and he's approved that proposed schedule you left with us last week. I told him we could always count on you to help with local problems and that, even if you couldn't do a good job in advertising, you deserve the order. However, I know you reach our market, and the manager completely agreed with me.

Of course, no station can survive if it depends upon this method of soliciting business. It is a poor station, indeed, that asks an advertiser to "take" a schedule on the station. The successful, professional broadcaster uses his public service work as an occasional door-opener, nothing more.

Daily listener mail is a valuable source of information. Secretaries, salesmen, and every other staff member should be taught to look for meaningful commentaries on the station and the community. By assigning one person to coordinate the continuing public survey, the licensee should have little trouble in establishing that he, indeed, is interested in community problems and makes worthwhile efforts to use his facilities to solve them.

RELATIONSHIPS WITH OFFICIALS

It is important to the licensee that he and his staff develop good rapport with local government officials. The better the rapport, the more effectively the station can work with government in terms of public service and news. In too many instances, police and other government officials believe that "reporter" means only newspaper reporter and that "press" means only the newspaper. The News Director who establishes solid contact with the Mayor, Police Chief, City Manager, and other prime news sources and then conducts himself as a responsible newsman eventually will earn as much respect as his newspaper counterpart. He will get his share of "news breaks," and these will grow in number, depending upon how he handles them. The licensee and his General Manager, as well as the News Director, where the station's budget will allow, must also maintain a rapport with high government officials, including Senators, Congressmen, and local representatives to the state government.

In his relationship with federal officials, every licensee should be a lobbyist. Congress established the Communications Act under which the FCC was born, and it is Congress which will change the Act in the future. Whether it will be for better or worse depends considerably upon how broadcasters work with Congressmen and Senators. If a Congressman or Senator declares he has no interest in a piece of legislation dealing with broadcasting, the broadcasters in his district haven't been doing their jobs.

PROGRAMING IN GOOD TASTE

Regardless of format, a station must always program in "good taste." Examples of programing in "bad taste" would include playing music with suggestive lyrics, announcers using obscene language or quoting obscenities. In the 7:00 A.M. newscast, for example, if a story deals with four persons killed in an auto accident, it is sufficient to simply report the names of the persons. It is not necessary to describe in detail the blood and gore surrounding the scene.

The Communications Act prohibits the use of obscene language on the air. If the law is violated, the FCC has the power to revoke operators' licenses and, in extreme cases, fine the station licensee or revoke the station's license.

McLendon decreed years ago that his stations would not program music with obscene or suggestive lyrics. Record distributors were required to submit lyrics in writing when they presented a record for consideration by McLendon Program Directors.

Some stations prohibit use of such words as "rape" (preferring criminal assault), "sleazy," "crappy," "cruddy," and most stations will not give the names of accident fatalities until they are certain the next of kin have been notified. Exceptions include celebrities and prominent persons.

For many years, many stations would not run some commercials during certain periods of the day. "Preparation H," a hemorrhoid remedy, had difficulty scheduling announcements during the breakfast hours on some stations and could not get on other facilities at all. The "good taste" operator avoids overemphasizing violence in newscasts.

It is not always easy to determine "good taste" programing. Dr. Barney McGrath, chairman of the Broadcast-Film Arts Department at Southern Methodist University, said, "Program matter must not get ahead of social mores; the broadcaster must make himself aware of what ideas and products the public has accepted." It is in "bad taste" to poke fun at ethnic groups. For example, Mexican-Americans have complained bitterly about commercials that employed Mexican accents. In the 1940s, it was in "bad taste" to program commercials dealing with feminine hygiene. Thirty years later, it was commonplace the hear such commercials. As Dr. McGrath said, program matter cannot get ahead of social mores.

The Staff and the Community

The smaller the market, the more necessary it is for the staff to become involved in community affairs. Participation is most vital in the major markets; however, some staff involvement indicates to the Commission that the licensee is abreast of community problems.

In a medium market of 300,000 persons for example, the staff involvement might include:

Manager-	Member Jaycees, Rotary Club, Chamber of Commerce.
Sales A-	Member local National Guard Unit.
Sales B-	Sunday School Teacher, member Lions Club.
News Dr.-	Member 20-30 Club, Optimists, Press Club.
Anncr. A-	Coach boys' baseball.
Anncr. B-	Auxiliary policeman.
Anncr. C-	Member Boy Scout Council.
Secy.	Member P.T.A.
Traffic-	Finance committee, Methodist Church.
Ofc. Mgr.-	Member local political party action committee.

The more involved the staff, the better picture the licensee has of the community he is licensed to serve. Not only must this impress the Commission, but it also puts station personnel in direct, personal contact with the business community. The smaller the market, the more advertisers buy on a personal, as opposed to professional, basis. The local appliance store leader is more likely to buy from George, his Lions Club buddy, than he is to buy from Pete-what's-his-name at the competing station. This, of course, speaks poorly of businessmen's buying habits, but the truth is there.

CKWW, located in Windsor, Ont., Canada, is a good example of how community involvement can make a station successful. Windsor, for years, had only two local stations. CKLW, with heavy U.S. ownership, programed essentially to Detroit. CBE, part of the Canadian Broadcasting Company, was government owned and, as is typical with most government owned stations, gave listeners what government planners thought they should hear. CKWW came along, in 1964, as the only local commercial station dedicated to serving the needs of Windsor and the surrounding area.

In the winter of 1964-1965, the Windsor-Detroit area suffered its heaviest snow storm in history. Drifts made streets impassable. People couldn't get to work. Ambulances couldn't run. Deliveries couldn't be made. CKWW staffers who lived only a few blocks from the station were able to report for duty, but those living in the suburbs were snowed in. The station preempted all regular programing and set up a message service and coordinated routing of emergency vehicles.

A woman called in to say she had no milk for her infant. This message, as well as the lady's name and address, were aired. A neighbor then called the station to say she had milk and would share if the woman's husband would come for it. Milkmen called to say their trucks were stalled at certain intersections. This information was aired, and patrons were able to walk to the intersections and get the dairy products. A local automobile dealer called to say he was making 5 Jeeps available for emergency purposes. He even supplied drivers, and during the two-day affair they took several pregnant women to the hospital.

Some five hundred such messages were put on the air during the emergency. Through this kind of programing and attention to local problems, and through heavy staff involvement in community institutions, people in Windsor began referring to CKWW as "our local station."

Of course, it's rare that a station has such an opportunity for service. But ownership and management should establish policy on what action will be taken in the event of an emergency. Under certain conditions, such as the slaying of President Kennedy in 1963, a station should, if it has facilities, go "news full time." This means all regular programing is preempted, and the station uses every means available to keep listeners informed of events. In other instances, all commercial matter may be eliminated. In such cases, advertisers usually allow the station to "make good," rather than demand credit for the commercials missed because of the emergency. Music is often toned down to the extent of programing nothing more than soft instrumentals. The event in issue might be **billboarded** throughout the day. For example, if a tank car explosion in a small town kills or injures forty persons and the station's facilities cannot cover the event directly, it might institute soft programing, eliminate commercials, and provide billboard-type news bulletins between records.

At KNOE, in Monroe, La., during a heavy sleet storm when streets became dangerously slick, the local Police Chief was provided with a mobile news unit so that he could go on the air directly and advise citizens which streets were impassable. This same station went full-time news once when the Ouachita River was threatening to overflow the levees. Had the levees broken, thousands of persons would have been displaced by the water. The station set up a mobile news broadcast center near the levee and continually interviewed inspectors during the night.

While no licensee in his right mind would wish for such emergencies, he should be prepared to act when they develop. Responsible action during emergencies builds confidence in and believability for the station.

THE STATION AS A PUBLIC FORUM

The modern broadcaster who doesn't adopt, at least to a limited extent, the philosophy that he is merely a leaseholder on his frequency, is likely to face a strike application or a hearing when he applies for a license renewal.

The Commission expects the licensee to make an affirmative effort to develop, through his facilities, dialogue on public issues. By affirmative effort, the Commission means for the licensee to go into the service area, learn about local controversial issues, and get all pertinent sides on the air. Often it isn't necessary for the broadcaster to make an effort; the issues come to him, demanding to be heard.

There are several ways in which the broadcaster may use the station to expose pertinent positions on a public issue. Some of these are:

1. The broadcaster himself can take an editorial position and offer equal time to the opposition.

2. The station can offer any number of broadcast periods (ranging from 30-sceonds to 60-seconds or more) to opposing sides, making certain that he gives exactly the same quantity and quality to each side.

3. The station can set up a round table discussion and include representatives from each side of the issue.

4. The broadcaster can set up a series of debates between representatives of the opposing sides.

5. The broadcaster can offer commercial time to all sides of the issue, making certain that each is offered the same quantity and quality of time.

6. Newscasts.

The Commission philosophy holds that licensees should editorialize, that licensees should involve themselves and their stations in public and political affairs. In the now famous Mayflower decision, the FCC discouraged editorials; and few were aired until 1949 when the Commission issued its "Fairness Doctrine." When the station serves as a medium for the discussion of political and or public affairs, the licensee must continually be aware of the duties imposed upon him by Sec. 315 of the Communications Act and by the Fairness Doctrine. The Fairness Doctrine deals essentially with the necessity of affording reasonable opportunity for the presentation of contrasting viewpoints on controversial issues of public importance. Generally speaking, it does not apply with the precision of the "equal opportunities" requirement of Sec. 315 of the Communications Act. In the case of the Fairness Doctrine, the licensee is called upon to make reasonable judgments in good faith on the facts of each situation, as to whether a controversial issue of public importance is involved, as to what viewpoints have been or should be presented, as to the format and spokesmen to present the viewpoints, and all the other facets of such programing. In other words, the Commission expects the licensee to exercise good judgment in such matters, and then be able to justify and defend his judgment when and if he is called to task by the Commission.

The essential requirements in Sec. 315 are fairly clear. They state that if the station deals with one candidate for public office, it must deal in the same manner with all other legally-qualified candidates for that public office. There is no option for the licensee. If he sells time to John Smith for Mayor, he must also sell time to Bill Jones for Mayor. He cannot charge a premium price for his political time. He must offer time at regular commercial rates to all candidates for the office in question, and the candidates are entitled to any discounts that are offered to regular commercial advertisers.

Station X in Florida during one election year decided that when a candidate used an advertising agency, the agency would not receive a commission. Agencies so involved were required to "gross" the applicable rate if they wanted to take a commission. Management of Station X illogically reasoned that a candidate who employed an advertising agency had an advantage over candidates who did not have such professional help, and that agencies in such cases were not entitled to the standard 15 percent discount. After several agencies complained to the Commission, Station X was advised, informally, to commission the agencies or face a hearing. It was simply a matter of Station X's not treating political accounts exactly as it did commercial accounts.

The lines, in most cases, are not so clearly drawn under the rules and policies of the Fairness Doctrine. The licensee must make "reasonable judgment" in many, many cases. It may be assumed that broadcasters keep the wires to Washington attorneys hot with lengthy explanations and the question, "Now don't you think that's reasonable?"

Example:

LICENSEE: John, on Sunday morning that usually calm Methodist preacher launched a dreadful attack on the school board. I didn't hear about it until I came to work early Monday morning. Briefly, the preacher accused the school board of sleeping through its meetings.

ATTORNEY: So, what's the problem?

LICENSEE: First thing out of the bag Monday, the school board members were pounding on my door. I agreed to let one man speak for the entire board, but they wanted three men to speak on three different occasions. I finally told them to take it or leave it...that only one of them could speak. Now they're threatening to take it to the FCC. On top of that, Joe Perkins who is very big in the Lions Club has demanded an opportunity to go on the air and defend the school board. I just told Joe to go to the devil, that the school board could speak for itself.

ATTORNEY: Anything else?

LICENSEE: Yeah. I don't even think there's a public issue involved here. All the preacher said was that we'd have better schools if the school board members didn't sleep through meetings. The preacher was arguing about the various values of Sunday School, and I guess the remark about the school board just slipped out.

ATTORNEY: Is that all?

LICENSEE: That's all.

ATTORNEY: Okay. Point one: Only one member of the school board may speak. You don't have to allow three of them on the air. One preacher, one school board member. Point two: Don't tell Perkins to go to the devil; advise him instead that you think the school board has adequate defensive talent and that you don't think he is needed to fight school board battles. Point three: I think you're right. You could forget it. I don't think there's a controversial issue of public importance involved. But give them equal time, just to be on the safe side.

As an afterthought, I'd caution the preacher against personal attacks of any nature unless he gives you forewarning. If he decides to jump someone else, you should require him to give you a tape or script in advance so you can make the affirmative effort to notify the person or agency being attacked.

LICENSEE: Thanks, John. See you later.

Actually, if the broadcaster understands that he must treat alike political candidates for any given office, and if he has a built-in sense of fairness, he can easily avoid trespassing on Sec. 315 and the rules and policies of the Fairness Doctrine.

The licensee may decide to handle a given controversy only in his newscasts. Suppose, for example, that the Mayor, on the 10:00 A.M. news, declares that the city council should adopt the water flouridation program. The licensee will have met requirements of the Fairness Doctrine if he carries, on the 11:00 A.M. news, a statement to the contrary by the president of the P.T.A., which opposes the program. To carry it further, and take affirmative action, the licensee might then seek out additional news interviews with members of the opposing parties. In his newscasts, he would give listener statements from both sides. If, in his opinion and good judgment, he devotes as much of his newscasts to the pros as he did to the cons, he's probably safe.

The telephone talk program is another sensitive area, and an alert, well informed moderator is necessary to keep the station in the middle and away from a Fairness Doctrine violation. It is possible, at any time, for a group of people to "gang up" on the moderator and present one side of a public issue. In such a situation, the moderator should urge opponents of the particular point of view to call in a voice for the opposing opinion. In some cases, the moderator himself might state the views of the opposition if he knows them. If an entire program should be dominated by only one side of an issue, the matter should be reported to management; and efforts should promptly be made to air the side of the opposition.

The licensee who carries reports from representatives in Washington or his state capital must be constantly alert to Fairness Doctrine violations. Generally, these capitol reports are harmless; but occasionally a member of the opposition will challenge a point and ask, or demand, equal time. The licensee then must decide whether the matter in question is of sufficient importance to justify the equal time requested or demanded. In any event, when the representative again becomes a candidate for re-election, he should be taken off the air, or the licensee should make arrangements to give his opposition equal time. The representative should be taken off the air the very day he becomes a legally qualified candidate for re-election to public office. Until the representative becomes a candidate, his program is logged PA (Public Affairs). The day he becomes a candidate, his program is given the dual designation of PA-Pol (Public Affairs-Political). Chapter VI of this text treats Sec. 315 and the Fairness Doctrine in more detail.

COMMUNITY ORIENTED PROMOTIONS

Regardless of market size, power, frequency, or relative standing in the community, the word "promotion" has come to be one of the most meaningful in radio's glossary of terms. There are sales promotions, station promotions, and client promotions; each has a different meaning, and each is designed to accomplish a somewhat different goal. Prior to 1950, promotion essentially meant a raise in pay or a step up in the chain of command. McLendon and the late Todd Storz, as they were resurrecting radio with nervy, noisy, and ingenious promotional razzmatazz, probably gave promotion its modern meaning.

Although each different kind of promotion will be discussed in detail in later chapters, each is involved to some extent in the community-oriented promotion. These promotions are valuable to the station because they involve the station on a face-to-face basis with people in the service area.

Listener Involvement

The community oriented promotion usually involves the public physically, KXXX's annual "family picnic" is a prime example of such a promotion. The Star Stations' "Bridal Fair" is another. In both cases, staff members are brought into direct contact with listeners. There are literally scores of other similar promotions, including the Annual Easter Egg Hunts, Tugs-of-War, and Fourth of July Celebrations. A community oriented promotion, then, is one in which the station invites listeners to come to a certain place to do a certain thing, with station staffers serving as hosts and hostesses. It is not necessarily designed to produce revenue; rather, it enhances the station's rapport with the community.

The annual picnic is effective, but difficult to execute. If the broadcaster can successfully assemble one of these, any others he conceives will be easy. Proper execution of the family picnic plan involves:

1. Announcements on the air inviting the first 200 (or any number) families to respond by mail to KXXX's First Annual Family Picnic. Listener interest is gained by offering free food drinks, and games for the children, such as sack races, bike races, or three-legged races. The date, time, and place are set in the opening announcements, and respondents are asked to tell how many members of their families will be present.

2. Prepare invitations and mail them to responding listeners. These invitations again should spell out details of the picnic, including time, place, menu, and activities.

(An important part of this promotion is to ask participants to assemble at a point away from the picnic site and drive in a caravan to the picnic grounds. Bumper stickers, antenna flags, or other suitable station identification should be placed on the cars in the caravan. Interviews via the station's newswagons are appropriate during the caravan assembly.)

3. Arrange to buy or "trade out" the food, drinks, and equipment needed to execute the plan.

4. Assign staff members specific tasks to perform on "P" Day. Be certain to involve air personalities in jobs that bring them into direct contact with listeners, such as supervising games or handing out hamburgers.

5. Ascertain that you have adequate public liability insurance.

Methods of Execution

As with any such promotion, attention to detail is critical. The General Manager should assign a coordinator to handle these details. The coordinator may be a member of the staff or someone from the outside, but there must be someone to "stay with it."

Rules of games must be determined. Jobs must be assigned. Menus must be planned. Preparations for entertainment (live or recorded) should be made early. If the station plans to conduct the promotion on a cash-free plan, the sales personnel must be sent out to make the trades. In the case of a family picnic, arrangements can usually be made with a local grocer for everything required. Dairies and soft drink bottlers might be dealt with separately.

Between the time of receipt of the 200 letters and the date of the picnic, the station should air announcements giving some of the names of respondents, crediting the trade-out suppliers, and generally telling everyone what a good time KXXX listeners are going to have at the picnic. If trade-out suppliers are credited in the promotional announcements, they must be logged under "commercial matter," as any matter which results in gains for any business or service must be logged "commercial."

On the appointed day, this should be the key topic of talk for air personnel left behind to man the station. The news unit should have half-hourly interviews. If there is no news unit, the telephone may be used for interviews, but it is essential to get them on the air. The announcers at the picnic, if possible, should make "cut-ins" during the day, describing the scene.

After the picnic, the station should broadcast the names of winners of games, the oldest and youngest visitor, the largest family, and the youngest family. Listeners are told how much fun everyone had at KXXX's first annual picnic!

The picnic might be an excellent opportunity for management to conduct a survey on community problems. This could be part of the station's continuing public survey.

The station that can be correctly identified as a "good citizen" of the community is not likely to be hit by a strike application at license renewal time, nor is it likely to suffer a business failure. The operator who sits in a corner doing "his thing" and ignoring the environment and people around him may suffer both.

Sponsor Involvement

Such promotions afford the station an excellent opportunity to show sponsors how it can motivate consumer response. Sponsors and potential sponsors should be invited as special guests. The grocer who has never advertised on the station might be persuaded to trade out the food. The department store manager might be invited to present a short show of outdoor fashions. Make the effort pay!

An entire how-to and what-to text could be written on the conception and execution of community oriented promotions. But from the foregoing, the student and new broadcaster should get a fair idea of the excellent exposure such promotions provide the station.

Saving Lives, Finding Missing Persons

Alert stations have saved lives, found lost children and pets, and prevented disasters. Many persons instinctively call their local radio station when they are in trouble. This is one reason the nationally recognized Call for Action program has been so successful. People identify with radio stations, consider the station and its air personnel as friends, and call upon those friends when there is trouble. Although there are certain hazards in being a good citizen, and these will be discussed later, there also are many rewards.

These are some ways in which a station may function as a good citizen!

1. Local hospital official calls and says a certain type blood is needed to save the life of a patient. The station

broadcasts announcements and asks those persons with that type blood to report to the hospital blood center. It is advisable to accept such requests only from hospital or police officials known to station personnel. Pranksters and mentally ill persons have been known to trick stations into broadcasting false alarms. Be sure the caller is authentic!

2. The police department calls to say certain streets and roads are impassable. The station airs announcements advising motorists to steer clear of the areas.

3. A woman calls the newsroom or control room to say she is about to commit suicide. The newscaster or engineer tries to hold her on the telephone while advising police of the situation.

4. A person is lost. The station assists the police in establishing search parties. Again, it is important that the project be under the direction of the police. Do not act on the tip of an "anxious" parent or anonymous caller. Too many persons have instigated such searches to embarrass or "get even" with the allegedly lost person.

5. Listener calls to say family pet has strayed. You might go on the air immediately with the problem or save it for a special program designed for this purpose. At least one station has a program called The Dog-Gone Bulletin Board on which all such messages are aired.

Natural, Civil Disasters

Radio stations can become Number One Citizen in times of natural and civil disasters. Stations have prevented or halted riots, been instrumental in the orderly evacuation of danger areas, or were of invaluable help to police or other governmental bodies when natural or civil disasters threatened. But it is important to the station that it work directly with official groups whenever possible as an arm of authority rather than as an independent do-gooder.

The Lousiana station which was called into action by local police and the Corps of Engineers when a flood threatened to break a levee and pour hundreds of tons of water into residential areas, set up an all night vigil. Official hourly bulletins were aired from the local National Guard headquarters via a two-way radio system. The station was completely at the disposal of local police, National Guard, and the Corps of Engineers.

In the mid 1950s, KLIF in Dallas went full-time information (News) when a tornado threatened the area and finally struck in suburban Oak Cliff. Newsman Les Vaughan was in route home in a mobile news unit and found himself caught in the middle of the disaster area. He immediately went on the air to describe the scene and advise listeners to keep out of the vicinity. Affirmative action on the part of station personnel was indicated, and Vaughan's alertness and sense of public service probably saved lives.

In the vegetable and fruit growing areas of the Rio Grande Valley of Texas and in Southern California, stations are often called upon to broadcast freeze warnings, thus enabling farmers to take early precautionary measures. A freeze in such areas could cause loss of crops and incalculable economic hardships.

Stations throughout the country have voluntarily initiated aid campaigns to help victims of floods, hurricanes, and fires. After hurricane Carla ripped up the Texas Gulf Coast in the mid-50s, dozens of southern and southwestern stations went on the air with appeals for blankets, food, and clothing. In some cases, stations were urged by local Red Cross operations to take the action; but usually the stations took it upon themselves to act. Such occasions afford stations a genuine opportunity to show advertisers the power and effectiveness of radio. Some stations have made arrangements with local food or service station chains to serve as depositories for donations of food and clothing. In no cases reviewed did any station actually make a profit from such situations, and announcements related to the aid efforts were not regarded as commercial matter.

Local Sports

Stations often become deeply involved in local sports. In one case in Indiana, a town's only radio station was a daytimer and, therefore, not able to broadcast night-time football and basketball games. So intense was interest in having the games broadcast that the station owner taped play-by-play reports and broadcast the tape the next morning, with full sponsorship!

In other instances, in markets of all sizes, radio stations are integral parts of the local sports scene. In small-to-middle-sized markets where there are, for example, four radio stations and four high schools, each station often contracts with one of the four high schools to carry all sports events. Lucky is the station that has a district or state champ, for his advertising will be easy to sell!

In the major markets, such as Chicago, Dallas, or San Francisco, there are few instances where high school sports are ardently promoted and followed. In these markets, college and professional sports are big attractions, and considerable revenue is involved in broadcast rights and commercial availabilities. Stations in college communities of every size bid for rights to broadcast major conference football games. Local stations fiercely compete for rights to set up state university networks and sell the play-by-play broadcast of the games to stations all over the state.

Participation in local-interest sports profit the station in at least two ways. First, financially. If the team is popular and on a winning streak, premium rates may be charged participating sponsors. Second, ratings. A hot game, such as a district play-off or an annual bowl game, will draw thousands of new listeners to the play-by-play frequency. Many will discover the station for the first time and will remain as steady, loyal listeners. The carrying station becomes to the listener the station that carries the Lions, the Cowboys, or the Tigers. This is an essential aim of any aggressive station: to become involved in people's lives.

For deeper and equally significant involvement in community sports, many stations form or sponsor amateur athletic teams. These may include basketball, football, baseball, and bowling. Ideally, staff members will dominate the team in numbers, but frequently a staff will yield only a few athletes, and the ranks must be filled by outsiders. Regardless, such activities give the station much favorable exposure and allow it to do some useful work in charity. Often, the station team will play a charity game against, for example, the local Junior Chamber of Commerce chapter. All proceeds in such instances should go to United Fund or some other local charity. When all money goes to charity, announcements promoting the event may be logged PSA. If participants receive any remuneration above actual expenses, the spot must be logged as commercial matter (CM); and an announcement must be made stating that players will share in proceeds.

The establishment of staff athletic teams also serves to build staff morale and teamwork. Staff cohesiveness is critically important to the operation of any successful radio station. The camaraderie developed through athletic teams contributes materially to the development of esprit de corps within the radio staff.

Public Utilization of Equipment

In addition to occasional official requests for equipment and air-time, most stations are, almost weekly, faced with requests for the loan of equipment. Some stations have flat policies against such loans, but others feel they must cooperate even at the risk of having equipment lost or destroyed. It is not uncommon for a local civic club to request stations to set up P.A. systems for club use. High School and college clubs may ask for turntables and P.A. systems for school dances. When churches are given air time to broadcast Sunday morning services, the station is often asked to provide microphones and remote amplifiers. The more sophisticated church organizations own and maintain such equipment, but more often than not, the station is expected to provide all equipment.

RELATIONSHIP WITH OTHER MASS MEDIA

In some markets, the atmosphere seethes with resentment and jealousy among mass media. Radio stations continually knock each other, thus putting down the entire industry. Newspaper reporters regard broadcast newsmen and advertising salesmen with contempt. There is no mutual trust or respect and no common understanding of the goals of mass media. In such cases of back-biting, back-stabbing, and mutual contempt, the public usually suffers. Strong, healthy competition is one thing; active mutual degradation is quite another. Where there is distrust among media, newspapers often refuse to help on any public project in which a radio station is involved. The station avoids mentioning the name of the newspaper on the air. The newspaper will never write the station's call letters in its columns, referring instead to a "local radio station." Such conduct, although childish and immature, exists, but since the mid-1960s has begun to abate.

In the ideal situation, there is considerable cooperation among media. Radio stations and newspapers execute trade agreements in which the station promotes certain features of the newspaper, and the newspaper provides display space for the promotion of station features. In most cases, there is no advertiser involvement. For example, the station might buy, under the trade agreement, a half-page ad to promote its hourly news but would not mention that the news is sponsored by First National Bank. The newspaper, on the other hand, could promote its sports or women's sections but could not promote a special section produced on behalf of a newspaper advertiser. Usually the agreement requires that neither station nor newspaper use the other as a tool to directly promote sales of time or space.

In other areas, such as news, the public benefits tremendously when there is cooperation and understanding between radio stations and newspapers. A small station with a weak or no news staff may arrange with the local newspaper to broadcast from the paper's city room.

Example: It's time now for the 8 o'clock news, brought to you by First National Bank. For the news, here's Joe Smith, reporting directly from the city room of the **Ourtown Daily Press.**

(Headlines, then a one minute commercial, followed by three minutes of news. Station's cue to take control will be: This is Joe Smith, reporting directly from the city room of **Ourtown Daily Press.** For complete news details, read today's **Ourtown Daily Press.**)

Under this plan, the station has access to the newspaper staff's news coverage, while the newspaper profits from the station's mention of its news source. An example to the contrary and one that causes the public to distrust all media is when the newspaper columns criticize a "local radio station" for erroneously reporting a story or when the station makes a similar attack on the newspaper. This has happened in hundreds of U.S. markets.

Several years ago, a newspaper columnist wrote a snide remark about a local broadcaster. The station responded by blasting the newspapter for carrying "whiskey" ads and using four letter words in its news columns. In the contest, there were no winners, only losers. Finally, the feud became so vindictive that the newspaper publisher called the station licensee and asked for a truce.

Commercially, there is less cooperation, but there have been instances when radio stations and newspapers have teamed to create excellent sales promotions.

Example:

BROADCASTER: Bill, we're planning a special promotion on the new shopping center. There are forty merchants involved, and I think we can do one heck of a job of promoting the center's grand opening. What would you think of a 4 or 6 page special section that would hit the day before the opening?

NEWSPAPER: Sounds great to me! Let's get together and plan it. We'll need a list of the merchants and the decision makers. You come up with the theme, and we'll use the same idea in our special section.

Just as often, the newspaper sales manager might call the radio station with the idea. In any case, the merchants and the public benefit from this kind of media cooperation.

There are other times when radio-print cooperation can vitally affect the welfare of the public. All media can join to promote the United Fund, make the public aware of an epidemic, clean up corrupt governments, and jointly promote the city's cultural offerings. There must be competition for dollars, readers, and listeners; but the competition does not have to be destructive.

There is perhaps more understanding between radio and television stations than between either and the newspapers because radio and TV stations have similar problems. Both sell time rather than space, Both have commercial availability problems at times, and both operate under the rules and regulations of the FCC. Often, radio and TV stations form unwritten and informal alliances to compete with print media. There are trade agreements in which the radio station promotes TV features.

Under common ownership, radio and TV stations often use one news staff, sales force, manager, and bookkeeping department. The joint sales force has been less effective because TV rates are usually much higher than radio rates and, for this reason, the salesmen tend to give radio a back seat. The same problem develops when stations set up joint AM-FM sales forces.

A practical solution to the problem is to separate at least the sales forces, even though all other departments work for both facilities. The need for cooperation between radio and TV stations is just as essential to community understanding of and respect for media as is the need for cooperation between radio and newspapers. As with gasoline wars, there is little profit in any area when medium fights medium.

Except in the allocation of advertising budgets among various media, there is little conflict between radio stations and billboard companies. The two may join in public service campaigns or may work together to execute a promotional campaign for an advertiser. There have been cases where radio stations and billboard companies formed agreements whereby each would use the services of the other to sell time and locations. For example, the station would allow the billboard company X number of announcements for X number of months. The station then, in presenting advertising packages, might offer X number of spots per month for X number of months, plus X number of billboards at no extra cost. The billboard company, on the other hand, would be able to offer a certain number of bonus radio spots in proposals to its customers. In such agreements, the station should be careful to maintain control over who may use the time and should, through its Washington attorney, or directly, if it has no attorney, file a copy of the agreement with the FCC . While there is no law prohibiting the bartering of time on a radio station, the Commission insists that the licensee maintain control and that such agreements be placed on file.

Summary

Rising generations of the 60s and 70s cried for involvement, change, and greater freedom to plan their lives. Fiery young spokesmen would not accept the platitudes and stock answers of the establishment. Youth and minority groups of all ages demanded to be heard. Liberal thinkers such as FCC Commissioner Nicholas Johnson joined the movement in efforts to unbend the traditional thinkers. It was inevitable that broadcasting become a target of the dissidents. Minorities throughout the nation struck out at licensees who ignored their needs. Lamar Life Broadcasting Company of Mississippi was denied license renewal under withering charges that its WLBT (TV) had discriminated against the large Negro population in its service area and had violated the Commission's Fairness Doctrine on civil rights matters by presenting the segregationist viewpoint only. In Washington, the Institue for Policy Studies published a 336-page report that encouraged the filing of protests against incumbent licensees. The United Church of Christ was deeply engaged in a campaign to open radio-TV programing and employment to blacks. The nation's licensees were faced with the most significant challenges ever to their rights to operate their stations as free enterprise businesses.

It became apparent that licensees must develop an acute awareness of community if they were to stay in business. Stations must operate as good, sensitive, unbiased citizens of the community if they are to operate at all. McLendon and scores of other professionals proved that it is possible to operate in the public interest and still reap enormous profits in money and aesthetic satisfaction. This chapter has attempted to describe in a general way the station's relationship with the community it is licensed to serve. Following chapters explain in considerable detail how and why the relationship must exist.

CHAPTER 2

Sales

The old axiom that "nothing happens until a sale is made" must have been written for the radio industry. For without sales, all the genius and creativity in the world can't save a station from commercial ruin. One of the most difficult points to make with programing and other non-sales personnel is that the product (station sound) must be geared (1) to meet FCC requirements, and (2) to the local marketplace.

It is not necessary, perhaps, that a station or its licensee have a definitive sales policy or philosophy; but circumstances and the personal character of the licensee must certainly produce at least some unwritten rules which govern the sale of time.

SALES PHILOSOPHY

Ideally, station management establishes policy that prohibits rate cutting, special deals to special customers, and a rate scale that can be lived with through good times and bad. Under such policy, salesmen are not permitted to quote rates "off the card." The advertiser gets the rate he earns and nothing lower. If the advertiser fails to meet contractual obligations, he is short-rated. If he earns a better rate than contracted for, he is immediately rebated in cash or time. There are no barter deals, no wholesale time deals. House agencies are accepted only when they perform the complete function of an independent advertising agency. This is a tough but completely honorable and businesslike sales policy. Many stations set such policies and stick to them. Others do not. Under a tough policy, there are no bonus spots, little or no "merchandising" support. The two-week cancellation clause in the standard advertising contract is strictly adhered to. Deadlines are observed and copy requirements are met.

Destructive Negatives

At the other end of the scale are the broadcasters whose philosophy is to "get the business, " regardless of methods or concessions. These operators are called the "whores" of the business. Under a "get the business" philosophy, there is little the hungry operator can't or won't do to sell time. The rate slash is only part of his ammunition. He can engage in the illegal practice of double billing. He can provide the advertiser with everything from trade-out hotel rooms, complete with food and liquor, to two-week vacations in the tropics. He can literally "buy" business from ignorant businessmen or unscrupulous time buyers and advertising managers, particularly when the buyer doesn't have to justify his buy to knowledgeable superiors.

Example:

SALESMAN: Look, I know we don't quite have the ratings of the other station; but considering the special deal we have this week, you'll get a better buy.

BUYER: So, what is your deal this week?

SALESMAN: Okay. You've got a $1,000 budget for February. I want it all, and we're willing to make it worthwhile.

BUYER: Are you talking about a rate cut?

SALESMAN: Yes and no. But actually it amounts to the same thing. You spend the "thou" with me. We'll bonus you 100 spots during the month and throw in three one-hour remotes on any dates you specify.

BUYER: Hey, that sounds pretty good. Now let's see, with the bonus spots, that brings my 60-second rate down to about $10. What would you say the remotes are worth?

SALESMAN: At least $200 each if we were selling them this month. And if you put that sort of value on the remotes, why your spot rate drops even more.

BUYER: Pal, according to Pulse survey, you reach only about half as many women as your competition. And while you're offering me rates at about half their price, I'm not sure they aren't a better buy--considering the results I need.

SALESMAN: Look, we've got success stories, too. Most of the time it's just a guessing game, and the success or failure of a schedule depends upon luck. The numbers in those rating services are just guesses, and I'm just as good a guesser as they are. And right now I'm guessing that you'd like to take your wife to Vegas for a week-end on our due bill. Now if that donesn't get your February budget, I don't know what will.

BUYER: My friend, I thought you'd never hit the right chord. You got the order.

Another common philosophy among unscrupulous operators is that if you can't out-program them and out-sell them, beat them to death.

Example:

(Scene One)

SALESMAN: You're not going to buy that station?

BUYER: Sure I am, but what do you mean by that station?

SALESMAN: Only this. It's the worst station in the market. They can't deliver ten customers a week because their programing is rotten, and they got no listeners.

BUYER: But they show up pretty good in the ratings!

SALESMAN: Forget the ratings. You can't believe a one of 'em. Why, you can buy a rating. I know a guy up north who paid a thousand bucks for the number one position. It's easy, believe me.

BUYER: Well, okay. Call me tomorrow and I'll let you know. You may be right.

(Scene Two)

SALESMAN: He said that about my station? That the rating services are crooked?

BUYER: Not only that, he also said your programing is rotten and that you really don't have any listeners.

SALESMAN: I can't believe it! The nerve of those guys. Their station is the biggest dog in the market. The announcers are all drunks, and they can't keep a salesman because they can't pay them.

BUYER: Is that right? I didn't realize things were so bad over there. Anyway, give me a ring tomorrow and I'll let you know something.

(Scene Three)

BUYER: Susie, (his secretary) call those radio bums first thing in the morning and tell them we've decided against using radio next month. And then call the newspaper. I've got to get something going on this campaign.

The Radio Advertising Bureau

The Radio Advertising Bureau has pleaded for years for broadcasters to stop knocking each other. Kevin Sweeney, president of RAB for many years, used to burn with rage when he heard one station knocking another, Sweeney's concept of selling was to go after the newspaper budgets. He abhorred the infighting and continuously exhorted fellow radio men to join RAB and "gang up" on newspapers and make joint presentations to the big department stores and grocery chains that spent 100 percent of ad budgets in the print media. The RAB makes dozens of such presentations each year on behalf of its members.

The broadcaster is sometimes faced with either going off his rate card with special deals, actually reducing and publishing a lower, more saleable card, or going broke. Too many operators choose the deal route, hoping the climate will improve and put them back on rate. But once the deals start, once the first under-the-table card is dealt, it is difficult if not impossible to stop. One lie leads to another, and soon the manager and sales staff are spending valuable time covering up for themselves and each other.

It probably is better in the long run to eat a little crow, admit to guessing wrong on rates, and simply rework the card and publish a lower rate. At least a special bookkeeper isn't needed to keep up with the one-time special deals to special friends and customers.

How do the rate holders compete against the rate cutters? "They know what their time is worth," might be one retort. Another, far more effective, is to advise the advertiser that he can't be sure his competitor hasn't gotten a better deal from the rate-cutter. Beyond this (and there are dirtier tricks to use), the local radio industry fares better when the salesman simply ignores the "other deals" and gets on with the business of selling the pluses of his station.

Most broadcasters are content to sell their station on its merits, rather than on the demerits of competitive stations.

No-Knock Policy

McLendon developed a "no-knock" policy in which salesmen were prohibited from selling on the competition's weaknesses. The station that sells its strengths rather than the competition's weaknesses is laying groundwork for future business. A radio time salesman should never use such negatives as:

1. KFFF is a dog. Nobody listens to it.

2. KFFF has power problems. It barely gets to the city limits.

3. KFFF is a rate cutter. You never know when you're getting the best rate available, but they'll cut rates at the drop of a hat.

4. KFFF can't deliver buyers. Your competitor used them last month and had no results from the schedule.

5. KFFF has a pretty good station, but its production department is no good.

And so on, ad nauseum. Meanwhile, KFFF salesmen would be saying the same things about other stations. Ultimately, the advertiser would surmise that NO radio station is worthy of his budget and decide to keep his business with the newspaper.

A salesman presenting his station's merits might say:

"Mr. Jones, I think you can reach more of your particular market on KXXX than you are doing on KFFF. You're selling small foreign cars, and the Overseas Survey Company's figures indicate that 70 percent of the buyers of small foreign cars are under 30 years of age. In my opinion, if you were selling big, expensive American-made cars, KFFF would be the right station for your budget. KFFF is the leading station in reaching men 35 and over. But, because of their format and type of music, they do not reach the under 30 buyers the survey shows you must reach to sell your cars. On the other hand, KXXX caters to adults 18-34 years old. ARB and Pulse both show that we reach about 60 percent of those persons in this age bracket. Again, I want to emphasize that KFFF is a great station, and it gets good results for advertisers who want to reach the over 35 market. But to sell small foreign cars, KXXX is really your best buy. Let's visit at your convenience, and I'll show you how it works out on a cost per thousand persons reached basis."

Whether or not the salesman makes a sale, he will have presented a good story on KXXX without destroying Mr. Jones' confidence in radio as an advertising medium. In some station sales tactics, there is no such thing as a "bad" radio station; some are more effective than others in selling specific products and services, but all stations are "good" buys when the advertiser bothers to study the station's format and potential audience.

Charity Rates

Some stations, including the McLendon group, have so-called charity rates. These may be from 25 percent to 50 percent lower than the applicable card rate and are offered to churches, schools, and other non-profit groups which have advertising budgets.

For years, many non-profit groups solicited free time from radio stations, while buying display space in the newspaper. The broadcaster, of course, felt they were being taken. As a result, many of them established firm policies regarding non-profit organizations.

Example:

Our station is anxious to support non-profit organizations. Each year, we provide such organizations with thousands of dollars in free time. We do it gladly and willingly as a public service.

If an organization has an advertising budget, then we insist that we get an equal share of the budget; and we will provide one free announcement for each one the organization buys.

If the organization does not have an advertising budget we will provide enough free time to satisfy the organization's need for publicity or promotion.

We will not provide free time to the organization that buys space in the newspapers, which are under no obligation to operate in the public convenience, interest, and necessity.

BUILDING THE SALES STAFF

The owner-manager of a small market facility was introduced to the manager of the top facility in a nearby medium market. "I'm glad to finally meet you, you so-and-so," said the small market broadcaster; "I've been training salesmen and announcers for you for years."

The larger markets, the more successful facilities, have always pirated personnel from the smaller markets and stations.

Example:

SALES
MANAGER: Boss, the competition has hired a swinging new salesman. He has all the earmarks of a real winner, and I'd like to go after him.

GEN.
MANAGER: How much experience in the market?

SALES
MANAGER: None anywhere, yet. But my every instinct tells me he's gonna' tear up this town.

GEN.
MANAGER: Okay. But let's wait about six months. Let them train him in the basics; then we'll slip over and hire him away.

The top five or six stations in a major market, such as Chicago, San Francisco, Dallas, or Detroit, have relatively little trouble in finding salesmen and setting up sales staffs. They simply hire, from among those already in the market, men and women with years of professional experience who "know where the bodies are buried" and who can join the staff and be productive the first day on the job. The salesman who makes a good appearance and can identify the buyers, account executives, and accounts of a market's major agencies can just about write his own ticket. In the major markets, he can earn from $20,000 to $50,000 a year and, unlike most executives, work only 30-40 hours a week. Usually, he works for a $1,500 to $2,000 per month draw, against a commission structure ranging from 5 to 10 percent of his net sales. Some stations pay salesmen salaries, but the majority use a draw-against-commission plan.

School Training

Colleges and universities are producing more and more graduates who are qualified to handle significant account lists. Other radio time salesmen are to be found in other selling jobs, such as insurance, stocks, real estate, and books. Radio time is often referred to as an "intangible," and many broadcasters feel they fare better when breaking in a greenhorn who previously has sold other intangibles.

Frequently, the "selling instinct" is in a man whether or not he is working as a salesman. Thus, the alert sales manager often can find top quality salesmen in unrelated fields. The successful sales manager of a Montreal station was "found" operating an elevator. A highly successful salesman in Dallas was "found" working as an ad manager for a bakery. Major sources of radio time salesmen are:

1. Local competition
2. Stations in neighboring markets
3. College and university graduates
4. Other fields in which intangibles are sold.

The perfect solution when management needs a salesman is to simply hire someone from another station. Failing here, the station must advertise for help. **Broadcasting Magazine**, of course, is one medium. This usually means an out-of-towner who must be oriented to the market. Sometimes, the local newspaper want-ad columns bring results. Not infrequently, a newspaper space salesman will apply. Further, the station may use its own facility to advertise for salesmen. On occasion, newsmen and announcers on the staff are "ready" for the big switch from programing to sales. The larger the market, the simpler the problem of finding "ready-to-produce" sales personnel. The industry "grapevine" operates with alarming efficiency.

Interviewing

If the job is a high-paying one, management will be subjected to a barrage of applicants. Some applicants' credentials sound impeccable. Some of the recommendations from friends and former employers are hard to believe. A man's "first appearance" may be startling. He may actually appear to live up to his recommendations and biography. Full of smiles, he will throw around names of buyers and account executives with a flair, whether or not he actually knows them or has called on them. He can sell his ability to sell the station. But most good general managers are adept at the practice of checking out applicants. They simply call a dozen top buyers in the city to find out how they like the guy; if the applicant is accepted and believed by the buyers, he gets their vote.

There are several areas in which the sales or general manager should dwell when interviewing salesmen.

DRESS: Does the man wear his clothes well? Does his appearance distract the interviewer? While clothes are important, the man himself must clearly come through the rags on his back. The applicant with the off-center tie, scruffy shoes, red socks, and rumpled suit wouldn't have a chance with most sales managers. His clothing should be suitable for the era and season but must not become a topic of conversation.

MANNER: Does the man come on too strong, or is he timid? Does he seem to have the personal appeal and charm that would make him acceptable to the buyers and ad managers you know? Sometimes the arm-swinging, desk-pounding, loud-talking guy will drive away business. Did he use familiar obscenities at your first meeting? If so, he probably will use them at his first meeting with some of your clients; and some of your most important ones will be offended. Is he a nail chewer, heavy smoker, wet-palm type? This type makes other people nervous. Do you feel easy with him?

PERSONAL: Is he married, with children? Does he own or rent his home? Does his sales background seem solid? Is his a compatible marriage, or is he on the verge of a breakup? It is important that the man be a basically "happy" person. If he isn't, he may well spend much of his valuable sales time fretting about or working to solve his personal problems.

FINANCIAL: The applicant's finances should be in fairly good condition. If he is heavily in debt, chances are the receptionist will be receiving a number of bill collectors. Furthermore, the heavily indebted individual may continually seek employment that pays more. In so doing he neglects the business.

A broadcast salesman or account executive who works on commission is, fundamentally, in business for himself. It isn't necessary for him to observe rigid office hours; he doesn't need to be in the office at 8:30 or 9:00 A.M. He could schedule appointments at those hours, check in with the receptionist or sales secretary, and come to the office anytime. Because of this necessary freedom, it is important that management find conscientious, responsible, self-starters to man the sales force. Although the sales manager looks for certain ideal characteristics in a potential salesman, what he really wants is a man who can produce revenue for the station. A top producer may wear red socks; he may never comb his hair; he may wear a full beard, and he may even speak contemptuously of the sales manager. But, under these circumstances, he'd better produce heavily and every day!

Orientation

Most stations regard orientation as a critical part of the new salesman's first few weeks on the job. A few operators will simply throw the man onto the street with the admonition, "Get out there and sell!" An effective orientation program, however, usually pays off.

1. Introduce the man to every member of the staff. He should know the announcers and when they are on the air. He needs to know traffic, copy, and production personnel because he'll have to work with them from the start. He should be taken around by the manager or sales manager and introduced with pride as "our new account executive."

2. If the salesman is to take over an established account list, he should be thoroughly briefed on each account and then be introduced to the principals.

3. The Program Director should brief the new salesman on the station's format. He should review personalities and saleable · program features. The salesman should have a good "feel" of the format before he makes his first contact with a client.

4. The manager or sales manager should relate the history of the station to the new man. He should be acquainted with every sales tool the station uses, including the rate card, coverage maps, audience surveys, target studies, market demographics, and the advantages or disadvantages of the station's power and frequency. It is critically important that the new man be advised of what he can expect in the way of competition. Who is the number one radio competitor? Who are the rate cutters? How strong is the newspaper and television station?

5. In smaller communities, it is important that the new account man be introduced to leading citizens, and he should make plans immediately to join a civic club or two. If he is a church-goer and hasn't joined a local church, the manager might introduce him to his denominational pastor.

6. The station's sales philosophy should be explained thoroughly to the new man. Older members of the sales force should be asked to talk informally to the new member, to explain and re-explain how the station wants the job done.

7. Details of his employment, including the pay plan, vacation periods, and other company benefits, should be explained before the salesman makes his first call. It is distressing to hear a salesman, in his first meeting with an advertiser, say, "I just started and don't know a thing about the company yet. But in a few weeks I'll be abreast of things and can explain why we're such a good buy"

The Army doesn't send men into combat without complete training and orientation. The same rule should apply to radio stations, and it does with the professionally operated facilities. Sending a new account man to visit an important account can be fatal. An experienced manager simply won't trust the new man immediately with his significant accounts. He'll make the calls on the account himself, or he will make the first several calls with the new man until he is sure the buyer has accepted the new station salesman.

DEVELOPING THE RATE STRUCTURE

Building a rate card for a new facility is about the same as building one for a recently taken-over property. Unless the taken-over property will be operated "as is," the card must be developed from scratch.

Competition has a heavy bearing on the card. A station can easily price itself out of the market if its rates are much higher than competition. Obviously, the first project to undertake in the development of a card is to make a complete study of competitive rates. Suppose, for example, that in a market of five stations the study reveals:

Station	Power-Freq.	Format	Audience Share	1x Open
Station A	1kw-620 kHz	C&W	14 percent	$20
Station B	5kw-830 kHz	MOR	6	15
Station C	1kw-1390 kHz	Network	5	18
Station D	5kw-1400 kHz	Top 40	20	25

The new station is the 5th facility and plans an expanded, more-music type Top 40 format. While Stations A, B, and C may be overpriced, each has a package that makes the average spot price $10, $7.50, and $9.00, respectively. On that basis, the pricing seems adequate. Station D holds firmly to the rate but discounts dramatically under a published TAP (Total Audience Plan) rate. The estimated average cost of minutes is approximately $15.00. Further investigation reveals that agencies and ad managers are not particularly displeased with the rates. The market has been fairly stable, and radio has been getting what appears to be a fair share of the advertising dollar. There are no outcries about radio being overpriced.

Although the new station management may believe it can take the Top 40 operation within three to six months, it probably should decide to start with a fairly low rate and build from that.

There is no law, yet, dictating how to charge for the commercial time on a station. Demand for time, as well as for ratings, helps to dictate rate structure. But on the first card, the new management should set rates it can live with.

Ultimately, it may reach a point where it can charge "what the traffic will bear."

Example:

LXXX Rate Card No. 1

(Effective May 1, 1974)

Time Classifications

Class A—7 A.M.-9A.M. & 3-6 P.M. Mon.-Fri.

Class B -- 10A.M.-3P.M Mon.-Fri. & 6P.M.-12 midnight-
Mon.-Fri. 6A.M -6P.M. Sat. & Sun.

Class C—All other times

CLASS A

Length	1x	52x	104x	260x	520x
60-sec	$15.00	$14.00	$13.00	$12.00	$11.00
30-sec	13.50	12.50	11.50	10.50	9.50

CLASS B

Length	1x	52x	104x	260x	520x
60-sec	12.00	11.50	10.50	9.50	8.50
30-sec	10.50	9.50	8.50	7.50	6.50

CLASS C

Length	1x	52x	104x	260x	520x
60-sec	9.00	8.50	7.50	6.50	5.50
30-sec	8.00	7.00	6.00	5.00	4.00

WEEKLY PACKAGE PLANS

10 announcements per week	104x rate
20 announcements per week	260x rate
30 announcements per week	520x rate
40 announcements per week	720x rate

(cont'd)

61

Five-minute news and headline news rates available upon request.
Rates for ID and 10-second announcements available upon request.

Rates are guaranteed for a period of three months only from the effective date of any rate increase, providing advertising is actually running at time of effective date of increase and providing that broadcasts continue without interruption.

This is one small market or low-rated station card. A thousand professional broadcasters would prepare a thousand different cards. It is advisable, at first, to keep the card simple, easy to understand, explain, and sell.

Frequency Discounts

Frequency discounts are earned by the advertiser who signs a long-term contract. Typically, a bank might purchase one 60-second AM drive time unit per day, Monday through Friday, for 52 weeks. It signs a 260x time contract and pays $12 per announcement. Should the agreement be cancelled after, perhaps, 26 weeks, the account would be short-rated. The station would then bill the bank for the "earned" rate or the one closest to the earned rate. In this case, it would be the 104x rate of $14. Assuming the banker had paid $12 per announcement during the Jan. 1-June 30 period, his last invoice would price last month's units at $14, and would include a short-rate charge of $2 per unit run during the Jan. 1-June 30 period.

Package Plans

The weekly package plans are designed for advertisers who run in short flights of ten to thirty announcements per week for two or three weeks. Because they are "flight" but heavyspending advertisers, stations normally give them a rate advantage. Package plans originally were designed to lower rates and to compel advertisers to put enough budget on radio to make the medium an effective sales tool. Too often, the advertiser would run four or five announcements on the local radio station, pay the 1x rate, and complain later that radio advertising was not effective. Newspaper budgets were ten, twenty, fifty times higher than broadcast budgets. As an inducement for the purchase of impact schedules, broadcasters came up with the package plans. These take many forms; some are obvious rate-cutting devices. In fact, one of the simplest means of lowering a rate is to devise and publish a new discount or package plan.

The TAP plan offers the advertiser x number of spots in each of the daytime parts of the program schedule. It might be a 20 plan, in which the advertiser would receive 5 Class As, 10 Class Bs, and 5 Class Cs. Under an ROS plan, the announcements are priced at the low end or low middle rate, with the station retaining the right to schedule them anywhere between 6 A.M. and 12 midnight.

In the case of the ROS plan, the rate for 60s might range from $5.50 to $11.00. In the TAP plan, the rate might be an average of the applicable Class A, B, and C rates, with a 10 percent discount off the average for buying announcemnts in all time periods. Stations use the TAP plan to encourage the purchase of other-than Class A time. When stations reach a sold-out position, Class A time usually is the first to go, which is one reason morning and afternoon drive periods carry premium rates. In the early 1970s, some stations were putting even higher premiums on Wednesday, Thursday, and Friday drive periods, primarily because of demand.

A look at an audience level chart in Fig. 2 will explain immediately to the student why premium rates are charged for morning and afternoon drive periods.

This pattern appears to fit most U.S. markets, regardless of format, where AM stations are concerned. It does not apply to FM operations, primarily because in the early 1970s few cars were equipped with FM receivers. Any really comprehensive audience study will include in-car, in-home, and in-store listening, as well as demographics. An FM average quarter-hour audience chart indicates greatest audiences in the 10 AM-3 PM daypart and the 7 PM-12 midnight daypart. Drive periods (6-10a 3-7p) show greater audience because of heavy in-car listening as people drive to and from work. Drive periods will vary from market to market and from station to station. One card may show 7-9a 5-7p as drive periods, while another may designate 6-9a 4-6p.

Program Rates vs. Spot Rates

It is doubtful that there is a widely accepted mathematical basis for the development of spot or program rate. In the final analysis, the average station charges as much as it can get. And any time the station program log indicates a sold-out

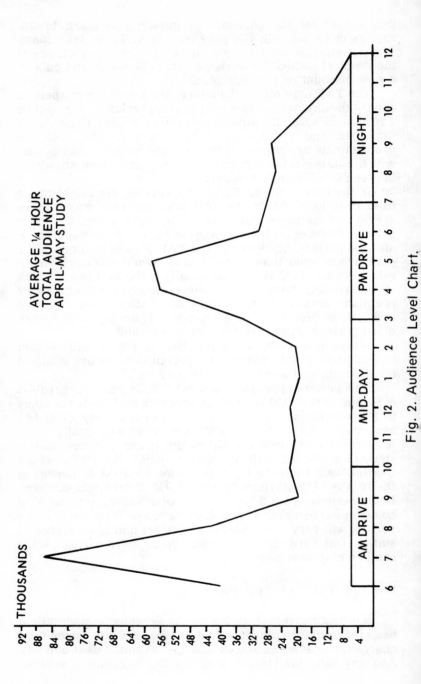

Fig. 2. Audience Level Chart.

posture, the advertiser can shortly expect some kind of rate increase.

The rate card developed here would indicate a five-minute newscast rate of $30, or twice the applicable 60-second rate. The headline news rate might be 1½-times the applicable minute rate. In establishing 15-minute, 30-minute and 60-minute rates, the area and arithmetic of the spot level are largely disregarded. With a $15 1-time open rate, there might be justification in charging $50 for a quarter-hour show, $75 for a half-hour segment, and $125 for a one-hour segment. Although hourly rates are not often published, they should be made part of sales policy, because if for no other reason, they may be needed during the next political campaign, assuming that blocks of time are sold.

Most radio stations include talent and production charges in the quoted rate. Should they decide to charge extra for studio work, the charges would be published on the rate card.

Remote Broadcasts

In the major markets, at least, the day of the "remote" is about gone. A few still push the idea of having personalities and equipment on the scene; but, for the most part, this device has about lost its appeal. It worked fine when radio station air staffs were made up of god-like personalities and when listeners listened to programs instead of stations. Now, major market listeners are too busy to follow station personalities to remote broadcasts.

In the small and medium markets, remotes are still sold and executed with great noise and precision. Hundreds of stations have remote studios, vans, or mobile homes that are completely equipped to feed the program line with good quality sound. The remote broadcast works best for grand openings, shopping center promotions, special sales, and close-outs. Some stations have perfected the remote gimmick to the point of using high-frequency FM transmitters to transmit the remote broadcast from the scene of action back to the station for pick-up and rebroadcast on the main facility. They are costly to the station and the advertiser, but they can produce some gratifying results. Stations that use remotes usually have a fixed price of X dollars per hour, plus lines and talent.

Remote Broadcast Presentation:

SALESMAN: Mr Buyer, here's what we can do for your shopping center promotion. We'll bring our remote unit out from 9:00 A.M. until 7:00 P.M. on Saturday. The unit is equipped with turntables, cartridge machines and racks, air-conditioning--the works. We'll order in a "balanced" line and sound just as good from the remote unit as we do from our studios downtown.

Monday through Friday preceding the Saturday promotion, we'll run 10 announcements daily promoting the fact that you're having the sale and that we'll be there live on the scene. We'll mention that the DJs will be there to wave at the crowds, that we'll give away free records and that you'll have new specials every hour.

Now, during the broadcast, the center will receive three one-minute spots per hour, not mentioning the adlibs we'll throw in as the DJ talks between records. We'll have two men on duty during some of the remote period, and one of them will do brief interviews with patrons of the center.

Mr. Buyer, we'll stir up so many customers for you that the clerks won't know what hit them!

While such promotions usually get excellent results, the student is warned that the FCC's program logging rules may be repeatedly violated unless extreme caution is exercised. Every word said about the center and the promotion must be logged as commercial matter.

National vs. Local Rates

Research has turned up no completely valid reason or logic for a differential between local and national rates. Some broadcasters justify the higher rate for national advertisers because, in the case of a product with general distribution, the advertiser gets the benefit of the station's total coverage. On the other hand, they argue, the local retailer profits only from the station's coverage of the market's trade area. Others argue that since all national business comes through an agency and a national rep, it is more expensive to handle and, therefore, should carry the higher rate.

There is no consistency in major, middle, or small markets in the establishment of local and national rates. Half the stations in a major market might operate under a "one card" system, while the other half would have the "two card" system, with national rates ranging from 10 percent to 30 percent higher than local rates. Most broadcasters, in major markets at least, will admit that the one-card system is desirable because it is simply easier to operate with one card. The fewer rates the station has to deal with, the less the paper work and the chance for billing errors.

Many stations are "trapped" with the two-card system and realize that it will take years to reach the one-card plan. When the station has been receiving an average of $75 per one-minute spot from national agencies, and an average of $45 from local agencies and advertisers, it is in a legitimate dilemma. The manager might lower the national rate (Heaven forbid!) to $55 and raise his local to $55 (and lose 50 percent of his local advertisers, and bring the national and local into even balance). He might, but he won't! Over the years he hopes to keep edging the local up to the national level, but almost every time there is an indication for an increase in local rates, the same indication applies to the national.

It is far easier in a major market to eliminate one card or the other and operate under the one-card system because the metropolitan advertiser is accustomed to paying the higher rate; and the station can more easily justify the higher rate on the basis, perhaps, of cost-per-thousand persons reached. But in the small market, where the station averages $5 per announcement locally and $15 per announcement nationally, the problem is quite different. The solution, if there is one for stations stuck with the two-card system, is to gamble on a slightly higher local rate and bring the national down to meet it.

There is no complete justification for the two-card systems. While a 50kw operation may cover eight states or more, its area of dominant influence is only within its local service area. The nationally distributed soap product, therefore, actually gets no greater effective penetration than does the local grocery chain. Radio is essentially a "service medium" and can effectively serve only those persons in the immediate area.

The Chicago station that reaches into the Rio Grande Valley of Texas isn't likely to sell much of anything because Rio Grande Valley residents are interested in Valley stations, service, moods, and music. The geography covered by a radio station is no longer a big selling point. So long as the station covers the trade area, it can provide just as good a service as the 50kw powerhouse.

MERCHANDISING AND SALES AIDS

Merchandising is a vague term that means everything from a legitimate way to cut rates to adding impact to the broadcast schedule. The agency buyer for a soft drink account may promise a substantial spot schedule provided the broadcaster can develop enough merchandising support.

What sort of support does the buyer want? There are several things the broadcaster may do if he desires:

1. Point of Sale signs. The broadcaster may print, at his own expense, a "shelf talker" to be placed on the account's displays in retail stores. The sign might say, "XXXB Beer, as advertised on KXXX."

2. The station could provide the local beer distributor with incentive prizes. The prizes would be offered to the driver-salesman who shows the greatest increase in sales during a given period of time.

3. Letters describing the campaign and asking retailers to put the product "up front" may be sent out by the station manager. These are called a "mailing-to-the-trade.

4. The station might do an on-the-air promotion for the client, giving him broadcast exposure in addition to the purchased campaign. For example, the station might develop a campaign in which listeners compete for a two-week, expense-paid vacation.

Listeners would send in their names and addresses along with a bottle top (or a reasonable facsimile, to comply with the anti-lottery law). At the end of a certain promotional period, the station would conduct an on-the-air drawing to determine the winner. The trip, of course, is a big prize. One alternative might be several cases of the product, coolers, motorbikes, boats, or cars.

It is not uncommon for a small "tear-'em-up station" to trade out a boat and a motor, then approach an advertiser with a plan to let him "give it away" during an advertising campaign. The idea is for the merchant to go on the air with a series of announcements asking listeners to come to his store and register for the prize. The station traded "unused" air time for the boat and motor, then converted the package into a cash sale. It is a hard way to develop revenue, but it has worked for hundreds of small operators.

5. Another favorite merchandising gimmick of small operators is the remote broadcast. As an incentive for the advertiser to put most of his budget on a given station, the station agrees to "give" the advertiser a remote broadcast.

6. Some stations have "merchandising agreements" with large chains and use the contract effectively in developing product advertising. Station KXXX may have an agreement with Super-Duper Grocery Chain. In the agreement, KXXX guarantees to run X-number of announcements per week for Super-Duper, in exchange for Super-Duper's setting up special product displays as ordered by the station. Station KXXX then calls upon the buyer for Brand-X and proposes that Super-Duper's twenty-five stores will build gigantic displays of Brand-X for one, two, or three weeks if Brand X will buy a certain number of commercial announcements on the station.

7. When a station has built a group of on-air personalities, these personalities often are used to swing sales. Popular DJs make personal appearances at the retailer's place of business to sign autographs and give away records.

The merchandising effort is limited only by the broadcaster's imagination. There is no historic rule of thumb for merchandising; it is done primarily when the station's audience is inadequate to influence sales or when competition in the market has forced all stations to "throw in extras." There is nothing illegal about merchandising, and it will probably remain in radio's bag of tricks for a long time to come.

The salesman, regardless of his field, needs "something in his hand." Newspaper space salesmen have layouts. The vacuum cleaner peddler has, at least, a vacuum cleaner. The insurance man has a brochure extolling the main points of his policy. Not only does "something in hand" offer something for the prospect to see and feel, but it also provides the sales representative with a degree of confidence necessary for him to close the sale.

There are a few instances when no sales aids are required. Salesmen for the only auto dealership in town probably will not spend much time demonstrating cars; they simply sit in the office and take orders. The only advertising medium in town, or a station whose ratings are obviously far superior to that of the competition, may need no sales aids, except perhaps, a rate card. But in most cases, sales aids are needed because competition is present, and the successful broadcaster must present his station in every favorable light.

The rate card is a necessary basic tool, though certainly not·the most important. The rate card may be a plain inexpensive mimeographed sheet, or it may be combined with art and color and printed expensively on fancy paper stock. Some broadcasters regard this expense as wasteful; others think a printed card is necessary to help convey the station's image. More often than not, however, finances determine the design of the rate card. It may contain information other than rates. Many stations include a coverage map. Others add current audience estimates and print new cards every time a new survey is issued. In all cases, the station's frequency, power, and rate protection policy should be included.

Surveys and Survey Analyses

There are at least two bona fide reasons for a buyer's placing time on a given station. The first is the station's relative position in an acceptable rating service's audience estimate. The second is experience with the station. The No. 1 station isn't necessarily the best buy for a particular product; it depends upon that station's reach (unduplicated audience) within the client's target audience.

In less sophisticated markets—100,000 to 500,000 population—experience with a station is often the buyer's most valid reason for making a particular buy. This is particularly true of the ad manager or store owner. If the local C&W station generated business, there is little the Top 40 operator with No. 1 position in the market can do to switch the client's buy. Among sophisticated buyers and account executives in agencies in markets of all sizes, the survey is a key in media decision making.

So far as radio stations are concerned, there are three rating services which are used extensively by agencies in media buying. These are C.E. Hooper, Inc., The Pulse, Inc., and ARB (American Research Bureau). Each service's methodology is significant to the student's understanding of the role surveys play in radio time sales.

ARB Methodology

ARB conducts continuing television and radio audience studies, using both the diary and telephone measurement techniques.

All U.S. television markets and the top 150 radio markets are included in the annual survey schedule. In measuring television, each sample household receives one diary for each television set in the home. A personal listening diary is used for radio with one diary sent to each person 12 and over in the sample family. Arrangements for placing the diaries in selected homes is normally made by trained ARB telephone interviewers. In the New York City metropolitan area, information is also obtained by an electronic device attached to television sets. This system is called ARBitron, and the data from it is reported weekly.

The frequency of television surveys ranges from a minimum of three nationwide "sweeps" of all 205 ADI (Area of Dominant Influence) markets, to as many as eight surveys annually for New York, Los Angeles and Chicago. In addition, a July sampling is taken in all ADIs to provide the estimates upon which the annual SUMMER MEASUREMENT INDEX is based. ARB Radio Reports are issued four times a year for the top eight markets and at least once a year for all 150 markets surveyed.

ARB also offers telephone coincidental surveys during which trained telephone interviewers gather viewing and-or listening data while programs are on the air.

The duration of a survey is four weeks. The total sample is divided into approximately four equal parts so that each household in the sample records its viewing activity for one week of the survey. However, when a survey period covers fewer than four weeks, the same size sample is used as for the longer period; but the sample households are divided by the number of weeks in the survey period.

In addition to keeping a written record of the family's viewing, for sample household furnishes other pertinent information such as the age and six of each family member, and the family's consumption of a number of categories of products and services widely advertised on television.

Stripped to essentials, each Television Market Report contains three basic elements: the Metro TV household rating and share of audience, and the ADI television household rating and share of audience; estimates of the number of television households viewing in the Total Survey Area, together with the Total Survey Area audience broken down into demographic categories; and ratings for age-sex categories of the audience within the ADI.

The ARB Radio Market Report is compiled in essentially the same fashion as the television reports except that the diary is a personal record of the listening activity of each person age 12 and over in the sample household. Estimates are provided for a number of demographic categories of listeners, and the reporting of average quarter-hour listening estimates and some audience estimates for both the Total Survey Area and the Metro Area.

The Hooper Radio Audience Report identifies the Homes Using Radio (HUR) and Share of Radio Audience for radio stations in the report area.

The data for the report are gathered by means of telephone interviews. The universe for the Hooper consists of all persons age 12 and over in the survey areas.

In essence, the procedure allocates interviewer work units to counties as primary sampling units with probability proportionate to size.

For a particular work unit, for coincidental interviewing, three sections are defined in a telephone directory that has been selected for the sample, after any parts of the directory corresponding to places located outside the defined market have been eliminated. Within each section, a page is designated, at random, which marks the starting point for a cluster of six consecutively listed telephone homes eliminating multiple listings within the cluster. Thus, the work unit for coincidental interviewing is defined as 17 dialings with a 15-minute interval or 68 dialings per hour.

Interviews are conducted during a 16-hour period, 7:00 A.M. to 11:00 P.M., Monday through Friday and from 8:00 A.M. to 11:00 P.M. on Saturday and 10:00 A.M. to 11:00 P.M. on Sunday. This interviewing is conducted for seven consecutive days during each month of the reporting period. The person who answers the telephone reports on current sets that are on at the time of the call, as well as the sex and age of the listener for each set. The phone answerer is directed to physically observe or ask other members for station information. Homes not responding to the telephone are counted as not listening.

The interviewer begins the interview by stating: "This is the Hooper Research Company calling. Is there a radio on anywhere in your home?" If yes, she asks: "What program are you listening to?" (program personalities, type of music). Then she inquires: "Would you mind looking at your radio and telling at what number the dial is set? Do you know what station you receive at that number?" The interviewer then determines the sex and age of all listeners, the same information regarding a second set in the home, and the race of the household.

Each response is edited to verify each station response. This is a highly time-consuming but important procedure, since respondents will sometimes identify a station incorrectly. Each data card is logic-checked and internally cross-totalled by computer to identify keypunch errors showing up as invalid codes for a column or a self-contradictory condition.

Race weights are then applied, bringing the sample into the metro population proportions of white vs. Negro. This compensates for lower telephone ownership among Negroes in many markets, which would otherwise cause an under-representation of Negroes in any telephone sample.

Stations not on the air during an entire interview segment are projected to that segment and that is noted on the report.

The final report or index is published once a month, two to three weeks after interviewing. Each Hooper Radio Audience Index is based on two months' moving averages and shows Homes Using Radio and Share of Radio Audience for each station in the market.

Pulse Methodology

Pulse Methodology uses the personal interview method: Interviewers are sent to pre-selected areas with instructions to interview respondents in their homes. The interviewer is instructed to procure both in-home and out-of-home listening for "yesterday." A cumulative estimate is also obtained by asking to what stations those interviewed have listened in the "past week."

The selection of a sample involves many intricate statistical techniques. The goal is to eliminate possible bias in the survey. The county is the basic unit of organization in the sampling procedure. The total number of sampling points decided upon for the survey is distributed among the counties in proportion to their household distribution. Two sampling procedures may be used. Sampling Frame I is a Telephone Starts method. This is not to be construed as a telephone survey based on telephone homes, as this could present possible bias by eliminating non-phone and unlisted phone households. Both phone and non-phone homes are included in the sample, and a procedure for statistically weighting them is used, based on the probability of phone vs. non-phone households found in each sampling point. Sampling Frame II is an alternate method generally used for Ethnic Samples and for large geographic regions. It is based on Census data in which blocks or civil divisions are selected by statistical procedures.

The IBM-360 Data Processing System is employed for completing the audience estimates. In addition to the phone-non-phone weighting, surveys are weighted for ethnic balance, county distribution, age, sex and time spent at home. This last weight is an adjustment factor for those people who were not at home at the time of the interview.

The audience measurements are estimates of audience size. Results are reported by Ratings and Shares, and projections into Persons.

Use of Surveys

Most major market stations and many small to medium ones subscribe to one or more of these radio audience survey services. Other subscribers include station representative firms, advertising agencies, firms specializing in media buying, and advertising departments of large companies which provide their own ad services. Charges to media range into the thousands per year, while agencies may pay only a few dollars per report.

The survey is a valuable sales tool, but it must be recognized for what it is, an estimate of a station's audience. Furthermore, when the results of a survey are published, the Commission requires that a disclaimer also be published:

> Any figures quoted or derived from audience surveys are estimates subject to sampling and other errors. The original reports may be reviewed for details of methodology.

The term "publish" means mimeographed sheets, brochures, or mass media...anything that is printed and distributed. The same restrictions apply to broadcasting results of a survey. If a station is No. 1 in total audience in the 6AM-10AM period, the promotional announcement must specify that time period. The survey results must be presented in such candor that it is clear to listeners when and how the station is No. 1. If the results are presented in a manner which implies that the station is top throughout the broadcast day, recriminations may result from the competition, the survey company involved, and the Commission itself.

Non-subscribers to a particular survey may not, of course, publish the results. Many stations "bootleg" surveys by using them quietly, without identifying their call letters with the figures. Bootlegging is only a polite term for stealing. If the station does not pay for a subscription to the survey, it exposes itself to legal action for violating the protective copyright laws.

The following sets of dialogue indicate how surveys are used:

HOOPER

BUYER: Bill, I've already decided to buy time on your station because Hooper puts you in the top spot. But I want time on three stations in the market. Can you tell me the next two ranking stations in afternoon drive?

SALESMAN: Well, let's see. The opposition Top 40 is No. 2, 6 A.M. 7P.M., but in afternoon drive the black-oriented operation is No. 2. The No. 3 rated station in that period is the network affiliate.

BUYER: What are the shares, Bill?

SALESMAN: The Top 40 has a 17 percent share and the network affiliate has 12. We have 28, as you know.

BUYER: That's it, Bill. Mail that Hooper to me, will you?

In this case, the buyer is interested only in audience "shares." Blair Radio, one of the nation's most respected Radio Rep organizations, defines a share as "the percent of all people who are listening to radio that are tuned to a specific station." This, then, is the relative piece of listening pie going to each station.

If a total of 20 persons of 100 surveyed indicate they are listening to some radio station, and 5 of those are listening to Station A, Station A would then have a 25 percent share. A Blair paper dated November, 1970, showed this formula:

People Listening to Station : Share All People Listening to Radio

$$\frac{5}{20} = 25\%$$

A typical Hooper Radio Audience Index showing in-home audience only:

	Mon.-Fri. 7A.M.-10P.M.	Mon.-Fri. 10A.M.-3P.M.	Mon.-Fri. 3P.M.-7P.M.
Homes Using Radio (HUR)			
	22.9 percent	12.8 percent	15.2 percent

SHARES OF RADIO AUDIENCE

Station			
A	6.0	9.2	7.4
B	0.7	1.8	0.9
C	14.3	12.1	14.8
D	25.7	21.3	29.0
Other	1.4	3.8	2.8

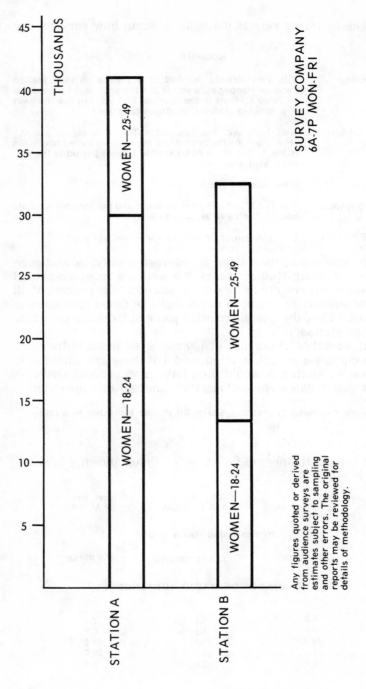

THOUSANDS

SURVEY COMPANY
6A-7P MON-FRI

WOMEN—25-49

WOMEN—18-24

WOMEN—25-49

WOMEN—18-24

STATION A

STATION B

Any figures quoted or derived
from audience surveys are
estimates subject to sampling
and other errors. The original
reports may be reviewed for
details of methodology.

Fig. 3. AQH Women 18-24, 25-49.

When all stations in the survey area are included, the total of each column is 100 percent. Each survey carries an explanation of any extraordinary circumstances surrounding the study. The asterisk by Station C's morning and afternoon drive figures might explain that the station is a daytimer and did not begin broadcasting until 7:30 A.M. and went off the air at 5:30 P.M. There may have been technical problems causing the station to be off the air during parts of the survey period; this also would be explained if the station notified the survey company. If any station aired a special promotion during the survey period, and if the survey company knew about it, a statement to that effect would be appended to the survey report.

Hooper's audience index shows only the average quarter-hour audience. No attempt is made to indicate the cumulative audience. To translate Hooper shares to actual homes, it would be necessary to know the base population in the area taken. The Blair paper used 100 persons as an index. Twenty of the listeners were tuned to some station; the HUR, then, is 20 percent. Of these, five were listening to Station A, giving the station 25 percent of the market. Translated, this same set of figures in a market of 100,000 homes, would show 20,000 homes using radio, with Station A averaging 5,000 of these per quarter-hour.

Sales presentations using Hooper normally show only HUR and shares. ARB and Pulse presentations are much more elaborate and detailed.

Many "statistics-oriented" salesmen and sales managers delight in making graphs that indicate their station's relative position in the market. ARB and Pulse provide not only shares, but also ratings, people, and some of their demography. In recent years, "demographs" have become important to many agencies that buy specific target audiences.

If an agency were making a radio buy for a laundry detergent, and buying studies showed women 25-49 years of age as the heaviest users of such products, the agency buyer might determine from ARB and Pulse which stations reach the largest number of women in this age category. Fig. 3 illustrates how the buying decision might be made. The graph indicates that Station A has the greatest number of women listening, a total average quarter audience estimate of 41,000. Station B shows only 32,000 women, but this station reaches more of the target audience (25-49) than Station B. Therefore, the buyer probably will place the budget on the station estimated to reach more women 25-49 years old.

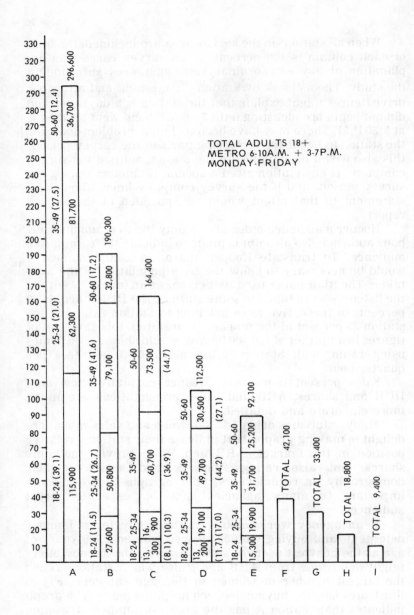

Fig. 4. Total Adults 18 and Over.

A toothpaste account probably would buy Station A because consumer studies show younger women to be heavy purchasers of such products. A chewing gum manufacturer would have no trouble making a decision. Neither would the maker of pimple creams. Their obvious choices would be Station A because of the superior audience of young women.

The ARB report is one of the most comprehensive studies available and is widely used by agencies in buying time on radio stations. Its report estimates who listens, when they listen, and how many there are. Some of the breakouts published by ARB are: Women, 18-24; 25-34; 35-49; 50-64; or over 64. The same estimates are made for men. Teens 12-17 also are indicated, but not by gender. These figures tell who is listening. Another section indicates when they listen, 6-10 A.M.; 10-3 P.M.; 3-7 P.M.; 7-12 midnight; on a Monday-Friday basis, along with Saturday and Sundary mornings, afternoons; and 7:00 P.M. to 12 midnight.

A beer account planning a 7-day weekly schedule, might ask for figures on adults 18 and over. Both ARB and Pulse make estimates for the 6 A.M.-12 midnight period, Monday through Sunday. Both estimate average quarter-hour (AQH) audiences as well as estimating cumulative audience. It is essential that the student understand the difference between Average Quarter-Hour listening and Cume listening. Blair radio explains:

> "Cume or unduplicated reters to the number of different people who tune to a station during a given period of time. This differs from average ¼-hour ratings, which refer to an average period; unduplicated or cumulative audience data refers to the number of different people reached during a broad period of time or a combination of broad time periods. This offers a second dimension to the advertiser in that the cume, as it appears in a report, tells an advertiser the number of different people who can potentially hear his commercial. There are differences among stations; some stations may have a small AQH audience and a large cume, meaning that a lot of different people are listening for relatively short periods of time. The opposite situation is a station with a large AQH audience and a small cume; in this situation, there is a hard-core loyal audience who listen for long periods of time."

The graph in Fig. 4 indicates cumulative audience and breaks down the audience demographically. A discussion of shares of audience requires an explanation of ratings, gross rating points, and People Using Radio (PUR). The Blair paper explains that a "rating is the percent of the population listening to a station during a time period. A rating may describe any single age group or a combination of several age groups.

If 100 men, representing a sample of the male population, were asked what station they were listening to, and five said they were listening to a specific station, that station would have a rating in men of 5.0. In other words, 5 percent of the men in that area were listening to that station. Ratings generally refer to the Metro Area and are not usually reported in larger areas. A rating can refer to average ¼-hour audience or cume (unduplicated) audience. It is most generally used to refer to average ¼-hour audience.

Translated to possible actual people, this means that in a Metro area consisting of five counties with a total male population of 500,000, the 5.0 rating would indicate 25,000 men in these counties were listening to this specific station in the average quarter-hour during the survey period.

Sophisticated agencies and advertisers show great interest in Gross Rating Points (GRP). Blair gives this definition:

"Gross Rating Points are used as a media planning and buying device to equalize advertising pressure in a group of markets. Since a rating is a percent of the market listening to a station, a target can be established in terms of total accumulated ratings. Therefore, if an advertiser wanted 100 gross rating points in a series of markets, his advertising in each market would be virtually the same in terms of the relative percent of impressions. Gross Rating Points for a specific schedule would be computed as follows:

Station	Average ¼-Hour Rating	Number of Announcements	Gross Rating Points
A	3.0	12	36.0
B	2.5	12	30.0
C	2.0	12	24.0
D	1.0	12	12.0
		Total Gross Rating for Market	102.0

FUR refers to the number of people listening to radio and can be expressed as either a number or as a percent of the population. It one hundred men, representing a sample of the male population, are asked whether they are listening to any of the radio stations, and twenty say yes then 20 percent of the male population is presumed to be listening. This can be projected into numbers of people."

Further refinement of the methods employed to buy "by the numbers" involves reach and frequency. Blair's gives this definition:

"The rating reports show the total unduplicated audience of a station. This does not tell you how many different people are reached by a specific schedule. For example, in the 6:00-10:00 A.M. period, Monday through Friday, there are eighty quarter-hour positions; and, theoretically, to attain a station's 6-10 cume, it may be necessary to utilize all 80 positions (buy 80 announcements). This is not necessarily the case. However, if an advertiser is buying eighteen spots during a period, he will not attain the total cume of the station. Using formulae or through special tabulations of data, it is possible to arrive at an estimate of the number of different people reached by a specific schedule.

"Frequency refers to the number of times that the average person hears a commercial. The gross rating points or gross accumulated number of impressions, divided by the station's reach, gives you the frequency."

$$\frac{\text{Gross Rating Points or people}}{\text{Reach}} = \text{Frequency}$$

Many times, buyers want to know only a station's CPM (Cost per thousand persons reached) to determine whether time is to be purchased and how much. This equation is simply arrived at and gives the buyer a quick analysis of the station's cost efficiency. CPM figures frequently preclude the purchase of time on the No. 1 station, and often show that the station with the lowest rates is not necessarily the best buy.

If Station A has a rate of $50 and an average quarter-hour audience of 50,000, the cost per thousand persons reached is $1. This formula is used.

$$\frac{\text{Cost of Announcement}}{\text{Avg. }\frac{1}{4}\text{-hour audience}} = \text{CPM}$$

Assume a time buyer is considering two stations. Station A has ¼-hour audience of 25,000, while B shows only 15,000. Station's A's rate is $50; B's is $30. On a cost-efficiency basis, Station B is just as good a buy as Station A if this is the only consideration. Station A's cumulative audience and consequent development of Gross Rating Points could make it a more attractive buy, in spite of the CPM.

While the professional rating services are widely used in the industry, broadcasters in smaller markets use other devices to determine how thoroughly they reach consumers. Mail pull and telephone calls from listeners provide one barometer. The telephone survey is another economical method of estimating audience.

From mail and incoming calls, station personnel may spot addresses on a city or area map. This indicates where listeners live and, in a wildly speculative sense, how many listen. The small-market advertiser may be impressed by such studies. The locally-conducted telephone survey is effective.

TELEPHONE SURVEY

(When the telephone is answered, ask the following)

1. When the phone rang just now, was your radio turned on?

(If answer is, "No," politely thank the person and hang up. If the answer is, "Yes," continue questioning.)

2. Do you know the call letters of the station you are tuned to?

3. About where is that on your dial?

So simple a survey can be useful. The numbers to be called are selected at random in the local telephone directory. For example, the first five residences listed on every tenth page might be called. This method of local survey indicates the number of people listening to all stations and each station's share.

Some broadcasters employ CPA firms or local women's groups to conduct the surveys and provide certification of the accuracy and lack of bias. This action logically makes the results of the study more believable to the advertiser.

Survey results mean different things to different buyers; many small-to-medium market advertisers refuse to believe any of them. Even in a market the size of Kansas City, one may hear an advertiser complain, "How can I decide which station is best for me if **everyone** is number one?" The advertiser in this case probably has not identified his target audience and, therefore, is confused when Station A is number one in total audience; Station B is number one in women 18-34; Station C is number one in men 25-49, while Station D is tops in women 35 and over. The advertiser who is ignorant of sampling techniques may become doubtful of all sales presentations aimed at his radio budget.

Such problems are rarely encountered in the major markets. Radio Reps in New York, Chicago, San Francisco, Dallas, Los Angeles, Detroit, and other markets of similar size are highly trained in survey evaluation techniques; and they sell to agency buyers who have similar skills. The sales presentations are conducted in the language of the industry.

Example:

REP: My station in L.A. jumped to a 4.5 rating in the morning That's up 1.5 since the last survey and now gives us a better CPM than the station you bought.

BUYER: That's true. But we don't switch stations on the strength of one increase. Let's see what the next study shows. If you're still at 4.5 or higher and the station we bought hasn't improved, we'll talk again.

REP: Thanks. Now, about that buy for XXX beer. Our PM drive went out of sight in this book, and there is no way you can pass us. I know what the client wants: men 18 and over and we got 'em in PM drive and at night. Our CPM in these day parts is lowest in the market.

BUYER: Okay. I'll call you Tuesday with the order.

This is called "buying by the numbers," and it isn't particularly important that the rep sell himself to the buyer, although good rapport between buyer and seller is always desirable.

In the smaller markets, it is absolutely essential that the buyer "like" the local salesman. Often, the salesman has to sell himself to the buyer before a sale can be consummated. Some old-line broadcasters believe an average of five calls on an account are necessary before a sale can be made. When the buyer (whether a store manager, ad manager, or agency buyer) doesn't appreciate or like a station's local salesman, another person should be assigned the account immediately. This is sometimes referred to as "personality selling." Numbers don't count. If the buyer likes the station, its music, its salesman, he will often place his budget there. This situation develops, of course, in small markets where there have been no surveys and where industry personnel are simply not trained to talk or act at such sophisticated levels as those used in the major markets.

Special Surveys as Sales Aids

Occasionally, a station employs one of the major survey firms to conduct a special study. The black-oriented station may wish to know (1) how many blacks in the market listen to radio and (2) what percentage of them listen to his station. Such studies are commonplace in markets where more than one station works with an ethnic format.

Another station may have developed a "teeny-bopper" image and, therefore, be unable to attract adult-oriented advertising from airlines, rubber companies, department stores, and appliance manufacturers. In one instance, after being passed on an airline buy, a station hired a professional survey firm to ask persons entering the advertiser's airplanes which local station they listened to most often. Everyone, in particular the advertiser, was surprised to learn the "teeny-bopper" operation fared best with the airline's passengers.

Another station posted interviewers at busy traffic intersections to ask motorists where their radios were tuned. In-school surveys have been used to determine students' favorite station.

A more sophisticated major market approach in making a target study is to define a product's buyer (such as women, 18-24) and then interview several hundred women in that age category to determine which station they prefer. While this study can be handled at station level, it is far more believable to the agency or advertiser if handled by one of the acceptable audience rating firms.

Personality Program Sketches

Some agencies and advertisers want to buy announcements in a station's top "personality" show. Stations, responding to such demands, publish program schedules and personality sketches. Such a sales tool might be printed on an 11 x 17" folded sheet, with the entire week's program schedule on the two inside pages, with personality sketches on the back, and other basic station data, such as power and frequency, on the front. An accompanying personality sketch with photograph might read:

THE JOE SMITH SHOW:

Joe has been on KXXX in the 6:00-9:00 morning slot for five years. His sparkling personality, quick wit, and topicality have made him number one in total audience in Hooper in 59 of the last 60 monthly studies. Joe's ability to get quick reaction on everything from department store advertising to appeals for the needy has made the 6:00-9:00 slot on KXXX one of the station's most sought-after shows.

Coverage Maps, Overlays

The use of coverage maps as sales aids has declined over the years as audiences outside a station's metro market have become smaller. In the so-called "golden days" of radio, the big 50kw station would cover not only the immediate trade area but might also effectively penetrate fifty other towns and cities. As more stations flocked onto the air after World War II and TV emerged as the prime entertainment medium, radio became more localized and more of a local service medium. Thus, it was no longer a big selling point if WBAP in Ft. Worth, for example, put a good signal into Greenville, Texas, because listeners in Greenville listened to the local station for local service.

Coverage maps, by the early 70s, were being used, not to show a station's superior coverage, but to indicate a competitive station's lack of coverage of the primary market. A highly directional station might cover the north side of a market with a city grade signal, while missing the south and east sides entirely. An aggressive salesman can get a copy of the directional station's coverage map through the station's Washington attorney or through other knowledgeable persons in Washington. As these maps are prepared primarily by Commission-acknowledged consulting engineers, they are fairly accurate in their reflection of a station's coverage. The salesman then prepares a sales presentation in which he compares his coverage with that of the competitor.

Testimonials, Written and Recorded

Testimonials are excellent sales aids if properly authenticated. If the owner of Furniture Store A writes that his schedule of announcements on KXXX sold twenty-five bedroom sets, the owner of Furniture Store B will likely be impressed if there is any similarity between the lines of the competing furniture companies.

The recorded testimonial also is effective. One technique is to record a telephone conversation in which an advertiser states that the station increased his business. Naturally, the salesman should advise the successful advertiser that (1) the conversation is being recorded and (2) the tape will be used as a sales aid.

Another technique of the testimonial is to suggest that a potential but reluctant client telephone an advertiser who, the salesman knows, had good results from a radio campaign.

A top-forty station, wishing to impress advertisers with the range of its audience, might run on-the-air testimonials from contest winners.

Example:

> This is Mrs. John Jones. I'm a mother of three and have just won $300 in KXXX's Cash Call contest. It sures pays to listen to KXXX.

This device not only gets a local name and voice on the air but serves also to indicate adult listenership.

Advertisers throughout the country have been treated (or subjected) to stations' "Secretary of the Day" or "Man of the Day" promotions. This may be a last-ditch sort of sales aid, but it has changed many minds as to who, if anyone, listens to radio. After being treated to the advertiser's vast knowledge of radio's death at the hands of television, the salesman advises the program department he'd like to make "Mr. Smart" the station's "Man of the Day." The program department prepares this announcement:

> Today is Mr. Smart Day in Ourtown. If you see Mr. Smart, give him a friendly greeting and congratulate him on being KXXX's "Man of the Day."

If Mr. Smart is well-known, the well-wishing begins almost immediately. The neighbors tell Mrs. Smart. Mr. Smart's business associates congratulate him. He can't believe so many people listen to that radio station! The same device may be used with Mr. Smart's secretary. This is particularly effective if flowers are sent to the secretary and displayed all day on her desk. This method can be detrimental if the boss or secretary so honored should be embarrassed by or resentful of the publicity. The list of honorees should not be prepared very far in advance; in case he should die or be seriously injured, it's easy to forget that Mr. Smart's name is on the list. This gambit, an effective sales aid in all markets with poorly-informed potential advertisers, is also effective as a station relations builder at sophisticated levels. Even though the buyer cannot justify a buy on the station, the salesman is certain to get a better audience the next time he calls for an appointment.

SELLING THE STATION TO ADVERTISERS

There was a period in which media did not cross-plug. Even the staffs of jointly owned radio stations, television stations, and newspapers fought each other. By the early 70s, however, it was commonplace to find independently owned newspapers and radio stations trading time and space or buying from each other. A station's best friend can be the market's number two newspaper or television station although the number two position is not necessarily a prerequisite to doing business.

External Use of Other Media

New stations or new formats in particular need outside media. Not only does a billboard, newspaper, or television campaign draw new listeners to a station, but outside promotion helps convince advertisers that the new station (or format) is being promoted and either does, or will have, listenership. Promoting a radio station is about the same as promoting any other product or service. It is simply an outside effort to influence people to try the station. All the billboards in the world can't help a poorly operated station. Promotion can move listeners to the frequency, but only the format can keep them.

In addition to local media, radio stations also use trade journals such as Broadcasting Magazine or data books such as Standard Rate and Data Service (SRDS). These efforts are aimed at national advertisers and their agencies. Industry ads are also used to intimidate and demoralize local print and broadcast competition.

Many stations employ advertising agencies to handle outside promotional activity. The agency performs the same service for a radio station as it would for a product manufacturer and often charges the station a retainer fee, plus whatever commissions may be generated on production and TV time space buying.

The prudent broadcaster, particularly in major markets, established a promotional budget to carry him through a given period of operation. As in any business, budgets allow the owner to plan. A typical promotional budget indicates the amount of cash to be spent as well as the amount of trade-out involved. The budget also gives the broadcaster another legitimate reason to turn down the hundreds of requests he gets each year to "participate" in special industry publications, special newspaper sections, school yearbooks and newspapers, police and fire department magazines, and football programs. If it isn't in the budget, and if the budget is a firm one, the money cannot be made available for such participation. Radio stations annually give away millions of dollars in time and still are asked to make cash donations to everything from United Fund to PTA spaghetti suppers.

A Typical Promotional Budget:

KXXX PROMOTIONAL BUDGET

Medium	Description	Cost	Cash	Trade
Billboards	100 boards, April May, June	$15,000	$15,000	
Newspaper (Daily)	12 ¼-page ads, one monthly	3,600	-	3,600
Newspaper (Weekly)	12 ½-page ads, one monthly	1,500	-	1,500
SRDS	Five 1-col x 5" ads, June, July, Aug., Nov.	2,500	2,500	-
Broadcasting	Eight full-page ads (Dates to be determined)	16,000	16,000	-
	Totals	$38,600	33,500	5,100

The outside promotion budget might also include the cost of sales aids, such as rating services, brochures, target studies, and special printing on rate cards. Any technique suitable for selling a product or service may be used in promoting the radio station. It is not uncommon to see a picture of a beautiful girl, clad in the traditional mini-bikini, stretched out cat-like on a billboard with copy extolling the sounds of a local station. Gordon McLendon once stirred up a commotion in Dallas with a billboard campaign that read, simply:

KLIF—The Station with One Hell of a Nerve.

A Chicago station, in the early days of psychodelic art, launched a billboard campaign that was a disastrous failure because the call letters were not discernable among the myriad of colors and swirls.

Sales Presentations

Most "pitches" by radio time salesmen (account executives or sales reps) are made informally. The climbing station with aggressive management and properly motivated sales personnel makes far more elaborate presentations than the busy station that fights to keep up with spot availabilities and simply handles the incoming business that years of high ratings have generated. But the sales problem itself often determines what sort of presentation or "pitch" is made to the advertiser or buyer.

The impromptu presentation is probably most commonly used by account executives. Any salesman who isn't prepared to give his station's complete "story" isn't doing his job. The impromptu presentation might occur in a coffee shop, an office, or a restaurant.

Example:

SALESMAN: Well, Mr. Johnson, I've been trying for several days to reach you by telephone, but no luck. You seem to stay busy.

JOHNSON: Who are you with?

SALESMAN: KXXX. I've had an idea which might be of some help on your advertising.

JOHNSON: I'm not familiar with your station, but now that we're talking, why don't you tell me what's on your mind?

SALESMAN: Well, I'm somewhat familiar with your business and your advertising. You have four dress shops, and you cater to the younger set. I've seen those big newspaper ads and I think someone has been doing a good job there. And while KYYY is a fine, well-programed radio station, I'm sure their format doesn't appeal to your market.

JOHNSON: We've never used much radio. And that schedule we have on KYYY was purchased mainly because I sometimes play golf with the owner. But how do you know they don't reach my market? Aren't all radio stations about the same?

SALESMAN: Positively not. You can't compare radio stations any more than you can compare your expensive ready-to-wear with dresses sold at a big discount store. The American Research Bureau (ARB) is an audience rating company,

	and they do two studies a year in this market to determine who listens to what radio station.
JOHNSON:	Are such studies accurate?
SALESMAN:	I think they are accurate estimates. Our station programs contemporary music; we appeal to the youth market. KYYY plays what we call middle-of-the-road (MOR) music, which appeals to an older group of people.
JOHNSON:	I see. And what does your ARB say that would interest me?
SALESMAN:	Just this. You're aiming for women, 18-34. ARB shows KXXX reaches an average of 18,000 such women during the average ¼-hour in morning drive. KYYY reaches only 6,000 during the same period. And as far as this age group is concerned, we reach more of them at any time of day than any other station in the market.
JOHNSON:	How far out does your station go?
SALESMAN:	Well, we're 5,000 watts non-directional day and night, and we easily cover Ourtown's entire trade territory. We have no signal problems, and our 1010 frequency is good. It's right in the middle of other local frequencies, and our listeners have no trouble finding us and keeping us tuned in.
JOHNSON:	Have any of my competitors ever used your station?
SALESMAN:	Oh, often. The Young Misses Shop is a steady advertiser. And Contempo Wear finished a successful anniversary campaign last week. The owner of Young Misses is a friend of mine, and I know he wouldn't mind discussing his results with you.
JOHNSON:	Look, I've got to run. But why don't you put something together for my stores? I'll gamble $500 with you on the sale we've got coming up.

In this case, the impromptu sales presentation involved no more than the salesman's knowledge of his radio station and some knowledge of the advertiser's business and his competition. He candidly discussed his station versus a competitive station, but he did not knock the competition. He admitted KYYY was a good radio station but pointed out that it simply did not reach Mr. Johnson's market. The salesman sold on KXXX's merits, not on KYYY's demerits.

The formal presentation may involve everything from color slides to produced commercials and jingles. It largely depends upon the size of the prize to be won if the presentation is successful. An account capable of spending $50,000 a year on a station would justify a considerable effort. The seasonal spender whose annual budget is $1,500 would get something less than the grand effort, depending upon market size.

Example:

Product: XXX Beer
Market: Ourtown
Budget: $50,000
Target: Men, 18 and older
(Note: The following may be accompanied by slides or flip cards that highlight principal points.)

The latest census report shows Ourtown has a population of 840,000 persons. Of these, 33 percent are men 18 years and older. We believe XXX Beer has made a good choice by deciding to enter the Ourtown market, for several reasons.

Ourtown is a blue collar market and a college market. There are 40,000 persons employed in heavy industry, and the market's three colleges have 18,000 male students.

Last year, local beer distributors grossed four million in sales. The top seller was X brand with 40 percent of the market; No. 2 was Y brand with 30 percent, and Brands A, B, and C shared the remaining 30 percent about evenly.

Of last year's total beer sales, 60 percent was bought in package and grocery outlets. The balance was sold in bars, taverns, hotels, and inns.

KXXX believes it can be a vital force in XXX Brand's effort to enter and capture part of Ourtown's rich beer market. Here's how KXXX rates with the market's males, 18 and older. All figures are from The Pulse, Inc., one of the nation's most respected audience rating companies; they denote average ¼-hour audiences, and cover the Monday-Friday period.

	6-10A.M.	10-3P.M.	3-7P.M.	7P.M.-12M.
Station KXXX	21,000	10,000	19,000	14,000
Station B	11,000	6,000	8,000	4,000
Station C	10,000	5,000	7,000	3,000

On Saturdays, KXXX has an average ¼-hour audience of 26,000 between 6A.M.-7P.M. and 18,000 between noon and 7P.M. on Sunday. Station B has less than half this audience, while Station C has about 30 percent.

Station KXXX proposes that XXX Brand use 40 1-minute announcements per week, distributed in this manner:

Day	Number of Spots	Time Period	Class	Unit Cost
Monday-Friday	(2)	10A.M.-3P.M.	B	$15
Monday-Friday	(3)	3P.M.-7P.M.	A	20
Monday-Friday	(1)	7P.M.-12M.	C	12
Saturday	(5)	6A.M.-7P.M.	A	20
Sunday	(5)	12N.-7P.M.	B	15

This schedule calls for 15 Class B announcements at $15; 20 Class A announcements at $20 and five Class C announcements at $12. The average CPM on Class A units is $1.00; $1.50 on Class B units, and around $0.66 on Class C units. Total weekly cost is $685 per week or $26,715 for the 39-week campaign.

While a similar budget on Ourtown's second-ranked station would purchase a few more spot units, the average cost per thousand persons reached would be $2.15, compared to KXXX's average CPM of $1.05.

KXXX has operated in Ourtown under the same ownership and format for 10 years. We broadcast at 1010-kHz on the dial and with 5,000 watts of power day and night. Our professtional news staff and weekly editorials have made KXXX one of the most respected radio operations in the state.

In the case of a beer advertiser, the station would not present proposed commercials, as most such advertisers have high quality, professionally produced material available. If such production is not available, the station, then, would logically present a series of so-called "spec" (speculative) spots to give the client an idea of how the station's production department can perform.

Most radio "pitches" fall somewhere in between the casual, impromptu presentation made in the coffee shop and the elaborate effort made with respect to the beer client. Extraordinary sales efforts are normally made in behalf of new accounts which have never used the station or for any account when the station is conducting a special sales promotion. Service is the mainspring of big revenue once the account is on the air. The professional salesman stays "on top" of his accounts' schedule, production, and sales. He checks with traffic to make sure spots are scheduled in the time slots ordered; he auditions production, when practical, to make certain his client is getting the best the station has to offer; and he maintains contact with the client to see whether desired results are being obtained.

Management as a Sales Force

The licensee who doesn't employ sales-oriented general managers and insist they involve themselves in daily sales operations is probably depriving himself of additional profits. Although there is no available study to indicate how many general managers have a background in sales and how many in programing, it is safe to assume that most financially successful stations are piloted by men and women with extensive sales backgrounds.

Only a manager with genuine sales experience can truly understand the problems of the salesman and know when he is being productive or when he is marking time. Program departments cannot be run by individuals with no experience in that field, and salesmen cannot often be motivated by managers who have not been "down the road." Aside from internal requirements for sales-oriented management, many accounts, particularly in small to medium markets, demand attention from top management. Some, in fact, refuse to deal with the ordinary salesman.

The aggressive general or sales manager stays ahead of his sales force through the use of midnight oil, planning, and constant attention to who is doing what in the market. Management is needed in preparing sales presentations to many accounts, and the involved manager often accompanies his salesmen on routine or special sales calls. When a direct account (no agency) is involved, store managers and ad managers usually are impressed when the boss of the station makes a call or takes them to lunch or cocktails. The manager with extensive background in sales can often sense an account's disinterest in the station. Only by involving himself to some extent in all major accounts can he know whether his station is getting a fair share of the advertiser's budget.

The "fat," unimaginative manager who defends his desk chair and prefers to operate from his ivory tower operates either a static station or one that is moving downhill. It is up to management to plan the sales effort and to increase or lower the rates through the packaging device. Management plans the sales promotions and provides the extra incentives salesmen need to bring in the business. It is a poor manager, indeed, who doesn't have something new for his sales force at each meeting.

Example of Poor Management:

SECRETARY: Okay, gentlemen. Time for the sales meeting.

SALESMAN 1: Oh, boy. Another hour to be wasted.

MANAGER: Good morning, men. How about that football game last night? Wasn't Rocky sensational?

SALESMAN 2: I'll say.

(The manager and salesmen then spend 20 minutes doing a post mortum on last night's game.)

MANAGER Look you guys. I've got a golf date with the owner this morning, so if none of you has any serious problems, let's adjourn the meeting. Business is good; ratings are holding; benefits are tight for the moment, so let's not overwork ourselves. Besides, the owner is happy with everything. See you guys later.

With five salesmen, the manager wasted a total of 2.5 man hours, not counting his own half hour. No business was discussed. Every man had a problem but couldn't classify it as serious.

Example of Good Sales Management:

SECRETARY: Okay, gentlemen. Time for the sales meeting. And be sure to bring your weekly reports.

MANAGER: Good morning, men. Say, Jim, before we start, how'd you make out on the pitch to Ourtown Department Store?

JIM: Don't know yet. KYYY was there first, and from what the ad manager's secretary said, it made a big impression.

MANAGER: Okay. See if you can get the ad manager on the phone after the meeting, and we'll take him to lunch. We're the best buy for them, and away from his telephones and staff members, maybe the two of us can sell him.

Okay, gents. Let me see your weekly reports. Glad to see you're up, Jim. That Firestone sale last week really helped your gross. Bill, you're looking better, but you shouldn't have lost that theater account. We'll have to get our heads together to plan a way to get it back or maybe activate some of the other newspaper-oriented theater accounts. Sam, you stood still last week. What happened?

SAM: I don't know. I think that cancellation demoralized me, and I just couldn't get traction. What I need is a big fat call-in (an account that calls or drops in with a surprise budget).

94

MANAGER:	Okay, okay. Now, let's get down to business. Our April local billing was 10 percent ahead of last year; so far in May, we're running slightly ahead of last year; but my projections show we're in trouble in June.
SAM:	Yeah, and I heard that KYYY is looking at the same problem in June. It isn't just us. I think business in general is headed downhill, what with the layoffs, and general economic conditions.
MANAGER:	Maybe so, Sam, but we're not buying that. I've got some ideas that may help put us back in the ballgame in June.
JIM:	So start talking, mastermind.
MANAGER:	Nothing masterful about my plan. We've been so busy looking after day-to-day business that we're not making enough new account calls.
JIM:	But...
MANAGER:	No buts! I read your sales reports every week, remember? All of you seem busy, but you're not making the new calls and developing the new business. You know, to get ahead, you need about 1.5 dollars in new business for each dollar you lose through cancellations or expirations. Now then, starting this week, I want each of you to call on five new accounts. I've set up a 40-spot weekly package I want you to sell. It's called the Total Audience Plan (TAP). We'll offer it during the summer months of June, July, and August. KYYY has the same plan, but they aren't pushing it.
JIM:	But what's so attractive about the TAP plan? Is it going to be offered at a lower rate?
MANAGER:	Positively not. The 40 plan I've devised calls for 20 Class A units at $25 and 20 Class B units at $15. The average unit cost is $20, and we're going to sell the package on that basis. Now, if we sell as many as 20 of those packages during June, July and August, the guy with the most new accounts sales will get $300 in cash and two days off. The low man will service the winner's accounts during his time off.

This, of course, was a better, more productive sales meeting. While the manager only came up with a simple package plan, there are literally hundreds of plans that could be developed to generate additional sales. It is the challenge of management to create sales plans that motivate salesmen to greater revenue production.

Public Relations

A California broadcaster once declared, "You can add your prestige, your public relations, and 10 cents, and have enough for a cup of coffee.'' Although a station's public relations are perhaps not that unimportant, only the largest and richest operations maintain separate public relations departments. Public relations are handled largely by every member of the staff, if the subject is the least bit definitive in the station's plan of operation. Any radio station, whether ownership and management are aware of it or not, is continually engaged in an effort to improve its relations with the public. The station and its staff literally live in a fishbowl and are subject to constant scrutiny by the general public.

A station's public relations may be determined by its ratings, what people say about it (or don't say), the extent to which people depend upon station services, and how often, perhaps, the station and its staff are called upon to help in civic projects. Ratings alone, however, do not insure that a station is well thought of in the community or that the licensee will not be challenged when his license is next up for renewal.

A station is said to have good public relations when it is known as a good citizen. Such an operation may be the lowest rated station in the market and, indeed, could be a financial loser. To reflect on the California broadcaster's remark, in this case, the station would need to add 10 cents to its prestige and public relations in order to buy a cup of coffee.

A realistic public relations department in a radio operation would:

1. Fill speaking engagements.
2. Handle all public service campaigns.
3. Function as the complaint department on all matters.
4. Design and execute advertising campaigns in outside media.
5. Handle the station's continuing public survey and build a file that will be helpful at license renewal time.
6. Maintain constant liaison with community leaders in all fields, including government, civic, religious, business, and cultural.
7. Coordinate with the program department on development of community-oriented station promotions.

Obviously, the maintenance of such a department would be expensive, and only a few radio-only operations budget funds for this purpose.

It is not uncommon to find such departments in a Newspaper-TV-Radio media complex. A department in such an organization would handle not only the seven areas mentioned, but also would probably handle any cross-plugging the different media might engage in.

Generally speaking, radio holds little for the student who wishes to operate solely in the field of public relations. The few jobs that do exist are held by broadcast pioneers who have been "kicked upstairs" into PR or by a rapidly diminishing group of experts employed only by major, old-line facilities or by the media complexes. The public relations function at most stations is handled by the staff, the manager, the announcers, and salesmen in particular. Anyone on the staff who has contact with people outside the station is dealing in public relations. Salesmen, in dealing with clients, have excellent opportunities to develop good public relations.

Example:

SALESMAN: Mr. Johnson, I just noticed the Lions Club plaque on your wall. Are you pretty active?

JOHNSON: Yes, as a matter of fact, I've just been elected publicity chairman.

SALESMAN: Well, I'm authorized to offer you whatever public service time you need to promote your projects. Our gal Sue handles most of the public service at the station, but if she happens not to be available, just give me a call.

Stations receive daily calls for help. Management and staff response to these calls determine, in large part, the level of the station's public relations. Here are ten situations which, if properly handled, will yield PR points for the station:

1. The police have requested that names of accident victims be withheld pending notification of next of kin. The station should comply.
2. The Kiwanis Club wants a speaker at Tuesday's luncheon. If any staffer is qualified to speak on the desired subject, the station should comply.
3. The PTA needs a public address system. If the equipment is available, it should be loaned. Extra points may be gained if an operator can be sent along. This action also would (1) ensure the equipment operates properly, and (2) prolong the life of the equipment.
4. A distraught woman visits the station saying her husband has disappeared, and she'd like to buy time to ask him to please come home. DON'T DO IT! BE SYMPATHETIC, BUT TELL THE LADY THAT ALL SUCH REQUESTS MUST COME THROUGH THE POLICE. While it may seem cruel to deny an individual such help, the station

will probably violate the Commission's rules against personal communications, and there is always the possibility that the station is being made part of a hoax or practical joke.

5. A local minister calls to ask if he can have thirty minutes of time each morning for a devotional directed to those who will not or cannot attend church. The station's religious schedule is filled, but at least one-half hour of the programing is devoted to a nationally syndicated, non-sectarian devotional. The station would be points ahead if it cancelled the out-of-town program and substituted the local one.

6. The local scout master calls and asks if some of his boys might tour the station. The station should make definite arrangements for someone to show the scouts around.

7. The station manager hears that the police are having trouble recruiting. The manager calls the police chief and offers public service time to help in the effort.

8. The school principal calls and asks the station to announce that, because of bad weather, the schools will be closed tomorrow. The station should comply immediately and ask how it may be of further service.

9. A group from the local bar association calls on the manager to complain about remarks made by an announcer about the district attorney's office. If investigation reveals the remarks were made, the station should make every effort to provide equal time to either the district attorney or his representative.

10. A listener complains that the station's editorial policy is too far right or left and that in most cases station editorials are unfair. The person hearing the complaint provides the listener with an explanation of the Fairness Doctrine or advises the manager of the complaint so that he may discuss the matter with the complaintant. If the salesman or the manager can provide the listener with editorials and rebuttals, the listener, while not completely satisfied, will realize that the station has at least been fair in broadcasting both sides of any important local issue.

The station operator who maintains a good, unbiased image in the community is not likely to be hit by a "strike" application at license renewal time. Most communities have minority groups, and they cannot be ignored. Black or Chicano elements must be given the same treatment as the station gives the majority group. The station cannot differentiate between black and white churches, civic organizations, or schools, nor can the minority elements be relegated to "special" times during the broadcast week. A station in

Georgia set aside the 6-9A.M. period on Sunday morning for use by local Negro churches. The 9-12 period was reserved for white churches. A delegation of local Blacks complained about the arrangement, and the broadcaster's Washington attorney advised him to integrate the religious broadcasts immediately, moving some of the Negro programs to the late Sunday morning period and some of the white programs to the early slots.

Stations, particularly in small to medium markets, are known by the staffers they keep. A shoe salesman for a local department store can tour the bars, land in jail, and the department store never seems to suffer. But if the morning man on a station is arrested for public disorder, it becomes a topic of conversation the next day. The department store clerk, if discussed at all, is identified by name. The announcer is identified as "the morning man at KXXX." If management can convince each staffer that he is externally in station public relations, chances are good that the operation's PR will remain high.

THE NATIONAL SALES REPRESENTATIVE

The careful selection of a National Sales Representative is every bit as important to the licensee as the selection of a general manager or sales manager. The National "Rep"' is an important member of the station's sales team, and the product of his work frequently makes the difference between black and red ink.

Just as good salesmen in major markets seek to work for the biggest revenue-producing station, aggressive Rep firms seek to represent nationally the major market's hottest station. The problem of the leading properties in the top twenty-five is not to find a rep, but to decide which applicant to accept. On the opposite side, the small market operator has as much of a problem in hiring a good rep as he does in finding and keeping a good local salesman. Most FM stations in markets of all sizes in the early 1970s were not able to get aggressive, productive national reps.

If a station is in the 200th or smaller market, a simple fact of radio life should be faced. If it has a quality rep, the rep will select the station, not the other way around. But if the station is in the top 100 markets, the broadcaster can expect to be solicited by at least one and possibly several firms.

The ideal rep firm will have offices in all major markets, especially in New York, Chicago, and Detroit. Secondary but professionally staffed offices will be maintained in San

Francisco, Los Angeles, and other top ten markets where national buys are made. In making a selection, top management should visit the main offices of the applicant rep firm. How many salesmen does the firm have to cover New York agencies? New York, after all, is the source of more advertising dollars than any other city in the country. How does the firm's number and quality of salesmen compare with other rep firms? What kind of background do individuals on the staff have? What sort of station "list" does the Rep have? If he represents top properties in the top ten markets, odds are good that he'll be a winner. If he has a list of second-best properties in the major markets, he probably has a second-best Rep firm. What sort of turnover has the firm had in stations? If the Rep has been playing musical chairs with stations, the firm has probably been jockeying for better properties, or the stations involved have been jockeying for a better Rep. If investigation reveals such movement, find out why.

The Rep Contract

A formal contract often binds the agreement between the station and the National Rep. The contract spells out commissions, protected territory (sales jurisdiction), and other conditions. In most cases, the relationship between station and Rep is friendly and is based upon mutual trust and respect. The contract, however binding, is used primarily to simply spell out or put into writing (to avoid misunderstandings later) the conditions under which the two will do business.

Sample Station-Rep Agreement:

Gentlemen:

We hereby appoint you to act as the exclusive national sales representative of Radio Station_____ , _____ , owned and operated by _____ . This arrangement is to become effective _____ , and you are to act in the capacity of national sales representatives throughout the United States with the exception as specified below, unless we specifically assign certain accounts to you within this territory.

You agree to exercise your best efforts in the sale of time and facilities of Radio Station _____ and the national promotion of the_____ market, and for this purpose will maintain a national organization, personnel, permanent office locations in the principal advertising centers, and do such traveling throughout the United States as is necessary. You are to pay all expenses in connection with the maintenance of these offices, personnel, and all matters incidental to obtaining national business for Radio Station_____ .

We agree to list your organization as our exclusive representatives in Standard Rate and Data, and in our own advertising and promotional material. It is mutually agreed that you will be consulted in the establishment of national rates which are published in Standard Rate and Data.

As compensation you are to receive a commission of 15 percent on the net amount of all national business accepted and carried by us originating in the United States, with the following exceptions:

A. Business originating from advertising agencies located within a 50-mile radius of the city of license.

B. Business which is currently under contract to us. At the conclusion of all current contracts, however, all business within the definition of this aggreement, if renewed, will become commissionable to you.

The net amount as referred to in this contract is defined as the actual amount billed and collected by us. Any product or service that is sold in two or more states under the same trade name is considered national business and is commissionable to your firm.

We agree to remit to you not later than the twenty-fifth (25th) day of each month all commissions due you, with a complete and detailed statement of all national business within the definition of this agreement done under the terms of this arrangement, in the preceding month, which statement shall set forth the names of all such national advertisers and the business done with each of such advertisers during the preceding month, and the amounts owing from each of said advertisers.

We reserve the right to terminate broadcasting under any contracts at any time and for any reason whatsoever, but agree to cooperate with you fully in the sale and service of both facilities and talent to advertisers whose business and products satisfy our requirements.

This agreement shall terminate on _____ , but shall be automatically renewed for the next successive 12-month period, and thereafter shall be automatically renewed from time to time for successive 12-month periods unless one of the parties notifies the other by mailing a written notice to the other not less than 90 days nor more than 180 days prior to the expiration of any such 12-month period of its desire that this agreement terminate upon the expiration of such period.

In the event of the termination of this agreement you shall be paid a commission on all business done under any contract then in existence until the termination or renewal of such contract.

If the foregoing is in accordance with your understanding, will you please indicate your acceptance of this contract by signing as indicated below.

Very truly yours,

_____

For RADIO STATION _____

By _____

Dated: _____

ACCEPTED:

_____

_____

For Radio Representative

Once employed, the Rep Firm becomes a member of the station's sales force and fits, essentially, into the organization (see Fig. 5). The solid lines indicate the flow of business from client, to agency, to salesman, to station. The broken lines indicate direct business, or sales derived directly from the client to the exclusion of the advertising agency. While the National Rep does not normally deal directly with the advertiser, it does happen. The dot-dash line indicates a house account, e.g., business handled by the manager and-or his secretary. Direct commissions normally are not paid on house accounts.

Keeping the Rep Informed

The radio sales manager of a New York rep firm became irate upon learning that one of his major properties had switched newscasts from the hour to the fifty-five minute spot. "How can we sell the station," he cried, "if the so-and-so's won't tell us what they're doing?"

The Rep must have the same tools as those provided the local salesmen. In most cases, there should be daily or at least weekly communication between station management and the Rep. The dollar volume being generated will dictate the frequency of contact, but regardless of the national sales level, management should establish a consistent pattern of contact.

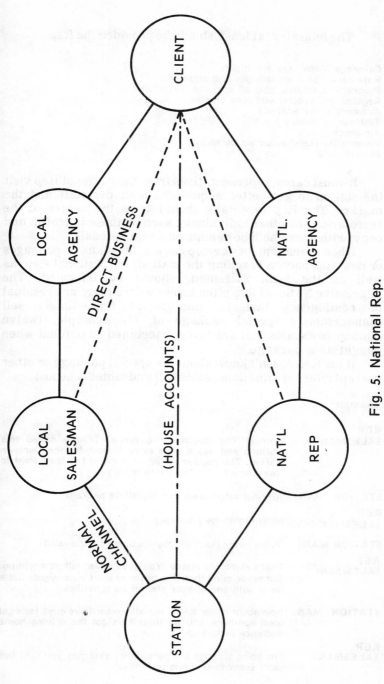

Fig. 5. National Rep.

103

The following, at least, should be provided the Rep:

Coverage Maps, day and night
Rate cards, plus all changes and additions
Program schedules, plus all changes and additions
Regular and special audience studies
Audience study analysis
Testimonial letters
Air checks
Personality sketches on air personnel
Market data

In most cases, representatives from the National Rep visit the station to get better acquainted with the staff and the market. The Rep especially should know the names of the secretaries and other individuals, such as those in traffic and copy, with whom he'll be dealing on a regular basis.

When management develops new sales plans or packages or new approaches to selling the station, the National Rep, as well as the local salesmen, should be informed. The aggressive National Rep often knows where there are residual or contingency budgets, and might immediately sell management's special package of, for example, twelve Sunday newscasts that are being discounted 10 percent when bought as a package.

If the Rep doesn't know about the special package or other current offers or situations, sales will undoubtedly be lost.

Example:

REP
SALESMAN: Jimmy! The Budweiser buyer at D'Arcy called this morning and has a little extra budget for the Ourtown market. The regular schedule is okay, but they want to play around with this extra money.

STATION MAN: Why not pitch them our nighttime package?

REP
SALESMAN: What nighttime package?

STATION MAN: Oh my gosh! Don't tell me you didn't get the word?

REP
SALESMAN: That's right, old buddy. You guys never tell us anything. But never mind fhat. The buyer doesn't want nights but a tie-in with one of your station personalities.

STATION MAN: How about Killer Kelly, our afternoon drive guy? He's got good numbers, and we think he's got the driving home audience locked up.

REP
SALESMAN: I'm going through the personality sketches you sent but can't seem to find one on Kelly.

STATION MAN: Oh, he's been here only three months. We probably haven't gotten around to bringing you up to date.

REP SALESMAN: (thoroughly hacked) Well, look. Have you guys done anything else we should know about? Like change the call letters or increase power?

STATION MAN: Okay, pal. I got your message. We'll get you up to date immediately. Sorry about the confusion.

Most middle-to-major market stations send a member of management on agency trips from two to twelve times annually. Where large amounts of money are concerned, the station man will often have an opportunity to present the station to the entire Rep sales team. It becomes a sales meeting, with the station manager making an effort to motivate the Rep sales force to sell his station. During such visits, which usually last no more than one week per market, Rep salesmen line up agency visits for the station man. An experienced Rep salesman, about to make agency visits with the manager of a medium market station, suggested the visitor come up with a brief but special tidbit about his market. "Anything," said the Rep, "that will help me keep your market foremost in the buyer's mind."

For the most part, the station man doesn't actually make a presentation to the buyer on the agency trips. Reps have been known to plan setups where the station man pitches the buyer and, to everyone's complete astonishment, makes a sale. There have been, however, legitimate cases where the Rep simply didn't have adequate market or station information; and the station man was immensely helpful in closing a sale. The local man would be helpful, for example, in a situation where the buyer was trying to make a decision between two properties in the same market where ratings were about even. The manager's presence, his intimate knowledge of his station, his ability to recite success stories and offer, perhaps, merchandising, could make the difference.

In New York and Chicago, particularly, visits by station men with agency buyers are infrequent and, for the most part, brief. The wise buyer, however, will give the station man some time, because here's a man who knows the market in which the agency may make a buy. The station man, for example, might mention that a certain industry's third shift ends at 8 P.M. and the information could indicate a buy of nighttime announcements in the market. The station man's knowledge of major market agencies and buyers makes it easier for him to discuss sales strategy with the National Rep.

Example:

REP
SALESMAN:
    X-Brand's agency is ready to make a buy this week, and Ourtown market is included. But it looks like KYYY will get the budget. The buyer has a short budget, but wants to concentrate it on news.

STATION MAN: Isn't the buyer Jim So-and-So?

REP
SALESMAN:
    The same.

STATION MAN: Look, when I was up there last time, Jim said he thought news adjacencies were just as good as being on the news itself. We can give him adjacencies to the 8:00 A.M. and 5:00 P.M. news at about half the rate of KYYY's news. Call Jim now and tell him we want that business and will be willing to provide the local distributor with a couple of sales incentive prizes.

POLITICAL SALES

Any discussion regarding the sale of time to politicians should be printed in red ink, because it is in this area of commercial activity that the broadcaster may get into the hottest of water. The Commission rules are fairly clear; Sec. 315 of The Communications Act spells out precisely how stations must handle political sales, and in 1966, the FCC issued its Section 315 Primer, which explained in considerable detail the courses stations may take in broadcasting political matter. (See Chapter VI.)

Political advertising is the single sales area, perhaps, that demands constant attention by top management, the licensee in particular, because he is the one who must answer to charges of Sec. 315 violations. Because they are so numerous, it is difficult to describe every situation in which station management has to make decisions based on an understanding of Sec. 315 and the Primer. Possibly, the best approach is to set down in writing a workable station policy that can be understood and adhered to by station personnel.

KXXX's Policy on Political Advertising

I. GENERAL—It is the policy of KXXX to accept political advertising and to adhere strictly to the provisions of Sec. 315 of The Communications Act and the Commission's rules that pertain to the act. Any employee who knowingly violates this policy will be subject to immediate dismissal.

II. **WHAT CANDIDATES MAY ADVERTISE**—Any person who has been declared a legally qualified candidate by a party's County Executive Committee may purchase time on KXXX, providing that station management has not decided to refuse time to candidates in that person's particular race. This is to say that while KXXX may accept time from qualified candidates in the race for U.S. Senator, it may refuse to accept time from candidates in the race for the State Legislature. There have been times in the past when KXXX simply could not accommodate all candidates for all offices; we, therefore, have established a policy in which we reserve the right to refuse advertising in certain races if we believe that to do so will overload our log with political spots.

III. **POLITICAL RATES**—When KXXX accepts political advertising, regular commercial rates will be charged. We do not have a political rate, per se. Any package plans that are available to commercial advertisers must be made available to the political advertiser. Agencies handling political accounts may take the normal 15 percent agency commission, as they do with commercial accounts.

IV. **PAYMENT**—All orders for political time will be accompanied by cash or certified check covering the amount of the order. While there is no rule that political advertisers must pay cash in advance, KXXX's experience has been that some politicans do not or cannot settle all accounts once an election has been held. This is particularly true of the losers. Therefore, if we require one candidate to pay cash in advance, we must require all of them to do so. It is not a matter of trusting the agency or the political advertiser; it is simply a matter of obeying the equal treatment implications of Sec. 315.

V. **PRODUCTION**—While most local candidates employ a professional advertising agency or public relations firm, or voice their own announcements, KXXX will make its regular announcer staff available to voice political announcements. Any announcer voicing a political announcement will use a straight, matter-of-fact delivery.

VI. **TRAFFIC**—The traffic manager will ascertain on a daily basis during political campaigns that political announcements are logged precisely as ordered. Program log entries for political announcements will indicate the name of the candidate, office sought, and party affiliation. Political announcements count as commercial time within a 60-minute segment, but are logged "Pol." indicating Political.

VII. **POLITICAL TIME ORDERS, CONTRACTS**—Each time order covering a purchase of political time will be submitted directly to the general manager, along with a regular station contract, advance cash or check payment as indicated previously, and a completed agreement form for political broadcasts. The agreement form must be complete in every detail. It is essential that station management have information on the form if we are to complete the Commission requirement for a report on political advertising. Staff members are familiar with procedures for completing our regular contracts and time orders. As the agreement form for political broadcasts is infrequently employed, we are reprinting a completed form to indicate the information we require. See Fig. 6.

Sec. 315 from the Communications Act, along with pertinent FCC Rules, are printed on the back of the form. Staff members such as salesmen, traffic girls, and announcers are urged to read the Act and the Commission's Rules on the subject.

VIII. FILES—The Agreement Form for Political Broadcasts, along with related time orders and station contracts, will be kept in the station's Public File for three years. The Commission requires that such records be kept for only two years, but KXXX's policy is to keep them three years. Naturally, in further compliance with Commission Rules, we will keep such information on file for an indefinite period of time should it relate to any litigation or controversy in progress. There is no requirement that we retain time orders and station contracts, but it is the intent of KXXX to provide full and complete disclosure on any political advertising should such a requirement be presented.

SPECIAL REVENUE TACTICS

When a retailer's inventory is not moved at the desired rate, he puts the merchandise on sale. Two-for-one specials are common in shoe stores, bakery shops, and department stores. The retailer realizes that it's better to sell on a no-profit basis today than to sell at a loss tomorrow.

There are times when the broadcaster, too, must resort to special sales devices if he is to stay in business. Under ideal conditions, the station sells spot announcements and programs, and published rates are strictly observed. There is no room for "hanky-panky" in a profitable operation. A price is named and the advertiser either pays it or doesn't get on the air. Unfortunately, all operations aren't financially successful, and these broadcasters must rely upon special revenue tactics to help the station survive. Special tactics

AGREEMENT FORM FOR POLITICAL BROADCASTS

STATION and LOCATION ___ KXXX, Chicago, Ill. ____ May 10 _____ 19 75

I, ___ John J. Jacobs ___, (being) (supporting) - _____,

a legally qualified candidate for the office of _____ Senator _____ in the

___ June 1 primary ___ election, do hereby request station time as follows:

LENGTH OF BROADCAST	HOUR	DAYS	TIMES PER WEEK	TOTAL NO. WEEKS	RATE
1-min	ROS	Mon-Sun	21	2	$18.00

DATE OF FIRST BROADCAST	DATE OF LAST BROADCAST
May 14, 1975	May 27, 1975

The broadcast time will be used by ___ The Candidate

I represent that the advance payment for the above-described broadcast time has been furnished by

___ Jones for Senator Comm. ___ and you are authorized to so describe the sponsor in your

log, or otherwise, and to announce the program as paid for by such person(s).

The entity furnishing the payment, if other than an individual person, is: ( ) (1) a corporation; (x) (2) a committee; ( ) (3) an association; or ( ) (4) other unincorporated group.

(a) The corporation or other entity is organized under the laws of ___ Ill. ___.

(b) The officers, board of directors and chief executive officers of the entity are: Tom Smith,

112 Wabash St., Chicago, Ill, Chairman; Laura Acres, 4516 Elm St.,

Chicago, Ill., secretary.

It is my understanding that: The above is the same uniform rate for comparable station time charged all such other candidates for the same public office described above; the charges above do not exceed the charges made for comparable use of said station for other purposes; and the same is agreeable to me.

In the event that the facilities of the station are utilized for the above-stated purpose, I agree to abide by all provisions of the Communications Act of 1934, as amended, and rules and regulations of the Federal Communications Commission governing such broadcasts, in particular those provisions reprinted on the back hereof, which I have read and understand. I further agree to indemnify and hold harmless the station for any damages or liability that may ensue from the performance of the said broadcasts.

For the above broadcast, I agree to prepare a script or transcription, which will be delivered to the station at least ___ 24 ___ before the time of the scheduled broadcast.

(Candidate, Supporter or Agent)

Accepted)
Rejected) by _____ Title General Manager

If rejected, the reasons therefor are as follows:

Accepted

This application, whether accepted or rejected, will be available for public inspection for a period of two years, in accordance with FCC Regulations (AM, Section 3.120; FM, Section 3.290; TV, Section 3.657).

Fig. 6. Agreement Form for Political Broadcasts.

include barter, outside sales forces, sale of production room facilities and talent, classified ads, trade agreements, per inquiry advertising, and record promotions.

Barter

A barter agreement is entered into when time is sold to an individual or company for resale to advertisers. All barter agreements must be filed with the FCC. There is no rule against making a barter deal, so long as the agreement specifies that the licensee will maintain control over use of the time involved.

Example:

BARTER SALESMAN: Look, Mr. Jones, if you're suffering a cash squeeze right now, maybe I can be of some help.

BROADCASTER: I don't see how unless you want to buy an awful lot of air time.

BARTER SALESMAN: That's exactly what I'm talking about. I'm prepared right now to write your station a check for $10,000. How does that sound?

BROADCASTER: Sounds fantastic. But how much of my blood do you want in return?

BARTER SALESMAN: Not blood, Mr. Jones. Time. I want time to sell to my clients. Your average rate on KXXX is $20.00. We're willing to pay you an average of $5 per spot, and we'll buy 2,000 of them right now.

BROADCASTER: If you're serious (and the barter salesman assures the broadcaster that he is, indeed, serious because he will re-sell the spots for $10-$15 each), I think we can make a deal. But I must be careful to stay within FCC rules on this deal.

BARTER SALESMAN: What rules? Don't tell me the FCC has a rule against selling time?

BROADCASTER: Not exactly, but one of my competitors ran afoul of the Commission's rules relating to barter or the brokering of time. The FCC does enforce Sec. 1.613 (c) of its rules which requires filing of all contracts relating to the sale of broadcast time to **time brokers** for resale. Brokerage agreements must contain a provision for licensee control of station operations.

BARTER SALESMAN: Well, what does this do to our deal?

110

BROADCASTER: It means we'll have to stipulate in the agreement that we have the right to approve all copy as well as the advertiser before we put it on the air. And, of course, we'll have to file the agreement with the Commission.

**BARTER
SALESMAN:** What else?

BROADCASTER: To protect myself, I will accept no orders on business presently running on the station and no orders from advertisers who have been on the station on a cash basis in the last twelve months.

Now, one more thing. Before your company attempts to sell any of the time involved in this contract, I want to see a list of your prospects. I do not want you calling on any of my regular accounts or on anyone I believe will be on the station anytime soon on a regular, cash basis. If you can agree to those provisions, I'll swallow my pride and sign the agreement.

Whether the barter salesman agreed or not is immaterial. The broadcaster has taken a big step into what is commonly known as station prostitution. A barter deal will result in quick, sometimes substantial revenue. But the broadcaster will be a long-time getting himself straight with the established advertising community; unless he's a masterful liar, he almost certainly will eventually be faced down by an irate client or agency.

In the late 40s and early 50s, it was not uncommon to find a station brokering time to local musical groups, ministers, and promoters. A string band might contract for a 1-hour slot every Saturday and pay the station $20, for example. Band members, then, would approach local advertisers and sell fifteen or twenty participating announcements at $5, thus realizing a substantial profit. These were the "innocent" little deals that ultimately led to the big money transactions, such as the one in the dialogue.

Barter is not the best way to increase revenue rapidly, but it is one way. And the technique indicated is only one of several approaches to consummating the arrangement. Merchandise, rather than cash, might be sent to the station. The merchandise could then be resold to local retailers or used in station merchandising plans. Such plans are limited only by the imagination of the station and the barter house, and the FCC provision that the licensee maintain station control.

Outside Sales Forces

Often, the broadcaster can employ outside sales personnel to sell a special station promotion and realize substantial profits from business firms that do not normally use the medium of radio. More often than not, the broadcaster hurts his station image with such promotions, depending upon the character of the special sales force. There are, however, highly efficient and well-managed special sales groups that bring credit to the station. One such group in the Dallas-Fort Worth area has for many years worked with stations throughout the Southwest, returning to the markets year after year and selling the same business firms again and again. Such "clean" operations are rare, but if the broadcaster can find one, he can be assured of a profitable campaign.

Usually, the station is approached by the manager of the outside sales force.

Example:

Mr. Jones, I know you've been bitten by bad operators in the promotional field, but I've got half a dozen good references and before we start talking, I'd like for you to call the manager at KYYY and ask him if he was pleased with our work. (The call was made and the recommendation was excellent.)

Okay, Mr. Jones, now that I know I'm not talking to a disbeliever, let me tell you what we think we can do in the Ourtown market. First, we set up a back-to-school safety campaign. We'll hang our sales presentation on that. We will not approach your regular advertisers; in fact, we want a copy of your regular sales force's protected list so we can be sure we don't step on any of your men's toes. We want to pitch only those accounts that have never been on your station.

We'll call on service stations, beauty shops, barber shops, machine shops—businessmen who normally can't afford to use your station or find radio an inappropriate medium for selling their product or service.

Our plan is to sell a package of ten back-to-school safety announcements for a flat $149.50. We'll also sell half-a-plan for $79.50. That'll let even the smallest business participate.

Now, under our way of doing business, we write all copy and collect in advance for the time. When a salesman closes a deal on the telephone, a collector goes immediately to the place of business and picks up a check to cover the order. These checks are made out to the station and are deposited by the station. Our people never handle cash. When we have sold as many advertisers as possible—or when you indicate you have no more time for us to sell—we'll settle with you. Our commission is 50 percent. That seems high. But remember, we're doing all of the work, including copy and collections; and we're selling only your unsold time. None of the time is sold "fixed position." Everything is ROS within a seven-day period, which means you may run the announcements at your convenience during the week.

At KYYY, we sold one hundred of the full packages and the station picked up a neat $7,500 for our efforts. It was all new business, and the manager told me he probably could convert several of our accounts into regular advertisers. Mr. Jones, this is an honest, effective way to use your unsold time and make some quick money. If you'll give us a chance, we'll start the campaign in two weeks. We need time to find work space, rent some furniture, and have the telephones installed.

If the outside sales force manager is truthful, his plan will work. The manager did check his one reference and, under the circumstances, might have checked others.

For comparison purposes, let's assume the outsider lied, that the reference he gave was a phoney one, and that his last deal was an absolute catastrophy for the broadcaster. Within a few days after KXXX's Back-to-School Safety Campaign opens, the station manager will receive complaints.

Example:

FROM A BAR: Mr. Jones, I'm holding a hot check for one of your salesmen. His name is J.B. Adams. You don't have a J.B. Adams? He said he worked for KXXX, and we usually don't have any problems with checks from your people.

A SALESMAN: Mr. Jones, you said those outsiders wouldn't approach our regular advertisers. Well, Big A Furniture bought one of those $149.50 packages today. Not only did he cancel his other schedule for next week, but he's mad because he let himself be pressured into buying the package.

A CUSTOMER: Mr. Jones, I bought one of those special packages and never did hear my spots on the air. I was told they'd be in prime time. What do you mean you don't see my name on the list of advertisers? I made out the check to your salesman, and I've got a receipt to prove it.

THE POLICE: That's right, Mr. Jones, we have four of your salesmen in jail for causing a disturbance at a rooming house last night. The charge is Drunk and Disorderly.

PHONE COMPANY: But, Mr. Jones, those telephones were installed as special KXXX lines, and we were told to send billing to you. Not only have the basic charges not been paid, but there's a big charge for long distance calls.

Had the promoter lied, these are just a few of the telephone calls the station might have received. And even with top, well-known references, the broadcaster still may be in trouble if the promoter does not know or cannot control his salesmen. The unscrupulous telephone solicitor will say anything to close a sale, get his commission, and leave the station to clean up after him.

Production Room

Income derived from rental of production facilities and personnel may be nil or significant, depending upon the size of the market, availability of commercial production facilities, the number of active advertising agencies, and competition among stations. In markets of from 300,000 to 500,000, the opportunities to make extra revenue through the sale of production room time may be many. Most advertising agencies in markets of this size do not have their own facilities, and there isn't enough business to support a commercial recording company. The station with adequate equipment and skilled personnel may charge up to $25 an hour for use of the production setup, and clear $200-$300 a week if an effort is made by station management to push the service. To the small station, struggling to make ends meet, this income can make the difference between profits and losses. Most stations do not add production charges to regular advertising rates. The production charge is made only to agencies that need taped announcements for other stations, both in and out of the immediate market.

Income from Real Estate

Some income can be derived from excess office and studio space. It is a fairly common practice for station owners to lease or build twice the space required for the station in order to sub-let or rent the balance for enough to make the mortgage or total lease payments. The principle is much the same when an individual buys a duplex house with the idea of living in one side and leasing the other for enough to make his payments. Some tenants can be extremely helpful to the station, such as a legal firm, CPA, printer, or advertising agency. A CPA firm, for example, might pay a certain amount of cash each month for rent and agree to handle the station's bookkeeping as part of the rental agreement.

A frequency and power requiring a great deal of real

estate for towers often can be made available to farmers and ranchers for grazing purposes. There are many stations throughout the country that require fifty to one hundred acres of land to accommodate their towers. After the towers and transmitters have been installed and properly fenced, livestock can safely graze the land without interferring with station operations.

An arrangement with a farmer or rancher could yield the broadcaster $1500-2000 a year, or more. Some broadcasters have made arrangements with farmers and ranchers to provide land maintenance in exchange for grazing privileges. More than one station owner has declared laughingly that he wasn't making money in radio, but he had just harvested his best alfalfa crop in years!

A Georgia broadcaster's construction permit required that he purchase tower space in an area adjacent to a business district. He directed engineers to use a self-supporting tower and put a good solid fence around it. He had his ground system covered with asphalt and then turned the entire space into a parking lot. It was rumored that the broadcaster made more money from the parking lot than from the radio station.

Album Promotion

No station is too large or too small to engage in the promotion of a special album of recorded music. The procedures are simple. The broadcaster first finds a producer for the album and contracts for X number at a fair price. He then arranges with a local retail chain to distribute them, in exchange for part of the profits. Once the contracts are signed and the albums are in the stores, he begins his on-the-air promotional campaign.

Assume Station A, number one operation in Ourtown, wanted to do something to increase revenue in January and February. The manager contacts a record manufacturer who agrees to produce an album of last year's hit tunes for $1.50 each. The manager and the producer believe the album will sell for $2.50 at retail, and that 10,000 copies can be sold during the four-week period between mid-January and mid-February. A chain of one hundred convenience food outlets agrees to handle distribution and will place point-of-sale signs in each of its stores. The chain manager wants 35 percent of the gross but finally agrees to accept 25 percent. Under this plan, if 10,000 copies of the album are sold, the record company will gross $15,000; the retailer will gross $6,250, and the station's revenue will be $3,750. On most stations, a $3,750 schedule in four weeks is regarded as good.

Again, it is important to obtain qualified references on the record company. Can it produce quality recordings? Will it make delivery on schedule? If the record company and the retailer perform with excellence in this promotion, it can produce the easiest revenue ever developed by a station. But if the station is harassed for six months after the promotion by irate listeners who paid $2.50 for a bad recording, the revenue earned won't be worth the time, trouble, and damage to station image.

There are several approaches management can take in developing such a promotion. Assuming the 10,000 album plan will be used, the station may agree to buy them outright or, if possible, arrange for the record producer to provide all or part of the albums on consignment. This simply means that if the records are not sold, the producer agrees to take them back and give the station credit. With the best of companies, a certain percentage of the albums will be faulty, and management should be certain the contract calls for the producer to give credit for all albums returned.

Another method of carrying out the album promotion is the telephone-mail sales system. The station broadcasts announcements selling listeners on the beauty of the album, invites them to send in a check or money order, and promises the album will be mailed to them immediately. Once the mail orders have slowed, special sales crews begin soliciting orders by telephone. This is the least desirable of the two systems because (1) the station's profit is usually lower and (2) it involves many of the unpleasant features of the special sales force and the problem of handling small checks and money orders. The fewer people involved in a promotion, the better the opportunity for bigger revenue and the less opportunity for damage to the station's reputation.

Classified Ads

Small market operations not only use the classified ad idea to develop special revenue, but some of them use the plan year-round. McLendon experimented, with FCC approval, with an all-ads operation in Los Angeles. He called the station K-ADS (FM) and broadcast classified ads around the clock. Whatever his reason for later changing the call letters to KOST (FM) and the format to "good music," it was probably the first time any broadcaster had attempted to derive revenue almost exclusively from the general listening public rather than from the business community.

The chief problem in selling classified ads is in collections. Each week, dozens of invoices for $3-$4-$5 are mailed to ad-users, and too often half of these take 60-90 days to pay or, perhaps, never pay. It is fairly simple for a station to keep up with a place of business; it is far more difficult to keep up with the consumer. But, some revenue can be derived from classified ads if management will set up a system and stick with it.

Housewives are the chief clients of classifieds-of-the air, so the Classified Ad Program should be aired sometime between 10:00 A.M. and 3:00 P.M., the time that housewives traditionally have time and do listen extensively to radio.

One approach is to put the women directly on the air. Listeners are asked to call a certain number at the station. A secretary records the caller's name, address, and telephone number, then switches the call to the control room where the announcer handling the show puts her on the air.

Example:

ANNCR: Now we have a lady with something to sell. Good morning. How are you?

CALLER: Fine, Jim; how are you?

ANNCR: Just great. Now what do you have for us this morning?

CALLER: I have a refrigerator to sell. It's a 10 cubic-foot white porcelain Norge, and I want $75 for it. It's frost-free, and we've had it about four years.

ANNCR: Now, how can our listeners see it?

CALLER: Well, I'm Mrs. Smith. My telephone number is 231-6788. I'd be glad to direct callers to my house if anyone is interested.

This technique is time consuming but develops greater listener interest than the straight announcer method. Under the latter plan, information from callers is typed on cards and delivered by the announcer. Each ad is run one or more times during a program, depending upon the rate system; and the conversation with the caller is not aired. Many stations run a Trading Post program during which listeners call in at no charge to buy and sell. In most cases, merchandise for sale includes household items only; no business firms are allowed to participate.

Per Inquiry (PI) Advertising

Want a PI deal? Stations often are confronted by this question and many manage to develop substantial annual revenues from the plan. There's nothing illegal about PI; it usually is just another way to cut rates. Under a PI plan, the station agrees to run announcements for a certain company and accept payment based on results of the advertising. For example, an insurance company may agree to pay the station $5 for each lead the station develops. The copy may ask listeners to write in for a special brochure, or call a telephone number for additional information. Each letter or telephone call would represent an inquiry, and the station would be paid on the basis of the volume of listener response. In other extreme cases, stations have made deals with automobile, furniture, or appliance dealers to broadcast promotions in which the station will receive a commission on all sales during a certain period. PI deals are not desirable, but if taking them means the difference between staying on or off the air, many broadcasters will accept this kind of business. A successful effort could result in the station receiving a higher than card rate. But in most cases, it means a rate cut and is not fair to other station advertisers.

Trade Agreements

Most trade agreements are consummated for reasons other than revenue. Stations trade out mobile news units, office supplies, office and studio space, and hotel and restaurant services. In these cases, the station is simply using unsold time to pay for needed materials and services. When the tradeout device is used for revenue purposes, it takes on a different complexion. One technique is to trade out automobiles and appliances and wholesale them in distant markets. Many dealers are anxious to make such arrangements because they receive a quantity of air time equal to the retail price of the goods. For example, if an appliance cost the dealer $100 and he received from the station $150 in airtime, he is, in effect, getting $50 worth of free time. While this special revenue plan is not recommended, it will work when the broadcaster is desperate.

SALES MANAGEMENT

Market size, the station's relative position in audience ratings, and the desires of top management determine the

118

nature and character of the sales organization. Certainly, someone must be designated to manage the sales effort, but there is no rule of business that requires that he be an executive type or that he work exclusively in this area. The general manager of a station may also be a sales manager; a salesman with a regular account list may be designated Sales Manager. Or, the station may employ a sales manager in the traditional concept and have him function only as an executive. Many larger stations employ national as well as local sales managers. See Fig. 7.

The smaller the operation, the more personnel management eliminates from the organizational chart. Regardless of the size of the staff, the sales manager's job remains constant. He initiates sales promotions, sets up and handles sales meetings, works with individual salesmen in developing account lists, maintains a master account list, rotates accounts among salesmen as required by circumstances, knows all station policy, is able to explain it to his salesmen, handles a personal account list, arbitrates disputes between salesmen, coordinates directly with the program director and traffic manager on availability lists, suggests advertising and promotional campaigns for the station, develops station-client relations, searches for new selling techniques, continually seeks testimonial letters, maintains extensive market files, maintains statistical files (demographic breakdowns, market studies), channels client complaints about programing to management, instructs salesmen to turn in complaint and praise memos to management, and may or may not handle regional or suburban business for the station (depending upon availability of a general manager or national sales manager).

In brief, the sales manager handles sales problems. He normally is directly responsible to the general manager, and his background in the business is primarily that of a salesman.

The ideal background for a sales manager:

1. One year as an announcer.

2. Two years as a salesman for the second station in a market of 100,000.

3. Four years as a salesman for the top station in a market of 500,000.

4. Two years as a rep salesman in New York or Chicago.

ORGANIZATIONAL CHART

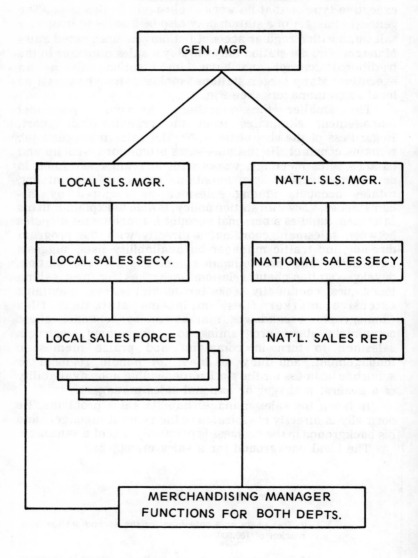

Fig. 7. Sales Organization.

The sales manager's personal attributes should include a good appearance, compatible family life, good credit, and membership in several community and industrial organizations. He should be a competitive individual and he should be ambitious. When employed, management should look for someone who eventually could become general manager of the operation. Too often, top management doesn't realize the significance of in-depth staffing. There should always be someone on the staff capable of, or in training for, taking over the position of News Director, Program Director, Sales Manager, or General Manager.

The sales manager's personal appearance is important not only to him as a working manager, but to the entire sales force. The sales manager sets the pace in work habits, in devotion to the sales problems, and in the staff's dress habits. Salesmen will imitate a neat, well-groomed sales manager. They also will ape the habits of a sloppy, careless leader.

Sales management is not a 40-hour per week job; effective management of a sales organization requires almost full-time attention from the leader.

Sales Manager Compensation

The sales manager for one of the top five stations in a major market usually earns around $25,000 to $35,000 annually. The income plan should always include definitive incentives to increase revenues.

Example:

1. Salary base (or draw against commissions) of $2,000 per month.
2. Two percent commission on net sales, providing, however, that there shall be no commission when local sales fall below $120,000 per month.

or

1. 1 percent commission on first $40,000 in local monthly billing.
2. 1.5 percent on next $20,000
3. 2.0 percent on next $20,000
4. 3.0 percent on next $20,000
5. 3.5 percent on next $20,000
6. 4.0 percent on all over $120,000

If the department produced only $120,000 per month in local revenue, the sales manager, under the second plan, would earn $2,400 per month or $28,800 per year.

Under the first plan, the sales manager's commission is a draw of $2,000 per month against a 2 percent commission, with the provision that he gets no commission if local sales drop below a certain point. That is his incentive. Under the second plan, which is, perhaps, more effective in inspiring the sales manager to produce, the average commission on $120,000 gross sales is 2 percent and yields the same income as the first plan. The difference is that plan number two offers intermediate goals for the sales manager and, therefore, is regarded as an improvement over plan number one.

Many old-line stations or stations in non-competitive markets use a simple salary plan for sales managers and salesmen, with perhaps a bonus at year-end if certain quotas are met. This is the least desirable plan because it does not provide for day-to-day incentives.

House Accounts

Often, the sales or general manager will handle certain advertisers as house accounts. These are accounts on which no one is commissioned. The sales manager may still get his override on total local sales, but no individual is commissioned on the house account. These develop, usually, when a salesman leaves the station, and management is faced with the problem of hiring a replacement or dividing the departed salesman's accounts among other salesmen. The question of how much servicing is involved usually determines when an advertiser becomes a house account.

The department store that requires four copy changes a week is not a good prospect for the house account designation. But the local soft drink bottler who provides produced commercials prepared by the brand's national agency is a good prospect for house designation. Little or no servicing is required. The schedule is prepared; the production company ships the commericals to the station, and they are logged without further problems.

Many stations require the general or sales manager to handle a certain amount of house business. The more such business is handled by management, as opposed to salesmen handling it, the less the station pays out in sales costs.

Assume that on net sales of $100,000 per month, the station pays $10,000 in commissions to local salesmen and an additional $1,000 to the local sales manager. If $10,000 of the net sales are converted to house accounts, salesmen would earn only $9,000; and the station will have reduced its overhead by $1,000 per month.

It is possible to go too far in establishing house accounts. The station manager who does so may find that he is competing with his salesmen, and the resentment this situation may create can destroy the sales effort. The safest approach is to make house accounts only of those advertisers which (1) require no selling or servicing or (2) cannot be serviced by local salesmen because the buyer is located in a distant market.

Sales Reports

Many sales managers require that salesmen turn in daily, weekly, or monthly sales reports.

A majority of radio stations use a sales report form similar to the one in Fig. 8. It has proved the most effective way for the sales manager to stay on top of his salesmen's activities. As most salesmen work with a **protected** account list, the report form is the sales manager's best means of determining whether the salesman is really working his list.

The alternative, of course, is to discuss the salesman's activities during a given period and to judge his sales production only on the strength of orders turned in. This might work, provided each salesman is a professional and is properly motivated to develop every available advertising dollar on his account list and provided the sales manager can find the time to hold weekly conferences with individual salesmen. The conference method is largely impractical in a professional sales organization, and most stations rely upon the written report.

After studying the weekly sales reports, the Sales Manager summons Salesman A to a conference as follows:

MANAGER: I note you made only 15 calls last week. What was the problem?

SALESMAN: I was bogged down in servicing. Every time I turned around it seemed I was getting a copy change or a kill or change order. I had hoped to pitch our special package to at least ten new accounts but just wasn't able to.

MANAGER: That happens, but if you'd make better use of the sales secretary you wouldn't get bogged down. Your job mainly is to sell; I can't have your talents swamped with non-revenue producing details. Susan isn't that busy, and I expect her to take this kind of detail off the shoulders of salesmen.

Example:

Name of Salesman_____

For Period ending_____

Date of Report_____

N - New

S - Service

C - Collection

CB- Call Back

Client	N	S	C	CB	Remarks
Smith Furniture	x				No radio now. Ad manager is Bill Smith. May try KXXX in May clearance sale
Rogers Agency		x			Picked up copy Johnson Motors schedule.
Clark Dept. Str.			x		Advised ad manager that account is 90 days in arrears; said would pay next week.
Auto Wash, Inc.				x	Third call on manager J.B. Jones. Believe he will buy week-packages in May.
Tyler-Smith Agency				x	Handling Home Show. Picked up $1,250 order for last week of April.

Sales Report Summary:

Number of calls made_____

Number of Sales_____

Amount of Renewals $_____

Amount of New Business $_____
Total Sales this period $_____
Salesman's comments _____

Fig. 8. Sample Sales Report.

SALESMAN: You're right, of course. It just seemed simpler at the time to handle the details myself.

MANAGER: So stop it and use the help we've provided you. Now, about Clark Department Store. You call the ad manager back and tell him we're cancelling his schedule unless we get a check by noon tomorrow. I'm tired of these people riding us for ninety or more days. We want their business, but we want to be paid on time from now on.

Without the sales report and the ensuing conference, the sales manager never would have known about the salesman's time-use problem. One important part of the sales manager's job is to insure that each salesman is devoting his time to selling, and not to administrative detail. During a sales meeting, a study of the sales reports will enable the sales manager to get to the heart of individual salesmen's problems.

Example:

MANAGER: Joe, I notice you haven't called on Jones Chevrolet in over three months. What's wrong?

SALESMAN: I just can't get through to the guy. He's stuck on KAAA and the newspaper, and I can't move him.

MANAGER: Okay. I've had trouble with him, too. If you have no objections, I'm assigning the account to Bill.

SALESMAN: Fine with me; obviously, I can't sell him.

MANAGER: Sam, your report shows Smith Furniture as a new account. Bill called on them last week and made a full presentation to the store manager.

SALESMAN: I talked with the ad manager, and he didn't mention that someone from the station had been by. I'll back off if Bill got there first.

MANAGER: Okay. So much for the sales reports. You guys are doing a fair job at calling on regular accounts, but you're not hitting enough new accounts. In this business, we can expect to lose a minimum of 20 percent of our so-called regular business each month, so we've got to continually develop new business to replace that which we know we're going to lose through business failures, changes in marketing plans, and so on. It doesn't matter at this point why we lose business; just believe me when I say we will lose it.

Now, Joe, I want to make some calls with you this week. I particularly want to call on Mr. Jones over at Car Wash, Inc. He should have been on our station six months ago, and while I know you've done a good job in presenting the station, it might be that Jones' ego will be boosted if the "boss" helps make a presentation.

125

SALESMAN: On the same subject, I could use some help over at the Rogers Agency. The new time buyer over there doesn't believe the rating services and is stuck on the salesman over at KGGG. I think we ought to call on the account executive and tell him how she's making her time buys.

MANAGER: You set up the appointment and let me know.

The sales report is a simple, efficient means of developing comprehensive communications between salesmen and management. The sales meeting is a means of extending and clarifying communications. Sales forces are much like motor cars; they require constant maintenance and repair. In most stations, the sales effort will simply drag to a halt unless management constantly stimulates and pushes sales personnel. The sales force thrives on new ideas and new approaches to sales problems.

Revenue Projections

The revenue projection, in its basic form, is simply a telescope that enables the sales manager to see into the future; it helps him to spot sags in the sales graph before they actually occur, and it enables him to lay plans to overcome the indicated revenue decline. The sales secretary or sales manager's secretary maintains the projection sheets, but the sales manager does the analytical work. Through his analysis, he can determine during early days of the first quarter of the year that business in the second quarter is falling behind that level of the preceding year. Only by such studies can he develop ways and means of keeping business ahead of the same period of the preceding year.

To maintain the projection sheet, it is necessary for the administrator to enter every order for new business, every change, every cancellation. Its accuracy is essential to management planning; it should be brought up to date each day and should be redrawn at the first of every month, eliminating the month just passed and drawing new totals for the months ahead. (See Fig. 9.)

In this case, the sales manager quickly determines that his current year projections indicate he is ahead of the same periods last year. He may determine, therefore, that no special sales promotions will be required for him to meet management-set quotas. He simply must continue to push his salesmen to sell available station time, programs, and packages.

Example: KXXX SALES PROJECTIONS—PAGE 3 January 1 ESTIMATES

ACCOUNT	JAN	FEB	MAR	APR	MAY	JUNE	JULY	AUG	SEPT	OCT
Schlitz Beer				$ 1,000	$ 1,500	$ 1,400	$ 1,200	$ 1,000		
Smith Furn	$ 650	$ 700	$ 700	700	700	700	700			
Auto Wash		500	400	600						
Gen. Motors	900	900	900	900	300	300				
Beneficial	1,800	1,800	1,800	1,900	2,000	2,000	2,000	2,000	2,000	
Ford	2,300	2,300	1,800	1,250	1,800	1,000				
Chevrolet	2,300	2,300	1,000	1,250	1,800	1,000				
John's Jeans	2,000									
Apex Nursary		900								
Clark Dept.		4,300								
Sears		1,200								
TOTALS	$190,000	$150,000	$130,000	$140,000	$110,000	$90,000				

Jan. 1 last year estimate $175,000
First quarter estimate last year $425,000
Second quarter estimate last year $300,000

Fig. 9. Revenue Projection.

127

By maintaining position charts or figures, the sales manager can know at all times what will be required in sales if he is to meet upcoming quotas. For example, if on January 1, last year, his second quarter business was $350,000, he knows from the projection sheet that at this point his second quarter sales are behind last year, and that he must plan an extra sales effort during the coming weeks.

The projection plan outlined calls for one person to collect data and enter it on the sheet (which may be a custom-designed form or a simple columnar pad). Another plan is for each salesman to maintain his own projection sheet and submit it on a regular basis to the sales manager who combines them to find his total projections. These may then be submitted to the general manager to combine with national sales projections.

Importance of Strong Local Sales

The National Association of Broadcasters (NAB) reported that in 1969 the typical station's revenue was 13 percent national and regional, while 87 percent was derived from local advertisers. In markets of 2.5 million or more and among stations grossing $1 million or more, national billing accounted for 48.5 percent of station revenue, with local sales accounting for 51.5 percent of revenue. In markets of 500,000 to one million, national dollars amounted to 35 percent of revenue and local sales amounted to 64 percent of the total. The ratio between national and local sales widened as the market size diminished. In the quarter to half million markets, national accounted for only 21.2 percent of sales while local revenues amounted to 78.8 percent of the total. In markets of less than 10,000, local was set at 89.9 percent, and national accounted for only 10.1 percent of total sales.

Even in the major markets, where national billing on top-rated stations reaches astronomical figures, local sales maintain their importance because local management can react more effectively to the local sales climate. For example, if a station loses its top-rated position in a market, national sales will plummet, and there is nothing local management can do except try to get the station back on top. While this effort is being made, national revenues may dwindle to zero. The station, therefore, must operate only on local revenues; and if the local sales force has not been nurtured and made strong, the station may face a financial crisis. National economic conditions often will cause national sales to drop and, again, there is nothing local management can do about the conditions. Local management can control only local sales and deal effectively with the local sales scene.

Many broadcasters in small-to-medium markets rarely project national sales, believing that the total effort must be directed toward local revenues, with any national dollars coming in to be considered "gravy." The smaller the market, the more prevalent is this attitude. The complete dependency in major markets on national business has led to many financial disasters.

One case history shows a daytime operation in a market of one million deriving 80 percent of its business from national sources and only 20 percent from local advertisers.

The station was the market's only black-oriented operation and paid only scant attention to local advertisers. Some advertisers complained they couldn't even get local salesmen to call on them. Others compalined the station refused to clear time for local advertisers.

As station management should have expected, but didn't, a competitive operation appeared and took the black audience. The daytimer's ratings fell to unsaleable levels, and the national dollars went to the new operation. The transition occurred in just a few months. Without a strong local base, without good rapport with local advertisers, the daytime operation failed. In such cases, the station either goes silent or is sold, subject to FCC approval.

Had the daytimer made room for local advertisers and depended less on national business, it might have survived the attack from the competition. It was unable to control the decline of national revenues and, because it had long ignored the local dollar and refused to plan ahead for the eventuality of strong competition, it was unable to survive. In this particular case, the station was purchased by a group interested in programing a country music format. Because it developed a strong local sales force and good rapport with local advertisers, it thrived.

THE CONTINUING SALES EFFORT

When McLendon was manager of KLIF, he once told the salesmen they would never be able to sit back, put their feet up on the desk, and smell the flowers. He was emphasizing that the sales force never had it made—that without a strong, continuing sales effort, no station can be financially successful.

Revenue Attrition

There is no such thing as a permanent account or an account that is locked in forever. A station loses business for six major reasons:

1. Business failures
2. Loss of ratings
3. Changes in marketing strategy, i.e., from radio to print or television
4. Aggressive, local competition
5. Salesman's errors
6. Administrative errors

The most frequently encountered reason for a schedule going off the air is a change in marketing strategy. A major brewery, for example, may decide this year to put the bulk of its budget into radio, with television and print being allocated only token amounts. Stations A, B, and C are allocated 25, 15, and 10 announcements per week for 39 weeks. Station A's total dollars from the schedule amount to $30,000; B's amount to $25,000, and C's schedule amounts to $15,000. The next year, the brewery purchases time only on Station A and has no budget for stations B and C. Most of the brewery's budget was allocated to television and print, with only a small amount going into radio. This lost revenue must be replaced, and only a continuing imaginative sales effort can keep gross dollars ahead of the previous year.

Occasionally, there are more subtle reasons for business leaving a radio station (or any other advertising medium). Radio broadcasters were not too concerned when the Federal ban on cigarette advertising became effective in January, 1971. Most broadcasters knew a year ahead of time that the business would be lost, and those with substantial tobacco budgets had plenty of time to develop other revenue sources. For those with none or only small tobacco schedules, no problem existed; that is, until the national television networks went to work in earnest replacing lost tobacco revenues. How did this affect radio stations?

Example:

BUYER: Joe, I'm afraid we won't be getting any local radio money this year. The Home Office says TV network availabilities have been reduced 50 percent in price, and the buys are just too good to pass up.

SALESMAN: But you had a $10,000 budget last year; this is a big blow to my sales picture.

BUYER: I can understand that, but I also understand what the company's national advertising manager is talking about. A network TV spot that cost $40,000 last year can be purchased now for $20,000. And because national TV delivers such huge audiences, he's taking the local dollars we had last year and putting them to work at national level. Sorry, Joe, but that's it.

There's nothing the station can do at the local level in such a situation, and the station is helpless when a client's business fails. But in most other areas, bright, agressive management can ward off many losses. When business declines because of ratings, local competition, and sales and administrative errors, something can be done. If a salesman alienates too many clients and-or agencies, he should be replaced or reassigned. If the bookkeeper costs the station business through billing errors, she should be replaced or retrained. Strong local competition is met with stronger competition.

An executive in a small group of stations once approached the manager of the city's leading contemporary music station and told him, "The group is planning to take the market. We're planning a Top-40 format; we're hiring five newsmen, including two of your best men. We are going to be top-rated in this market, and I'm telling you about the plan so you won't waste time and money fighting us."

The competitive manager could have reacted in one of two ways. He could have fought the coming onslaught, but his was a daytime station; and the new operation would operate around the clock; or he could have recognized the futility of resistance and determined to change his format and serve the community with a different one. He wisely decided on the latter, and his station continued to be financially successful, even though it lost the distinction of being number one in the market.

Prospecting for New Business

Recognizing that the development of new business every week is essential to continued prosperity, the aggressive sales manager will use every channel available to locate and sell new radio advertising prospects.

The following avenues present themselves:
1. Monitor other radio stations in the market.

2. Check local newspapers.

3. Check the Chamber of Commerce and government office for building permits, for new businesses opening in the community.

4. Read the business pages of local newspapers and magazines.

5. Monitor TV stations, particularly such spot-carriers as cooking shows and late movies.

6. Survey wholesalers for the possibility of available co-op money.

Monitoring competition is one of the most effective methods of keeping up with who is using radio. Often, the monitor will show the broadcaster than another station is getting more budget than his station, or that the competition has ferreted out business that his salesmen have missed. Who does the monitoring? Certainly, no one on the regular staff has the time. Often, the wife of a salesman or announcer can handle the monitor chores to pick up extra income. In other cases, the sales manager might employ an invalid who is unable to do other work. Regardless of who is hired to monitor the competition, there are certain techniques that must be employed. A form should be supplied the person employed to insure that the information required is supplied in the final report.

Example:

Monitor of Station.....................

Day and Date........................

Advertiser	Time On	Length
Coca Cola	6:55A.M.	60-sec.
Clark Department Store	7:02A.M.	60-sec. (In news)
Beautyrite	7:12A.M.	30-sec.
Chevrolet	7:15A.M.	60-sec.
Midget Car Races	7:20A.M.	30-sec.

In a major market, the sales manager might order the top five stations monitored every Wednesday, Thursday and Friday. Why late in the week? Because just about any advertiser will schedule spots on Wednesday, Thursday, or

Friday; if any days are to be skipped, they usually will be Monday, Tuesday, or the weekend. The monitors, once received at the station, are duplicated; and copies are distributed to each salesman. They should be discussed at length at the next sales meeting.

A monitor analysis is helpful in some cases. This involves another, more definitive format.

Example:

Advertiser	Sta A	Sta B	Sta C	Sta D	Sta E	Sta F
Coca Cola		X	X	X	X	
Chevrolet	X	X				
Ford			X	X	X	
Clark's Dept	X	X	X	X	X	

With this report, the sales manager can determine how deep each account bought and precisely what stations were used. If the manager of Station A thought Coca Cola and Ford were not in the local market, he was sadly mistaken. The accounts, according to the monitor analysis, simply didn't buy Station A.

The monitor analysis often can be used not only to develop new business, but also to get budgets increased. As an example, Clark's Department store might reach more unduplicated audience by increasing its schedule on Station A than by including Station E in the budget. If the buyer understands the concepts of reach, frequency, and Gross Rating Points, the mathematical calculations could easily prove the proposed increased budget to be more effective than adding another station to the buy list.

Checking Local Newspapers

To the eternal consternation of broadcasters, there still are many retailers who think only of newspapers when they think of advertising. The newspapers, therefore, are an excellent source of new client leads. One of the most common techniques for converting newspaper ads into radio spots is the presentation of a speculative spot (Spec Spot). With this approach, the salesman locates the ad, prepares a radio commercial, and presents it to the buyer with a suggested schedule.

Example:

SALESMAN: Mr. Jones, I saw your grand opening ad in the morning paper, and I've prepared a radio spot from it that I think can be very helpful in getting your business off to a roaring start.

MR. JONES: But I'm not interested in radio. We use only newspaper.

SALESMAN: It'll only take one minute of your time, and I've got the commercial cued and ready to play. All you have to do is listen.

MR. JONES: Okay. Go ahead.

(Plays recording of commercial into telephone.)

SALESMAN: So what do you think, Mr. Jones?

MR. JONES: Not bad. I like the music you put behind it. Makes our opening sound like a lot of fun. What sort of money are we talking about? Like I told you, we don't believe in radio.

SALESMAN: Mr. Jones, my plan is to run 10 spots daily, Wednesday, Thursday, and Friday. That's 30 units and our cost is only $600, about a third of what you paid for the full-page ad. This schedule could make the difference between a big grand opening and a moderate one. Our average quarter-hour audience is 25,000 persons—so you'll reach a heck of a big part of your potential market.

MR. JONES: (Ideally) Okay, let's go! Get them on the air as soon as possible today.

Getting the Jump on New Business

An occasional check with the local Chamber of Commerce or the City Manager's office will turn up unexpected new business potentials. The Chamber secretary may say he received an inquiry from X Company regarding the availability of building space for a new restaurant. A major grocery chain might inquire through the Chamber about the availability of space in a shopping center. The X petroleum company may have requested building permits for a string of new service stations. Once the salesman knows a new business is developing, he can make early contact and inquire about promotional plans. It usually is too late when the grand opening ad hits the paper or when the salesman notices the building under construction.

Experience has indicated it is easier to switch an account from one radio station to another than it is to switch a newspaper or television advertiser to radio. The competitor may assume the radio advertiser is already sold on radio, so the salesman has only to convince the advertiser of the merits of his station. The newspaper or television advertiser must first be sold on radio as an advertising medium, then on a particular radio station.

Sales Incentive Plans

It is strange but true that a salesman will find extra energy and devote extra effort to his job for a $100 bonus or prize when he won't make the same extra effort for his regular commission. An industrial psychologist might explain the anomaly by pointing to the basic human urge to win a prize. Whatever the psychological explanation, sales incentive plans work!

The incentive plan may be complicated or simple; it doesn't seem to matter as long as there is a special reward at the end of the contest. One waggish manager set monthly sales quotas and announced that any man making his quota would get to keep his job. He didn't announce the penalty for failing to meet quota, but the sales force perceived his meaning.

PLAN ONE: Sales quotas are set. If all salesmen reach quota, each will receive an extra 5 percent commission bonus. If any salesman fails to reach quota, there will be no bonus for anyone. Through this device, the strong salesman help the weak ones. It is remarkable how perfectly honest men will scheme and connive, for the most part, good naturedly, to earn extra dollars.

PLAN TWO: Involve salesmen's wives and other members of the staff. One such plan calls for setting up sales teams with a salesman at the head of each team. Sales Team No. 1 might consists of a salesman, two announcers, and the traffic manager. The "helpers" seek out leads for the salesman to call on. Other teams are established along similar lines.

The plan is announced at a staff meeting that includes salesmen's wives. It is held at a hotel meeting room where a number of prizes are on display. Prizes include everything from refrigerators to golf clubs.

At the opening of the meeting, everyone is asked to select a prize that suits him. The bachelor announcer may choose a set of golf clubs. The bachelor traffic manager may want the electric blender. The salesman's wife may select a washer, dryer, or refrigerator. Once everyone has made a selection, under whatever pretense the manager may decide to use, he then calls the meeting to order and announces how and when the prizes may be won.

Under this plan, a three-month quota is established for each team. If each team makes quota, everyone wins. If any team fails to make quota, no one wins. Staff members have been known to hold meetings independent of management to devise ways and means of helping each team make quota. This is an ideal situation where every member of the staff, not to mention salesmen's wives, are dedicated to making the operation a success. The prizes, while obviously expensive, may be traded out with a department store or appliance store. The only cash outlay might be the award party if every team makes quota.

PLAN THREE: This plan, one of the most difficult to execute, is designed primarily to develop new business and to sell program vehicles, such as weather and newscasts. The plan also helps to build nighttime and weekend sales. Under this plan, the manager establishes a total prize of $1,000 (or any figure that fits the station budget). Each salesman tries to win the largest share of the total prize. Formula:

New accounts (multiplied by) week-end contracts
(multiplied by) contracts for nighttime spots
(multiplied by) newscast contracts (multiplied by) total
billing.

The total of these calculations establishes the individual salesman's factor. If any salesman offers a zero in any category, his factor is zero. Assume, however, that Salesman A sold three new accounts, two week-end accounts, five nighttime accounts, four newscast contracts, and did a total net billing of $12,000. By using the above formula, A's factor would be 144. Other salesmen's factors are 90, 120, 160, and 115, all arrived at in the same manner. Add all factors, then divide the sum into the individual factor to get the individual salesman's percentage of the bonus. This is a workable plan; it assures each salesman of something unless he gets a zero in one of the categories. The plan forces the salesman to work the "hard" areas, such as week-end saturation and nighttime schedules.

Sales contests are planned for months that normally are lowest in local gross billing. If a station normally suffers a significant drop in January and February business, planning for the two-month sag should begin in November or December.

There is no limit to the size and scope of sales incentive plans. It depends entirely upon the imagination of the sales manager and the station's financial ability. The only object of such plans is to stimulate the sales force to greater revenue productivity. Further, when the entire station staff is involved, the contests build staff cohesion and esprit de corps, without which the station really can't realize its revenue potential. The station that is top-rated in a major market may not feel the need for sales incentive plans because salesmen spend much of their time searching for spot availabilities and trying to fit schedules onto the program log. But most stations have commercial time begging for sponsorship. The sales incentive plan is one way to fill the gaps.

Account Agency Switching

Most stations use the protected-account-list system. In this manner, each salesman is given a list of sales prospects and is expected to work the list. It is a protected list because other salesmen at the station are not permitted to solicit business from any client or agency on the list.

There should be no such thing as a permanent protected account list. For a variety of reasons, sales management should constantly study the productivity of each salesman and his protected list to insure that each list is yielding every possible dollar, and that no serious imbalance has developed between the quality of the lists.

Several years ago, four experienced and highly-skilled salesmen were employed by a west coast station. Each was given a protected list of one hundred prime accounts. Within eighteen months, Salesman A had 140 of the prime accounts; B and C were about even, and D was down to 60 prime accounts. Salesman D had the same skills as the other men, but the ebb and flow of accounts from one agency to another had worked against him. When one of D's agencies lost an account, it almost invariably would switch to one of A's agencies. One important result of this imbalance was that Salesman A had more active accounts than he could properly handle, and D was in a depressed state because he could not control the loss of his prime accounts. The sales manager could have prevented the problem by simply keeping up with account agency hopping and switching agencies from Salesman A to Salesman D when the imbalance became apparent.

New salesmen, particularly those with scant sales backgrounds, often are given poor prospects lists as part of the training program and, equally important, because the new salesman can do less damage to the station's sales picture with a low-budget advertiser than he can with a high-budget one.

Accounts and agencies are switched between salesmen essentially because a given salesman cannot sell a given account. Regardless of the reason, no salesman should be allowed to hang onto an account if he can't get that account on the air. There often are valid reasons why the salesman can't sell the account, and they range from personality conflicts to the salesman's inability to develop just the right strategy to sell the buyer. Some buyers want to be coddled by the salesman with lunches, cocktail sessions, and free tickets to sports events, concerts, and other shows. Other buyers will take no part in the social side of business, fearing it will obligate them in some way to make an unsupportable buy.

Nevertheless, the sales manager should switch accounts when it becomes obvious, through a sales meeting or conference, that the salesman assigned cannot sell them.

Example:

SALES
MANAGER: Bill, you've been calling on Ourtown Hardware for four
             months with no results. What's the matter?

BILL:	I don't know, really. I make the calls, present the guy with facts about our station, and he doesn't buy.
SALES MANAGER:	Okay. You obviously aren't getting through to the buyer, so I'm, as of today, assigning the account to Joe.
	Now, Joe. You apparently are having a problem with Ourtown Advertising Agency. The chief buyer called yesterday and asked me to assign someone else to call on them. What's the problem?
JOE:	Well, the other day I got just a little sick of getting the short end of the Home Show budget, and I let off a little steam to the account executive. He lives next door to the salesman from KFFF, and I know he's just playing favorites; he cannot justify his buy on KFFF.
SALES MANAGER:	Okay. You've just lost the agency. You cannot lecture account executives and time buyers, unless you've got that kind of relationship which you obviously don't have.
	Tom, you have a problem with the Ajax Agency. I had lunch with the account man for American Homes last week, and he said you have so far been unable to give them a presentation based on ARB demographics and cost-per-thousand-persons reached (CPM). The account man is a numbers buyer, and unless he can get the numbers, he isn't going to give us an order.
TOM:	Sorry, but I just don't have the background to make that kind of presentation.
SALES MANAGER.	Okay. You'd better start learning because more and more agencies want this kind of mathematical detail. I'm assigning the agency to someone else.

Regardless of the reason, when a salesman isn't writing business for an agency or account, a change should be made. The action is often called a "purge" of the protected account list; it rids the list of so-called dead accounts and attempts to activate other accounts by assigning them to different sales personalities.

Some firm policies are required to keep professional, aggressive salesmen from each other's throats, particularly when new business appears at the station. Once the basic list is established, each salesman makes an effort to add new accounts. These new accounts come from the basic development work discussed earlier in this chapter, and from call-ins. A call-in, simply, is an account that calls the station and asks for someone in the sales department. If the switchboard operator or sales secretary has instructions to rotate call-ins among the salesmen, there usually is no problem. But if the slightest favoritism is shown one salesman, the other salesmen will justifiably complain bitterly.

What happens when an account, active or otherwise, switches agencies? The salesman handling the losing agency loses the billing, and the salesman handling the winning agency gains the billing. While there should be a general rule of thumb that the salesman servicing the winning agency will get the new business, it would be imprudent to have this as an inflexible rule. For example, Salesman A, employed at a particular station, worked six months to get an account on the air. Three months later, the account decided to employ an agency being serviced by Salesman A. Three months later, the account became disenchanted with the agency and decided to switch to another agency. The other agency had no active accounts on the station and was serviced by Salesman B. In this case, Salesman A was assigned to follow the account he developed to the new agency. Properly handled, the sales manager can make such decisions and maintain a happy relationship among salesmen if he can show that he has been fair. Salesman B had been elated over the prospect of taking over the big account Salesman A had developed and received the following explanation upon learning that Salesman A had developed and received the following explanation upon learning that Salesman A would keep the account:

> "Bill, I know you've been servicing the new agency, but there's never been a dollar spent by them on radio. So you really aren't losing anything when I assign Joe to take it over. In this case, I'm simply protecting Joe because of the hard work he put into developing the account into a radio buyer. Now, if you think you're entitled to keep the agency and profit from Joe's labors, just say so and I'll give it more thought. But I think you'll agree that this is the fair way to handle the situation."

Hopefully, Bill bought the idea. The facts of this situation indicate that a hard, firm rule would inevitably result in an inequity that would do serious damage to salesmen's morale.

The Switch Pitch

The switch pitch might be any argument designed to transfer advertising budgets from one medium to another, but in the radio business it means an argument that favors one radio station over another radio station. A Chicago manager once called the station licensee with this statement:

"If we get the ratings we expect, we'll be switch-pitching all over the Windy City. I know of at least twenty budgets we didn't get because KFFF's showing comprised more adult women in the last ARB. And if we succeed in only half of the pitches, we'll pick up an extra $200,000 in business this year."

Assume that an agency had an account whose market is women, 25 to 49 years old. Station KFFF got the budget on the strength of its showing among women in this age group. The last Pulse or ARB indicated KFFF's average quarter-hour audience among women 25-49 was 25,000 persons in the 10:00 A.M. - 3:00 P.M. segment. Station KXXX was a close second with 21,000 such women. Figures were taken from the October-November study in the market. KFFF showed a figure of $2.00 as a cost-per-thousand persons reached, while KXXX's CPM was $2.80. KFFF obviously was the best buy for the product involved. At this point, KXXX might have engaged in a rate-cutting scheme to show a better CPM, but management decided to hold the rate and wait for ARB's next study. Meanwhile, KXXX program personnel went to work developing audience-building features for the mid-day housewife period.

In the next survey, KXXX figures showed 28,000 women 25-49, compared to 21,000 for KFFF. The station then was better armed to attempt a switch pitch.

Compensation Plans for Salesmen

Troublesome as it is, turnover among administrative personnel has comparatively little effect on the station's sales objectives. But the station with constant turnover among salesmen has difficulty in reaching its sales potential.

Management's first decision in hiring a sales force hinges on the station's potential in the market and the availability of operating capital. Does the station have the potential of capturing a substantial audience in a short period of time? Can station investors afford to bring in top-notch and highly-paid salesmen? Or, will it be a slow-build station that will ultimately reach a substantial portion of a given segment of the audience but will never be among the top three stations in the market? Or, is it a shoestring operation that must crawl before it can walk?

Assume the station is a full-time facility that definitely has the potential of gaining No. 1 position in the market within a few months, and that there is adequate capital to sustain operating losses over a long period of time. In this instance, management should go after the best, most experienced men it can get, regardless of cost. These will be men who probably have been in the market for a number of years, have earned top money for several years, and know where the business is and how to switch it to the new station. A thumb-nail sketch of four top men from Ourtown market might show:

SALESMAN A: Five years in the market, one with KAAA and four with KVVV. His billing climbed from $200,000 annually four years ago to $400,000 last year. Married, two children, membership in numerous clubs and organizations. Owns own home, in good health. Top recommendations from agency buyers throughout the city.

SALESMAN B: Three years in the market, all at KCCC. He previously was an account executive with a local advertising agency. Married, no children. He is 48 years old, plays golf and tennis. Expert in developing statistical support for his presentations. Has excellent rapport with agency management in city, due to family connections.

SALESMAN C: Young and aggressive. Bachelor, 27 years old. Graduate of State University with degree in broadcasting. Knows how to handle personal investments and is the responsible man-about-town type who travels in good company. Has one year with KLLL in sales, previously was in another major market and worked for a National Rep firm.

SALESMAN D: Former small market station manager who loves freedom from administrative responsibilities offered by sales job. Excellent track record, 38 years old. Something of a loner, but highly respected by agency buyers because of his apparent candor in evaluating competition. Has been known to refuse schedules when he didn't think station would reach advertiser's market.

Because of the availability of capital, each of the four might be hired and given a draw against commission of $1,500 per month. Expensive, but if management has guessed correctly on the station's potential, the plan will result in getting the station off to a fast, profitable beginning.

Every salesman is employed on a trial basis, usually for three to four months. Within that period of time, he is expected to at least "make his draw." A salesman makes his draw when his commission on sales or collections is equal to the monthly amount he is guaranteed. For example, a salesman would earn his $1,500 per month draw against a 10 percent commission on $15,000 in net collections. Some commissions, however, particularly in small-to-medium markets, are based on sales usually with a condition that if any sale becomes uncollectable, the commission paid the salesman will be withheld from his paycheck.

An explanation sheet, accompanying the salesman's commission check when commissions are based on sales might show:

Gross Sales	$30,000
Agency Commissions	4,500
Net Sales	25,500
Earned Commission	2,550
Less Monthly Draw	1,500
Commission Due	1,050

When commissions are paid on collections, gross sales for any given month are not considered. Ultimately, if the salesman doesn't continue to increase his sales, the lag obviously will be reflected in collections.

The explanation sheet when the commission system is based on collections might read:

Net Collections, March 1-31	$21,500
Commission at 10 percent	2,150
Less March draw	1,500
Commission due	650

There are times, of course, when collections lag far behind sales. For example, a salesman might know that he has billed an average net of $30,000 per month for the last eight months. He knows that his earnings, if the billing is collected, should eventually reach $3,000 per month. But during the same eight-month period, his collections have averaged only $20,000 per month, and he actually has been paid only $16,000 in commissions. He still has $8,000 coming when and if collections are made. Under this system, stations manage to maintain accounts receivable at a fairly low level because the salesman himself has a personal interest in seeing that the advertising is paid for. When salesmen are paid on the basis of sales, the inclination to collect isn't so strong. The decision to commission on sales or collections usually is determined by the economics of the station. The small-market, low-budget station that can pay only $400 to $600 in draws or advances usually must commission the salesman on sales rather than on collections because with a low draw, the salesman can't wait for the money to be collected. The high-budget station with a backlog of capital can afford the higher draw and the salesman can thus sustain himself until collections reach and exceed the draw.

Stations that use the collection system usually get fewer bad accounts on the air. The professional time salesman will not waste his time developing an account if he knows he isn't likely to be paid. On the other hand, the salesman working under a commission system based on sales may be inclined to put any account on the air, knowing he will be paid anyway. So the collection system is superior from a pure business standpoint because (1) the salesman himself will run a credit check on the account, and (2) the salesman will make the extra effort to collect should the advertiser become delinquent.

In many stations, regardless of the commission plan, no account is put on the air until the credit manager approves the order. Unless the station has a credit manager, or someone who wears that hat, bad credit risks are certain to get through and be on the air before anyone realizes there may be trouble in collecting.

If, after three or four months, the new salesman hasn't reached the required level in billing, he should be called to a conference with the sales manager. The sales manager may simply explain that the salesman doesn't appear to be able to sell the station and therefore should be discharged. There may be extenuating circumstances, and if they exist, they should be considered when evaluating the performance of the salesman. He may have had some extraordinary cancellations; he may have suffered a death or some other misfortune in his family that has made him emotionally unable to sell. There might be any number of legitimate excuses. But if there are no extenuating circumstances, the salesman probably should be replaced. Some managers favor putting the salesman on straight commission in cases like this. Under this plan, the salesman gets no draw, only commissions on sales or collections. But if a man is unable to produce under a plan that is workable for other salesmen, he probably can't produce under a straight commission system.

The well-managed operation does not play games with sales personnel. Salesmen either produce according to quotas or they leave. In small markets, where salesmen of any caliber are often difficult to find, management sometimes will overlook deficiencies in order to keep men on the streets.

Enlarging the Sales Force

It is possible for a sales force of three or four men to find itself saturated with business. That is, the salesmen are incapable of handling additional accounts. They are too busy servicing existing accounts to get out and develop new business. Or, management may decide that the sales force is getting fat and lazy. This often happens when men have spent four or five years at a successfully programed station and are earning substantially larger sums of money than others in the field. This situation, coupled with the sales manager's knowledge that salesmen are not making calls on new accounts, indicates the need to broaden the station's local sales base.

Assume that each of four salesmen last month grossed $35,000 each. None have earned less than $30,000 per year for the last four years. One technique would be to hire a fifth salesman who would spend his time seeking out new business. He would start with no active accounts. This is the least desirable approach, as the four old timers still would have no incentive to get out and develop new dollars. The practical approach would be to take, perhaps, $5,000 in active monthly billing from each of the four present salesmen and simply give it to the new man. The $20,000 in active billing wouldn't be enough to satisfy the new man; he'd still need to find new advertisers. And the loss of $5,000 in base billing by the four other salesmen would encourage each to get back on the street and ferret out new money.

There is always the possibility that one or more of the four salesmen will quit, but the loss to the station will be minimal if the departing salesman was, indeed, simply servicing established accounts and making no effort to create new sales. Almost anyone with a background in time sales can service an account. It requires a skilled, aggressive, "hungry" salesman to service and sell.

Rate Increases

When and how does station management decide to increase rates? How many advertisers will the station lose when rates are increased? Can the salesmen justify the increase to active accounts? What happens if the new rates simply cannot be sold? These are only a few of the perplexing problems management must face and attempt to solve before effecting a rate increase. When the station reaches a sold-out status, it probably is time to increase rates. The manager and his salesmen know how much business has been turned away due to lack of spot availabilities. Assume that KXXX enters July with no time available during the morning and afternoon drive periods, and that half-way through the month the mid-day and nighttime availabilities have disappeared. The average drive time rate is $25; the average mid-day rate is $20, and the average nighttime rate is $23. Management notices that the sold-out position actually began in March, and, through its projection sheet, realizes the condition will exist at least through August. The present rate card guarantees rates for three months, provided there is no interruption of schedule. This is to say, that if the soft drink bottler is paying $25 for morning and afternoon announcements, he will continue to pay that rate for three months after the effective date of the rate increase, provided he doesn't take a hiatus during the three-month period. An advertiser takes a **hiatus** when he cancels his schedule with the intent of resuming it shortly thereafter. If he stops the advertising and has no intention of resuming it, it is a cancellation.

When rates are increased, low-budget advertisers are likely to cancel or reduce the number of units scheduled. Only if it knows where to find replacement business, can management safely make the move. Circumstances under which management will consider increasing rates are:

1. Sold out status.

2. Rates are below those of comparably rated stations in the same market.

3. Rates are below those of comparably rated stations in similar-size markets.

4. Management simply believes it can get more for station time.

When management of a high-rated station observes that a lower-rated station is charging and getting a higher rate, it may assume that if the competition can sell the higher rate, surely the top-rated station in the market can do so. Often, a station will begin business with an extraordinarily low rate in order to attract trial business. This is especially common when a station has changed formats and has not had a survey to indicate its relative position in the market.

In one case, a 50,000 watt network operation dropped the network and adopted a Country & Western format. To introduce advertisers to the new sound, the station offered spots on a Run-of-Schedule plan for $7 each. The rate was absurdly low, but within days, the log was full and the station was sold out. Advertisers were getting startling results from their schedules and had been warned by salesmen that the $7 rate was an introductory offer, that if the station audience grew as expected, there would be frequent and substantial rate increases. Within four months, average station rates had risen to $30, slightly higher than those of the competing C&W station.

Suppose that the leading station in Ourtown, which has a population of 200,000, has an average rate of $15. The leading station in Theirtown, a market of about the same size and located 300 miles away, has an average rate of $20. This may be an indication that the Ourtown station is under-priced and should increase rates. Local economic conditions, established practices, and competition from other media would ultimately determine whether the Ourtown station was, indeed, underpriced.

An Arizona broadcaster once said he set his rates "according to what the traffic will bear." "How much will the advertiser stand for?" he asked. Often, this is the case, once management has decided how much it will charge and how much it must sell at these minimum rates to either survive or make a profit.

For example, suppose the station has an operating overhead of $20,000 per month. Between 6:00 A.M. and 6:00 P.M., Monday through Friday, it has 1,080 minutes of time it considers best to sell (18 minutes per hour, 12 hours per day, for five days). At an average rate of $5 per 1-minute of commercial time, the station would have to stay 100 percent sold-out in the daytime periods just to break even. Management decides it can sell at least 50 percent of the available commercial time, which means it must average at least $10 per 1-minute sold. While this price would enable the station to break even, it would have to sell considerable nighttime and week-end business to show an operating profit. Based on these estimates, management might decide on a rate structure that would average $15 per minute of commercial time during the day and offer package plans for nighttime and week-end slots.

Extraordinary Sales Techniques

It is one thing to utilize special revenue tactics, such as the outside sales force and the album promotion. It is quite another to develop extraordinary sales techniques and use them on a day-to-day basis. The top stations in medium-to-major markets will make little use of such devices. The struggling station in markets of all sizes must employ specials to survive.

The most common method employed by the bottom stations is the rate cut. "I know our rate is $10, but this week we're offering a special rate of $5," the salesman explains. This, outside of the illegal practice of double billing, is one of the most insidious, harmful practices in the industry. Once the stations in a given market begin selling off the card, it is difficult to stop. However, advertisers, particularly in small, unsophisticated markets where the advertising-agency-media industry is largely unprofessional, encourage it. It often requires a brave, well-financed station to suddenly call a halt to rate cutting and begin selling strictly off the card. On occasion, managers of local stations form an association and decide not to fix rates but to simply stick to the published ones. Any rate-fixing scheme surely would violate anti-trust laws. But there is no law preventing stations from agreeing to sell at published rates.

There are many ways to cut rates honorably. The most widely used is the package plan, discussed earlier in this chapter. The station that has lost top position in the market or has suffered revenue losses for other reasons, can legitimately establish and publish package plans that offer rate reductions. To publish, management simply mimeographs, or has printed, the new rates and offers them to everyone, on top of the table. This method of rate reduction is understandable. It is the sly, under-the-table rate cut that does irreparable injury to radio broadcasting's image.

Many stations conduct monthly or annual sales promotions in which the advertiser gets something extra for purchasing time on the station. One of the most profitable sales promotions in recent years is the nationally syndicated and copyrighted Bridal Fair. In a period of four years, its use has grown from ten to seventy markets, and is used mainly by contemporary music stations. The basic sales idea is to give the advertiser participation in the Bridal Fair if the advertiser will spend X number of dollars on the station within a given period of time (usually, January and February). The station promotes the Bridal Fair, which consists of four fashion shows and panel discussions in a two-day period. Bridges-to-be are invited to see the latest in fashions and to participate in discussions with doctors, home economists, bridal consultants, and ministers.

Prospective advertisers include florists, commercial photographers, jewelry stores, auto dealers (particularly those with compact cars), travel agencies, bridal shops, banks, furniture stores, and department stores. Not only is the sales promotion designed to encourage regular advertiser spending during weak months but also to serve as a tool for the development of new advertisers. The Bridal Fair promotion and many others of its kind are protected by copyright laws, and nothing similar should be independently developed by any medium.

One of radio's most difficult sales tasks has been to sell itself to staunch users of newspapers. The problem of selling the medium exists not only with the ad manager but also with the professional advertising agency. An Oregon broadcaster developed a plan whereby station management and sales personnel would host a "critique" luncheon for the creative personnel of leading local advertising agencies. At the meeting, the creative personnel would criticize station programing, sales approaches, and perhaps the station's rate structure. Once the station learned specifically what the agency felt was "good radio," enough of the recommendations might be adopted to induce the agency to give the station a trial run. At other meetings, station personnel would deplore an agency practice of preparing one piece or one set of copy for several different stations, all with different formats and audiences. Copy that is suitable for the audience of a Top-40 station may not be effective with a C&W station's audience. "Copy," the broadcaster argues, "should be tailored to fit that station's audience."

The most common of extraordinary sales techniques is entertainment. This function can range from the salesman buying lunch for a time buyer to providing the ad manager or account executive with a free week-end in Las Vegas. Too often, such entertainment practices amount to nothing less than bribery. It won't work, of course, with the buyer or ad manager who must justify a station-buy to his superiors. But it does work effectively when the buyer or ad manager has the last word on which medium gets the budget.

One station in Chicago built a small screening room in its building and invited time buyers to view first-run movies, complete with cocktails and snacks. Chicago's communications industry is highly sophisticated and professional, not usually subject to outright bribery; but the parties did serve to improve rapport between station salesmen and the buyers.

A northern station once offered a free trip to Las Vegas with each $3,000 package of advertising purchased. The promotion was widely publicized and sold well. The free trips were traded out with a feeder airline and several Las Vegas hotels and were offered only to the decision-makers within the companies approached by salesmen.

An FM station in Indiana offered a free FM radio to every new advertiser. One significant problem the FM station had encountered was that advertisers didn't have FM sets and, therefore, couldn't hear their spots. The free receiver at least answered that particular objection to buying time on the FM station.

SUMMARY

The student shouldn't kid himself about the importance of sales at a radio station. **Art gratis art** may be appropriate for foundation or publically supported educational facilities or for government-owned facilities in Canada or England, but commercial radio in the U.S. depends upon sales for its survival. As one ethnic station manager declared, "That's where it's at, baby." Another operator said, "The name of the game is money." McLendon, in the early years of his group operation, warned his managers to "take care of the sales; don't force me to get involved in selling. My principal job is programing and I can produce a saleable product. Just make sure you can sell it." The combination of McLendon and his sales-oriented managers obviously worked, because he became one of the most successful group operators in the country. It is not enough that the student knows how to write commercials, public service announcements, prepare balanced program schedules, and understand the music of a given format. If he can't relate these creative aspects of the business to sales, he will be something less than an effective member of the team. The old sales admonition that "nothing happens until a sale is made" is startlingly true in commercial broadcasting.

CHAPTER 3

Programing

Just as many motion picture and stage performers become typed as villains, comedians, or character players, many career broadcasters develop reputations as Country and Western operators, Top 40, or ethnic specialists. These are broadcasters who, because of their success with a given format in one market, will buy into another market and try to make the familiar format work in the new area. The Ebony Group is, perhaps, a prime example of how a broadcaster was successful with an ethnic format and made it function profitably in several markets.

The reasons behind such specialization are several. First, the profit motive. If a formula worked well for an operator in one market, it follows that it will succeed in other similar areas. Chain grocery stores use the concept. Another reason is that the broadcaster feels comfortable with the format and with the individuals who staff such formats. It's much like the retailer who has always sold women's ready-to-wear; he'd feel out of place selling western or men's wear.

Until he entered the Oakland-San Francisco market, McLendon was known as a Top 40 specialist because he had been immensely successful with the format in other markets, including Dallas, Houston, Shreveport, Milwaukee, and San Antonio. His reason for stepping out of character, deciding to abandon the contemporary music approach and serve the Bay Area with so-called good music, adult-oriented news, humor, and information, was based upon formidable local Top 40 competition and his inborn desire to try something different.

In the mid-to-late 1950s, licensees of Top 40 operations stood in fear of having a McLendon or a Storz buy a station in their market. These operators were of the uncommon variety and enjoyed success with their rock music and audience-building stunts wherever they located. Twenty years later,

AVERAGE QUARTER-HOUR

	AVERAGE PERSONS — TOTAL SURVEY AREA, IN HUNDREDS											STATION CALL LETTERS	AVERAGE PERSONS — ME				
TOTAL PERS. 12+	MEN					WOMEN					TEENS 12-17		TOTAL PERS. 12+	MEN			
	18-24	25-34	35-49	50-64	TOTAL	18-24	25-34	35-49	50-64	TOTAL				18-24	25-34	35-49	50-64
134	5	13	33	29	63	6	17	18	5	51		KBOY	121	4	11	32	24
36	4	4	1		9	1	5	17	2	27		KDUX FM	32	4	4	1	
												KBUY	9				
												KFJZ	18	3		2	
												KFWT FN	32		11	1	2
83	6		3	11	20		27	14	10	63		KIXL	56	8		2	10
84	7	12		12	31		14	22	14	53		KIXL FM	77	7	9		12
32	4		15	1	20	1	4	2	5	12		KKDA	24	2		14	
357	68	16	10	24	118	93	43	37	20	205	34	KLIF	215	28	13	9	17
												KNOK	106	19	21		
												KNOK FM	26	8		7	
												TOTAL	132	27	21	7	
8	5				5						3	KNUS FM	4	2			
294	6	2	36	42	134	3	6	53	53	160		KRLD	163	6	2	24	18
36		1	6	7	16			5	8	20		KRLD FM	22			6	6
22			5	1	9	3		3		13		KSKY	12			5	
13		1			1	2	7	1	1	12		KVIL	13		1		
32			9		9	6	15		2	23		KVIL FM	31			9	
45		1	9		10	3	22	1	3	35		TOTAL	44		1	9	
55	6	24	4		34		5	7	2	21		KYAL	16		1	2	
												WBAP	28			3	6
												WBAP FM	15	2		1	4
173	12	6	42	14	83	12	21	21	17	88	2	WFAA	60	11	1	12	3
89	3	2	14	17	37	4	12	14	14	50	2	WFAA FM	35	2	2	10	2
64		7	10	17	36	2	6	7	11	28		WRR	57		7	6	17
39			10	7	18		1	10	3	16	5	WRR FM	32			10	7
												TOTAL LISTENING IN METRO SURVEY AREA	1304	113	85	171	136

FOOTNOTE SYMBOLS: (*) means audience estimates adjusted for actual broadcast schedule. (†) means AM-FM Combination was not simulcast for complete time pe

AMERICAN

154

Listening Estimates

| Y AREA, IN HUNDREDS | | | | | SHARES—METRO SURVEY AREA | | | | | | | | | | | | | |
| WOMEN | | | | | | | MEN | | | | | WOMEN | | | | | |
25-34	35-49	50-64	TOTAL	TEENS 12-17	STATION CALL LETTERS	TOTAL PERS. 12+ %	18-24 %	25-34 %	35-49 %	50-64 %	TOTAL %	13-24 %	25-34 %	35-49 %	50-64 %	TOTAL %	TEENS 12-17 %
16	16	5	47		KBOX	9.3	3.5	12.9	18.7	17.6	13.6	4.8	11.9	7.9	3.3	6.6	
5	13	2	23		KBOX FM	2.5	3.5	4.7	.6		1.7	1.0	3.7	6.4	1.3	3.3	
	7	2	9		KBUY	.7								3.4	1.3	1.3	
	1		7	6	XFJZ	1.4	2.7		1.2		.9	4.8		.5		1.0	11.3
4	4	7	18		KFWT FM	2.5		12.9	.6	1.5	2.6		3.0	2.0	4.6	2.5	
7	11	8	38		KIXL	4.3	5.3		1.2	7.4	3.3		5.2	5.4	5.2	5.4	
14	19	13	49		KIXL FM	5.9	6.2	10.6		8.3	5.1		10.4	5.4	3.6	6.9	
	2	5	8		KKDA	1.8	1.8		8.2		2.9	1.0		1.0	3.3	1.1	
23	26	16	120	28	KLIF	16.5	24.8	15.3	5.3	12.5	12.3	46.2	17.0	17.8	10.5	17.0	52.8
8	19	1	61	5	KNOK	8.1	16.8	24.7			7.4	24.0	5.9	9.4	.7	8.6	9.4
4	1	5	10	1	KNOK FM	2.0	7.1		4.1		2.8	5.5	3.5	.5	3.3	1.4	1.9
12	20	6	71	6	TOTAL	10.1	23.9	24.7	4.1		10.2	24.0	8.9	9.9	4.0	10.0	11.3
				2	KNUS FM	.3	1.8				.4						3.8
5	19	34	89		KRLD	12.5	5.3	2.4	14.0	13.2	13.6	2.9	3.7	9.4	22.4	12.6	
	2	6	9		KRLD FM	1.7			3.5	4.4	2.5		1.0	3.9		1.3	
		1	6		KSKY	.9			2.9		1.1			.5		.8	
7	1	1	12		KVIL	1.0		1.2			.7	1.1	5.2	.5	.7	1.7	
15		1	22		KVIL FM	2.4		7.1			1.7	5.5	11.1		.7	5.1	
22	1	2	34		TOTAL	3.4		1.2			1.9	7.7	16.1	.5	1.5	4.5	
5	6		13		KYAL	1.7		1.2	1.2		.6		3.7	1.0		1.8	
1	1	3	15		WBAP	2.1			1.8	4.4	2.4	1.9	.7	.5	2.0	2.1	
	2	5	6		WBAP FM	1.2	1.3		.6	2.9	1.1			1.0	3.3	1.1	
3	11	6	29	1	WFAA	4.6	9.7	1.2	7.0	2.2	5.5	1.0	2.2	5.4	3.9	4.1	1.9
4	6	2	17	2	WFAA FM	2.1	1.8	2.4	5.8	1.5	2.4		4.0	1.0	1.3	2.4	3.8
4	6	11	25		WRR	4.4		8.2	3.5	12.5	4.9	1.9	3.0	1.0	7.2	3.5	
	7	2	9	5	WRR FM	2.5				5.8	5.1	3.9		3.4	1.3	1.3	9.4
135	203	152	707	53													

means refer to Special Notice on Page 5.

RESEARCH BUREAU

Fig. 10. ARB ¼ Hour Report.

rather than being the exception, their procedures were the rule. In fact, stations, particularly in major markets, had abandoned stunts that had become threadbare and were concentrating on sophistication, programing to a specific, target audience, and trying to live with ever increasing pressures from the FCC for more problem-solving programing.

Audience Identification

In order to effectively program and sell his station, the modern operator must decide with considerable precision the exact audience he hopes to attract to his sound. The advent of such audience survey firms as Pulse, and ARB have helped stations immensely in determining the age and sex of listeners to a given station. To further identify a station's audience, Brand Rating Index (BRI) provides an in-depth study that describes age, sex, educational level, income, and buying habits of radio audiences by format. ARB and Pulse publish, among other estimates, average quarter-hour demographic breakouts that describe, at least, to the satisfaction of most professional advertising agencies, a station's audience (see Fig. 10).

Inevitably, the contemporary music station, such as KLIP in the example, will develop or attract a high audience in the 18-34 age group. There was a time when Top 40 operations were called "teeny bopper" stations because they were top-heavy with the 12-17-year-old audience. After a station had been programing contemporary music for 15 to 20 years, it was discovered that its teeny-bopper audience had grown to be 27 to 37 years of age. It still attracted teen-agers, but its original audience had not changed its taste in music and, therefore, had grown up with the music of its age. Thus, the advertiser whose product or service was marketed to people aged 18-35 sought out availabilities on contemporary music stations. In the case of KRLD in the example, the audience under 35 is relatively small. It programed considerable news and middle-of-the-road (MOR) music that included big band, and sophisticated combos that played music written and published twenty years ago. The advertiser whose product or service is aimed at persons 35 or older will select availabilities on the adult-oriented station.

This dialogue may help the student understand the relationship between commercial music and people:

WOMAN-Age 30: I listen to KBBB and have for 15 years. I like the music; they've always kept up with the hits. Call it rock, pop, horrible, or what have you; it's still the same type of music year after year. I like music with a definitive beat, and as long as KBBB programs music with a beat, I don't care if it's an original Elvis Presley or something new like Sly and the Family Stone.

WOMAN-Age 46: Not me. I grew up in the era of the big bands like T. Dorsey and Benny Goodman. Presley hadn't come along, and the wildest thing we had was Dixieland Jazz, progressive jazz by Stan Kenton, and later, Bill Haley and the Comets. I can't stand outfits like Sly and the Family Stone. All that screaming gets on my nerves.

MAN-Age 40: Well, you may have liked Dixieland, Kenton, Jazz and the like—but I always liked it slow and easy. And when Presley started the rock-and-roll era, I thought I'd go into shock. My music has got to be beautiful (to me), and memorable. It's got to remind me of something pleasant. You can have your modern junk; give me Percy Faith doing a new arrangement of "Moonlight Bay" or "I Could have Danced All Night."

MAN-Age 30: You all are wrong about "good music." I like the country variety. Jim Reeves, Eddie Arnold, Roy Acuff—they're the musicians I like. I grew up with country music and plan to listen to C&W stations until I die. You'll never convince me that there's anything beautiful or memorable about Percy Faith or anything interesting about Sly and the Family Stone. Furthermore, everyone know and associate with likes country music.

WOMAN-Age 28: You're crass, all of you. You talk about cheap, commercial music when, in my opinion, none of it really is music. Bach, Beethoven—they were musicians and produced my kind of music. The simple, childish beats of pop music just leave me unmoved and cold. A Strauss Waltz is, to me, an example of pure music.

The broadcaster must first understand that every music taste exists in virtually every market in the country. His research objective should be to determine which is the largest group. His programing objective, then, would be to supply music to the largest number. This study, of course, deals only with music, not with other needs, tastes, and desires of the community. These must eventually be dealt with, but are not necessarily the first to be considered.

In a market of 1,000,000 persons, an estimate of a given county by sales management might show:

Black..............................	15 per cent
Spanish Surnamed...........	2 per cent
American Indian..............	1 per cent
White & Other.................	82 per cent

The broadcaster immediately sees two things. First, the black audience can be commercially significant. Second, the Spanish market, insofar as audience potential is concerned, is relatively insignificant. And, while he must consider this minority group's problems, he need not necessarily consider its music tastes.

Sales management figures might further show the market by age groups, as follows:

0-17..............	25 per cent
18-24..............	11.5 per cent
25-34..............	11.8 per cent
35-49..............	32.2 per cent
49-64..............	11.0 per cent
65.................	8.5 per cent

This, of course, is not necessarily a typical market. A city in southern Texas, New Mexico, or Arizona might show as much as 50-75 percent Spanish or Indian, with few or no blacks. A city in Alabama, Michigan, Mississippi, or Illinois, might show as much as 30-60 percent black.

Whatever the racial or ethnic distribution, the broadcaster must be aware of it if he is to serve the needs, interests, and tastes of the service area. Not only does such awareness benefit the broadcaster commercially, but the FCC's policy requiring licensees to know community problems makes it an absolute necessity for the modern broadcaster to understand his market.

Age and racial distribution, however, are only part of the picture. How do citizens earn a living? How many are in industry? How many are in government or retail sales work? What is the average family income? How many are agricultural workers? What are their buying habits?

There are many sources for such information. The Census Bureau's reports furnish considerable information about the characteristics of the people in a given city, county, or state. Sales Management's Survey of Buying Power is another source of information. Standard Rate and Data Service (SRDS) further breaks down buying power. Brand Rating Index (BRI) describes the characteristics of radio audiences. And, as indicated, Pulse and ARB studies are helpful in determining audience listening habits, as well as being indispensable to the broadcaster and advertiser in estimating a station's relative position in a market.

Brand Rating Index, among other studies, shows that the more formal education a person has, the more money he is likely to earn. This characteristic is spelled out in BRI's study of radio audiences.

In a nationwide sweep study of the top 25 markets, a BRI study might show the following:

Type Format	High School Graduate	Grade School or Less	Income $5,000	Income $10,000	Under $5,000
Contempo	80 percent	9 percent	75 percent	10 percent	7 percent
C&W	60 percent	25 percent	60 percent	2 percent	30 percent
Ethnic (black)	61 percent	22 percent	55 percent	1 percent	40 percent
Classical	94 percent	5 percent	85 percent	14 percent	1 percent
MOR	82 percent	7 percent	77 percent	12 percent	6 percent

The characteristics of a market's population and a potential radio audience are related to the geographics of the area. A sourthern market (Mobile, Ala.) will differ considerably from an eastern market (Baltimore, Md.), and these will differ from a west coast market (Los Angeles). Strong differences in population characteristics will also be found in northwestern, midwestern, and northern markets. The Southwest has yet another set of population characteristics, not only in music tastes, but also in terms of other needs, tastes, and desires.

A programing philosophy, therefore, must stem not only from the talents and desires of the licensee, but also from the location of his market, family income and education, and ethnic composition.

Market Size and Format Considerations

As a rule of thumb, the larger the market, the more specialized must be the station's format if the licensee is to realize profits from his investments. The days of a station being all things to all people in major markets disappeared years ago. The major market station's format must lend itself to quick and easy definition. Just as the general store has vanished in the heavily populated markets, so has the general purpose radio station.

Example of the number one C&W station's program schedule in a major market:

Program Schedule
Monday-Friday

News and Weather	6:00 - 6:05 A.M.
The Cowboy Jolson Show	6:05 - 6:30 A.M.
News Headlines	6:30 - 6:33 A.M.
The Cowboy Jolson Show	6:33 - 7:00 A.M.
News and Weather	7:00 - 7:05 A.M.
The Cowboy Jolson Show	7:05 - 7:30 A.M.
News Headlines	7:30 - 7:33 A.M.
The Cowboy Jolson Show	7:33 - 8:00 A.M.

The smaller the market, the greater the licensee's "safe" latitude in laying down programing philosophies.

The Cowboy Jolson Show	6:00 - 9:00 A.M.
Eddie Davis Show	9:00 - 12:00 noon
Tommy Thompson Show	12:00 - 3:00 P.M.
Dave Schmidt Show	3:00 - 6:00 P.M.
Michael Williams Show	6:00 - 9:00 P.M.
Teddy Malloy Show	9:00 - 12:00 midnight
Ernie Arnold Show	Midnight - 6:00 A.M.

The same routine of scheduling news and headlines might continue throughout the broadcast day, with only the personalities changing. The skeletal form, with **program inserts** not included, would appear:

Shows may be set up on a three- or four-hour basis, depending upon budgets or available capital. News, headlines and weather, sports, and other features are entered on the program log as **program inserts**. The standard-formula-station-program schedule contains these elements, plus whatever extras or program inserts management may decide to include. Hundreds of variations have developed as operators sought to beat competition. Newscasts have been scheduled at the :55 (five minutes before the hour) so the station may program music at a time when most other stations are starting newscasts. Headlines and weather have been scheduled for the :25 for the same reason. Other stations have set up 20-20 news; that is, five minutes of news at 20 minutes past the hour, and three minutes of news at 20 minutes before the hour. It has long been known that a youthful audience will change stations if there is an alternative when news is presented. For this reason, broadcasters have done everything imaginable to keep the news brief and still present a comprehensive picture of what is happening locally and around the world. Elaborate news introductions have been produced to add excitement to newscasts. As many listeners keep radio music in the background, the news introductions serve also to alert the listener to the upcoming news.

While the formula station may be found in markets of all sizes, competition in the major markets dictates rigid adherence to a specific format. The weaker the competition, the less rigid the format of the leading operation.

In a single-station market, the problem of format selection is less difficult. The broadcaster simply "feels" his way, to a large extent, until he finds the proper format. In a farm community, more than likely, he will program Country and Western (C&W) or other locally traditional music. The County Agent is a must for at least five minutes each day, preferably fifteen minutes.

In this schedule, emphasis has been placed on religion and agriculture. The early morning, Monday-Saturday, music will be C&W. At 9:00 A.M., when it is presumed the woman has the house to herself, the programing is directed to her. The music may be easier and the talk will be geared to her minute-to-minute problems. The homemaker show is another must. In small farm communities, experience and surveys indicate that over 50 percent of the audience is forty years or older. Therefore, gospel music might be well received.

As school is dismissed in most communities around 3:00 P.M., programing for teen-agers should begin at that time. Popular local students make excellent disc jockeys or announcers for this purpose. It is desirable to keep five or six of them in training after they have acquired proper operator licenses.

Sample Monday-Saturday schedule:

6:00-6:01	Sign-On
6:01-6:30	Country Melodies
6:30-6:32	News Headlines
6:32-6:45	County Agent
6:45-7:00	Country Melodies
7:00-7:15	News
7:15-7:30	Country Melodies
7:30-7:32	News Headlines
7:32-7:45	Morning Worship
7:45-8:00	Country Melodies
8:00-8:15	News
8:15-8:30	Country Melodies
8:30-8:32	News Headlines
8:32-9:00	Country Melodies
9:00-9:05	News
9:05-9:30	Time for the Ladies
9:30-9:32	News Headlines
9:32-9:45	County Demonstration Agent
9:45-10:00	Time for the Ladies
10:00-10:05	News
10:05-10:30	Swap Shop
10:30-10:32	News Headlines
10:32-11:00	Swap Shop
11:00-12:00	Gospel Music
12:00-12:15	News
12:15-12:30	Markets
12:30-1:00	Country Hits
1:00-1:05	News
1:05-1:30	Afternoon Melodies
1:30-1:32	News Headlines
1:32-2:00	Afternoon Melodies
2:00-2:05	News
2:05-2:30	Afternoon Melodies
2:30-2:32	News Headlines
2:32-3:00	Afternoon Melodies
3:00-3:05	News
3:05-3:30	Afternoon Melodies
3:30-4:00	Teen Show with Bill Dixon
4:00-5:00	Teen Show with Bill Dixon
5:00-5:05	News
5:05-5:30	Teen Show with Bill Dixon
5:30-5:32	News Headline
5:32-5:55	Teen Show with Bill Dixon
5:55-5:59	News
5:59-6:00	Sign Off

6:00-6:01	Sign-On
6:01-6:05	News
6:05-6:30	Gospel Riders
6:30-7:00	The Baptist Hour
7:00-7:30	The Catholic Hour
7:30-8:00	Silhouettes
8:00-8:30	Gospel Music
8:30-9:00	Local Quartet Live
9:00-10:00	Sunday School Hour
10:00-10:30	The Episcopal Hour
10:30-11:00	Church of Christ
11:00-12:00	Methodist Church (Live, Remote)
12:00-12:15	News
12:15-12:30	Local Jaycees
12:30-1:00	Farm News Roundup
1:00-1:05	News
1:05-1:15	Report from Washington
1:15-1:30	Report from Austin
1:30-2:00	Music for Sunday Dinner
2:00-2:30	Tabernacle Choir
2:30-3:00	Teen Music with Grant Smith
3:00-3:05	News
3:05-4:00	Teen Music with Grant Smith
4:00-4:05	News
4:05-5:00	Teen Music with Grant Smith
5:00-5:05	News
5:05-5:55	Teen Music with Grant Smith
5:55-5:59	News
5:59-6:00	Sign-Off

The schedule above would be suitable for a small farming community. If the community has an ethnic composition, such as a German settlement, the music might range from polkas to operas. Perhaps one or two newscasts could be delivered in the German language. If the community is predominantly Black, music should be selected according to the tastes of the majority of Blacks who listen.

Only the broadcaster who is bent on going broke will try to cram a format down the throats of his community. A farm community of poorly educated, low-income citizens, doesn't want good music, classical music, or 100 percent rock-'n roll. The format must be tailored to meet the needs, tastes and desires of the broadest possible number of people in the service area.

It is relatively simple to build a format in a single-station market. The broadcaster can do anything he likes, so long as he is certain his efforts serve specific purposes.

The picture changes when a market has two or more stations. The more stations serving a market, the more difficult the programing. Typical radio dial for a market of 500,000:

Pct. Market	Frequency & Power	Call Letters	Format	Hours
10	570 50kw	WBXX	CBS - Block	24 hours
34	840 5kw-d-1kw-n	WAAA	Contemporary	24 hours
6	900 51kw-d	WBBB	MOR Hits	Sunup-Sundown
30	920 10kw-d-1kw-n	WCCC	C&W	24 hours
10	1020 1kw-d	WDDD	Ethnic-Negro	6:00A.M.-Sundown
3	105.6 100kw ERP		Classical Music	24 hours
4	107.7 25kw ERP	WFFF-FM	Standard Music	24 hours
3	96.8 100kw ERP	WGGG-FM	Religion	18 hours

If a consulting engineer has found a new frequency for the market, the broadcaster must study competing formats carefully to determine the format he will propose to use in the market. He may wish to aim at becoming the No. 1 contemporary music station (going for the numbers) if the proposed frequency is a full-time one. In this case, he would argue that there is only one contemporary music station in the market and he proposes to offer listeners a choice. He might propose more local news (noting that the competing contemporary music station broadcasts only 300 minutes of local news weekly). He might propose a telephone talk show that would make the format different and would offer something new to the market. He might propose to use mobile news units or to provide more time for public service, churches, and cultural institutions. Regardless, he must propose to provide the market with some new service, keeping strictly in mind that the FCC will expect him to do almost precisely what he proposes. He must keep in mind, also, that to develop a significant flow of revenue, he ultimately must get better ratings than the established station. To be competitive, he must try to attract advertisers. To get that audience and those advertisers, he must do a better job of executing the contemporary music format.

In a major market, such as one with 1,000,000 population, the broadcaster cannot expect to have the top-rated station in the market if the facility is daytime only. In this case, he would select a specialized format. It might, for example, be "good music," which appeals strictly to educated adults. While the station probably would get no business from soft drink and chewing gum companies, it should do well with big ticket advertisers, such as auto or appliance dealers. An adult-oriented daytime station can provide a genuine service and can be financially successful.

If the owner has chosen to buy an existing station in the market, his problems will be different. He may wish to simply upgrade an existing format and try to improve the revenue in this manner. He may sense the need for a complete format change, in which case he must explain the change in the application for transfer. In the previously outlined sample market, there is only one Black-oriented station, with 10 percent of the audience. The market has 200,000 Blacks, and the present Black-oriented station is doing a poor job of programing. Either a new station or one of the existing stations, would have an excellent chance of knocking off the present Black-oriented station because (1) it is a daytimer and (2) it does a poor job with its format.

It is better, of course, to select an entirely different format, particularly if the present stations are successful. In Dallas, after KLIF had been the leading contemporary music station for many years, KBOX copied the format and tried, without appreciable success, to out-program KLIF. After many years of futile effort, KBOX owners gave up, changed the format to C&W, and were immediately successful. Its only competition was KPCN, a daytimer licensed to a suburban area. KBOX took the C&W audience by storm. Advertisers flocked to the new format and soon KBOX was giving KLIF more competition for the advertising dollar than it had done as a Top 40 operation.

In Buffalo, McLendon fought for years against WKBW for a share of the Top 40 audience. WKBW had been established for many years as the leading Top 40 operation, but McLendon felt the format was poorly executed. It was, but when WYSL hit with a new format, WKBW sharpened and tightened its sound and became a formidable competitor. It took years for McLendon to turn a profit at WYSL, and he never did completely take a plurality of the contemporary audience from WKBW.

In another case, McLendon bought an existing station in Shreveport, La., changed the call letters, established a Top 40 format, and took the competition in less than a month, according to Hooper. A daytimer had been the number one operation for several years and was making money. Under pressure of the McLendon format, the daytimer ultimately changed format and took another seat in the market.

While McLendon struggled in Buffalo, he was eminently successful in most other markets he entered. His KILT in Houston was top-rated in total audience. KABL in San Francisco was never number one, but his unique format gathered enough adult listeners to make it one of the most desirable advertising mediums on the West Coast. In this case, McLendon romanced the market with beautiful music and minimum talk. In every case, he either developed a different format for his new market, or he "outprogramed" an existing one. His success as an innovator is legendary.

Music Selection Policy

The FCC does not require that a station's music selection policy be on file at the Commission, but leading Washington attorneys advise licensees to have the policy in writing, on file at the station, and in circulation among those staff members who are assigned to select the station's music.

There are two obvious reasons for having such a policy in writing and available for immediate inspection. First, the station's program department needs a guide established by management. Second, if the station is ever accused of payola or plugola, it should be prepared to show the Commission that while the offenses may have occurred, they were in violation of station policy. A statement of policy governing selection of music to be played on the air may read:

> 1. Music at KXXX is selected by the music director (who also is a disc jockey). All records programed by KXXX must show sales action in at least one of these sources: Billboard, Cash Box, and the Bill Gavin Record Poll. If a record receives reports of sales action in the station's immediate service area, it may then be added to the

playlist. Occasionally, the music director may add "ear" picks to the playlist. These are records which have no sales justification, but are, in the music director's opinion, good additions to the playlist. These picks are held to a minimum.

2. Each Wednesday afternoon, the music director previews in the presence of the program director, all the records added to the playlist. At that time, the list is either approved as is, or with omissions and additions.

3. Announcers may play any records from the current playlist and from the file of classics (old hits). Playing a number that has not been approved and added to the playlist is grounds for immediate dismissal.

4. All announcers are required to keep a log of the music played during their shift. Records are categorized on "A" or "C" lists (depending upon their popularity) and the ratio of play is preset by the program director. These logs are kept in the program files for ninety days.

5. All disc jockeys are allowed to do outside record hops when prior approval is obtained from the general manager. They may not give promotion to these hops on the air unless they are for nonprofit organizations and the hops are open to the public. None of KXXX's disc jockeys promotes his own dances, shows, or hops on the air.

This is only one example of how a music policy is written. The policy is prepared and published in accordance with station format, established procedures, and under advisement from the licensee's Washington attorney.

DEPARTMENT ORGANIZATION

There may be many variations of the organizational chart shown in Fig. 11. In many cases, the news department, for example, may be a separate organization with the news director answering only to the general manager. Traffic and copy, while working under professional control of the program director, may be under the administrative control of the general manager. That is, hours and wages, days off, overtime, leaves of absence, would be controlled by top management. The general manager may or may not be in direct supervision of the program director. There may be, as indicated by the chart, a station manager or operations manager who deals with the program director and his problems. The organization of the program department depends largely upon the licensee's concept of management and the station's income. If the station produces large revenues, a more elaborate organizational structure may be required. If the station is a small revenue producer, a more

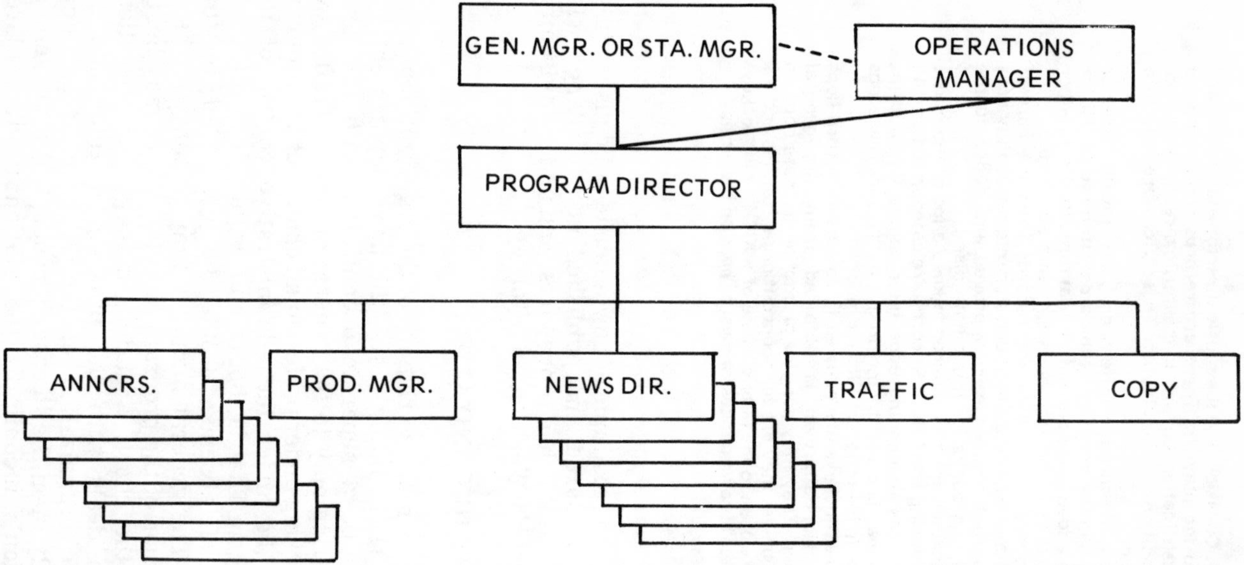

Fig. 11. Program Dept. Organization.

simple organization would be indicated. Whatever the structure, the licensee's management must have knowledge of and control of programing procedures.

The Program Director

In most cases, the program director is assigned to carry out programing policies of the licensee or his top management. He is not necessarily required to be creative, but it is necessary that he be industrious and attuned to station policy and FCC rules, regulations, and policies. The program director, in other situations, is creative and has absolute control over the station's sound. This absolute control may give him authority to reject commercials that he considers incongruous with that station's format, discharge announcers or other air personnel he regards as incompetent, and generally decide what may or may not be broadcast. The ideal program director has several years of on-air experience, preferably at several different stations, with the station's type format. He should be creative, energetic, and capable of managing the announcing and production staff. He should be able to establish rapport with top management and function as a station executive. Additionally, he should be capable of performing every task required of the staff announcer or disc jockey. Many stations have program directors who have neither experience on the air nor the capability of handling any announcing or on-air task. But usually, program directors are super-smart and super-experienced disc jockeys or announcers. One problem with an off-air program director is that he cannot fill in for other announcers during vacations or illnesses.

The program director should be a competent writer and planner. He should qualify as a program innovator, and he must be able to construct a successful station promotion from its conception to the voicing of promotional announcements and final execution. He should be able to take an old threadbare promotion and revise it for current exposure. If any single background consideration is more important than another, it is experience with a given format. The individual who has labored with a Top 40 or C&W format in another market, is far more valuable to the station than one with little or no definitive experience in a specific format.

KXXX'S Announcer Work Schedule

ANNCR	MON AIR	MON OTHER	TUES AIR	TUES OTHER	WED AIR	WED OTHER	THURS AIR	THURS OTHER	FRI AIR	FRI OTHER	SAT AIR	SAT OTHER	SUN AIR	SUN OTHER	TOTAL HOURS
A	6-9am	9-1	6-9am	9-2	6-9am	9-2	6-9am	9-2	6-9am	9-2	6-12n	off	off	off	40
B	9-12n	12n-4	9-12n	12-5	9-12n	12-5	9-12n	12-5	9-12n	12-5	12-6p	off	off	off	40
C	12n-3p	9-12 3-4	12n-3p	9-12 3-5	12n-3p	9-12 3-5	12n-3p	9-12 3-5	12n-3p	9-12 3-5	off	off	6a-12n	off	40
D	3-6p	11-3	3-6p	10-3	3-6p	10-3	3-6p	10-3	3-6p	10-3	off	off	off	off	40
E	6-9p	2-6	6-9p	1-6	6-9p	1-6	6-9p	1-6	6-9p	1-6	off	off	12n-6p	off	40
F	9-12m	3-9	9-12m	4-9	9-12m	4-9	9-12m	4-9	9-12m	4-9	off	off	6p-12m	off	40
G	12m-6a	—	12m-6a	—	12m-6a	—	12m-6a	—	12m-6a	—	12m-6a	off	off	off	36*
H (PT)	—	—	—	—	—	—	—	—	—	—	—	—	12m-6a	—	6

"OTHER" INCLUDES:
ONE-HOUR MEAL BREAKS
PRODUCTION OF COMMERCIALS & PSA's
PRODUCTION OF STATION PROMOS
WRITING STATION PROMOS
MUSIC DIRECTOR DUTIES
SHOW PREPARATION
PUBLIC APPEARANCES
OTHER DUTIES, SUCH AS MONITORING COMPETITION, AS ASSIGNED BY PD

*THE ALL-NIGHT DJ
MAY WORK FOUR
ADDITIONAL HOURS, AT HIS
CONVENIENCE, USUALLY, IN
SHOW PREPARATION OR
SPECIAL PRODUCTION.

Fig. 12. Announcer Schedule.

Duties of the program director (PD) generally are as follows:

1. Establish format or execute established format.
2. Set up announcer work schedules.
3. Organize production department and schedules.
4. Handle a share of the air shifts (optional, of course, at discretion of general manager and-or licensee).
5. Supervise commercial copy and traffic manager.
6. Plan and execute station promotions.
7. Coordinate with sales department in development of commercial or sales promotions.
8. Select or supervise selection of music.
9. Interview, hire, and discharge air personnel.
10. Adjust format, (Major adjustments usually require concurrence of top management. Major changes in music, news, public affairs, and "other" type programing, must be cleared with FCC before execution).
11. Hold air staff meetings to inform announcers of changes in program policy and procedures and of significant shifts in FCC rules, regulations, policies, and thinking. Must be continually aware of Commission interest in programing.
12. Monitors competitive stations, keeping attuned to their formats, promotions, and personnel changes.
13. Supervise preparation and scheduling of public service announcements (in the absence of a full-time public service director).
14. Responsible for studio security, as well as the security of station's secret program material and policies.
15. Responsible for keeping a backlog of applicants for department jobs.
16. Recommend or grant salary increases.
17. Have and maintain extensive knowledge of format music.

Different formats will dictate different job descriptions for program directors. The program director of a small market station may also be a salesman, a disc jockey, or the job may be combined with that of general manager. The PD of a network station may be only an extension of the arm of the general manager, with few or no executive functions. He may be a detail man—assigned specific day-to-day tasks and, in this case, would be required to get permission for any change he might wish to make in the format.

The program director of a good music or classical music station may have few executive qualities. His forte would be his extensive knowledge of the format's music. Management might waive executive ability in order to find and employ a PD with this knowledge. Obviously, there are more men and women available in the Contemporary, Popular, and the Country and Western fields than in the Good Music and Classic fields.

The Announcers

The outsider and broadcast neophyte often glamorize and envy the lucky guy who works only a three-hour air shift. This is seldom the case, even with the so-called "gods of the air." These are air personalities whose local fame is well established and whose services have become so valuable to the station that they can get away with murder. Even the "gods" must spend endless hours preparing for a three-hour air shift and often are required to pitch in and help with production and station promotions. Most announcers are employed on a 40-hour-per-week basis, even though they may do only 15 to 20 hours per week on the air. The balance of the work week is devoted to handling off-air production or promotional chores. Again, the size of the market and the revenue of the station will generally dictate announcer duties. The work schedule in Fig. 12 indicates one station's use of announcer time.

This, of course, is only one schedule. It is designed for a 24-hour personality formula station that plays Contemporary, Country and Western, Middle-of-the-Road, or any other specific kind of music on a consistent basis. The daytime-only station, broadcasting from, for example, 6:00 A.M. to 6:00 P.M., has fewer problems in establishing an announcer schedule and can do it with far fewer people. The formula for a daytime station schedule may appear:

6 - 9 A.M.	Johnson
9 - 12 noon	Smith
12 - 3 P.M.	Jones
3 - 6 P.M.	Williams

Johnson and Smith may work six hours each on Saturday, with Jones and Williams taking the two six-hour program periods on Sunday. The remainder of their 40-hour week would be absorbed by production and-or news duties. Management may elect, on the daytime operation, to set up 4-hour air shifts and use only three full-time announcers and two part-time announcers. In very low budget daytime-only operations, the manager and three salesmen can handle all air and production chores. It is not uncommon in a small market to find such situations, which may include one of the men's wives working as traffic manager, bookkeeper, receptionist, and program director. A full-time engineer is not required on low power non-directional stations, and often management elects to keep a competent engineer under contract to (1) do maintenance and (2) inspect the transmitter five days per week. In cases like this, however, it is essential that anyone doing air shows has a third class ticket so that he may keep the operating log. (See Operator Requirements, Ch. V.)

In other cases, air personalities may be employed under a simple performance contract and have no duties other than the air show. These individuals sell their services and normally are not affected by wage and hour laws. They earn from the minimum hourly wage to $100,000 or more per year.

Off-air assignments may range from handling newsroom shifts to writing commercial copy. Few stations can afford to have announcers idle during their off-air hours, and most announcers are loath to handle just an airshow. One of the most important extra assignments that can be given an announcer is the job of music director. In many instances, the program director himself handles this task. But in other cases, the job is assigned to the announcer who appears to know most about the station's music.

The Music Director

The music director is responsible for the proper execution of the station's music policy. He makes daily and weekly checks on the relative popularity of his format's music, talks with representatives from record distribution firms, publishes the hit chart (if any), and generally makes sure his station is programing the very newest in format music. Regardless of whether the station programs Rhythm & Blues, Country and Western, Contemporary, or Middle-of-the-Road, the principle is the same. The music director may also be a full-time employee who does not carry an air show and has no other responsibilities. He may share the job with another announcer or with the program director. Whatever the arrangement, one or more persons in a station having a format must have the responsibility of keeping the station's playlist up-to-date.

If a hit sheet is published, it usually is the responsibility of the music director to make weekly changes. Hundreds of thousands of records are sold weekly to the public on the strength of stations' Pop Charts. In a major market, when a record reaches the top 10, sales may be astronomical. When a record first hits the air, music directors pay close attention to sales and elevate or lower the record's position on the chart in accordance with sales. Local record dealers usually are anxious to cooperate with the music director and will give him weekly sales figures, hoping to get more air play for a particular record and thus increase sales. If a record is selling well locally, and if the so-called national charts (Billboard, The Gavin Report) also indicate increased sales, the record is slipped ahead a notch or two on the Pop Chart. It may jump one position per week for several weeks until it hits the top 5 or 10, or it may explode into popularity overnight and become number one in a matter of days. It is the essential job of the music director to make sure his station is on top of the ebb and flow of record sales and that only the best sellers are included on the playlist.

There has been no study made on the question, but it is reasonable to assume that most stations assign the announcer with the greatest interest and knowledge in music to handle the duties of the music director.

Typical dialogue between the Program Director and an announcer being considered for Music Director:

PROGRAM DIRECTOR:	Tom, I'm much too busy with programing details to handle these record salesmen. I need some help, and I think you've got the necessary background to be music director. Weren't you MD at your last station?
ANNOUNCER:	No, I was assistant music director. I helped, but didn't make decisions. My recommendations were generally followed, though.
PROGRAM DIRECTOR:	Good. Now, you should read our music policy. That'll help you understand the procedures we use here. What I want is a guy who will work and not become overly impressed with his title. First of all, make it known to record people that you'll see them on Wednesday afternoons only. You can't do the job with those guys bouncing in here at their convenience. Find out what they're selling, and question them on how specific records are doing in the area. Spend the rest of the week doing your record store survey, studying Billboard and the other surveys, getting the Top 40 sheet prepared, printed, and distributed, and preparing the play-sheet for the announcers to use.
ANNOUNCER:	No problem. My experience has been that there is usually some new music available to us every week. Do you want me to use my own judgement as to when a new piece goes on and when an old one has run its course?
PROGRAM DIRECTOR:	Generally, yes. But for awhile, until we can get ourselves on the same frequency, let's talk first about the changes you want to make. I really have confidence in you, but I want to see how you work before I give you too much rope.
ANNOUNCER:	Fair enough. Now, about albums. We're getting more and more playable cuts on new albums, pieces that have never been out on singles. In my opinion, we should pay careful attention to these new albums, and maybe even publish the Top 10 albums of the week.

PROGRAM DIRECTOR:	My thinking, exactly. And this is where the record salesmen can be helpful. Question them if they don't volunteer the information, on which cuts are breaking where. I've known of record companies to sell a ton of singles on a particular piece after it had been out on album.
ANNOUNCER:	Right. There's no way to second-guess the public 100 percent of the time.
PROGRAM DIRECTOR:	Another thing. Keep the record room locked. We have a file of a million sellers that goes back ten years. It is absolutely vital to this format that we maintain and protect this file; we never loan records to anyone; we do not allow people to wander around the record room. And on the discards, give them to the sales secretary. The salesmen like to use them as giveaways to clients with youngsters. Keep a close eye on the hot albums we store in there. Some of them are irreplaceable, like Bloodstone III. Chicago, Sly and the Family Stone, and others like that.
ANNOUNCER:	Think I got the picture. I assume you'll arrange with engineering to get me a good turntable, amplifier, and speaker system. I've always felt I needed top quality equipment for auditioning records.
PROGRAM DIRECTOR:	No problem. Now get to work.

Production Director

Often, an announcer will be assigned the job of production director in addition to his air shift. When available finances permit, the production director may handle that job exclusively. Regardless of whether it is a full-time or a part-time assignment, the qualifications are about the same. In most stations, the production director is primarily responsible for the production of commercial matter (spots, spot announcements, commercials). He may also produce certain program material that is not related to the commercial requirement. This material would include station promotional announcements, contest material, and PSAs.

The word **production** has many meanings, but in the commercial radio business it generally means the writing and recording of program or announcement matter.

In larger stations, the production director may be just that; he may direct the activities of writers and sound engineers. But in many cases, he is a working production director whose duties include writing and sound engineering. The production room itself may be as elaborate as the station's master control room, in terms of available equipment. In other cases, it may be as simple as an arrangement of one recorder, one turntable, a microphone, a mixer (small console), all situated in one room. As usual, the size and productivity of the production room depend upon the licensee's financial ability and the income of the station.

A fairly typical production set-up in medium-to-major markets would include a combination writer-operations director and a production director. The operations director receives time orders, scheduling instructions, copy instructions, and completed production from national or full-service agency accounts. Under supervision or instruction of the operations director, the production engineer prepares tape cartridges for delivery and use in the control room.

A production order is little more than one person's instructions to another to perform a task in a certain way. Any form, or no form, will do—so long as the communication is completed. Fig. 13 is a sample production order.

```
┌─────────────────────────────────────────────────────┐
│              PRODUCTION ORDER                        │
│                         Date _____     │
│                                                       │
│  Account _____   │
│   ☐ 60-sec     ☐ 30-sec     ☐ Other                  │
│                                                       │
│                                                       │
│  No. cuts _____  spots start _____ stop _____  │
│  Rotation sequence _____  │
│  Production instructions _____  │
│                                                       │
│  _____    │
│  _____    │
│  _____    │
│                                                       │
│              _____                 │
│                        Signature                      │
│                                                       │
└─────────────────────────────────────────────────────┘
```

Fig. 13. Production Order.

Typical Production Problem:

SALESMAN: Jim, I've just sold Main Street Ford a big schedule and I need some good production.

OPERATIONS MGR: Okay, what have you got?

SALESMAN: Here are my copy notes. This weekend they're offering big discounts on demonstrators. And the sales manager wants to get away from straight-sell spots; he wants some pretty dramatic production. You know, with two or three voices, some music, and maybe some sound effects.

OPERATIONS MGR: Well, let's see. Let's do an interview type spot. Four different ones ought to do, wouldn't you say?

SALESMAN: Four will be enough. But what do you mean by **interview** spots?

OPERATIONS MGR: Well, I'll write the dialogue, and we'll dub in a light crowd noise as though one of our announcers were in the display room at Main Street Ford. The announcer will interview one of the salesmen or the sales manager. Announcer No. 1 will ask questions, and Announcer No. 2 will give the answers. In this way, we'll get all points of the weekend sale across to our listeners.

SALESMAN: Sounds okay. The client wants to hear them, if you don't mind, when you finish.

(Two hours later)

OPERATIONS MGR: Tom, here's a production order and copy for Main Street Ford. As you can see, we'll need two voices, some crowd noise, and let's use the open and close of the national Ford jingle to get into and out of the commercial.

PRODUCTION MGR: Good idea, Jim. That national jingle is good and is a real attention-getter. I'll just use the first three seconds to open, and the stinger to end it.

OPERATIONS MGR: Fine. And get Williams and Perry to record the spots. I think Williams will be best on interviewing. Let Perry imitate the salesman at Main Street Ford.

PRODUCTION MGR: No problem. They're both on production duty from 1:00 to 3:00 this afternoon.

OPERATIONS MGR: Now, Tom, please notice that we want four different commercials. Put all of them on one cartridge because we want even rotation on all of them. And when you've finished, make a dub for the salesman. He wants to play them for the client before they go on the air. We'll need the dub first thing tomorrow, and the schedule starts the next day. If you have any questions, and they aren't answered on the production order, give me a call.

PRODUCTION MGR: No problem.

Once the copy has been produced, the production manager will "cart" the spots, give them a "rack number" that has been designated by the operations manager, and deliver them to the control room.

Cartridge label:

```
Main St. Ford - 60-sec. - 4 cuts
May 12-16                                    118
```

Under the Operations Manager-Production Manager system, the sale-to-control room sequence is:

Sale is made.
Copy and details to operations manager.
Operations prepares copy, provides "rack" number, instructs production.
Operations enters "rack" number on program log.
Production "carts" announcements, delivers carts to control room.

This is a basic procedure and would vary according to the desires and organizational abilities of the personnel involved. The "rack" in most station control rooms is a wire carrousel or pigeonhole cabinet that is designed to contain standard size cartridges. These, especially at heavily commercial stations, are numbered so the announcer on duty can easily locate them when a particular commercial comes up on the log. The program log number entered by the operations manager corresponds with the number he put on the cartridge label when he delivered the copy and production order to the production manager.

The production manager's primary qualification is his ability to handle the equipment (console, turntables, tape machines), and he must have a talent for mixing the various sounds required in the production of a commercial. It is desirable, also, for the production manager to have an air voice and equipment maintenance capability. The production manager who can clean recording heads, repair turntable motors, handle other minor repairs, and voice a spot can obviously save the station time and money.

The Music Library

In the early days of radio broadcasting, virtually every station had a record library of unbelievable size. Almost every record that came into the station received a file number and was cross-indexed by title and by artist. When a station passed from seller to buyer, the inventory inevitably included several thousand dollars for the record library. And the station had either a full-time record librarian, or the job was assigned to someone in the program department as an extra duty. In those days, particularly among the network affiliated stations, every show was planned to each piece of music and virtually each word that was spoken. The engineers often would get his copy of a show script, go to the record library, and ask the librarian to pull his music.

Even today, some stations cling to the practice of maintaining huge music libraries. But most libraries contain only hits of the past few years. To get into the modern station's library, a record must have made it big on the charts and must have been purchased by at least a million fans. These are the "goldie oldies" so often heard on Top 40 stations and hits of the past heard on C&W formats. If a record doesn't achieve hit status, it goes into the station junk box and is either thrown away or given away free to anyone wanting it. In those early days, most stations purchased their music from record stores or from the producer. Record manufacturers had not yet learned that when a record got big play on a radio station, sales zoomed.

It is rare today when even a slightly successful station has to purchase music. Record manufacturers and distributors literally flood Top 40, C&W, and ethnic stations with demonstration samples, not for sale. The problem is not in getting the samples, but in deciding upon the one or two out of every hundred received which will eventually grace a station turntable. And this decision-making is one of the primary duties of the modern-day music director.

Specialty Personnel

In medium-to-major markets, many stations employ specialty personnel such as talk show moderators and investigative reporters. In both cases, these people may or may not have other duties, depending upon station revenue or available capital.

The **talk show moderator** must be a well-informed, quick-witted individual, who has a good sense of timing and fairness, and who is highly articulate. The talk show has become a favorite vehicle for airing conflicting views on important and unimportant public issues. The FCC has accepted such programing as part of a station's public affairs commitment, and it is one of the few PA programs that actually builds a station audience. Whether it is an audience builder or killer, depends almost entirely upon the moderator. Untold different situations develop during a talk show that demand of the moderator fairness, acute perception, and vast knowledge of current events. The following are a few problems that may develop:

1. On a 90-minute show, virtually every caller is opposed to making possession or use of marijuana a felony. The moderator keeps the dialogue going smoothly and continually, but without success, asks for opinions from the other side.

Solution: The moderator himself takes the view that the possession or use of marijuana is sufficiently serious to be considered a felony, or he talks in a telephone interview until someone he knows supports this view.

2. A caller criticizes recent attacks in the newspaper on the director of the local poverty program.

Solution: The moderator should realize that he is about to be drawn into a discussion on a hot local issue. If he is prepared to discuss details of the issue and elaborate upon statements made by both parties, he should proceed. If he is not prepared, he has the option of hoping spokesmen for both sides will enter the discussion, or of cutting off all discussion on this particular show, with the explanation that he will have spokesmen for both sides in the studio on the next show for a full and fair discussion of the issue. If he allows a one-sided discussion on the show, the station likely will receive a demand for equal time and will have to provide it. The demand legitimately could be made under the Fairness Doctrine.

3. A caller refers to a certain public official as a dirty, rotten fink who should be impeached.

Solution: The moderator should sharply reprimand the caller and hang up on him, explaining to listeners that the station doesn't tolerate the use of such immoderate language. He might add that if a caller wants to criticize anyone, his remarks should be based upon known facts, and that he should refer to a specific point of failure on the part of the public official, and should express his opinion more graciously.

4. A caller uses a four-letter word that is considered vulgar by the moderator.

Solution: The moderator hits the program cancellation button. Most telephone talk programs are aired on a 7-second delay recording tape. This means the moderator has 7-seconds to react when a caller uses vulgarity. The program is actually recorded, on an endless tape cartridge with seven seconds of tape on it, and rebroadcast in seven seconds after a word is spoken. This is the only practical method of editing out the dirty words that are bound to be used eventually by a caller.

5. A caller wants to ask personal questions about the moderator, whom he says he has learned to hate.

Solution: So long as the questions relate to issues that are under discussion or that have been discussed, the moderator could legitimately discuss personal matters. These would include, for example, the moderator's experience or background that might qualify him as an expert on a given subject. Some callers have been known to call moderators a dirty this-or-that (based upon religion, race, etc.), and the moderators have been justified in dismissing the callers as idiots or bigots.

6. A caller brings up a topic completely apart from the issue under discussion.

Solution: Dismiss the caller with the explanation that the subject is not relevant and may be discussed later.

7. A caller starts reading a long, dull, uninteresting article that is not related to anything in particular and that the moderator feels is killing his audience.

Solution: Interrupt the caller, if possible, and get him off the line. Every show has its quota of regular "nut" callers, people who are mentally or emotionally unbalanced. The moderator either "handles" them or allows them to completely disrupt the program. Some criticism will be generated when the moderator is rude, but no one has yet found a polite way to get such callers off the telephone. Some such callers are intelligent and articulate and must be heard; others simply waste everyone's time.

8. No calls are received when the show is on the air, and the moderator is struggling to keep it alive with a monologue on the issues of the day.

Solution: Have the engineer break the show with a commercial or a PSA. The moderator then calls someone and has them "hooked in" and ready to discuss a current event when the break is concluded. This doesn't happen often, particularly in large markets, but the moderator should always have someone on tap to help him stimulate discussion.

9. A caller demands answers which the moderator is unable to provide about a particular issue.

Solution: The moderator admits his ignorance and asks for help from listeners. If this fails, the moderator simply promises to get the answers and provide them on a later show. In this case, he either researches the issue or arranges for an expert to appear on a later show. This is a farily common and generally effective method of getting to the heart of an issue. For example, a caller complains that the local bus service is inadequate and wants to know why. The moderator gets the president or some other spokesman of the transit company on the telephone or arranges for him to appear in the studio, take calls, and defend his company's position.

10. A caller wants to discuss in candid terms a subject that the moderator may regard as taboo, such as sex, abortion, premarital relations.

Solution: If enough listener pressure is applied, the moderator must allow discussion on the subject, but he can do it on his own terms by either getting experts on the telephone or inviting them to the studio. By bringing in ministers, physicians, or other professionals, the moderator probably can keep discussion on a **taboo** subject at tasteful yet informative levels. Such subjects as marital sex usually may be discussed openly and in detail if the moderator is able to develop the theme along professional lines and can include doctors or qualified marriage counselors.

Telephone talk shows, if well done, may be scheduled at any hour without destroying station ratings. In most cases, however, they are scheduled between 7:00 P.M. and midnight because this is not regarded as prime time on radio. A bad or unpopular talk show would do less damage here than to highly-saleable day time periods. Logically, more persons are available at night to make telephone calls and participate in the show. In many cases, if a station's nighttime audience is behind competition, a well-done telephone talk program may put the station in number one position. Some stations even use the program in the prime morning drive slots to build audiences.

In other cases, the program may originate on an AM station and be broadcast later on a commonly owned FM station, or vice versa. Still other operators broadcast such programs simultaneously on AM and FM facilities. A programer should know, however, that the FCC regards any program that is broadcast both on an AM and FM station within 24 hours of each other as a **simulcast** This policy was established to prevent commonly owned AM and FM stations from completely duplicating programing and therefore retarding the development of FM stations. Without the rule, an operator might record the entire AM broadcast day and repeat it the next day on his FM facility. The Commission requires that at least 50 percent of a dual operation's FM programing in cities of 100,000 or more originate with the FM station.

Investigative Reporting is a relatively new function in commercial radio stations. It doubtless has been practiced for years by some operators, but only in recent years has it become widespread. The investigative reporter is qualified to do original research and does not necessarily rely only on the usual news sources. For example, a remark is made that certain city council members have taken bribes from road contractors. No confirmation of the rumor or report of any official investigation can be obtained from detectives, the city manager, or anyone else. The station's investigative reporter, then, might be assigned to check it out. He would proceed to function as any other private investigator, though not with the license given the ordinary "private eye."

There is no law prohibiting the private citizen from investigating a rumor. But the libel and slander laws protect the person or thing being investigated from false or malicious attacks on the air and otherwise. The truth generally is a defense against slander over the air, but stations that engage in investigative reporting should maintain the legal services of quality counsel and ample insurance against a slander suit. (See Ch. VI.) The reporter checking out the bribery rumor should thoroughly document every fact obtained, as to names, places, and dates. If a city hall clerk has knowledge that will help expose the accused, his statement should be made in the presence of witnesses; and his signature should be witnessed by a notary public. Stations throughout the country have exposed corruption in government by these methods, but it obviously is dangerous in that it subjects the licensee to possible legal action or physical harm.

Other specialty personnel in the program department may include part-time or full-time editorial writers, fashion reporters, political analysts, and sports editors. The inclusion of such personnel will be dictated by financial and format considerations.

Other Program Staff Members

The job of **continuity director** may or may not be a full-time staff position. It may be combined with the job of operations manager, production manager, or engineer. Qualifications include a good command of the language, a spritely imagination, and willingness to work odd hours at home and in the office. Some stations, particularly in markets where local agencies are extremely active, pay scant attention to the position. In others, where most local business is direct (no agency), the continuity director fills an important slot.

Example:

SALESMAN: Marion, Big Town Furniture has an anniversary sale coming up, and they want something special in the way of copy and production. We've got two weeks to plan the approach, but our getting the budget depends almost 100 percent on what you can dream up for the commercials.

CONTINUITY DIRECTOR: Just give me the facts, Bill; I'll plan some dazzlers that might even get the budget increased.

SALESMAN: That's what we like...confidence! But remember that the store is an old one, been here 50 years. You'll have to be careful about using wild music and mod language. I'm afraid the president will rule us out if we try that approach.

CONTINUITY DIRECTOR: Just give me the facts and I'll **create** something that'll reflect the store's image and still sell some merchandise.

Radio stations have traditionally referred to traffic clerks, copy writers, and production personnel as **directors**. The title is probably inappropriate when the traffic manager is the only person in traffic, and there is no one to manage or direct. But the directional titles remain in station jargon and are harmless.

The traffic director may be the most important post in the program department. An ignorant or stupid traffic director (or clerk) can create more problems with a single day's log than Washington attorneys can clean up in a year. The traffic personnel must be thoroughly familiar with the FCC's rules and regulations on keeping program logs. Otherwise, serious problems can develop.

Example:

MANAGER: Young lady, we're in trouble. You apparently have had your mind on something else lately, because a number of logging errors have just been brought to my attention. If you'll have a seat, I'll enumerate some of them.

TRAFFIC CLERK:	Yes, sir.
MANAGER:	First, you cost us $500 in **cash** last week when you failed to log that Saturday and Sunday schedule for Big Town Apartments. **Second**, you logged the Congressman's report as political when it should have been logged as Public Affairs. **Next**, you left five PSAs off the air and caused us to violate our promise to the FCC. **Fourth**, you scheduled 21 minutes of commercial time in the 7:00-8:00 segment. We promised the Commission that we never would exceed 18 minutes in commercial matter, except during political campaigns. Now we probably will have to notify the Commission of your oversight. You must watch these things and help us to stay out of trouble with the FCC. **Fifth**, you failed to note on the log that we are on Central Standard Time. Maybe you think this isn't serious, but the Commission **does require** such an entry. **Sixth**, the 3rd page of the yesterday's log was missing. The announcer did the only thing he could; he made up a special sheet and made entries on the commercials and PSAs he **thought** should run. It was a mess, and if an FCC inspector had walked in at the time, I'm sure we'd have received a citation.
	The announcers have complained that you are scheduling competitive advertisers back-to-back on the log. Our people can handle this sort of situation because they are professionals, but they shouldn't have to handle such matters; you should know better than to put Budweiser and Schlitz commercials in the same quarter-hour period. You **know** we guarantee each of them 15 minutes separation from the other. Generally speaking, your work is not acceptable. The program logs must accurately reflect the material we broadcast. Thirty-second spot announcements must be logged as such; the same with 60s and 10s. We must be sure to log and run 24 PSAs per day. We must be sure that all of our public affairs and religious programs are logged and aired. There is no specific Commission rule that says we must run any certain amount of this program matter, but we **promised** that we would do so. If we don't keep our promises, we could be subject to losing our license. Do you understand?
TRAFFIC CLERK:	Yes, sir.

Obviously, this traffic clerk has been inadequately trained, has lost interest in the job, or has encountered so many personal problems she could not concentrate on her responsibilities.

The traffic director must be capable of deep concentration and should have an office or work area that is conducive to such concentration. One station manager laid down the following qualifications for a traffic director:

1. Ability to concentrate, and in good health.
2. Happy personal life without emotional entanglements.
3. Husband or wife and other members of family in good health.
4. A desire for a career in broadcasting, as opposed to someone who is just working to get out of the house or be with people.
5. The ability to read and understand Commission. rules regarding program log requirements.
6. Highly accurate typing skills.
7. Sufficient integrity to prevent unauthorized logging of commercial matter and to withstand pressures of sales personnel for special scheduling favors.
8. Ability to work with salesmen on availabilities, with announcers and other production personnel, and with clients who call and ask for specific times announcements have been logged.

Other program personnel include secretaries, assistant traffic managers, log typists, specialists in station promotions, and assistant continuity writers and directors.

Types of Staff Organization

Staff organization, obviously, depends upon station format, available financial resources, market size, competition, equipment, and the particular mentality of management. The staff of a network operation will vary drastically from that of the formula C&W operation. The organization of a staff for a live MOR format will in no way compare with the staff for an automated station staff. Staff or employee organization is much like that of the military. Personnel are organized and trained to do certain jobs in certain ways, and, as no two stations are precisely alike, it is unlikely that one will find two identical staff organizations.

The organization plan for a Top 40 staff will apply to virtually any formula station that uses live talent 100 percent of the time and which has a format that calls for the development of personalities. A formula station is one that has rigid on-air performance requirements. In the selection of air personnel, voice quality is not always a critical criteria. In this case, personality and the ability to communicate are prime considerations. The music may be Top 40, R&B (soul), MOR, or C&W—it doesn't matter. The basic staff structure will be about the same. The other duties assigned to staff announcers (or DJs) will vary, of course; but the basic personalities will have strong similarities, and the professional performance requirements will be about equal. The meaning of staff organization essentially is how many and what sort of people and personalities are required to develop and execute a given format.

Basics of a Formula Station:

1. Personality announcers, sufficient in number to cover 24-hour operation.

2. Maximum 3-hour shift, except on week-ends.

3. Announcers capable of doing production, promotion, planning.

4. No strict voice quality requirement.

5. Announcers under direct control of program director.

6. No announcers with extra duty in other than program department.

7. Top-notch morning man employed under special contract.

8. No announcer to appear in any way on competing station.

9. Announcers required to make public appearances, so announcer's personal appearance will be a consideration.

10. Above average knowledge of format musi.c

All News Format Basics:

1. Announcers with deep, authoritative voices only.

2. Two (or four) announcers per shift, alternating newscasts.

3. Announcers must have writing and editing capability.

4. Names may or may not be used, but personality development will be minimized.

5. Announcers sufficient in number to staff air operation in six-hour shifts, 24 hours daily.

6. Staff reporters covering actualities and making remote or telephone reports will not be required to possess same voice quality as studio news announcers.

7. Above average knowledge of local, national, current events.

Automated Station Format Basics:

1. Operators with first class tickets sufficient to man 24-hour format in eight-hour shifts.

2. Voice quality sufficient only to deliver brief newscasts, time checks, weather reports, and news bulletins.

3. Two full-time announcers with top quality voices to prepare commercials, public service announcements, pre-tape newscasts, weather reports, and other program matter.

4. Female office personnel, when practicable, with first class license (ticket).

5. Sales and management personnel with voice and operator capabilities, when practicable.

Block Format Basics (Network):

1. Sufficient resonant voices to staff station for 24 hours daily in eight-hour shifts.

2. No personality requirements, except for all-night announcer.

3. Must be capable of delivering authoritative newscast.

4. Must have writing and production room capability.

5. Staff will include woman's editor, with writing and voice capabilities.

6. Program director will pull airshifts only during vacation or illnesses.

The Block Format Staff (No Network):

1. Specialty announcers. One C&W, One Top 40, two inside newsmen for newsblock announcing, one woman's editor, three staff announcers.

2. Newsmen and staff announcers must have top voice quality.

3. C&W and Top 40 personalities. Voice not big consideration.

4. Woman's editor also handles public service.

5. Staff announcers will have voice capability, handle MOR shows, production room chores.

The MOR Format Basic Staff:

1. Five full-time, one part-time announcers, all with quality voices.

2. Announcers will have writing and production room capabilities.

3. Announcers may hold part-time employment elsewhere, as no personalities will be developed.

4. Announcers will handle all news, making news ready during 12-minute music sweeps.

5. Program director will take air shift.

Changing a Format

Assume a station has operated as a network affiliate since it first went on the air. The air staff consists of four middle-aged but deep-voiced announcers who have been pulling the same air shifts for the last ten years, an equally middle-aged and "fixed-in-their-ways" sales staff, along with a record librarian, a woman's editor who is very popular locally, and two very professional and authoritative newsmen who write editorials and cover the local and area news. The station has ridden the network for six to eight hours daily, with the balance of the schedule being made up of musical interludes, discussion programs, religious, agricultural, and sports programs. It has been, in short, a stuffy, antiquated operation that has not kept up with change. The licensee decides to change format, eliminate the network, and go for the numbers with a Top 40 operation. He has the following discussion with the general manager, who is agreeable, but doubtful:

LICENSEE: Bob, we're losing money to that little daytime operation across town, and I'm about ready to update our sound and see if we can make some money. At the NAB convention last week, I talked with a friend of mine in another market who was getting clobbered by the competition until he changed formats and started programing for mass audience. Our format has been the same for the last twenty years. We just haven't kept up with the times and, as a result, our ratings are nil and we aren't making a profit. Now, we're going to change to the Top 40; you can adjust to the idea and help me put it together, or you can resign. What do you say?

MANAGER: I'm game. But I hope you realize that a lot of our long-term employees will have to go because they just can't cut a Top 40 format.

LICENSEE: I realize that, but it can't be helped. And I'll help those we have to release find jobs elsewhere; I'll do just about anything to help them find new positions, but we've got to make this change or go broke. There is no other choice, as I see it.

MANAGER: I hope you realize also that we aren't equipped to run a Top 40 operation. We don't have the cartridge equipment; our newsroom is inadequate for the job, and we have no personnel or equipment for doing on-the-spot coverage of news.

LICENSEE: Again, I'm ahead of you. I'm prepared to make the investments required. You put the plan together; tell no one what we're up to, and that includes the staff. We'll spring it on everyone when we're ready to make our move.

MANAGER: Just one more thing. You'd better talk with the Washington attorney about...

LICENSEE: That's my department and I've already covered it. The lawyers think the Commission will accept our proposal for a new format because the only other contemporary station here is a daytimer and can't do an adequate job. So just proceed on the assumption that we will get the Commission's blessings.

The manager has a difficult and emotional experience in front of him. He must replace personnel who are not equipped to work in a station with a Top 40 format. Here are some of the steps he must take to develop the plan:

1. Make contact with an electronics equipment company and get advice on the equipment that will be required. The equipment will include new turntables, five cartridge playbacks and two recorder units, two-way radio equipment for a mobile news unit, a vehicle to serve as mobile news unit, a new console for the control room, another for the production room, and a smaller one for the new newsroom that must be built.

Total cost: $28,000.00

2. Call a trusted broadcast friend in a distant market and get the names of three top quality program directors who may be willing to join the station and who have the capabilities for establishing a winning format. One of the new PD's first jobs will be to locate six Top 40 announcers, three of whom he may be able to hire away from the local competition.

Total increase in monthly announcer salaries: $6,500.00

3. Locate an agressive, experienced news director who can take over and manage the news operation for the new format. He will have to employ four men to handle inside mike work and outside news gathering.

Total increase in monthly newsmen salaries: $3,000.00.

4. Plan a promotional campaign for newspaper, television, and outdoor exposure of the new format.

5. Plan personnel changes. Traffic, copy, bookkeeping, and secretarial employees will be unaffected. The sales staff will remain the same temporarily, except for one man who has been a strong anti-Top 40 spokesman ever since the competition daytimer went on the air. This man will be released immediately and replaced by a working sales manager who can be lured away from another local station with a better commission deal. The new sales manager will then decide which, if any, of the other salesmen must be replaced.

Of the two newsmen presently on the staff, the manager may decide to recommend one of them for outside reporting duties. He will recommend the other for a station news job in a nearby market. If this fails, he will recommend that the licensee give the man two months serverance pay upon dismissal.

Of the four men on the present announcing staff, he may decide to keep one on the staff as a production engineer. He will try to help the others find non-radio jobs in the market. It is possible that one of them could make it on the sales staff, but he decides to let his new local sales manager make the decision.

6. Contact the national representative and give him details on the impending format change. He might also ask the rep to help find jobs for the displaced personnel. The rep deals with stations all over the country and often knows where job "plums" can be found.

7. Take his plan back to the licensee.

Once the manager has his plan on paper and the wheels turning, he would report to the owner:

MANAGER: Okay. You expected the investment and the increase in operating costs. We can have the equipment here in fifteen days and the engineering department sworn to secrecy at this point, will need another week to install it.

The news director will report here for work on the first; he came in last week at our expense to discuss the format and find a place for his family to live. About the same schedule for the program director, who has three DJs lined up to start on the first of the month. One of our local competition's men has agreed to join us, and we can work short a man or two for a couple of weeks if we don't get the full complement of announcers on board by the kickoff date.

I've scheduled newspaper ads, a 100-board outdoor campaign, and TV spots to start on the first. We should have a staff meeting at the earliest possible date to explain what we've been up to. And I think you ought to break the news to the staff.

LICENSEE: Fine. Set the staff meeting up for Wednesday afternoon at 3:30. I'll do the talking, though I must say I don't look forward to cutting people from this staff. There is no easy way to tell a man he must look for another job.

The personnel problem varies according to the market, the size of the company, and the capabilities of the personnel involved. In a single-station operation, the problem is acute because the station owner actually has only the staff jobs to offer. In an AM-FM set-up, at least there usually are two staffs; and in some cases the displaced personnel can be shifted to the other station. In an AM-FM-TV-Newspaper complex, the transfer of personnel would not normally constitute a big problem. The same would be true of the licensee who owns and operates other businesses, even though unrelated to broadcasting. Whatever the situation, when dramatic format changes occur, people are displaced and the problem of treating them fairly must be faced.

STAFF DEVELOPMENT AND MAINTENANCE

An announcer once complained that his application for employment was accepted so quickly that he was thrown into the control room for an air shift before he knew the call letters of the station. This may happen in realistic situations, if management is desperate to just "hire a body" and get it on the air, but the intricacies of modern programing are such that a thorough orientation is necessary before the new announcer goes on the air. The new employee should be briefed not only by top management as to policy and community relations, but also by the program director as to details of the format, equipment, work schedules, and staff relations. The employer is cheating himself and the new announcer when he doesn't do everything possible to inform and instruct him on station operations.

Typical Schedule:

1. Program director interviews and decides to recommend hiring the applicant.

2. Recommendation goes to general manager, who then conducts an interview with applicant. Discusses, among other things, salary, raises, management expectations, fringe benefits such as hospitalization and vacations.

3. General manager concurs with program director and the new employee is taken to the bookkeeping department to complete required personnel forms.

4. Program director then takes the new man on a tour of the facility and introduces him to other staff members.

5. New man is assigned to monitor station for two days to get the feel of the format. These two days also to be used for the new employee to get his personal housekeeping in order. This would include finding a place to live, ordering utilities, and other domestic chores.

6. A copy of the station policy book is given to the new employee to read. He is instructed to study a history of ratings and maps to acquaint himself with the geography of station coverage. He is told to check the pronunciation of streets and suburbs, prominent citizens' names, and neighboring towns.

7. In some cases, the new announcer is introduced to key advertisers. This may be especially true in the case of a personality announcer.

Training Announcers in Depth

The more jobs an announcer can perform, the more valuable he is to himself and to his employer. The announcer with writing and production room capability is usually worth more money than the announcer whose only asset is his voice. The announcer who has bothered to study for and obtain a first class license is worth still more where stations use combination operator-announcers.

At the earliest practicable date, the new announcer should start working or learning other air shifts to understand the sometimes subtle change in music and attitude required to execute the format. The early morning man, for example, might do the 9 A.M.-12 noon show, or the afternoon drive show, on occasion, to increase his familiarity with the overall format and equip himself to handle such shows successfully during illness and vacations.

Each announcer should be capable of handling production room duties. He should understand the equipment, how it is assembled, be familiar with the sound effects and the production music library, and be capable of turning out a quality commercial announcement.

It is frustrating and wasteful to have an announcer who cannot type, does not know about or understand the production room equipment, has no writing capability and, indeed, can only do his air show. The more financially successful operators may operate with such specialists, but in most stations management must have air personnel with multiple talents. It is desirable to employ individuals with other than on-air abilities, but this is not always possible. It is, however, possible and practical to establish training procedures to broaden the work base of each air employee. In addition to instruction on working other shifts and handling the production room, it usually is possible to train announcers in news reporting, reporting election returns, and handling play-by-play broadcasts of sports events. In all cases, it amounts to on-the-job training and should be done under the supervision of a competent staff member. Most stations do not have the time for an academic approach to training; the product of the instruction should be usable and-or saleable.

Continuing the Search for Air Personnel

Only the foolish program director or general manager will say to himself, "Now, my staff is permanent. I don't need others." No staff is permanent as long as there are other operators who can and will pay more money and as long as humans remain vulnerable to sickness and retain the quality of becoming lazy and disinterested. A continuing effort must be made by management to locate and establish rapport with new and different on-the-air talent. The competent program director will know the names of air personalities on competing stations, the amount of their earnings, and the salary offer required to "bring them over."

If there are no desirable individuals working for the competition, the program director should monitor neighboring city stations and advertise in trade journals for off-the-air tapes, using blind box numbers. One way or the other, the program director should equip himself to deal with the problem of unexpected resignations, incompetence, and illness. The announcer who is content today will be discontent tomorrow if he gets an offer of $150 more per month from another station. The announcer who is adequate today may have to be fired on the spot tomorrow for incompetency. This does not say there should be a barrier of suspicion between management and staff, but there is the continuing probability that sooner or later management will have to make adjustments in the staff.

Inter-Staff Conflicts

One of management's most gnawing problems is inter-staff conflicts. These result from salary differences, preferential treatment of one staff member over another, personality conflicts, personal problems, and individual sensitivity. It is not always possible to detect an individual's personality problems when he is being interviewed for the job. Some of the staff conflicts that arise will stagger the imagination.

One case history involved an announcer from Florida and another from New Jersey. The Southerner had a slight accent off the air, but was able to conceal it on the air. The New Jersey native had what the Southerner thought was "yankee arrogance." Ultimately, the two engaged in a fist fight in the main control room, and both were fired.

Other situations that create inter-staff conflict:

1. Overtime assignments given to favored announcers.

2. PD socializing with some announcers, avoiding others.

3. Pay increases given on personality rather than merit basis.

4. Assignment of unpleasant jobs to less favored staff members.

5. Failure to praise as well as criticize.

6. Rewarding incompetence.

The program director may avoid staff conflicts by making an educated estimate not only of the individual's professional capability, but also of his ability to fit in with the members of the staff. The announcer with a chip on his shoulder may not be able to take the kidding handed out by his fellow workers. He may be too serious for a particular group of individuals, or he may be too cavalier in his attitude toward his profession. When management begins to hear complaints from multiple sources about a staff member, he would do well to begin a quiet watchfulness. Complaints and rumors may include:

1. The guy's too cocky. Thinks he is network talent.

2. He's pleasant at work but drinks like a fish and causes trouble in public places.

3. Too quick to criticize fellow announcers.

4. He's dirty. I can't stand to be in the control room with him.

5. He's vulgar. He tells dirty jokes to the girls in the office.

6. He takes station music home with him and is building a personal record library at station expense.

7. He never talks to anyone. He's a loner. He won't participate in station functions such as bowling, softball, and staff parties.

8. Continually knocks the station, equipment, format, personnel to anyone who will listen.

9. Refuses to take instruction and cannot follow orders.

When management detects such conflict, it should move immediately to correct the problem. The solution may be found in talking with the offender. It may also be necessary to discharge the offender and replace him with someone more in tune with the entire staff. This doesn't mean the staff will decide who may or may not be employed. On occasion, a staff can become so entrenched at a station that a clean sweep is required.

Example:

MANAGER: Now, Bill, it seems you aren't getting along too well around here. I've heard nothing but complaints about you since the day you arrived.

NEW MAN: I don't doubt it, Mr. Jones. You have a program director and five other announcers and I've never seen such an incompetent clique anywhere; and I've worked in several pretty good operations. Even if I wanted to, it would be impossible to break into their little circle.

MANAGER: What do you mean, incompetent? I understand how people form tight little circles and while I don't like it, I don't know how to correct it just now. But I don't understand what you mean by **incompetent**.

NEW MAN: Well, I'll tell you since you asked. The morning man is unable to read a newscast. But this is passed over because he and his wife are constant companions of the PD and his wife. Since I've been here, the morning man has overindulged several times, was unable to make it to work on time, and the PD filled for him.

MANAGER: I've heard nothing of that.

NEW MAN: Of course you haven't, because the PD covers it up. And furthermore, only one of your men is capable of handling production. He doesn't like it, so I've been getting all production room assignments. And in case you haven't noticed, I've been recording most of the commercials since I came here because the salesmen and their clients don't like the work of the other men. And look at the way they dress. I've yet to see one of them wear a tie and coat. And the morning man often wears a gym suit to work. The control room is like a pig sty when I go in for my show. I can't tell you how to run your radio station, but this is one case where you'd better check the complainants, before you look into complaints about me.

Such situations do develop, and it is the fault of top and middle management, rather than the fault of the staff members involved. The problem of cliques can be avoided if management takes an active, daily interest in the conduct of the department. In the case cited, the manager should have known about the freeze-out being given the new man. He should have inspected the control room and learned for himself that it was like a pig sty, and he should have listened to his station enough to know when a newscast was poorly done or when the PD was filling in too often for a particular announcer. Top management simply cannot afford to allow little kingdoms to develop within a staff. It stifles competition, destroys creativity, encourages ineptitude and laziness.

Incentive Plans

It is not difficult to devise incentive plans for salesmen. They are profit-oriented, and any plan that offers them extra cash or merchandise usually will be successful. It is more difficult to stimulate an air staff because their personal motives are different from those of the salesmen. The announcer is, inevitably, moved by the same factors that move an actor; he is, essentially, a performer, and it is this one characteristic that permits management an opportunity to incite him to improve his work. Recognition and reward bear heavily on the subconscious of the air personality. Reward is important, but recognition is paramount.

Typical Incentives:

1. Person-to-person talks. Congratulating the announcer on his ratings, his ability to interpret the format, and the results he has gotten for advertisers.

2. Small but regular pay increases for the announcer who continually performs above average. This often will stimulate others to match his performance.

3. Promotional announcements on one show promoting the personality on another show. This is recognition.

4. Cash bonus if a certain audience share is reached. Instead of cash, management may use merchandise, travel, or local entertainment.

5. Some freedom to exploit himself in outside functions, such as teenage dances, public speaking, or lecturing.

6. Some freedom of expression often may be given an announcer to motivate him to perform better. Some formats tend to cramp an announcer or personality and thus render him incapable of performing.

7. Advertising in other media. A picture of the DJ in a local

newspaper ad or an appearance in a television commercial for the station, may bolster his ego.

There is a certain management magic, also, in keeping an air staff's morale high. A licensee, listening to his station one day, declared that the "announcers sound like the number two station in town and until they start sounding like they are number one, they'll stay in the number two position in the market." Often, it is possible to tune across a dial in a market and detect the top-rated station just by the on-air attitude of the disc jockeys. Being top-rated often is sufficient stimulation for an air staff, but even here it is necessary to keep the pot boiling with praise, pay increases, and recognition. While these management actions are desirable in most businesses, they are essential in radio broadcasting. A station, after all, is little more than people making a sound that is interesting, entertaining, and informative to the general public. Thus, we see 50,000 watt stations with a million dollars worth of land and equipment running behind a thousand watt "coffee pot" whose staff is spirited, motivated, and challenged.

McLendon was one of the first broadcasters to ever offer cash bonuses to announcers for increased ratings. Any formula may be devised, of course, but McLendon offered a certain amount of cash for each tenth of a percent increase in audience share.

The bonus idea, while not in use at his stations today, served to make a specific point: Announcers will do a better job if they are motivated by challenge and reward. McLendon's men were motivated to more carefully select from the playlist music for their particular shows; to keep the cues tight between music, voice, commercials and other program matter; to prepare timely remarks, and to generally improve the pacing and movement of their shows.

Announcer Conduct Requirements

The station's announcing staff has a responsibility to the licensee and management that goes beyond its duties within the offices and studios. The public tends to develop a special regard for any performer, whether stage, screen, television, or radio. And whether the air personality is liked or disliked, he is nearly always set apart from others by the public. The announcer, therefore, has a special responsibility to protect his own image and the image of his station. It is incomprehensible but true that, to the mass audience, the announcer is the station; when the public is pleased with the announcer, it is pleased with the station: If the announcer is a "nogoodnik," the station is similarly categorized. An individual, new in the market, can pop into many stores, identify himself as an air personality with KXXX, and cash a check or obtain immediate credit. If the station has a good reputation in the business community, almost anyone associated with the station can obtain special favors. The smaller the market, the more prominence the average local air personalities can achieve. It obviously is not necessary for the announcer to walk the narrow line of abstinence from all things evil, but it is absolutely essential that he practice his vices with great discretion if he is to protect himself and his station.

Sample Station Policy Statement Regarding Announcer Conduct:

1. KXXX announcers, in public appearances, will be neatly dressed in tie and jacket. Long hair and other attempts at developing a highly individual appearance will not be tolerated.

2. Any announcer who is arrested for brawling or drunkenness in any public place is automatically suspended. KXXX positively will not tolerate announcers making public spectacles of themselves.

3. Announcers will remember that they represent KXXX at all times and will be careful to conduct themselves in a manner that will bring praise rather than criticism upon the station.

4. An announcer's personal life is his own, so long as it has no negative reflection upon the station.

Any such policy, of course, must be written to cover the individual station's situation. The recognized leading station in a market of 100,000 has far more to protect in the way of a local image than does the tenth-rated station in a market of 1,000,000.

THE PRODUCTION DEPARTMENT

As discussed earlier in this chapter, the production department is an important part of the programing effort because so much of the program matter is created and developed here. Fig. 14 is a typical production room layout.

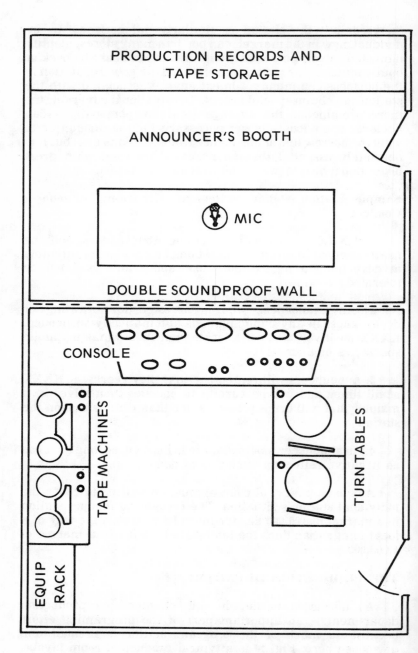

Fig. 14. Sample Production Room Layout.

The best production rooms are laid out to separate, by a soundproof wall, the announcing booth from the equipment room. The primary reason for this separation is to help the production director (or engineer) get a proper mix between voice, sound effects, and music. For example, a commercial might call for an opening with crowd noise; a segue into music, which is faded for the announcer's voice. By separating the live voice from the equipment and the recorded material, the engineer can get a balanced mix. That is, he can hear crowd noises derived from a tape on the tape machine and music derived from a disc on the turntables, and set his console volume levels in proper balance with the announcer's voice.

Production Aids

Any production department must have certain production aids if the station is to build excitement into its sound. The following list represents an ideal situation. Any station could operate on less, but the better the aids library, the better the station sound.

1. Modern sound effect library.

2. Merchant jingle package. This asset is particularly important to small market operations where revenues and talent are usually inadequate to do a professional job. A jingle package includes open end commercials that provide space for the advertisers's name, address, and specials. Such packages usually include special jingles for drug stores, department stores, jewelry stores, and other retail organizations. One practice is to prepare a spec spot for a given retailer, using the special jingle, and offer it to the advertiser on an exclusive basis.

3. Commercial bed package. This is simply a series of 30- and 60-second musical beds suitable for use in the background of any advertiser commercial. These may be purchased in ready-to-use form or may be gleaned from any album of instrumentals by the production engineer.

4. Production albums. Most stations receive from manufacturers and distributors albums that are not suitable for regular air play, but which contain music that is excellent for commercial backgrounds. The soundtracks of movies are

in many cases excellent for commercial background. This music is more dramatic and expressive in many instances and is useful frequently in emphasizing the tone and nature of a given business.

5. National advertiser musical commercials. These include professionally produced commercials for Ford, Chevrolet, Coca-Cola, Frigidaire, and hundreds of other nationally distributed products. They can be extremely useful to the station when making a proposal to a local retailer. A speculation spot is prepared for the local Ford dealer, and the national agency spot is used in part to give the commercial a familiar and professional sound.

6. List of outside talent. In most markets there are good male and female voices that may be used effectively in the production of special material. A top 40 station, for example, may have no heavy voices on the staff. The local amateur theater, again for example, may have several members with really excellent voices for a specific type commercial. The same is true when the station needs a female or child's voice. It is better to charge the advertiser for special production costs than it is to say, "We can't do the commercial the way you want it."

7. Instrumental versions of hit songs, present and past. These often are useful as background music for commercials.

8. Carbon microphone. Although this is not a library item, it is often useful in producing a dialogue commercial where a character is talking on the telephone. In many cases, the local telephone company may wire a regular phone circuit into the station equipment for this purpose.

9. Echo chamber capability. Most experienced audio engineers can build the echo capability into the recording equipment. This also is used when the commercial requires a special sound. If the technique is not known to a station's engineer, the equipment manufacturer usually can supply details.

10. Telephone recording facility. This enables the production room to record **on-the-scene** interview type commercials. For example, an announcer may be assigned to visit a furniture store that is having a special sale. The announcer might interview the sales manager who would give

items and prices. The same method may be simulated with a carbon mike in the studio, but the excitement of an on-the-scene interview may be lost.

Production Techniques

Production methods range from straight copy to copy with (or without) musical background to elaborate scripts involving several persons, several different sounds, musical backgrounds, crescendo openings, and stinger closes.

Example of Elaborate Production:

CLIENT:	Smith Furniture
LENGTH:	60-seconds
USE:	April 15-25
PRODUCED:	April 8

SOUND:	Excited female crowd noise, up three seconds, under for:
ANNCR NO. 1:	There's plenty of excitement these days at Smith Furniture in downtown Ourtown. The reason?
SOUND:	Suspense music, up briefly, then under and out for:
ANNCR NO. 2:	Smith Furniture is having its annual birthday sale, and prices are at rock bottom. Just listen to some of these marvelous values.
SOUND:	Light, bright music, up briefly, then under for:
ANNCR NO. 1:	Name-brand living room sets that were priced at $399 are on sale now for $299. Platform rockers that regularly sell for $129.95 have been marked down to $99.00 during Smith's birthday sale. But there's more.
SOUND:	Excited female voices, up and out for:
ANNCR NO. 2:	Dining Room sets are being discounted 50 percent during Smith Furniture's big sale. **Big Name** laundry equipment that normally sells for $239.50 is priced now during the sale at $199.50.

ANNCR NO. 1:	And bedroom suites that usually sell for $199.00 have been reduced to $149.50. And these suites include full-size bed, box spring and mattress, vanity, and a huge chest of drawers.
SOUND:	Excited female voices.
ANNCR NO. 2:	Yes, it's really exciting these days at Smith Furniture Company's big annual birthday sale.
SOUND & ANNCR NO. 1:	(Echo effect) Smith Furniture Company. 1212 Main Street, in downtown Ourtown.

A successful production effort results from close cooperation and coordination between the client, salesman, continuity writer, production engineer or director, and announcers. The salesman must be careful to make his production presentations within the capability of the continuity writer and the production department. The salesman should not, for example, propose using a female voice in a commercial if the station has no female voice available. He should not propose the use of elaborate commercials if the production room can't deliver them.

Too often, everyone involved will take the easy way out. Basic notes will be turned over to the continuity (copy) writer, who will hack out a dull, routine, price-filled spot and turn it over to the production room. A disinterested announcer will then apply his "golden tones" to the script, and a routine, low or non-sell spot will be produced and put on the air. Stumbles and kicks will be allowed, along with bad copy interpretation and mispronunciations. If the program and production staff is alert, professional and proud of its effort, no bad commercial production gets on the air. Somewhere along the line, at least one person should be a bear on production. The continuity writer may insist that copy be well done and that announcers interpret it correctly and without reading errors. The announcers themselves may reject weak copy and may insist that the engineer allow retakes until the copy is right. Finally, the program director may insist that all copy and production meet his rigid standards before it is allowed on the air. Some program directors will insist that the copy and production fit the format.

On a good music station, for example, the program director may allow no commercials that use contemporary music and a hard-sell approach. On an underground, progressive rock, acid rock format, the program director may insist that no "old" language be used and that all commercials and public service announcements be delivered in a low-key, matter-of-fact tone. It becomes a matter of professional pride on the part of at least one person in the production chain.

Generally speaking, top management decides the quality of production by establishing policy guidelines. Such guidelines include a prohibition against exceeding the ordered spot length. A 30-second announcement runs 30 seconds, not 35 or 40 seconds. A 60-second announcement is given the same treatment. Program log entries for commercials usually are made from time orders and these specify the length a spot will be. While the Commission makes no rule on the length of commercial matter, it does insist that if a spot is logged 60-seconds, that it run that length and no more. Ninety-second spots are allowed, but most stations, particularly those with formula formats, will not accept them because they delay by 30 seconds the resumption of music. Another guideline management may lay down is a prohibition against the use of unprofessional voices except where the script calls for testimonial lines by housewives or other consumers. Some stations may prohibit hard-sell; others may require that all commercials be produced with music, sound effects, and other devices designed to excite the listener. The Commission itself has advised against the use of sirens or bulletin news introductions for commercials. Essentially, the Commission doesn't want the station to fool the listener into giving his attention to what sounds like an important news item when in reality he is about to hear a commercial.

Examples of What Not to Do:

SOUND: Police Siren, up three seconds and under for:

ANNCR: Your attention, please. Smith Furniture Company is having a fire sale.

ANNCR: Here is a Bulletin from KXXX (pause). Smith Furniture announces its annual birthday sale.

Attention-getting devices are acceptable, as long as they do not attempt to get attention under false pretenses. And these devices need not be loud or nerve-rattling. Attention may be gained, on a Top 40 station for example, by the announcer's simply opening the commercial quietly and directly. Crowd noises, such as cheering from a football stadium, may be acceptable, along with racing auto engines, referee whistles, music of any kind, or loud or unusual voices.

In recent years, the advertising industry has made a considerable effort to tone down dramatizations and use the straight, candid approach to selling merchandise and services because it was discovered that consumers praised production techniques but couldn't remember the product or service being advertised. Many announcers are capable of doing other voices, such as an old man, old woman, child, grandpa, grandma, or using dialects to depict a character of Italian, Oriental, Mexican or Jewish origin. One morning man at a southwestern station developed a character named Granny Emma. So effectively was she employed that many listeners never realized she was a figment of the announcer's imagination. She specifically was called upon to do commercials and other on-air chores. Often, when the announcer wanted to criticize or make fun of something, he would use "Granny" and thus escape bringing reaction to himself. He would blame Granny for the statements. If such characters are well-done and popular, the sales department often can close sales by offering the services of one of the on-air characters. In some cases, however, stations and advertisers create public relations problems for themselves by the use of such devices. The Mexican-American community, for example, may resent any character with a Mexican or Spanish accent. The same might be true of Negro, Italian, Jewish, or Oriental accents. Law enforcement organizations have complained about characters that make officers appear stupid or ignorant. And, although station management may not agree with such evaluations, good public relations dictate discontinuance of objectionable characters on the air. People may still laugh privately at themselves and their race, but find little humor in hearing their accents being held up for the general public snickers.

THE NEWS DEPARTMENT

A news department may range in size from no professional newsmen and no equipment, other than a wire service printer, to dozens of staff members and unlimited equipment facilities. The Commission does not require that a station have a news department or that it program any particular amount of news material. But upon reading FCC forms for applying for Construction Permits (301) and the form for applying for license renewal (303), it becomes immediately apparent that the Commission desires, hence, requires that a certain amount of news be programed.

FCC Policies

In FCC Form 301, Section IV-A, Part III, Paragraph 14 (1), the Commission asks that the applicant state the number of hours and minutes of news he proposes to broadcast each week and the percentage of the total broadcast week this time absorbs. Paragraph 15, Section IV-A, says:

> "Submit in Exhibit No. _____ the following information concerning the applicant's proposed news programs:
>
> A. The staff, news gathering facilities, news services to be utilized; and
> B. An estimate of the percentage of news program time to be devoted to local and regional news during a typical week.

There are instances where a licensee or applicant for a new station may propose to broadcast no news, stating in his application that other stations in the market provide a more than adequate news service and that he proposes to broadcast, for example, only classical music, telephone talk shows, or employ some other highly specialized format. Even though there may be some precedent for such a proposal, there is no guarantee that the applicant's Washington attorney will submit it or that the Commission will agree that other stations provide a more than adequate news service. Again, there is no rule that an applicant must propose to broadcast news, but there is considerable evidence that the Commission wants such matter on the air. And if there is a rule as to how much news a station must carry, the applicant himself makes the rule when he proposes to carry a certain number of hours and minutes of news per week. If he proposes to broadcast 10 hours and 30 minutes of news, that figure becomes the rule for him.

Radio vs Press

Broadcast journalism still is not as trusted and respected as print journalism, though a majority of Americans will admit they get their news from radio or television. Even at this late date, with radio in its sixth decade of operation, many persons still regard the press as newspapers and newspaper reporters. Radio news is sold to news sources and the general public only by professional competence, and literally hundreds of stations in the last ten years have crossed the line separating insignificance from significance in news reporting. It isn't easy or cheap to build a competent, responsible, respected news operation. It takes trained personnel, expensive equipment, and months and years of consistent, effective work to produce a department that listeners can and will depend upon.

Even the "rip and read" news departments with no professional news personnel can do an adequate job of news reporting if management will establish firm policies regarding editing and delivery. Such policies include requirements that every newscast be "woodshedded" by the announcer before he puts it on the air. To "woodshed" a newscast is to simply rehearse it, checking pronunciation of names of persons and places, making certain that all sentences are complete and intelligible (that they "read") and that none of the news matter is offensive. Wire services often will note at the top of a news story: "The following material may be offensive." This might include stories involving unusual deaths, such as mutiliation in an auto accident, or sex crimes in which offensive details are used to tell the story.

Even with no professional news personnel, it is possible for the low-budget station to cover local news and localize certain national or area stories that are received over the news printer. Some stations make arrangements with local newspapers for local news. Others may assign announcers to telephone news sources and get stories during their off-air hours. A national story, for instance, that deals with a reduction in strength at certain military installations, may be localized by getting a statement from the mayor or some other public official on the effect the reduction will have on the local economy, and tying it in with the national story.

Example:

WASHINGTON—THE PENTAGON ANNOUNCED TODAY THAT THE 48TH ARMORED DIVISION WILL BE TRANS-

FERRED FROM FT. SMITH TO BERLIN. THERE ARE
20,000 MEN IN THE DIVISION, WHICH HAS BEEN
STATIONED AT FT. SMITH FOR TWO YEARS. HERE IN
OURTOWN, KXXX REPORTERS ASKED CONGRESSMAN
JIM JONES FOR HIS REACTIONS TO THE PENTAGON
ANNOUNCEMENT. THE CONGRESSMAN SAID THE
LOCAL ECONOMY COULD BE SERIOUSLY AFFECTED
BY THE TRANSFER UNLESS ANOTHER DIVISION
COULD BE MOVED INTO FT. SMITH.

If the station is only minimally equipped, it might use a
news actuality in which the congressman's voice is recorded
and his comments inserted into the news story. This effort
requires only that the telephone company provide a recording
hookup that enables the newsman to feed a telephone conversation into a recording machine.

Building a News Department

Assume that a station has been making the minimum
effort in reporting the news, and decides to build a complete,
professionally staffed news department. And, further assume
that the news director will run the department and will report
only to the general manager. In some cases, news departments are so strong they report only to the licensee; but in this
case, the news department won't have that range of authority
immediately.

The first consideration is a news budget, not only an
operating budget but also a budget covering the initial investment in equipment and quarters.

Example of Initial Investment:

1. Remodeling of Studio A as newsroom $2,000
2. Recording machines, console, other
       technical equipment.. 6,000
3. Two mobile news wagons (cars)...................... 6,000
4. Two-way equipment.. 4,000
5. Legal fees for two-way licensing...................... 300
6. Radio monitors for mobile units.......................... 1,000
7. Flares, other emergency equipment for mobiles....... 500

8. Typewriters.. 700

Other one-time costs might include management's agreement to pay moving costs to bring certain newsmen into the market or the payment of employment agency fees if this method is used to find a staff. Once the initial investment budget is estimated, management should then decide how much it will spend monthly to operate the department. These costs might include:

News Director Salary	$1,200
Salaries for 10 newsmen	8,000
Two-way maintenance	200
Mobile Unit maintenance	500
Direct lines to city hall, county court house	100
Long Distance Telephone calls	500
UPI Audio service	500
Weather Wire	100
Stock Market Wire	100
AP Broadcast Wire	800
UPI Broadcast Wire	800

News Policy

A basic operating policy for the news department should be set down in writing before the staff is employed so that adherence to management's wishes may be made a part of the employment contract. A professional news director may wish to add to or delete from the policy, depending upon whether his views agree or conflict with those of management.

Basic News Policy that might serve as the foundation for a later, more detailed policy:

KXXX NEWS POLICY

1. Firearms are never kept in the station, newsroom, or mobile news unit.

2. Families of victims of dog bites frequently telephone with a plea for broadcast appeals to help in finding the missing animal. KXXX's policy is to assist the victim in the search but only during the final three days of the incubation period of rabies. Ten days from the bite, the rabies shots usually begin. KXXX will begin broadcasting the appeal on the eighth day following the bite, but not before. KXXX is sincerely concerned about these cases and will make every effort to be of valuable assistance, but because of the volume of requests, it

must wait until the eighth day. Police say most animals are found, without radio assistance, during the first seven days.

3. Only in the event that police suspect foul play will KXXX broadcast a missing persons appeal. Management prefers that a policeman actually record the broadcast. If that is not practical, the news editor in charge must have the appeal verified by someone of whom the editor has personal knowledge at the police department. If the editor has the slightest doubt about the authenticity of the appeal, **IT WILL NOT BE AIRED.** Pranksters sometimes sound authentic. If you are working by telephone, get the report from the officer; then call him again through the police switchboard.

4. Appeals for blood will be made only on request from a hospital or police official.

5. Names of accident victims will be withheld pending notification of next of kin. Police generally will give guidance in this area.

6. Keep routine news copy no more than thirty days. Should you quote "A" in an attack on "B," you should maintain this copy for an indefinite period in a special file. You should also notify "B" of the attack and get his reaction for your follow-up stories. "B" may be an individual or institution (See Fairness Doctrine).

This policy, obviously, deals only with the operation of the department and has nothing to do with how the news will be presented. Programing and delivery techniques are discussed later in this chapter.

The News Director

The selection and employment of a news director is management's first critical decision.

Qualifications of a first rate news director:

1. Degree in Journalism.
2. Experience as reporter in general news on daily newspaper.
3. Quality, authoritative voice and experience in newscasting.
4. Vast interviewing experience, both radio and newspaper.

5. Command presence, ability to direct work of others.

6. Good health, highly energetic.

7. Ability to write news, detect and develop editorial subject.

8. History of highly responsible performance.

9. Demonstrated news judgement.

10. Willingness and physical capability of working long hours.

11. Good understanding of the Fairness Doctrine, state criminal codes, government organization at all levels.

12. Sufficient bearing and stature to represent the station to any public official or at a public or governmental function.

A news director with all these qualifications is the sort of person management dreams about but rarely finds. At the minimum, however, the news director must have experience as a professional broadcast newsman and possess all of the basic qualifications of a reporter. It is vital also that he be able to set examples for and lead other members of the news department. The news director's experience should be with a format similar to that of the station employing him. If the station is a network operation that attempts to deliver news in a slow, expanded manner, a man with Top-40 news experience would have to make many adjustments to fit the network format. By the same token, a newsman with only standard delivery experience probably would have difficulty adjusting to a Top 40 format.

The News Staff

Once the news director has been employed and filled in on management's policy. it then becomes his responsibility to hire a news staff.

Example:

Inside editors, broadcasters............................ 5
Mobile news reporters...................................... 4
Local government reporter.............................. 1

The inside editors must have top quality voices and be capable of writing news, editing wire reports, conducting telephone interviews, editing voice tapes and fitting them to written reports, and delivering the news in an authoritative, fast-paced style. They must have a sense of good news and be able to evaluate the importance of a story to the local area. They must be able to detect when a national or regional story can be localized, and have the initiative to handle localization when it is indicated.

The mobile news reporters need not have top quality voices, although this is desirable because they should be capable of working the news desk and microphone inside during illness and vacations.

These reporters will handle all local coverage, such as accidents, shootings, and other violence. They must be capable of interviewing government and other community leaders, as well as visiting celebrities. They should know their way around law enforcement agencies and be able to develop and protect a large variety of news sources. They should develop rapport with newspaper and television reporters and arrange to swap news tips. They should be capable of reporting a story from notes, or without notes if the situation demands. Some stories require a play-by-play effort, much as in a football or basketball game. Such a play-by-play technique might involve reporting from close in the progress of a tornado or reporting a shoot-out between police and bandits.

A classic example of on-the-scene reporting occurred in 1963 when Jack Ruby killed Lee Harvey Oswald, suspected slayer of President Kennedy, as Oswald was being transferred out of the Dallas City Jail. In the confusion that followed, one radio reporter repeated his opening line three times. He had difficulty orienting himself because each time he would speak the opening line, the crowd would knock him to the floor. Upon getting back on his feet, he would repeat the opening line.

The local government reporter handles city council meetings, important civil trials, county and state government stories, and covers the political scene. While he should have a quality voice, his knowledge of the interworkings of government and politics is more important. This man may also be used by the news director and by management to write and deliver station editorials. Editorials critical of or containing praise for government officials or other politicians should be written by someone who is well-grounded in the subject and who is acquainted with the personalities involved. The most embarrassing thing a station can do is broadcast an editorial that contains errors in fact.

Scope of Coverage

Management, in the hypothetical case discussed, might decide that with its new facilities and an eleven-man staff, it will concentrate on local and regional coverage and will depend as little as possible upon the wire service's coverage of these scenes. News editors will be permitted to call anywhere in the U.S., Canada, or Mexico to get actualities on tape. Arrangements are made to exchange stories with reliable stations in San Francisco, Chicago, New York, Philadelphia, Dallas, and other major markets of the country. If, for example, an earthquake hits the San Francisco area, the station will not have to depend exclusively upon the wires for stories. The San Francisco station, under the arrangement, can give KXXX an exclusive report directly from the disaster area. Emphasis also will be on the development of exclusive local stories and getting them on the air at the earliest practicable moment. The deadline for getting an important story on the air is immediately after the reporter gets the facts. If the station has promised the FCC it will program a certain amount of local and regional news, the promise must be strictly observed.

Programing the News

News, in this situation, will be programed five minutes on the hour and three minutes at the half-hour, inclusive of commercials and-or public service matter. This means three and one-half to four minutes of news on the hour and one and a half to two minutes on the half-hour. If the newscast contains a one-minute commercial or PSA, then only one minute of time is deducted from the news program. If the newscast is sponsored, and contains a commercial open and close as well as a one-minute commercial, then one and a half minutes are deducted from the program. Under Commission policies, only the actual news in a newscast may be counted; commercial or other non-news matter must be deducted. A five-minute news program may be logged, but if the program contains a one-minute commercial, then only four minutes of news may be counted when the operator evaluates his program log for license renewal purposes.

All regular newscasts will originate in the newsroom, with special broadcasts coming from city hall or the court house via the special lines or from the mobile news units.

In a newsroom equipped and staffed as elaborately as the one shown in Fig. 15, the news can be gathered, prepared, and presented authentically and dramatically. Mobile news units can be cut in during a studio newscast. Mobile reports can be prerecorded onto tape cartridge and inserted into newscasts. The newscaster himself has control of the equipment through the news console, and, therefore, can keep the newscast tight and fast-paced. Police and fire department radio monitors may or may not be cut out during the newscast, depending upon the level of background noise desired by the programers. In many cases, stations want the authentic newsroom noises of teletype machines, radio monitors, and typewriters behind every newscast. This adds to the excitement of the presentation. It gives the listener the impression that he is part of the scene at KXXX's newsroom.

Typical News Department Work Schedule:

Johnson	Newsroom 5:30 - 2:30
Jones	Newsroom 6:30 - 3:30
Williams	Newsroom 10:30 - 6:30
Adams	Newsroom 2:30 - 10:30
Wheeler	Newsroom 4:30 - 12:30
Byers	Mobile Unit 5:30 - 2:30
Wilson	Mobile Unit 9:30 - 5:30
Thompson	Mobile Unit 2:30 - 10:30
Evans	Mobile Unit 4:30 - 12:30
Masterson	City-County 8:30 - 5:00

In addition, specific schedules may be set up to indicate which man or which two-man team does which newscasts and when each individual newsman takes a lunch break. The overlapping of work schedules is necessary so that telephone beats can be covered, stories can be written and edited, and telephone interviews and mobile reports recorded and edited for use inside newscasts.

In this suggested schedule, Johnson would prepare and broadcast the 6:00 A.M. newscast. Jones, arriving at 6:30, would assist Johnson in preparing and broadcasting the important 7:00 and 8:00 A.M. newscasts. The half-hourly headlines and weather broadcasts may be handled by either. Williams, arriving at 10:30, would take over editing and

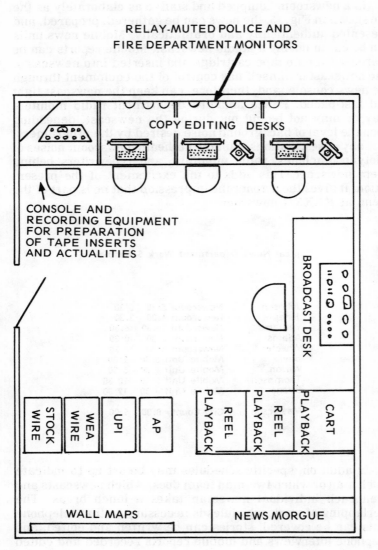

Fig. 15. Sample Newsroom Layout.

broadcasting duties while Johnson and Jones made their "telephone beat," wrote news stories, and taped interviews. One or the other would be assigned to check UPI audio for taped reports to use in connection with the national and international material being delivered on the UPI Broadcast Wire. Johnson and Jones would take one-hour lunch breaks separately, so that only one would be out of the newsroom at a time. Williams would continue handling the broadcasts through the 3:00 P.M. edition. At this point, he would take over writing, rewriting, and tape editing duties from Jones. Adams, reporting for duty at 2:30, would brief himself on the day's news, and prepare to handle the 4:00 P.M. edition by himself. Wheeler, reporting at 4:30, would work with Adams in preparing and delivering the important 5:00 and 6:00 newscasts. The 7:00, 8:00 A.M., and 5:00 and 6:00 P.M. newscasts are regarded as important because usually at these times a station has its greatest audience. Adams would be off at 10:30 P.M., and Wheeler would work through the 12:30 A.M. headlines. As Wheeler departs, he should leave with the announcer on duty a copy of the day's most important local news items. The announcer would get the remainder of his all night news from the wire services. He is alerted to news bulletins by a flashing light actuated by the news service, and would handle all newscasts from 1:00 A.M. through the 5:30 headlines.

Mobile reporters are scheduled so that two will be on duty through most of the day, 6:00 A.M. until 12:00 midnight. The city hall and court house reporter's schedule is set to fit the office hours of his prime sources, such as the major and city manager, court room, district attorney, and others in government installations. The news director may or may not develop his own beat. Regardless, he must be capable of doing any job required in the news department and of replacing any one of the reporters. In many cases, the news director will schedule himself to do at least two of the day's most important newscasts. Regardless of how much of the day's routine he handles, the news director has a multitude of duties to perform if he is to keep his department "ahead of the game." These duties include:

1. Monitoring competing stations to determine what, if any, news has escaped his own department.

2. Checking daily newspapers for the same purpose, but also to double check the accuracy of story facts.

3. Monitoring his own staff's newscasts to determine whether (1) newscasts contain all major news stories, (2) there is a good balance between types of stories used, and (3)

local and area stories are in the proportion proposed to the Commission in the last license renewal application.

4. Monitoring quality of delivery and interpretation of his own staff's newscasts, making sure each man is pronouncing local and area names and places correctly and that no individual newscaster is consistently kicking and stumbling through the news.

5. Maintaining high-level liaison with such sources as the mayor, police chief, congressmen, senators, state governor, political party leaders.

6. Representing station at official press functions, such as membership in radio news associations, press clubs, and certain press conferences involving high level government, political, social figures.

7. Devising the work schedule and ascertaining staff compliance.

8. Serving as liaison between his staff and station management.

9. Maintaining files on news stories and tapes that are or may be involved in controversy.

10. Running a double-check on all newsbeats, getting to know sources personally, ascertaining that staff reporters have respect of and are getting maximum cooperation from sources.

11. Handling public speaking chores of department and of station when appropriate.

12. Handling administrative duties such as approving timesheets, recommending salary increases, and ascertaining that staff has completed company insurance forms.

13. Handling public complaints relative to the news operation.

News Importance

A station's news department rarely pays its own way; but it, nevertheless, is a critically important part of most stations' program format. That listeners look to radio for news is evidenced by the success of the all-news formats that were started in the late 50s and early 60s. Such formats are tremendously expensive, and some fell by the way because they were not profitable. Others were able to generate sufficient audience to justify advertiser confidence and so continued. In any event, establishment of an all news format in a given market inevitably resulted in competing stations doing a more comprehensive job with the news and serving the listener better.

Literally hundreds of contemporary music stations get and hold adult audiences because of superior news coverage. McLendon's KLIF in Dallas is a classic example. The station was one of the first in the country to adopt the controversial news and music format. Adult listeners complained that Rock-and-Roll music was played ad nauseum, but the news department was alert, professional, and aggressive. Listeners were brought to the edge of their chairs by the locally famous "first news, first" mobile news introduction that featured a police siren.

Mobile News Format of KLIF:

SOUND: Police Siren, up and under for:

ANNCR: (Excitedly) First news, First! KLIF now takes you to the scene of a major accident in Dallas.

MOBILE: Jim Smith here for KLIF (pronounced Cliff) News. We're at the intersection of Peak and Haskell streets where a two-car collision has just occurred, injuring two women and a small child. Police are here, and Patrolman Bill Johnson is handling the investigation. He has identified the injured as Mrs. Mary Brown, 35; her daughter, Sue Brown, age 6; and Carolyn Adams, age 20. Patrolman Johnson said Mrs. Brown and her daughter were in one car traveling east on Peak—colliding with the other car driven by Miss Adams and traveling south on Haskell. None of the injuries appear serious, according to Patrolman Johnson. JIM SMITH HERE FOR KLIF NEWS.

SOUND: Police siren, up gradually for:

ANNCR: KLIF News has just taken you to the scene of another major accident in Dallas. Stay tuned to KLIF for First News, First.

The station had two mobile news units, black station wagons with white lettering, patrolling the streets at least eighteen hours a day. Police and sheriff's radios were used by the mobile reporters to gain information on traffic accidents and other violence. Often, the mobile news units would reach the scene before the police. Each unit was equipped with oxygen, stretcher, and first-aid equipment and often was used as an auxiliary ambulance. Mobile coverage was not limited to traffic accidents. Reporters were on the scene of shootings, explosions, tornados, building cave-ins, and other civil tribulations. Interviews were conducted with visiting dignitaries and public officials. Reporters accompanied detectives on narcotic raids. If the soap operas, Jack Benny, Fred Allen, and Captain Midnight constituted the Golden Days of Radio, then mobile news coverage in the late 50s and early 60s constituted the Sizzling Days of Radio. From these sensational methods of covering the news, radio gradually has refined the process with more and better trained newsmen, more sophisticated equipment, and clearer minds at the helm. Radio news still is exciting, and radio still is the first place most people turn when they hear of disaster. There are few jobs in the business that are more rewarding or exciting.

PROGRAM DEPARTMENT FACILITIES

It is true that some poorly equipped stations out-program and out-draw stations with unlimited equipment and facilities. But there is a point below which no station can go if it expects to develop a sound that will attract and hold listeners. Better than adequate equipment often is required to get and hold competent air personnel. Not only is adequate equipment required, but quality maintenance must also be performed routinely and when otherwise necessary. Such equipment refinements include top quality turntables, cartridge machines, reel-to-reel recording machines, and audio consoles that have adequate inputs and controls to handle the format. The physical plan is equally important, not only within a given work room, but within the program section of the building.

Any professional broadcaster will say he can design a better program department layout. He may design a different one, but not necessarily a better one. The student can visit and inspect 500 different stations and will find no two layouts the same.

In the program department layout in Fig. 16, we have placed the news and production rooms adjacent to master control. This arrangement enables the news broadcaster and announcer on duty to exchange visual as well as verbal cues. When a tight format is employed, this visual contact is necessary. It is not absolutely essential that the production room be adjacent to master control, but the arrangement is helpful and, indeed, essential when there is a prolonged equipment failure in master control. Operations may be immediately switched to the production room until repairs in master control are complete. In this case, also, the subcontrol and auxiliary production room has been placed so that it also may be used as a control room in emergencies. While live studio interviews are relatively rare, there are occasions when studio space is needed for that purpose. A prime example is when a station programs a telephone talk show. The subcontrol room is ideal for that purpose in that it provides a separate, out-of-the way place for the moderator to work and for him to seat experts who come in to talk with listeners.

The news director and program director have their offices near the actions they control. Traffic and copy, of course, are deeply involved in production and program logs; and their close proximity to production and control is desirable.

The music director's work area may or may not be immediately adjacent to the other program offices and studios, but this is desirable as the program director often works with him in listening to and evaluating a piece of music. And while the lounge may appear to be a luxury item, it does give off-duty personnel a place to hang their hats and prevents their spending non-productive time in the work areas. Most plans separate programing and production from sales, engineering, and administration. Traffic and copy should be the two offices that lie between sales and programing because it is in these offices that liaison is most often accomplished. Time orders and copy notes flow from sales to programing through traffic and copy.

Fig. 17 is a sample station layout showing the relationship between programing and administration. These facilities cannot be regarded as luxurious, but neither do they constitute the minimum. Some stations operate entirely in two or three separate rooms. Others are spread out over thousands of square feet of space, are highly departmentalized and staffed with one-job specialists. In the small operation, such as a daytimer, the master control may be used to program the station during the day and serve as a production room at night. This is doing it the hard way, but such situations exist, and they provide all the challenges and excitement of the big operations. In such instances, the traffic director may also be the bookkeeper, copy writer, receptionist, and woman's director. The general manager may pull an air shift and handle all sales and engineering. Experience has shown that staff and facility are important to the station's quality of service, but there are many stations that provide excellent listener service with an irreducible minimum in staff and facility. It reverts again to the concept that radio stations essentially are people, not wires, transmitters, buttons, and turntables.

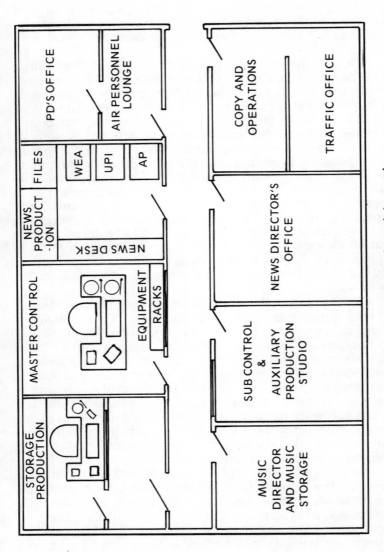

Fig. 16. Program Department Layout.

222

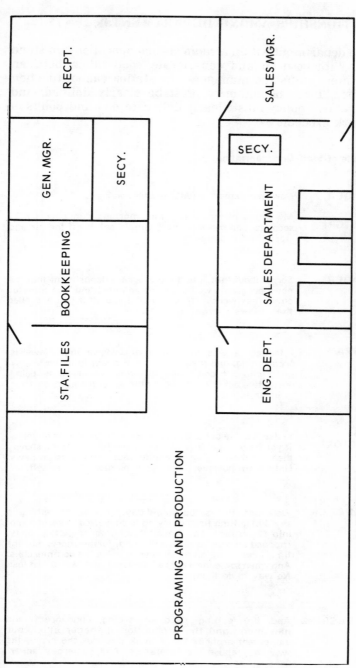

Fig. 17. Sample Station Layout Showing Relationship between Programing and Administration.

RELATIONSHIPS AMONG DEPARTMENTS

No department within a radio station operation can stand alone. Without deep and considerate cooperation between department staffs and managers, the station cannot function smoothly. Lines of authority must be clearly defined, and management policy must clearly delineate **do's** and **don'ts** in the work procedures.

Example of Staff Disorganization:

MANAGER: Now, gentlemen, what's the trouble?

NEWS DIRECTOR: My seven o'clock news this morning ran over by 30 seconds, and the announcer simply cut us off the air and started programing music.

MANAGER: Sorry about that. I told the program department that the news programs would be five minutes and five minutes only. They were instructed to cut you off if you exceeded that. Guess I forgot to tell you.

PROGRAM DIR: I thought I was in charge of programing. News is programing, and it seems to me it ought to be under my jurisdiction. I don't like the way the news is being presented, but I haven't been able to get the news director to listen to me.

NEWS DIRECTOR: Listen, you've got enough trouble with those DJs of yours. If you have the ability to correct the flaws in their shows, then maybe I'll give an ear to your comments on news. Until then, however, keep your opinions to yourself.

PRODUCTION MGR: Well, since this is "be candid day," I've got something to say. I'm getting tired of trying to squeeze a 90-second spot into 60 seconds, and I'm getting tired of getting dirty, chopped up copy to work with. And, furthermore, half the time I can't find an announcer to voice the commercials. And when someone wants a two-voice spot, we're just lost. No way to do them.

ENGINEERING: And I'm getting tired of seeing announcers and newsmen...and the production manager...kick our equipment around. You'd think this was the army, the way they abuse the turntables. And yesterday an announcer kicked a cartridge machine trying to make it work. He even made some nasty remarks on the air about the maintenance here. We can keep the equipment in good repair if the people using it will remember that this is electronic gear; it's delicate and it's expensive.

TRAFFIC MGR: If the salesmen don't start getting orders in before 4:00, I'm just not going to put them on the air. They are very inconsiderate. I have to work until six o'clock most days to complete the next day's logs just because those guys turn orders in late. Can't you do something about that?

SALES MANAGER: Well, I wish we could get together. Half the time, it seems, we can't get a client's schedule on the air because of bad or no production or because the traffic manager forgets to log the spots.

This kind of situation, unless corrected, can destroy a station. It is an example of total disorder resulting from laziness or stupidity on the part of management. Not only should operating policies exist, but they should be in writing for frequent reference purposes. And when the policy is changed, the change should be noted in all copies of the operating manual. Here are just a few rules that will correct the problems indicated in the dialogue:

1. The news director has complete charge of the news department. He answers only to the general manager.

2. News and programing will cooperate in following program lengths precisely as indicated on the log. Announcers are instructed to begin their shows at exactly five minutes past the hour and three minutes past the half-hour.

3. The time order deadline for schedules starting the following day is 2:00 P.M., Monday through Thursday, and 12:00 noon on Friday. The copy deadline for schedules starting the following day is 3:00 P.M., Monday through Thursday, and 1:00 P.M. on Friday.

(Note: The Friday deadline is different because on Friday copy and traffic must prepare commercials and logs for Saturday, Sunday, and Monday; more time, therefore, is required.)

4. Only the chief engineer or a member of his staff may make repairs on any equipment. Any non-engineering staff member will be subject to immediate dismissal if he so much as speaks harshly to station equipment.

225

5. All copy will be 120 words or less for 60-second announcements or 60 words or less for 30-second announcements. The production engineer is instructed to return continuity to the copy department if it exceeds these standards.

6. Effective station operation requires staff cooperation. We have no room in this operation for prima donnas, malcontents, or other ineffective or inefficient personnel.

The issuance of the operations manual may be made at a general staff meeting or at a meeting of department heads who will be instructed to pass copies along to members of their departments. However the information is disseminated, it should carry friendly but fair warnings from management that strict compliance is expected.

It is not uncommon for the program or news department to demand autonomy from top management. The program director often wants no management or administrative limitations placed on listener contests, station promotions, music played, personnel hired or fired. "I'm the program director and as such I should be free to program the station according to my own beliefs, experience, and knowledge," he might argue. The news director may come up with similar arguments, explaining that news production should be totally free of entertainment, commercial, or political considerations.

In some cases, these department heads may be right. But, generally, management must maintain tight control over the programing and news operations to (1) satisfy FCC requirements that the licensee run his station, (2) make certain advertisers are not driven from the station by insensitive news or program actions, and (3) ascertain that listeners are not offended by program or news indiscretions. With regard to the FCC and programing, the PD may wish to eliminate a block of news that would cause the station to violate its promise to program only a certain amount of news. Before such changes are made, top management must be consulted, and permission must be obtained from the Commission if the change significantly alters the station's proposed news programing. Advertisers may be driven from the station by news and program blunders. An announcer once, upon playing a Pepsi Cola commercial between 6:00 and 7:00 A.M., suggested it was too early for soft drinks. "Let's all have a cup of coffee," he said. At this point, an irate agency account executive called the manager and cancelled the schedule. It happens that coffee is a soft drink bottler's biggest competitor.

Any criticism of an advertiser, however mild it may appear, should be cleared through management. This is not to say a station should protect an evil influence in the community just because the influence happens to be an advertiser, but it should be management's decision over that of the program director or an announcer. Such autonomy in programing may cause damage beyond the commercial area. An announcer's criticism of the police department can ruin years of work by the news department in establishing reliable and friendly news sources.

Management also must set policy on the quality of music to be played on the station. This would not include the banning of certain artists or beats, but would include the banning of music with lyrics that may be considered loud or suggestive or to extol the virtues of illegal use of drugs. In fact, the Commission has issued warnings to stations to avoid exposing lyrics that play up the use of drugs. The Commission requires that licensees maintain a strict control over operation of their stations and over the material that is broadcast. Licensees can maintain such control only by establishing strict policy and then by constant policing of the policy.

A classic example of how unpoliced programing may bring disaster to a station occurred in 1960-61 to WDKD in the now-famous Charlie Walker Case. The Commission set a hearing on the station's application for license renewal to determine, among other things, "(1) whether the licensee maintained adequate control or supervision of program material broadcast over his station during the period of his most recent license renewal, and (2) whether the licensee permitted program material to be broadcast over station WDKD on the Charlie Walker show, particularly during the period between January 1, 1960, and April 30, 1960, which program material was coarse, vulgar, suggestive, and susceptible of indecent, double meanings."

At the hearing, the Commission produced verbatim transcripts of material broadcast by Charlie Walker. The transcript included the following monologue:
"Next Saturday night it is we gonna have the big grand opening over at the New W.P. Marshall store in Greasy Thrill (Greeleyville) and we gonna come over there and let it all hang out. Course, if we let it all hang out in Greeleyville, there ain't gonna be enough room over there for nothin' else, is there?

"He says: 'I believe that old dog of mine is a Baptist.' I asked him why he thought his old dog was a Baptist and he says, 'you know, Uncle Charlie, it is that he's done baptized every hub cap around Ann's Drawers (Andrew)'. You say it is that all the hub caps in Spring Gulley is going to Heaven?"

As a result of this sort of material being broadcast, and the Commission's determining that the licensee, indeed, did not maintain control over programing, the application for license renewal was denied.

It is doubtful that many managers or licensees involve themselves in the minute, creative aspects of station programing. McLendon is one exception, of course, because he has always been his company's chief programer and innovator. But in most cases, management can only hope to manage the efforts of program staff members and keep them within the limits of the law and local social boundaries.

Communication among management, news, and programing is essential if the station is to reach its goals of public acceptance, high ratings, profitable revenues, and complete compliance with FCC rules, regulations, and policies.

SUMMARY

Programing is another word for **product**. It is a result of ingenuity, necessity, invention, and good management. It cannot please every citizen; it cannot meet every need of the community. And there will always be complaints. In the 1920s, Lee De Forest, heavy contributor to the technical development of radio, addressed a convention of broadcasters with these words:

"What have you done to my child? You have made him the laughing stock to intelligence, surely a stench in the nostrils of the gods of the ionosphere. Murder mysteries rule the waves by night and children are rendered psychopathic by your bedtime stories. This child of mine is moronic, as though you and your sponsors believe the majority of listeners have only moron minds."

Forty years later, Newton Minow, Chairman of the FCC in the early 60s cried out: "To twist the radio dial today is to be shoved through a bazaar, a clamorous casbah of pitchmen and commercials which plead, bleat, pressure, whistle, groan, and shout. Too many stations have become publicly franchised jukeboxes."

In both cases, the critics were talking about highly popular, mass audience programing. The broadcaster, somehow, must develop programing that meets the entertainment needs of listeners, yet appeals to audiences' higher, cultural instincts. The product of programing efforts must satisfy the requirements of the Commission; it must be attractive to the community and it must be saleable. It must also be a source of pride to the people who produce it. Good programing develops from the broadcasters' sensitivity to listener needs. In spite of tightening government regulations, it is possible to entertain as well as inform with station programing. Many a courageous actor has wowed audiences while suffering terrible physical pain. "The Show Must Go On," has long been a truism in theater. It is equally applicable to radio broadcasting.

CHAPTER 4

Administration

The term **administration** is probably the least definitive in the broadcaster's vocabulary. If anything, administration is a catalystic process that tends to hold the station and staff together. Administration is defined as the performance of executive duties of an institution or business. It is paperwork, policy, policing, forms, payrolls, accounting, billing, invoicing, collecting, moderating, negotiating, compromising, license renewal applications, files, personnel, and about anything else that occurs within a station that is unrelated to sound and sales. Even here, in these highly creative divisions, competent administration is necessary. Individuals are in radio programing, radio sales, radio management; but rarely are they identified as being in radio administration. But the administrative personnel and processes are there just as surely as Webster defined the term "performance of executive duties." Too much administration can mire a station into zero productivity; too little, and the operation will collapse. Administrative functions should be subordinated to sales and program functions. Effective administration is the invisible, unoffensive, unobtrusive force that melds and channels station staff actions into a viable, productive, creative force.

ADMINISTRATIVE RESPONSIBILITIES

The general manager of a radio station is usually the chief administrative staff member. He may be assisted in this function by an office manager, operations manager, assistant general manager, bookkeeper, accountant, personnel manager, or secretary. But, in most sizable organizations, in spite of his assistants, the responsibilities are his. It is often said that the buck passing stops at the general manager's office, and this is true if the general manager has been given the authority necessary to make and execute management decisions.

230

The General Manager

The general manager should be a broad-gauged individual with extensive experience in all phases of radio broadcasting. While there are a few top station executives whose primary backgrounds are in programing and engineering, most general managers are sales oriented and worked their way to their positions through the sales channels. This is not to say that people who enter the industry through programing departments cannot become general managers. On the contrary, an individual is better equipped to function as head of a radio station if he has moved through programing and sales to the top post. Hundreds of case histories could be cited showing that people enter radio through the backdoor as week-end announcers or newsmen or even mail boys, and ultimately become licensees or occupy high posts in management teams.

The ideal background for a high caliber general manager:

1. One year as a newsman
2. One year as a disc jockey or staff announcer
3. Two years as account executive in an advertising agency.
4. Two years with a national rep firm
5. Two years as a local salesman
6. Two years as a local sales manager
7. Three years as general manager of smaller station
8. A degree in law with a minor in psychology.

In terms of experience, this man should be ready to tackle the toughest challenge the industry has to offer. But the ideal general manager must have more. He should be civic minded, have an overt personality, a strong sense of justice and fair play, and still be able to discharge staff members who do not or cannot do their jobs. He should be a moderate drinker, able golf player, sports fan, and solid family man with children and a house mortgage. He should be able to converse easily with publishers, public officials, FCC members, attorneys, ministers, educators, militants, students, leaders of Women's Lib, policemen, doctors, and irate listeners who call to complain about the programing. While one is inclined to view this list of qualifications with tongue in cheek, the student should remember that the ideal manager is probably nonexistent. The challenge for owners, stockholders, and licensees, then, is to select a top operating executive with as many of these qualities as possible.

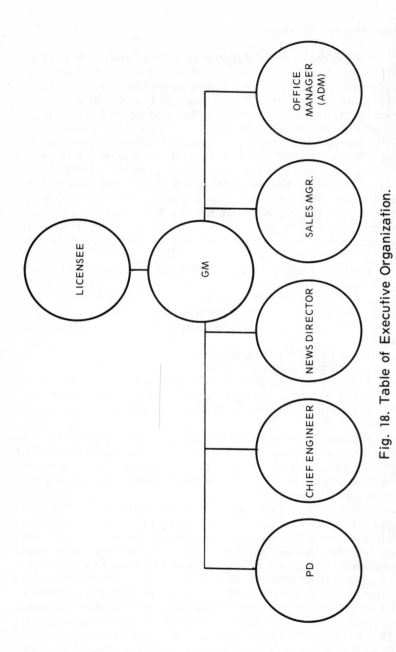

Fig. 18. Table of Executive Organization.

There are several staff members whose function is critically important to the licensee, but none quite so critical as that of the general manager. The FCC holds the **licensee** responsible for the actions or inactions of the staff. If a general manager permits a crooked contest or engages in some other illegal practice such as double billing, it is the licensee who is brought to task by the Commission. The general manager can get off free, while the licensee may lose the station. It becomes apparent, therefore, that the licensee should exercise extreme caution and conduct exhaustive background studies before turning his radio station over to a general manager. The licensee can assign the operational work load to a general manager, but he cannot delegate final responsibility to him because the Commission denies him that leeway. If the licensee is an individual, he personally must sign applications for construction permits or for license renewal. If the licensee is a corporation, the applications must be signed by an officer of the corporation. The general manager, unless he is also the licensee or an officer, may not sign the application, although he is permitted to handle virtually every other detail of the application.

Executive Organization

There is no firm rule governing the precise duties of the general manager. He may, in fact, hold such a title and still not have general control of the operation. The strong general manager is answerable only to the licensee, whether it is a corporation, a partnership, or an individual. In the organizational table shown in Fig. 18, all station personnel are responsible to the general manager through the department heads he has selected. Such a table of organization indicates a strong and well organized GM.

In this organization, regardless of whether the staff is 10 or 50, the licensee deals with one person, the general manager. The GM deals with five persons, as indicated. Traffic, copy, production, and all announcers are responsible to the program director. All engineers answer directly to the chief engineer. Newsmen report to the news director and salesmen answer to the sales manager. Accounting, reception, utility secretaries, building maintenance personnel are responsible to the office manager. There may be additional departments, such as public relations, public affairs, or promotion. These may report directly to the general manager or to a department head. In any case, the lines of control should be clearly

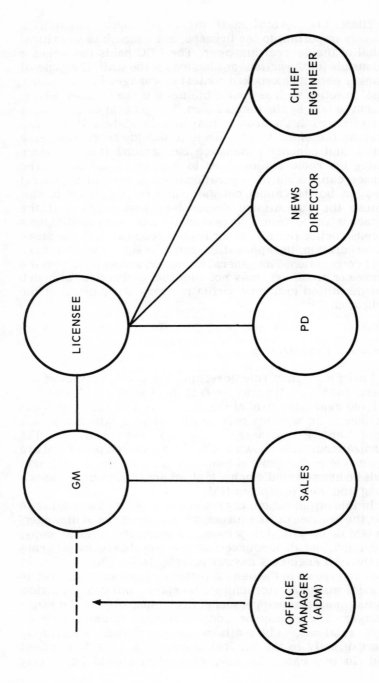

Fig. 19. Alternate Executive Organizational Plan.

established, and personnel should be discouraged from crossing these lines. An alternate plan of organization might be as shown in Fig. 19.

Under this plan, the licensee's chief executive may carry the title of general manager, but is, in fact, a sales manager or station manager. In a very large organization, there may also be included a national sales manager and a station manager. The national sales manager would occupy a position adjacent to other department heads; the station manager would answer to the general manager. All other department heads would report to the station manager. He might also direct the work of all departments except sales. Virtually any table of organization will function productively so long as everyone understands how the staff is organized and who has what authority.

Lines of Authority

The licensee who goes around his general manager to criticize or correct the work of staff members is undermining the authority of his manager. The manager who breaks the chain of command and goes directly to employees is undermining the authority of his department heads. Such actions on the part of management tend to set precedent for employees to go directly to the top when they have questions, problems, or need decisions. The end result of such activities is the ultimate destruction of middle management and the possible burdening of top management with day-to-day decisions to such an extent that it cannot meet the challenge of the larger and more crucial problems.

Indications of Little or No Staff Organization:

1. Newsman tells program director that outside men are not doing their jobs. PD advises newsman to report this to the news director. Newsman replies, "He doesn't have enough control over the staff to correct it." PD advises newsman to try again or report the situation to the general manager.

2. Traffic Clerk goes directly to the general manager with a traffic problem. "Give this problem to the program director," said the GM. "He knows nothing about traffic," the clerk replies, "and refused to help."

3. Accounting department head calls licensee with request that new billing forms be devised. "You should check this out with the office manager," said the licensee, "or the general

manager." Accounting replies: "They've ignored the request for months and apparently are not interested."

4. General Manager goes to traffic and production and schedules a station promotion. "I knew nothing about the promotion, until I heard it on the air," said the program director.

5. Two new newsmen are employed. "I learned about them when they showed up for work," said the news director.

6. The all-night announcer reports to the general manager that he was criticized and fired last night by the licensee.

7. The licensee and general manager decide to purchase a new transmitter and place the order. The chief engineer learns of the decision when the transmitter arrives.

8. An announcer sets up a listener contest for his show only, giving away a substantial prize. When questioned by the general manager, the program director said he knew nothing about the contest.

Such destructive, nonproductive situations have developed and will continue in any organization unless the licensee insists upon positive definition of duties, authority, and lines of communication. A strong, well-defined organization does not pre-suppose a cold, computer-like operation. People within any organization should be competent to converse productively without chipping a link out of the chain of command. A conversation among management and staff members may be conducted between, for example, the licensee, a salesman, a newsman, and the production engineer.

Example:

LICENSEE: Well, the staff seems to be doing a good job these days. Billing is up and the station sounds good.

SALESMAN: Thanks. We've had some great sales promotions this year—thanks to the planning done by the manager.

LICENSEE: Yes, he's a good man. He has my complete confidence.

NEWSMAN: One thing we need, though, is a new mobile news unit.

LICENSEE: I don't know about that, but I'm sure the news director would. He makes all such recommendations to the general manager who makes the final decision.

NEWSMAN: But you're the owner. Why can't we put our request directly to you, and get away from this chain of command routine? You'd think we were in the army.

LICENSEE: Because, young man, I pay the general manager to make those decisions. I trust his judgment and know his decisions will be in the best interest of the station and my pocketbook. And while we're certainly not in the army, we can learn a lot from the army's organizational systems. After all, they've had a couple of hundred years to work the wrinkles out of their methods. I've had some time in the army, and I think the chain of command idea is sound. No one person is given more men to control than is necessary. For example, in a company-size organization, there is a company commander. The company commander works directly with four platoon leaders. The platoon leader works directly with the platoon sergeant and four squad leaders. Each squad leader works with an assistant squad leader. The company commander can't control the work or efforts of 200 men, so the army provides him with four department heads, so to speak, in the form of platoon leaders. Now the platoon leaders can't control the movements of 50 men, so again, the army has provided this department head with an assistant (the platoon sergeant) and four squad leaders. And so on down and up the line. That's the way I try to run my organization, though certainly in a more democratic manner. I don't want my general manager directing the work of the news department, though I certainly want him to know what's happening in the department, and I want him to thoroughly understand the work of the department. And the same applies to programing, engineering, and administration.

PRODUCTION ENGINEER: I was about to ask if you'd okay some new equipment for the production room, but guess I'd better take that little problem to the chief engineer. Right?

LICENSEE: You have the picture, young man. See the chief. Enjoyed the talk, gentlemen. Let's get together again some time.

BUILDING THE ADMINISTRATIVE STAFF

Small stations with staffs of from five to fifteen normally would not have titled office managers. In larger operations, this position is often occupied by a woman, and it is important that her duties and authority be carefully defined. An especially talented woman is required to fill such a post because her job often requires that she exercise some authority over the men in the station. And, although there are many competent office managers who successfully fill such posts, it is safe to say most men resent a woman telling them what to do or not to do. The problem is not so acute with other women, but even here a great deal of tact is required on the part of the office manager. One major radio chain has used the office manager system successfully for many years. It is employed primarily to relieve the general manager of most administrative detail, so that he may concentrate his efforts on sales. The office manager is, in effect, an assistant general manager or a station manager. She has **administrative** control over the entire staff, except the general manager. She is responsible for billing, collections, traffic, reception, payrolls, payables, sales commissions, and the secretarial pool. As she has these responsibilities, she must necessarily have enough authority to meet them.

If she is doing her job, she can correct a salesman who has made a mistake on a time order, such as misfiguring the cost of a schedule or applying the wrong rate to the account. She cannot fire the salesman for the error, but it is within her jurisdiction to correct him on administrative matters. She cannot tell him how to sell; she cannot tell him his office hours, but she can require that he check invoices before they are mailed or that he check commission figures before a commission check is requisitioned from accounting. The office manager may reprimand an announcer who can not complete his time sheet correctly, or the chief engineer if he fails to make out purchase orders for engineering supplies. She sets rules and work hours of the receptionist, the switchboard operator, the sales secretary, the traffic clerk, and the building maintenance personnel. Her duties and responsibilities may include interviewing, hiring, and discharging administrative personnel.

Many women are fully qualified, by temperament and training, to handle such positions. Others fail miserably.

Example of Ineffectiveness in an Office Manager:

OFFICE MANAGER:	Jim, won't you ever learn to fill out a time order correctly? You've been here a year, and you're still making mistakes that foul up the traffic and account departments.
	(Worse, she makes her critique in front of the sales secretary)
SALESMAN:	(Grimly) What mistakes are you talking about?
OFFICE MANAGER:	Here. You misfigured the total dollars involved, and you show a start day of Monday the 15th when Monday is the 14th. Just when do you want to start the schedule, or do you know?
SALESMAN:	Look, girl. I happen to be the top salesman on the station and if you so much as speak to me again in that tone I'm going to the general manager and have it out. One of us will be leaving, and I have an idea my sales are worth more to the operation than your continual nit-picking. Now you just mind your manners and we can get along; but you criticize me like this again and you've had it. If you were a man I'd belt you.

Such situations can easily be handled tactfully and effectively.

Example:

OFFICE MANAGER:	(Pleasantly) Mr. Jones, may I speak with you for a moment?
JONES:	Sure, Miss Smith, what's up?
OFFICE MANAGER:	I'm afraid I've been remiss in my duties. When you came aboard several months back I was supposed to explain to you how we keep our time sheets. We never had that talk and I suppose that's why I have to re-do your sheet every week.
JONES:	Ahhh, I hate those things anyway. Details!
OFFICE MANAGER:	Yeah, I agree. But Uncle Sam's Wage & Hour Division says we gotta keep them...so please help me.
JONES:	Okay. Guess we can't fight city hall. So, how can I help you?

With an extra minute of time, and a few well-chosen words, the office manager managed to make an ordinarily fractious individual sympathetic to her. **She** had a problem and conned the morning man into helping her solve it. And she blamed the whole problem on the government! The situation called for tact, compromise, political know-how. She solved the problem without rancor, without creating a scene, and without sacrificing her authority or position. As in any management situation, each employee at the radio station must be dealt with differently. The office manager may be able to tear the hide off one employee and make him feel more secure because of it. In another case, she must tread lightly or face the possibility of a resignation or a front office battle that could cost her the job.

An office manager is employed, usually, to place administrative problems under an expert wing, thus relieving the general manager or licensee of this non-revenue producing burden. The office manager should be qualified to function expertly in every job she supervises. These include bookkeeping, billing and invoicing, payrolls, traffic, telephone, switchboard, and secretarial duties such as typing and shorthand. She could be capable of completing all periodical reports to the FCC. If any single factor will make her an acceptable administrative boss at the station, it is **knowledge** and **training**. Even for the man who resents female bosses, it is difficult to argue with accuracy of facts.

The office manager is only one member of the administrative staff, but doubtless is the most important from an organizational standpoint. She basically heads the **support team** for programing and sales. Her team forms the supply lines for the front line, the salesmen on the streets and in the agencies and stores and the announcers at the microphones. They soon would cease to function if the office manager didn't keep the paperwork flowing smoothly.

The Bookkeeper

In a multi-station or chain operation, the station bookkeeper may be, in actuality, a billing clerk, with formal and legal bookkeeping and accounting procedures being handled at a home or central office. And, depending upon the personalities involved and the desires of the licensee, the bookkeeping department may answer directly to the general manager, the licensee, or the office manager. The functions of the bookkeeping department are explained later in this chapter. The discussion here regards how the bookkeeper figures into a single station staff operation.

In hiring a bookkeeper, management should look not only for formal training, but also experience in broadcasting. It is not necessary that the bookkeeper be a certified public accountant because most stations utilize a CPA firm to do monthly or annual audits, profit and loss statements, and tax reports. If someone with broadcast experience cannot be located, and this often will be the case, then someone with formal bookkeeping training at a college, university, or business school should be sought. The bookkeeper, especially in a larger operation, should not only be able to do the work, but also supervise others in the department.

The responsibilities of the bookkeeper may include keeping the sales journal, general ledger, accounts receivable, preparing profit and loss statements, billing and invoicing, preparing credit and debit memos, collections, sales and rep commissions, preparing affidavits of performance, preparing the payroll and maintaining payroll and personnel files, filing tax reports, and preparing the annual financial report to the FCC. All of these duties will be dealt with separately later in this chapter, but it should be remembered that much of the work of the bookkeeper is subject to audit by a CPA or a CPA firm, unless the bookkeeper is a licensed CPA. The annual financial report mentioned is required by the FCC, and must be filed on or before April 1 each year. In a large corporation, particularly one that is publicly held, stockholders and-or investors require an annual financial report.

The larger the operation, the more intricate the bookkeeping department and system. A Kansas broadcaster once declared he didn't have a bookkeeper. "I collect for the advertising, pay my employees and other expenses, and put what's left in my personal bank account. Once a month I take my check stubs and paid bills to my CPA and he does all the formalizing." This "shoebox" or "hippocket" system may work for small operations, but even then it is not recommended. The Commission requires explicit information on the station's financial situation every year and especially at license renewal time. Sloppy records could result in a delay in obtaining a renewal, an investigation, or, indeed, a hearing. Experience shows it is better to keep too many, rather than too few, records.

Other Administrative Personnel

Receptionist: This is the first person a visitor sees upon arriving at the station. It usually is a woman, though not always one employed full-time as a receptionist. She may be the switchboard operator, a secretary, or anyone whose job does not require absolute freedom from interruption. In a small station, the receptionist may wear several hats, including copy, traffic, bookkeeping, and secretarial. In the larger operations, she may be a switchboard operator who receives vistors as well as helps with typing and bookkeeping overloads.

In some instances, station management uses the receptionist's job as a training base. Women hired here are gradually trained to handle one or more of the more important jobs such as traffic, sales or general management secretary, or bookkeeping. In any case, it is an important job because often the first impression a visitor gets of the station is through the efficiency of the receptionist. If she is reading a book, or filing her fingernails when the visitor arrives, the station may get an immediate bad rating. If, however, she is occupied at the typewriter or the switchboard or some other assigned function, and if her greeting is friendly and open, she can give the immediate impression that the station is a well organized, business-like operation. Not many, if any, stations need a full-time receptionist because there just aren't that many people who visit the station. Some advertisers have patronized a station for years, yet never visited the offices and studios. In most cases, therefore, the receptionist is an extra girl who does any number of worthwhile odd jobs. And while she may be an "odd job" expert, her function as a receptionist can be critical.

Example:

RECEPTIONIST: (With a friendly tone and smile) Good morning. May I help you, sir?

VISITOR: Yeah. I wanna see the owner of this station.

RECEPTIONIST: Oh, that's Mr. Johnson. And he's out of town today. What is your name, sir?

VISITOR: Wallace. Jim Wallace. And I've just about had it with this station.

RECEPTIONIST: Oh? I'm sorry, Mr. Wallace. Since Mr. Johnson is out of town, perhaps you'll tell me something of the problem you're having with the station and I can direct you to another of our executives.

VISITOR: Well, I wanted to see the owner. But when he's out of town, who's in charge here?

RECEPTIONIST: Our General Manager, Mr. Ellis. But he's out of the office until noon. Are you sure I couldn't be of some help?

VISITOR: I doubt it, girl. It's about that editorial yesterday. I didn't like what you said about labor organizations, and I'm about ready to punch someone in the nose.

RECEPTIONIST: (Smiling, sweetly, still) Oh, Mr. Wallace, you don't seem the type to go around punching people in the nose. Anyway, I think I know just the person for you to talk with. How about the man who wrote the editorial?

VISITOR: Who's that?

RECEPTIONIST: Our News Director, Paul Astor. Let me see if he's in.

VISITOR: Fine. He's the guy I'll punch in the nose, writing those things about labor.

242

While, hopefully, the effective receptionist would have talked away the visitor's hostility, this receptionist didn't do badly. She might have further incensed the man by arguing with him, by vigorously undertaking to emotionally defend a station editorial position without the real ability to do so, or by reacting rudely to his apparent rudeness.

Secretary: Secretaries are helpers, **thinking** assistants to executives, who provide extra eyes, hands, minds, and motion. A good secretary keeps records, handles correspondence, and often is a superb liar, all, of course, in the interest of the individual or company she serves. In most radio stations, secretaries are necessary for the general manager, and the sales manager or sales department. In large, high income operations, secretaries often are found in the program, engineering, and news departments. In other situations, there is a utility secretary who handles correspondence and files for several department heads. In small operations, the traffic manager or bookkeeper may also serve as the general manager's secretary. Many secretaries to general managers often graduate, silently and imperceptibly, to the post of office manager. The GM secretary must be highly knowledgeable about the station and its departments and, because of her close work with the top executive, she often is rated as the office's "mother hen" or number one girl. Her prestige among other members of the staff is often as high as that of the manager himself. Being secretary to top management requires in itself a management knack. One secretary will know when to defer to the GM and his department heads, and when to speak out. This is the one who becomes almost irreplaceable. The other never speaks at the proper time and ultimately ends up with another company or in a less prestigious post. These generalities serve only to indicate the secretary's importance in the organizational structure of a radio station.

Qualities of an ideal general manager secretary:

1. All office skills, including the ability to type, take shorthand, operate adding machines and calculators, mimeograph machines.

2. Excellent command of the English language, written and spoken, ability to spot mis-spelled words and poorly constructed sentences.

3. Good political instincts that enable her to properly handle her boss' friends and enemies, business and social.

4. An organizational ability that enables her to quickly find anything in her files at any time.

5. An extraordinary knowledge of the radio business, the FCC, local laws, and the advertising industry.

6. The ability to get on a first name basis with important clients and other friends of the station.

7. The ability to transmit an order from the general manager to a subordinate without offending the recipient.

8. Ability to anticipate the needs and desires of the general manager and willingness to meet those needs and desires.

9. Knowledge of how to write copy, handle the traffic department, ability to voice commercials, and make sales calls.

10. Ability to write advertising contracts, interpret agency and National Rep contracts and time orders, and translate them to local time orders.

Being secretary to top management in broadcasting requires, at best, a professionally oriented woman. Hers is a job that is challenging and rewarding and is an excellent training post for management. Many ambitious women in the industry started as secretaries and wound up as general managers, sales managers, and, in at least one case, became a corporation secretary and an important member of a group station management team. One Idaho female served her station as office manager, but would never accept the offered general manager's post because it would take her away too much from her family. In 15 years, she said she trained 15 managers to handle the job that she herself had so often declined.

Station secretaries should also have certain personal characteristics. Good health is essential because the station needs her during every business day. She should not be a clock watcher because often her responsibilities cannot be met in an 8-hour day or in a 40-hour week. If she is married and her domestic situation requires that she be home by 5:30 PM every work day, she should perhaps be placed in a job that is less demanding. A New York broadcaster, after determining that a secretarial applicant had the basic skills, would ask further questions in an effort to determine the emotional balance of the applicant.

> Is yours a happy home?
> Does it bother you being divorced?
>
> Do you like to work with other girls?
> Do you have marriage plans and do you plan children immediately?
>
> What are your hobbies?
> How often do you date?

Some women may resent such questioning, believing that answers to questions such as these are none of the employer's business. "If I do my job," they will say, "it shouldn't matter what my hang-ups are." But it does matter.

No manager wants to hire, train, and develop a trust in a compatible, efficient secretary, only to find six months later that she is getting married, getting divorced, hates working with other women, has boy-friend trouble, or some other involvement that either takes her away from the job or renders her inefficient while on the job. It is impossible to anticipate every problem an employee will have, but management is learning to look for signs that indicate a short-term employee, troublemaker, congenital liar, and other undesirable traits. Some stations, in fact, are using industrial psychologists to examine potential employees before they are hired. While these exams are not 100 percent conclusive, they do sometimes indicate whether a person is aggressive, passive, honest, or ambitious.

Department Head Assistants

Staff organization often includes assistant chief engineers, assistant sales managers, assistant traffic managers, assistant news directors, and assistant production engineers or managers. At times, the title is no more than an honorarium. In other cases, the work load is such that the assistant really earns his title and position. Many general managers employ assistants for department heads in order to train someone to buck for or someday take the job of the department manager. This is called in-depth staffing. Politicos preach that voters should elect lieutenant governors or vice presidents because the top post is only a heartbeat away. The idea has merit. And many companies maintain heir-apparents for all important station positions, from the general manager on down. Not only does the assistant slot have merit for the company, but it is good for the ambitious employee as well. Where else but in the number two position can an individual learn a job to perfection?

Other Administrative Personnel

Building Maintenance: While this function falls in the area of administration, it is not necessarily part of the professional staff. The maintenance may be handled by an honest, steady individual, or by a professional maintenance company. Clean working quarters are important to the morale of the staff and often will indicate to a client visitor how efficiently the station operates. One broadcaster is fond of replying, when asked what he does for a station, that he is janitor and general manager. Often, in small stations, this is literally true. Some budgets simply cannot be stretched to cover building maintenance. Others are so well-maintained that employees don't even have to clean their desk tops.

Mailboy: This is another administrative function that does not require professionalism. In many cases, management will deliberately employ a youth for this job with an eye toward training and promoting him to more important functions. Mailboys, like copy boys at newspapers, grow up to become salesmen, disc jockeys, managers, even licensees.

Temporary Help: The famous Kelly Girl is often employed to help in overload situations, and she becomes a part of the administrative pattern during her tenure. She may be employed only for a few days to replace a secretary who is ill, or late in the month, to assist the bookkeeping department in getting the billing prepared and mailed. Temporary help usually can not be used in traffic, copy, or operations, because of the requirement for vast background knowledge of the day-to-day routine. These posts are usually filled by assistances or by other staff members who have been trained in these jobs. The receptionist, for example, may be trained to handle traffic during illness and vacations, while a temporary worker may be called into handle the less-technical post of receptionist. Outside help often is required when the station executes a sales or station promotion. She might handle a heavy influx of mail or perhaps prepare a mailing in connection with a sales promotion.

ADMINISTRATIVE OFFICE QUARTERS

Spacious, well decorated and properly arranged office quarters are important to the morale and efficiency of the administrative staff. Cramped, make-shift quarters often lead to high, expensive turnover in employees.

It isn't always possible for management to provide ideal working quarters, but when it is possible every effort should be made to make people comfortable and to arrange offices in a manner that will minimize the number of steps required to accomplish a given task. In the plan outlined in Fig. 20, individuals who do business with each other are situated adjacent to each other. Salesmen prepare time orders and turn them in to the sales secretary. The sales manager approves rates and credit, and the sales secretary then distributes copies of the time orders, as follows:

1. Bookkeeping (first copy, usually) for billing purposes
2. General manager, for his revenue projections
3. Salesman who wrote the order
4. Traffic, for program logging
5. Copy and production, for continuity, recording and scheduling
6. Local sales manager's operating files.

The sales secretary can quickly, under this plan, distribute four copies of the time order to administrative offices. The other two copies go to the programing and production departments, offices that are adjacent to each other (traffic and copy). No wasted motion is required. The administrative plan here called for a conference room. Often, such space is needed when several members of a client organization come by to audition commercial announcements. Staff meetings may be held in the conference room, and it may be used also as an extra office, work area for special projects such as sales and station promotions or license renewal. The bookkeeping office should be close to the general manager and the sales offices because of these offices' frequent requests for billing or collection information.

A direct access door between the general manager's secretary and the bookkeeping department is convenient because it gives the general manager immediate access to P&L statements, accounts payable, accounts receivable, and

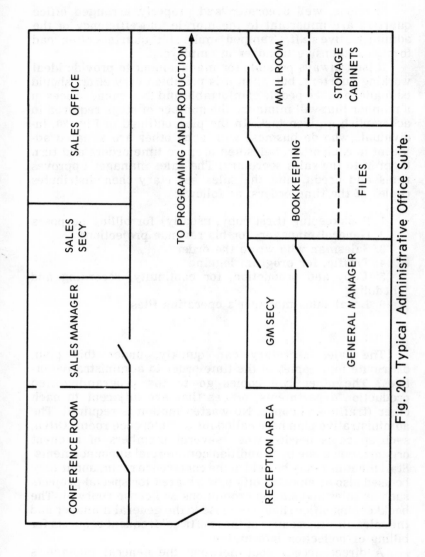

Fig. 20. Typical Administrative Office Suite.

The labels within the figure read:

CONFERENCE ROOM

SALES MANAGER

SALES SECY

SALES OFFICE

RECEPTION AREA

GM SECY

GENERAL MANAGER

BOOKKEEPING

FILES

MAIL ROOM

STORAGE CABINETS

TO PROGRAMING AND PRODUCTION

other bookkeeping material that he may require to keep himself abreast of the overall operation. The mailroom and employee lounge (not shown) should be somewhere in the middle as they belong neither to administration or programing but are utilized by both.

Too often, a station has inadequate space for employees. Bookkeepers work in the distracting atmosphere of the sales office; traffic managers may be officed in bookkeeping, and the manager may have to office with his secretary or with the salesmen. In some uncomfortable situations, programing and administration are mixed helter-skelter with no consideration given to any worker's need for quiet and privacy. Traffic, bookkeeping, and copy should have environments conducive to concentration. Mistakes in these areas can be costly; too many or too few spots logged for a given client, an invoice error, or incorrect price in a piece of commercial copy are serious. An office that is noisy or in a traffic pattern increases the possibility of such errors. Where well organized quarters are available, most stations make a practice to minimize person-to-person contact with traffic, bookkeeping, and copy. For example, the sales secretary may be instructed to take time orders to traffic and bookkeeping once or twice a day, rather than interrupting the personnel every time an order is turned in. Many copy writers simply cannot function under operational interruptions.

Good administration in a radio station requires good planning, skilled employment practices, and day-to-day attention to the implementation of plans and systems. Where possible, top management should not be encumbered with or by the basic administrative function; it should be handled by middle management. Individuals must be accepted and treated as such; they cannot be made to function like payroll numbers. Top management often doesn't have the time or patience to deal with secretaries who develop personal problems, or the bookkeeper who gets upset because time charges are computed erroneously. Some **one person** should be designated to head the administrative functions, if not full-time, at least as a part-time assignment. Without good administrative support, the best programed and highest revenue producing station can come apart.

Not only will good administration help insure continued top ratings and high sales, but it is invaluable in keeping expenses at a minimum and profits high. The general manager and the licensee must have at least one middle manager to control expenditures. Without a tight rein on expenses, the station can be "nickled and dimed" to death. Purchasing procedures should be established and administered. Some stations use the purchase order plan. Others assign the purchasing chores to one person with all requests for office supplies, magnetic recording tapes, records, production aids, and other non-technical items going through that person. Under this plan, no bill or invoice may be paid until the purchasing agent has approved it.

ACCOUNTING DEPARTMENT

The bookkeeping department is one of those silent operations that may function unnoticed for years and becomes obviously important only when critical errors are made. The purpose of any accounting or bookkeeping system is to tell the dollars and cents story of a business enterprise. Weekly, monthly, or annual summary reports, made up from the accounting records, reveal whether the business has been making money or losing money and how much. From these records of past operation, management has the material which serves in part as the basis for planning the future of the operation. Two basic accounting statements or reports provide the needed information. One is the **income** or **operating** statement, which summarizes the record of the financial operation of the business during a given period of time. From an operational point of view, the income statement (or profit and loss statement) is the basic accounting report. The second statement is the **balance sheet** which shows, as of a given date, the relationship between assets on the one hand and liabilities plus ownership interest on the other. A comparison of these and similar reports for previous periods gives a picture of the financial trend of the business.

The National Association of Broadcasters has available to members an accounting manual for radio stations. Much of the material in this section is taken directly from the manual and in some instances is quoted verbatum. The manual gives an example of an accounting system but, as with this section, makes no attempt to teach accounting per se. Clearly, it is not possible to lay down a bookkeeping system or method that will fit every radio station. Many factors cause individual station accounting needs to vary greatly. Among them are the size of the station, organizational structure, operating philosophy, and, most important, the amount of detail required by management and ownership. One operator may be completely satisfied by the "hippocket" or "shoebox" procedure and may be able to satisfy investors (if any) and government taxing agencies with these simple methods. Another broadcaster, even though it may be a relatively small operation, may want a complete system that includes everything from P&L statements and balance sheets to accounts payable journals and general ledgers.

There are two approaches the broadcaster may use in setting up his bookkeeping system. One is the **cash** approach in which no transaction is recorded until cash is received or paid out. The other is the **accrual** method in which income is recorded as earned and expenses recorded as incurred. Most accountants agree that as a practical matter, most systems involve parts of both approaches; there is no such thing, then, as a pure cash or a pure accrual system.

Department Organization

Setting up a bookkeeping department involves the employment of from one to three or four persons, depending again upon how much detail management wants. In our example, three persons will be employed. The number one person may be called a head bookkeeper, accountant, or controller. In large stations the number one bookkeeper may earn from $15,000 to $20,000 per year. The two assistants each will earn around $6,000 per year, depending upon local pay levels for such work. The figure may be slightly higher in the North and East, and perhaps slightly lower in the South and Southwest. The department head need not be a certified public accountant (CPA), but he should have the equivalent experience and training. The minimum background would include a degree in accounting and hopefully some experience with another company. Assistants need not have degrees in accounting, but some experience at handling accounting detail is desirable, although not essential, assuming the department head has the time to train them for the job. Some accountants prefer competent "greenhorns" whose "minds are not cluttered by someone else's system."

In this discussion the terms **accountant** and **bookkeeper** are used interchangeably. The only time there is differentiation is in the use of the term certified public accountant, which is an individual with extensive training who can legally certify a financial statement. The CPA or **auditor** is an **independent third party** who audits a company's books.

Most companies, even small ones, employ these independent third parties to conduct at least annual audits and prepare annual balance sheets and operating statements.

The Books

In the department cited here, there is a sales journal, accounts receivable ledger, general ledger, a cash receipts journal, general journal, and a cash disbursements journal. Some companies keep an accounts payable journal, but in this case it has been deemed unnecessary.

The **sales journal** is kept in a double-page, multi-column binder of entry sheets. An **entry** indicates the month and date in which the business ran on the air, the account name, the invoice number, or, in case of a credit memo, the CM number. These entries are made across the page, in the designated columns, from left to right. The amount of the invoice is **debited** to accounts receivable in the sales journal. This is the accountant's language for entering the charge figure. So far, four columns have been used. To further identify the charge figure, most systems describe whether the billing is from local or national advertisers, whether it is program or spot sales, network revenue, or political broadcast income.

Other columns might indicate whether all or part of the billing is from "sale of talent," "sale of program material and facilities," or "other operating revenue." An invoice for $1,000 might be broken down as follows: Sale of time to local advertiser, $800; production costs, $30; agency commission, $120; and salesman commission, $50. Had there been a "talent" charge, this, too, would have been entered. Had the billing been in connection with a trade agreement, it would have been entered in the "trade" column. Once all entries have been made for a given billing period, the figures are totalled and balanced across the bottom, and these totals are posted to the general ledger. Then, **each** gross billing figure in the sales journal is entered on the client's page in the accounts receivable ledger. The bottom figures from the sales journal would indicate immediately to management that, for example, $75,000 of the month's billing was local; $50,000 was from national advertisers; $2,500 was for production room facilities, and $300 was for talent. Once the bottom line figures were totalled, management also would know precisely how much of the month's gross revenue would go to agency and salesmen commissions and what portion of the revenue was non-cash or trade income. It is important that trade accounts be tagged as such and recorded in every detail along with the cash business, because, for tax and music licensing purposes, it is income even though no actual dollars were received. Stations must pay tax and license fees (to BMI, SESAC, and ASCAP) on all income, whether it is in cash, goods, or services.

Credit memos also are listed in the sales journal. Assume that an account was overcharged $50 in a previous month's billing. The account, naturally, won't pay the erroneous figure and it must, somehow, be removed from the accounts receivable ledger. A credit memo is prepared, signed by the manager, and entered into the sales journal. The figure is later entered in the accounts receivable ledger as a **credit** to the client. It usually is set off in red or in brackets, to indicate that it is a credit rather than a debit. Debit memos, on the other hand, are used to increase an erroneous billing figure. If accounting failed to include, for example, production charges, the difference could be made up either by a simple debit memo or by a separate invoice covering the difference and entered into the sales journal under "sale of program material and facilities" or "other operating revenue."

The **accounts receivable ledger** gives management an accurate picture of money owed the station. In this ledger, each account is given a separate page and entries are made into the AR ledger from three sources:

Example of Aging Sheet:

ACCOUNTS RECEIVABLE
(As of June 30, 1972)

Account	Total	June	May	April	March	Salesman Agency Rep
Smith Furniture	$5,000	$1,000	$1,000	$1,000	$2,000	BBDO
Budweiser Beer	4,000	4,000				D'Arcy-Blair
Ajax Plumbing					500	Johnson
Rialto Theater		350				Williams

1. Sales journal, invoice credit memo figures.
2. Credit for payments from the cash receipts journal.
3. The general journal (miscellaneous corrections).

The **gross** amounts are posted in every case, even though the **net** amount was paid because cost accounting cannot be done accurately unless total billing and total costs are known. From the accounts receivable journal, an **aging sheet** is prepared to indicate which accounts are current, 30-60 days delinquent, 60-90 days delinquent, and 90-120 days or over delinquent.

The aging sheet continues until all accounts are listed. At the bottom of the last page, each column is totalled, indicating to management June's total billing (except for cash in advance accounts), and providing a report on which accounts are delinquent, how long delinquent, and the name of the salesman, agency, or rep firm involved. The following dialogue from a sales meeting indicates the use of the aging sheet:

MANAGER: Johnson, what's with Ajax Plumbing? They ran a schedule last March and still haven't paid the bill.

JOHNSON: I told bookkeeping last month that the company has folded and that the $500 should be written off. The owners have skipped town.

MANAGER: Okay. But I want you guys to check the aging sheet from time to time. Bookkeeping prepares a new one every month from the accounts receivable ledger and they keep it current by putting a red circle around the figure when a payment is made. Watch your accounts because you are responsible for collecting them when they become delinquent. And the older they get, the harder they are to collect.

The **general ledger** is kept on a standard form and contains a variety of information. It is divided into two primary sections. One shows assets, liabilities, and capital; these figures are used to make up the balance sheet. The other sections describes income and expense accounts; these figures are used to make up the operating or profit and loss statement. Normally, the general ledger shows total figures; the breakdowns are contained in subsidiary ledgers. For example, the general ledger might indicate $1,000,000 in land or building, and a subsidiary ledger would describe in detail the land and buildings.

The **cash receipts journal** is kept on a standard, multi-column double page spread sheet. It is used to record the net amount of customer payments. If the net payment is less than the gross charge, the difference is indicated in the CR journal as commissions deducted by the agency or by the national rep firm, if the firm happens to provide a collection service for the station.

The CR journal carries a miscellaneous column to accommodate such incidental revenue as the sale of equipment, rental of transmitter sites for grazing or other purposes, and any other extraordinary situations. Once all entries have been made for a given period, the columns are totalled and balanced across the bottom of the page; the totals are posted to the general ledger, and the individual customer payments are posted to accounts receivable.

The **cash disbursement and voucher register** is kept on a form similar to the CR journal and is simply a record of money paid out by the station. It may be as detailed as management desires, but should contain columns for all types of commissions. It could, for example, include all major expense account numbers. Each check written and entered may be put in a column under **programing, administration, sales commissions, salaries, or engineering.** When this breakdown is maintained, management can quickly determine what percentage of expenses belongs to each department.

The **general journal** may be described as a book of original entries for use in recording non-cash transactions and adjustments. Non-cash transactions may include depreciation and amortization figures and accrued bills **not paid.** Such other matters as taxes, interest, insurance and rent due may also be recorded in the general journal. All adjusting and year-end closing figures are entered in this journal. The graphs in Fig. 21 indicate the flow of paperwork within a radio station bookkeeping department.

A study of the typical **profit & loss statement** (operating statement) serves to cover several subjects, including the **chart of accounts,** specifics on station income and expenses, and P&L statement analysis.

Some P&L statements are "backed up" by a detail sheet showing precisely what each charge covers—salaries, specific engineer purchases, specific newspaper costs and printing costs in a sales promotion campaign, and details on taxes, insurance, interest paid, and other general and administrative expenses. The P&L statement in Fig. 22 indicates the last

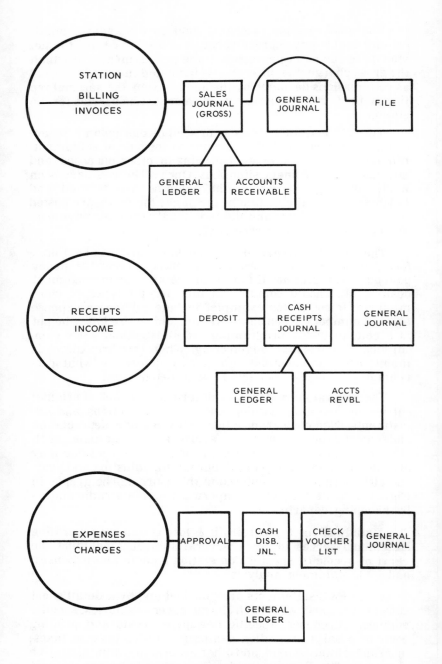

Fig. 21. Bookkeeping Paper Work Flow.

PROFIT & LOSS STATEMENT
June, 1972   INCOME

AC-No.	This Month	Same 1971	Year to Date	This Date '71
301 Local Sales				
302 Natl. Sales				
304 Network Sales				
305 Political Sales				
306 Other				
Totals & Rep	DIRECT EXPENSES (Deductions from revenue)			
401 Agency-Comm				
402 Cost of Talent				
403 Pg Materials				
404 Rights-Roytalties				
Totals	ENGINEERING EXPENSES			
501 Salaries				
502 Power-L-H				
503 Rep Bldg-Cnds				
504 Rep Tech Equi				
505 Trans Line				
506 Outside Eng				
Total	PROGRAM DEPARTMENT EXPENSES			
601 Salaries				
602 M-R Studios				
603 News Serv				
604 M-P Other				
605 Royalties				
606 Records				
607 Travel-E				
Total	SALES DEPARTMENT EXPENSES			
701 Salaries				
702 Sales Comm (1)				
703 Adv.				
704 Sales Promo				
705 Tvl-Ent				
Total	GENERAL & ADMINISTRATIVE EXPENSES			
801 Salaries				
802 Rent				
803 Light-Heat				
804 MR Office				
805-10 Tvl-Ent				
811 Tel & Tel				

Fig. 22. P&L Statement Form.

INVOICE

No. 3104

THE McLendon STATIONS

WYSL W-NUS KLIF WWWW-FM KOST-FM KABL
BUFFALO CHICAGO DALLAS DETROIT LOS ANGELES SAN FRANCISCO

2120 Commerce, Dallas, Texas 75201
Area 214 - 747-9311

sales:
XTRA
over Los Angeles **TERMS: NET CASH**

DATE September 30, 1972
Amount This Invoice
$ 1,500.00

Metropolitan Advertising Agency
1415 Metropolitan Ave.
New York, N.Y.

BAL. DUE $1,500.00

TOTAL $2,000.00

FOR Continental Milk Company (Dept 4-22)   SALESMAN Blair/Jenkins

SCHEDULE OF BROADCASTS

Mon.	(2) 6-10 A60 / (2) 3-7 A60
Tue.	(2) 6-10 A60 / (2) 3-7 A60
Wed.	(1) 6-10 A60 / (1) 3-7 A60
Thur.	(3) 6-10 A60 / (3) 3-7 A60
Fri.	(3) 6-10 A60 / (1) 3-7 A60
Sat.	
Sun.	

DAILY ITEMIZATION OF BROADCASTS COVERED BY THIS INVOICE PER YOUR ORDER

	1	2	3	4	5	6	7	8	9	10	11	12	13	14	15	16	17	18	19	20	21	22	23	24	25	26	27	28	29	30	31	TOTAL
1				4	4	2	6	4			4	4	2	6	4				4	4	2	6	4									60
2																																
3																																
4																																

1 For 60 broadcasts $ 25.00 rate per broadcast $ 1,500.00 Total

2 For _____ broadcasts $ _____ rate per broadcast $ _____ Total

3 For _____ broadcasts $ _____ rate per broadcast $ _____ Total

4 For _____ broadcasts $ _____ rate per broadcast $ _____ Total

STATE OF TEXAS
COUNTY OF DALLAS   **AFFIDAVIT OF PERFORMANCE RADIO STATION KLIF**

Subscribed and Sworn to Before Me

_____Julia Scott (Signature)_____ being duly
sworn, says that she is the Bookkeeper of KLIF, a radio broadcasting
station, and that according to the official station log the above programs or announcements were broadcast.

this 30th day of September A.D., 19 72

_____(Signature) A.D. Moore_____
Notary Public in and for Dallas County, Texas

Fig. 23. Invoice Form.

monthly revenue and expenses, compares them with the same month last year, shows the total for the year, and compares this year's total with those of last year at this date. With such figures, management can quickly determine whether revenues are higher or lower than last year, and if the latter is true, why. Income may be down, and expenses up. Income may be steady or equal to last year, with expenses up. Only by careful study of the operating statement can management make decisions necessary to adjust income and expenses.

This particular operating statement is one of hundreds that may be devised. Each such statement has the common purpose of communicating information to management, but there is no standard form. A business devises an operation statement to conform to management's need for information. In this example, columns were provided for comparatives. Another operator may figure he needs less information, and, therefore, would ask his bookkeeping department to provide only monthly and year-to-date information. Comparatives may be drawn from last year's P&L statement for a given month. Some operators may not want "direct expenses" indicated in the manner shown. Instead, they may want sales and rep commissions listed in a sales department account; another might want all travel and entertainment expenses lumped under general and administrative; another would ask that all travel be broken down by department so that he could determine precisely and quickly how much travel and entertainment each department head is doing. Finally, it is simply a matter of the bookkeeping department devising a reporting form that suits the owner or manager.

Billing

While some of the journals and ledgers may not be absolutely essential to the successful operation of the station, all must be conducted competently. Foremost among these is the monthly billing procedure. Each broadcaster has his own idea of how to economically and efficiently "get out the billing," and no two systems are alike. The crux of the matter is to determine precisely what ran on the air for the customer, then transfer the information to a statement or invoice, and provide sworn statements to support the claim. The billing process begins when bookkeeping receives its copy of the broadcast order. One practical system requires that when the time order is received, the invoice is "headed up"; that is, the advertiser's name and mailing address is typed onto the form.

Then, the schedule "as ordered" is types into the appropriate section.

The sample invoice provided in Fig. 23 contains an affidavit of performance in which the bookkeeper affirms that the schedule ran as indicated on the invoice. Her signature is attested to by a Notary Public, usually someone in the bookkeeping or administrative department. As someone often is required to "swear" that the time ran as indicated, careful checking and cross-checking must be done on each order and invoice. There are several ways to ascertain that a schedule ran as ordered. One almost foolproof technique is to check the program logs daily for each advertiser's schedule. If the announcer signed the log and if bookkeeping finds a time check by the log entry, it is safe to assume that the announcement was aired. Another technique is to work from a control sheet. The traffic manager, in making up the program log, first enters the advertiser's name and the number of spots or programs ordered. A different control sheet is required for each day, of course.

Example:

CONTROL SHEET

Day and Date   Mon., Sept. 4. 1972

ADVERTISER	ORDERED	LOGGED	CHECKED	RAN	
BORDEN MILK	4 60's	1111	1111	7:40a 8:20a	3:30p 5:30p

In this case, traffic has logged the four units as ordered and has double checked to make certain one has not been omitted. When the day's effort is finished, the control sheet is routed to bookkeeping. The next day, the completed program log is routed to bookkeeping, where the "ran" column is completed.

When the clerk has completed the task of comparing the control sheet with the actual program log, she turns to the invoices that were already "headed up" when bookkeeping received the time order. She has the relatively simple task, then, of transferring information in the "ran" column to the daily itemization section of the invoice. This may seem to the student a rather involved way of handling the billing, but because radio cannot provide tear sheets, as the print media, such detail is necessary. The exact times a schedule ran may not be necessary in every case, but when an advertiser demands an affidavit of performance that shows exact times, the only way the station can comply is to have someone **look at the log!**

In an earlier section of this chapter, duties of the receptionist were described. One of her duties might be to "head up" billing or, in some cases, check the control sheets against the program log. It is important, also, that bookkeeping receive a copy of the daily discrepancy sheet which usually is a blank sheet attached to the back of the daily program log. Announcers are instructed to note any mechanical or other problems on the "discrep" sheet. The log checker may believe a certain spot ran at a certain time, only to discover later on the discrepancy sheet a notation by the announcer that the spot didn't run because of a jammed cartridge. It happens! And every possible step should be taken to prevent an erroneous invoice from being mailed to an advertiser.

The billing method outlined here is neither the most complicated or simplest to be found in the industry. Small stations often will simply send out statements indicating X number of spots ran at a certain price and showing the total of the charges at the bottom of the page. There is nothing wrong with such systems if the advertiser accepts them and pays the bill.

Computers

Other, more sophisticated operations, have gone to computers or huge accounting machines that turn out logs, program avails, and monthly billing. These are usually found in big AM-FM-TV combinations where the work load is heavy enough to justify the investment. Most of the systems employ punched cards and some require more, rather than fewer, employees. One operator had four employees doing logs and bookkeeping. After installing a machine accounting system that used punched cards, he discovered he needed six persons to handle the work. In another case, two persons were able to handle the work of four, using the same plan.

Computer programers have become more adept in developing systems for broadcasters, and some computer organizations now offer "time share" plans to broadcasters. The day may be just around the corner when even the small broadcasters can indeed have economical access to computers that do everything except gripe. Most operators who use computers and machines enter the area one step at a time. For example, a system may be tested only with program availabilities. Next, the program logs might be committed to the equipment. If the broadcaster has been successful at this point, he might then have his billing done automatically. Automation in broadcasting **works**, but it has not eliminated the necessity for skilled personnel to do the thinking.

Collections

Bookkeeping departments often are given the responsibility of running credit checks on every new advertiser and ultimately for collecting the money. In less sophisticated operations, this responsibility is given primarily to the salesman making the sale. He alone makes the credit check and handles collection problems. One system is as good as the other, probably, so long as the station collects for the time it runs.

The collection system depends upon staff organization and locally accepted practices. In the small market, where everyone is known, less severe systems are used. To rile an advertiser in a small town may be to alienate him forever. In the larger markets, where personalities often are not a consideration, more direct techniques may be used. There are numerous choices of procedures.

Example:

1. The bookkeeping department runs a credit check on each new account. Working on "references" supplied by the salesman, the department simply calls the newspaper or radio station where the account has done business and finds out how promptly the account pays its bills. In other cases, bank references are used. The bookkeeper calls the bank and asks for a balance check. While banks do not give precise figures, many will indicate the level (such as an average balance in the high four-figure or low five-figure area) of the account or how promptly the advertiser has paid off bank loans in the past.

2. Many stations send out monthly billing that does not indicate previous balances. Often, under this plan, the advertiser will pay the May and skip the April or earlier portion. The inclusion of previous balances helps to keep the accounts receivable figures down to a workable level.

3. Other invoice formats include "second notice" sheets. These normally are in snap-out packages and are mailed out, for example, on the 20th of the month if the advertiser hasn't paid by that date.

4. Some companies have developed a series of collection letters that are sent routinely to delinquent accounts. The first letter is a mild reminder that the bill is past due and payable immediately. The second letter expresses a raised eyebrow. The third demands payment, and the fourth, perhaps, indicates that the account is being turned over to attorneys for possible legal action.

Whatever the system, it is necessary to maintain pressure on delinquent accounts. Cash flow is important to any business. And cash flow is developed through the collection of station billing. Stations have been forced to borrow money to meet monthly operating expenses because they couldn't collect from advertisers. Various shock techniques have been used in collections. One method is to start adding interest (unless a state or local law prohibits this) after a bill becomes 30 days delinquent. Another is to employ a collection agency that will "stalk" the account until the money is paid. One desperate broadcaster, feeling that he was being taken advantage of by advertisers in a medium market, simply doubled the amount each delinquent account owed and mailed the statements. He got an immediate reaction from advertisers who knew they had been over-charged and were willing to immediately pay the lesser but correct amount. Such "stunts" are not recommended, but may be expedient when to do so may eliminate a trip to the bank for the purpose of making a loan.

Sales Commissions

A vast majority of stations pay salesmen on a commission basis. The reasons for the plan are discussed in the chapter on sales, and the task of calculating such commissions usually falls to the bookkeeping department. There are two basic plans. One calls for a commission on net or gross sales. The other calls for commission on net or gross collections. A third but far less popular method provides a salary for salesmen with, perhaps, a bonus of quotas met or exceeded at the year's end. In small budget stations, management often has to pay a **draw against commission** on local sales, rather than collections. Small market operations, as one would expect, have low billing; and even a few slow-paying advertisers could hold up sales commissions for months. In the large markets and at successful stations, the individual salesman's cash flow can be built to a substantial level.

Examples of five fundamental sales commission plans:

(A)

```
Total   Individual  Sales.................................$5,000
Commission, 20 percent ...............................  1,000
Less  Draw  of  $500..+.................................    500
                         Amount due salesman  $  500
```

(B)
```
Total   Individual  Sales.................................$5,000
Less Agency  Commissions...............................   300
Sales Commission, 20 percent..........................   940
Less Draw of $500.......................................   500
                         Amount due salesman  $  440
```

(C)
```
Total  Individual  Sales.................................$40,000
Total collections, March 1-31..........................  35,000
Less  Agency  Commissions...........................   3,500
Sales Commission, 10 percent  .....................   3,150
Less Draw of $1,500....................................   1,500
                         Amount due salesman  $ 1,650
```

(D)
```
Total   Individual  Sales.................................$10,000
Less  Agency  Commissions...........................  1,000
Sales Commission, 15 percent  .....................  1,350
Less Draw of $800.......................................    800
                         Amount due salesman  $  550
```

(E)

Total Individual Annual Net Sales............ $120,000

Salesman Annual Quota......................... 100,000

10 percent Commission on all over $100,000........ 2,000

Salesman's Annual Salary........................ 10,000

Amount due salesman at end of year $ 2,000

While it was indicated above that the collection or billing period was a given month (March 1-31), there is no obvious necessity for setting such periods. It may be more convenient for the bookkeeping department and the salesman to establish a cutoff date of, for example, the 25th of the month. This may enable bookkeeping to determine commissions before the end-of-the-month billing period swamps the department. It also may enable the salesman to collect his commissions at a time when most of his bills are payable.

The bookkeeping department should provide the salesman with a duplicate of the computation sheet so that he will be completely satisfied that he has received full compensation for his work.

Example of computation sheet:

SALES COMMISSION REPORT

Salesman's Name: William Williams
Rate: 10 percent
Period: Feb. 26 - Mar. 25 collections

Account	Month	Gross	Agency	Net	Commission
Smith Furniture	May	$1,000	$150.00	$850	$85.00
Ajax Plumbing	March	500	Direct	500	50.00
Miller Sausage	Jan.	1,500	225.00	1,275	127.50

Total earnings for above period.........................$3,150
Total draw during March................................ 1,500
Attached check, less standard deductions................ 1,650

Note to Salesman: Should you find any discrepancies on this commission report, please report them to the bookkeeping department no later than the 15th of the current month.

_____

For KXXX Bookkeeping Department

A frequent question, where commissions are paid on sales, rather than on collections, is what happens when an account goes bankrupt or for some other reason fails to pay the advertising bill on which the salesman has been commissioned. Some operations may wish to write it off; others may decide to deduct from the salesman's next commission check an amount equal to the commission he was paid on the account that went sour.

Payroll, Personnel Files

Insofar as station morale is concerned, there is no function in the bookkeeping department so **unimportant** as the payroll until is is late; then management becomes certain the payroll is the real cement that holds the staff together.

The preparation of payrolls is guided by local, state, and federal laws. Stations have the option of paying by check or cash and may decide whether to produce the payroll manually or with the use of machines. Beyond these options, management is guided by statutory provisions, primarily, and sometimes by the added advice of whatever labor unions happen to be representing all or parts of the staff. When a new organization is being formed, management should have legal or CPA advice in setting up the payroll plan. Any of the local, state or federal departments of labor also will supply ample guidance, but may explain fewer options than a skilled attorney or CPA could find. The sample payroll in Fig. 24 is intended only to show the student one particular form. There may be others like it, but in no case should an employer attempt to use the form without legal counsel.

There is no set rule or practice among stations to pay by the week or semi-monthly. The pay cycle is determined by

Station KXXX City Our Town, Texas

Pay Period Ending Page No.

Name and Account No.	Overtime Hr	Overtime Rate	Total Ovrtime	Regular Salary	Other	Gross Salary	S.S. Tax	W.H. Tax	State Tax	City Tax	Insurn.	Other	Total Deduct	Net Pay	Check Number
501															
John Smith	4	6.94	27.76	400.00		427.76	22.24	44.30					66.54	361.22	
701															
Jane Doe				350.00		350.00	18.20	48.80					67.00	283.00	
TOTALS															

Fig. 24. Payroll Sheet.

local custom, management's past practices, or by the station's economic situation. A good administrative practice is to pay semi-monthly by check (rather than cash) and distribute the checks to employees in sealed envelopes. The semi-monthly pay periods involve less paperwork in the bookkeeping department, and payment by check enables both management and employees to keep more accurate records. Checks should be so designed to show gross earnings, less deductions for income tax, FICA, insurance, and possibly a pension or profit sharing plan.

Taxes

Tax problems (and they **are** problems) fall within the jurisdiction of the bookkeeping department, particularly if the head of the department is a CPA or has equivalent training. If not, an outside auditor must be employed to make station tax estimates and provide counsel. The most common taxes faced by any business are payroll (FICA), ad valorem (property), and the federal government's tax on the station's **net** income. Others may include sales (rare), state, and local income taxes.

There may even be personal property taxes charged ownership on such items as office equipment, chairs, tables, and desks. Most group or chain operators are careful to get advice on local taxes they may be liable for. Taxes on real and personal property usually are fairly stable and can be estimated accurately for the year ahead. This figure would be entered in the general journal and is subject to payment when due. The Internal Revenue Service, in most cases where income is substantial (and IRS determines when revenue is substantial), wants to tax the income as earned or in advance, rather than at the end of the year. For example, the head bookkeeper estimates in January the company will owe $5,000 in taxes at the end of the first quarter. This amount probably will be required by IRS. At the end of the tax year, IRS will permit adjustments. If the company has estimated and paid too much, a refund will be due. If it has paid too little, the shortage will be requested by IRS.

RECORD KEEPING, GENERAL AND LEGAL

Aside from the plethora of normal operational business files, the licensee also must keep in precise and accurate order two particular files under rules of the FCC. One is the so-called **public file**. The other is the **political file**, which is part of the public file. The two files are similar because both may be inspected by anyone under certain conditions. A distinction between the two is made because an annual political report must be made to the FCC. And while both are subject to public inspection, one file helps meet a specific demand of the Commission for certain information (political), and the other enables the station to meet specific demands of the public for information about the licensee.

The Public File

In recent years the FCC has emphasized the importance of licensees maintaining a public file, i.e., a file that is open during regular business hours for inspection by members of the public. In this case, the "public" means anyone desiring to look at the public file may do so if he applies during the station's regular business hours.

The following is a typical station policy regarding the public file:

"Anyone coming into the station and requesting permission to see our public file is entitled to do so. He does not have to identify himself or give his reason for wanting to see the file. If he appears between 9:00 AM and 5:00 PM Monday through Friday, take the visitor to the conference room where the file is kept. We are under no obligation to make copies of any document. If he asks for a document that should be, but is not, in the file, call the Washington Attorney immediately and make arrangements to have the document available to the visitor at a later time. We may not question the visitor about his reasons for wanting to see the file, but we are entitled to observe his review of the documents and to note the documents that seem to attract his interest. If several persons appear and ask to see the files and if we cannot accommodate that number of persons in our conference room, make arrangements for them to inspect the files in small groups of two or three. No document may be removed from the conference room for any reason by the visitor."

Types of Applications and Reports
Which Must Be Kept in the Public File

A. All applications to construct new stations (Form 301) or for extensions of time to complete construction of a new station (Form 701).

B. All applications for major changes in facilities (Form 301). Generally, if a Section IV-A (Programing section) is submitted with the application or if local notice by publication and broadcast is required, then the application must go into the PF. Typical applications involving major changes or changes in station locations, changes in frequency, and changes in power which materially affect the area served. Applications which make a slight change in antenna height, or a change in equipment are considered to be applications for minor changes. You are not required to keep copies of such applications in your files. When in doubt, the safest procedure is to keep a copy of the application in the local file.

C. Every application involving a change in program service.

D. Applications requesting Commission consent for transfer of control or assignment of license (Forms 314, 315, 316), whether voluntary or involuntary and regardless of whether there is a substantial change in ownership or control. Until the sale is consummated, it is the seller's duty to have both the seller's and the buyer's parts of the application in the public file. After the sale has been completed, it is the buyer's duty to see that all necessary documents for the file have been obtained from the seller and placed therein. Responsibility for the public file always falls upon the person who is currently the licensee.

E. All ownership reports (Form 323) and contracts which are required to be filed with the Commission relating to ownership, control of use of station facilities, such as stock pledge agreements and time brokerage agreements.

F. All applications for renewal of license, including copies of program and transmitter logs for the composite week.

G. The regular political file.

H. All network agreements filed (with the Commission) after May 1, 1969.

I. Annual employment reports.

With respect to each of the above-mentioned applications, or reports, all exhibits, amendments, Commission correspondence, including all initial and final decisions, and any other pertinent documents must be maintained in the public file. Exceptions to this rule are as follows:

1. Information pertaining to an application which is already in the file, usually because of some previous ap-

plication or report, need not be duplicated. Instead, an appropriate reference may be made to the location in the public file at which such mentioned documents will be found.

2. Engineering sections of all applications need not be included, **provided** the following information is put in its place:

a. The state, county, or town and street address of the proposed transmitter location.

b. The same information, if known, for the main studio.

c. Copies of any contour maps that were in the engineering section.

Because the engineering portion of renewal applications (Form 303) is only two pages, there is no real advantage to removing it from the public file. Although standard broadcast stations are required to submit transmitter logs with their renewal applications, copies of the logs do not have to be part of the public file.

3. If a Petition to Deny is filed against any pending application, the petition itself need not be included in the public file. However, a statement must be placed in the file that such a petition has been filed with the Commission. This statement must list the name and address of the party that filed the petition. Under the rule, the following applications and reports need not be placed in the public file:

a. Documents which are treated as confidential by the Commission such as the Annual Financial Report (Form 324) need **not** be put in the public file, unless referred to by some document already in the file for information such as a response in the financial section of the application. This "incorporation by reference" makes the formerly confidential report a public document. Network affiliation agreements, formerly treated as confidential by the Commission prior to May 1, 1969, are no longer given secret status. Consequently, any renewal or modification of a pre-May 1, 1969 network affiliation agreement, automatically requires that the basic agreement as well as the renewal or modification, be placed in the public file. As stated earlier, all network affiliation agreements made after that date, must also be placed there.

b. Applications for licenses to cover construction permits (Form 302).

c. Applications for extension of time to complete construction (Form 701), except those relating to construction permits authorizing new stations.

d. Applications for STL, remote pick-up, and base stations (Form 313).

e. Applications by FM stations for subsidiary communications authorizations (Form 318).

f. Applications for remote control authorizations (Form 301-A).

The public file must be maintained in the community in which the station is licensed at any one of the following places:

1. The main studio.

2. Any other accessible place in the community to which the station is (or is proposed to be) licensed, such as public registry for documents, an attorney's office, or the licensee's business office, if this differs from the main studio.

3. The file must be available for public inspection at any time during regular business hours.

4. A multiple owner must maintain a separate file for each of its stations in the community in which each station is licensed. If, for example, the multiple owner's principal offices are in Chicago and it has a station in New York and a station in Los Angeles, it must maintain a separate file in New York for the New York station and in Los Angeles for the Los Angeles station. The New York file need not contain any information concerning the Los Angeles station, and vice versa. If it also has a station in Chicago, then it would be required to maintain a separate file for the Chicago station.

5. The Commission requires that the ownership data and the applications file be kept together in one place; i.e., the general public cannot be made to go to more than one location to obtain all of the data which the Commission requires in the public file.

All material contained in the local public files must be retained by the licensee for a period of **seven years**, or until the second renewal following the filing of the material in question is finally acted upon by the Commission, whichever is later. Where, however, an application "incorporates by reference" material in a document due to be discarded, the material referred to must be retained until the referring document is itself seven years old. For example, an application filed with the Commission in 1970 refers to a Section II (Legal Qualifications) filed with an applications in 1966. In 1973, the 1966 application may be discarded, **except** for Section II, to which the 3-year old 1970 application refers. To this 7-year rule, however, there are the following exceptions:

A. Applications not granted by the Commission may be discarded when finally denied or dismissed, and all court action has terminated; i.e., when the application is a completely dead issue.

B. When the technical mode of operation of a station is changed, (i.e., increase in power, change in transmitter, change in antenna height), engineering material pertaining to the former mode of operation need not be retained more than three years after the day the station starts operating under the new mode pursuant to Commission authority.

C. Material contained in the political file need be kept only two years.

D. Material in the public file which is related to a private claim against the licensee or any affiliated corporation, or which has a substantial bearing upon a Commission investigation or a complaint to the Commission must be retained in the public file until the claim is resolved or the processes surrounding the Commission investigation have been completed, regardless of time. This requirement applies to any earlier documents "incorporated by reference" into the materials in question. Under such circumstances, it is conceivable that the materials will be retained in the public file well in excess of seven years—those materials having substantial bearing on such matters must be retained until the licensee is notified in writing by the Commission that the material may be destroyed, or, in the case of a private matter, the material must be held until either the claim has been satisfied, finally adjudicated, or barred by the statute of limitations.

E. If the licensee voluntarily wishes not to discard materials in the public file more than seven years old, he does not have to keep them located in the public file, but may, instead, move the old documents to a place more convenient for storage, or they may be transferred to microfilm. However, for as long as the licensee possesses the information, a member of the public still has the right to see such materials. In order to do so he must make a written request to the station and arrange a time and place suitable and convenient to the licensee as well as to himself. (Unlike the regular public file, there is no requirement that this material be made available during regular broadcast hours.)

Political File

An accurate, up-to-the-minute political file is an absolute necessity in every radio station. Commission rules require that "every licensee shall keep and permit public inspection of a complete record of all requests for broadcast time made by or on behalf of candidates for public office, together with an appropriate notation showing the disposition made by the licensee of such requests, and the charges made, if any, if the request is granted."

The following procedure is recommended when anyone makes a request for political time under the above rule:

1. Ascertain that the candidate is indeed a **bona fide** candidate for a political office.

2. Does station policy permit the airing of announcements by the candidate in this particular office?

3. Have the candidate, or the person applying on the candidate's behalf, complete the "Agreement Form for Political Broadcasts."

4. Have the candidate, or the person applying on the candidate's behalf, sign a regular station contract which spells out in every detail the schedule of time to be aired.

5. If it is the station's practice to collect from **any** candidate in advance, then **every** candidate must pay in advance.

Experience has shown that a political file can't be too complete. Copies of the agreement form, station contract, agency contract, station time order, station invoice and affidavit of performance, any correspondence relating to any of these documents and a copy of the check covering costs, should be included in the political file. While one broadcaster may think this is excessive, another might foresee the following situation in which every piece of paper in the file will be needed.

VISITOR:	I'm here to get information on Senator Smith's campaign for re-election. Can you help me?
MANAGER:	You'll want to see the political portion of our public file, I believe.
VISITOR:	Yes, that's what I was told. First, I'd like to see the **time order** to determine the times the schedule was supposed to run.

	Second, I wish to know the name of the person signing the **agency order** for the time.
	Third, who signed the **Agreement Form for Political Broadcasts**? I also need the names of the organization and-or individuals who supplied money for the time.
	Fourth, I wish to see the **Affidavit of Performance** and the **Station Invoice** to make sure the time ran as ordered.
	Fifth, I understand that the Senator himself contacted you by letter regarding this schedule, and I'd like to see that letter and the station's reply to him. We have a copy of the Senator's letter, but would like to confirm that it is in your files.
	Sixth and last, I wish to know who signed the check that was used to pay for the time.
MANAGER:	Fine, but what's this all about?
VISITOR:	We have reason to believe that the Senator has received some illegal contributions to his campaign fund, and we simply want to know the names of persons and organizations involved in his campaign. We also have reason to believe that the Senator was charged minimum rate on the station, that he was given better times than our candidate recieved, and that the station owner actually gave Senator Smith some time during the campaign.

Fantasy? Several broadcasters across the U.S. would attest that the dialogue is reasonable and realistic. It **does** happen! With adequate information, the manager might nip this inquiry in the bud. With inadequate information, the unsatisfied inquiry might wind up being adjudicated by the FCC or by a court of law. Don't skimp! Keep the file complete and up to date.

Th station political file, as a practical matter, should also contain complete information on local campaigns involving **issues** as opposed to live candidates. Lively controversies revolve not just around candidates for public office; they also include hot arguments over bond issues, water fluoridation, local liquor laws, tax increases, and other issues not involving candidates. Where there are no candidates involved, Sec. 315 would not apply. Instead, the station would be bound under the rules and policies of the Fairness Doctrine. But in the event the station is charged with being unfair to **either** side, complete records would be required if the licensee is to successfully extricate himself.

The well-run station, regardless of revenue or market size, maintains complete commercial files including, but not limited to, agency contracts, station contracts, time orders, kill orders, change orders, renewal orders, and any correspondence relating to these documents. The ideal situation, of course, is a central filing system where every piece of paper is cross-referenced in a card file. But as a practical matter, few of these systems are found because of the necessity of employing a full-time person to maintain them. The cost cannot be justified except by the most extensive combines.

The sales department secretary, the general manager's secretary, bookkeeping assistants, and the copy production director are responsible for keeping most commercial files.

The sales secretary may keep a folder on **each** local account, even though the account may be on the air only once or twice a year. She may file by **account** in every case, with agency matters not relating to the client going into a separate file. The account file will contain all contracts issued by the agency on behalf of the client, all time orders written by the salesman in executing the agency orders, all kill and change orders (which should include rate changes), and any correspondence relating to a particular contract. Some stations prefer that the file folder contain a metal binder and that each item filed be in chronological order. A typical account file may contain, in this order, the following:

Agency letter requesting rates and availabilities
Station salesman response
Agency contract
Salesman's time order
Agency kill order
Salesman's kill order
Agency renewal
Salesman's new time order
Agency change order
Salesman's change order
Salesman's letter regarding rate increase
Agency acceptance of rate increase
Salesman's kill order showing old rates
Salesman's new order showing new rates

The file folder tab might show: OLD TOWN BEER, with the name of the agency, Stanfield Agency, in parenthesis immediately below the account name. The system might also indicate the name of the salesman handling the account, although this may be impractical if the market has a high turnover in salesmen and agencies.

The sales secretary also should keep a file of each salesman's "proposals," whether formalized or in simple letter form. These may be kept in a catch-all file that is assigned to a specific salesman, or in an alphabetized general file for local salesman correspondence.

Staff organization would determine who keeps similar files on national sales. The sales secretary may function for the national sales manager, or he may have his own secretary. In some cases, the general manager handles national sales and, in this case, his secretary might maintain national files. Indeed, there may be a pool of two or three sales secretaries who would handle files for both sales areas, assuming the sales volume will justify a secretarial pool. The essential requirement of any filing system is that records be placed where they can be retrieved with minimum time and effort. There is no rule as to how long such files should be kept; a good rule is to "clean out" the files after 12 to 18 months. If the 1971 file on the Wrigley Gum account can be closed, that is, if the agency has paid as billed and there are no disputes over rates, invoice, or times run, it is safe to either destroy the file or move it to a basement-type permanent file area. Never kill or destroy a file if the account or agency hasn't paid for the advertising. Each document may be needed to prove your case in court!

The bookkeeping department should keep a file of monthly invoices, along with related station documents (such as affidavits and copies of requested co-op copy) and bookkeeper correspondence. There are several systems and techniques that are efficient and helpful. Some of them are:

1. A copy of each invoice is bound into a monthly file and retained for two years. Affidavits of performance and requested co-op copy would be included, as they would be a significant part of that particular account's invoice.

2. A copy of each invoice is placed into a loose file, and is destroyed when the invoice is paid. (Permanent records of the transactions, of course, are kept in various ledgers and journals in the bookkeeping department.)

3. The bookkeeping department maintains a file similar to the one kept by the sales secretary. This file would contain bookkeeping's copy of the time order; a copy of the invoice for the order; copies of affidavits of performance mailed out, along with copies of requested co-op copy. Naturally, any correspondence regarding delinquency or inaccuracies would be contained in this file, particularly if the bookkeeping department is responsible for handling such matters.

Log Files

The station's program logs should be filed in or near the bookkeeping department because this is where a finished log normally ends its circulation. It is used by bookkeeping employees to prepare affidavits of performance and to determine specific times a particular schedule ran on the air. These should be kept in a precise chronological order and for a period of two years. The exception is where the station has broadcast material incident to a disaster or communications incident to or involved in an investigation by the Commission, of which the licensee has been notified by the Commission. In such cases, the logs must be retained until the licensee is specifically authorized in writing by the Commission to destroy them. If the logs are incident to or involved in a claim made against the station, and of which the licensee has had notice, then they must be retained until the claim or complaint has been fully satisfied or until the applicable statute of limitations for filing suits upon such a claim has expired. Logs, or copies of them, that make up the composite week in applications for license renewal, must be kept for seven years, along with other portions of the license renewal.

Copy and Production Files

The copy and-or production director must maintain files containing copies of all commercial and political matter run on the station. This file is divided into three parts. One is for recorded material; another is for live material submitted to the station for production, and the third is a file of production orders.

As copy and recordings are routed to the production area, the production or copy manager assumes responsibility and relates each piece to his copy of the broadcast time order that will specify its particular use. A production order is prepared, the order executed, and the materials returned to the issuing department. The materials would include the live copy or agency produced recording, live tags, finished production on cartridge, and the signed copy of the production order. The production order would be filed alphabetically by **client**. The live copy would be filed by **client**. And some workable system, such as a large metal cabinet or special filing case, should be used for the filing of agency production (whether on tape or disc).

Example of use:

SALESMAN: Jim, six months ago Goodtime Lake Development ran a schedule involving what they regard as some unique copy ideas. They want to use the same approach next week, but can't find the copy. How about putting your super filing system to work and see if you can locate it?

JIM: Hold on a sec. (checks production order file) I've got the production order here, but that material came in from the Smith Agency and was on tape. We have the tape, but there's no transcript. If the account wants to borrow the tape, okay; but we want it back and you'll have to sign for it.

SALESMAN: Beautiful. By the way, how long were the spots?

JIM: They were 60's, with 5-second tags. We have the tags in the live copy file.

It is easy to imagine the dialogue if a salesman requested such information from a production department that didn't maintain files. Careless, to-heck-with-it employees often throw away tapes once they have been put on cartridge. Others will prepare notes rather than live copy and throw away the notes once the spot has been cut. Although there is no law relating to the length of time commercial matter must be kept on file, as a practical matter it should be kept for at least one year. If monthly chronology is maintained, for example, December copy from 1971 may be thrown away at the beginning of December, 1972. If annual chronology is employed, in another instance, all 1971 copy might be placed in an isolated file for six months as the 1972 copy file is being built.

As burdensome as some consider elaborate filing systems, many well ordered broadcasters demand them. Business often demands that situations be reconstructed. Only with a well organized filing system can this be done.

Public Service Files

The daily mail brings letters of complaint or praise regarding something the station has or has not done. The public service director, whether full-time or part-time, should keep a file of these letters, especially those that commend the station for its effort in a particular public service campaign. Complaint letters should be directed to the general manager's office for possible resolution. One specific purpose in keeping a file of congratulatory letters is to have them available for inclusion in the next application for license renewal. The station must convince the FCC that it has indeed rendered significant public service, and the letters serve as testimonials in support of the effort the station has made.

Some stations maintain a file of public service resumes. Each public service campaign is documented as to the organization helped, time given to the organization, and the results. In too many instances, stations simply run the promised quota of PSA's and drop it there. The station files bulge with thank you form letters from the local Red Cross, Parent Teachers Association, State Employment Commission, or the Ladies Auxiliary of the Veterans of Foreign Wars. There is nothing wrong with these files; but they indicate only that the station ran announcements supporting these organizations. A file of public service resumes spells out the effort and may indicate the station made an affirmative effort to provide better than average help in a given situation.

In the example shown in Chapter I, the public service director indicated it was an affirmative effort, as opposed to a responsive effort. This means, simply, that Mr. Jones heard about the project, contacted the club, and offered the station's help. This report on the Lions Club project, along with supporting letters to and from the club, provides excellent support of a station's claim that it has, indeed, looked into and helped solve community problems.

At license renewal time—or should the station's public service performance be challenged by "strike" organizations—the file could be used as a dollar weapon of defense. The station could show, for example, that the 10,000 spots ran during a 12-month period has a value of $200,000.

Volumes one and three (I & III) of FCC Rules and Regulations should be kept up-to-date in station files, preferably in the general manager's office. The general manager's secretary may have the responsibility for keeping the file current through posting of the Commission's "Transmittal Sheet." These sheets provide substitute pages for those on which rules and regulations have been amended, deleted, or added.

While the availability of these rules in no way suggests that station personnel are qualified to interpret them, enough information may be gained from them to indicate whether a Washington attorney is needed in a given situation. Sometimes, local non-communications attorneys may be helpful in interpreting the R&R's, and considerable help may be gained from reading Commission primers on certain subjects. Primers, available through the Superintendent of Documents or the FCC, include:

1. Primer on **Ascertainment of Community Problems** by Broadcast Applicants, Part I, Section IV-A of FCC Forms.
2. The Fairness Primer (This deals with interpreting the provisions of the Fairness Doctrine).
3. The Section 315 Primer (This deals with interpreting the rules and statutes concerning political advertising).

The Fairness and Section 315 Primers are dealt with in Chapter VI.

Obviously, any correspondence with anyone at the Commission on any subject should be carefully catalogued and kept in the general manager or licensee's files. In addition, FCC files should include:

Notices of Proposed Rule Making
Report and Order(s)
Citations
FCC Bulletins

Any listener correspondence with carbons to the FCC should be kept in or near the FCC file drawer, along with the station's response to the letter. Citations for any violation the Commission inspectors find when examining a station, along with detailed information on how the complaint was disposed of, should be kept with meticulous detail.

Contractual agreements, other than those dealing with the sale of air time, should be kept by the general manager's office. These include land, equipment, and building leases; network agreements; trade-out contracts; brokerage contracts (which must also be filed with the FCC); wire service contracts; union contracts or agreements, and employment contracts with specialty personalities or artists where conditions of employment are different from those of other employees. The general manager's office obviously should keep an in-depth correspondence file, along with documents prepared by the National Association of Broadcasters, the Federal Trade Commission (which treats of consumer rights), and other documents and data that may be helpful in the general manager's effort to keep himself informed.

If the station does not employ a personnel director (most do not), the general manager's office also should keep a detailed file on applications for employment, along with a copy of the station's policy regarding training, hiring, and promoting employees or potential employees who are members of minority groups. This file should also include copies of employment advertisements run in any publication, especially if the publication is oriented to a particular minority group. Anything relating to the station's employment practices should be retained in this file, as it will be needed at next license renewal time when it must be proved the licensee has followed a nondiscriminatory course in hiring, firing, training, and promoting members of minority groups.

OFFICE EQUIPMENT

Every radio station has an inventory of office equipment, including typewriters, adding machines, duplicators, desks, and filing cabinets. In the case of office machines, some effort at standardization should be made to simplify servicing and procurement of expendable supplies. Often, considerable money may be saved if every piece of office equipment is purchased from a single manufacturer. It's the "cheaper by the dozen" concept and may result even in lower prices for supplies.

The business world seems to demand that every operation have a copier of one sort or another. While the development of efficient copiers has, in many instances, eased the staff's work load, costs often soar as employees make wasteful use of them. One broadcaster cut his copier costs in half by requiring that anyone using it make an entry on a log showing the department, purpose, name of individual, and number of copies run. This quickly stopped those who made 20 copies of cartoons to send to friends, and ladies who copied favorite recipes for distribution to the staff. Another operator saved money by putting the copier in a barely accessible corner of his building's basement. These appear to be "penny pinching" tactics, but there is no question that unthinking employees can waste and destroy thousands annually in paper, supplies, and copier materials.

ADMINISTRATIVE POLICY

A station with no definitive administrative policy, preferably written and distributed to all employees, is like a ship with no rudder. Many broadcasters provide handbooks for new employees explaining station policy on the pay plan, wage and hour rules, company benefits, and detailing what is expected of each employee. The handbook is an excellent way of communicating considerable information to the new worker and cuts down on inadvertent violations of company rules.

Wage and Hour

In establishing salary scales for the different jobs in a radio station, management must take into consideration Federal Wage and Hour laws, as well as any local or state laws on the subject.

First, the pay plans should avoid any forms of discrimination because of sex, race, or religion. The Department of Labor, Wage and Hour Division, publishes a Notice to Employees, dealing with the Fair Labor Standards Act; this notice should not only be posted in the employment office but its language should be reproduced in the station handbook (policy book, operating book). It is safe to say that most U.S. stations are affected by the Federal Wage and Hour laws. The National Association of Broadcasters has available to member stations interpretatives on the Wage and Hour laws, insofar as they deal with broadcasters and station job descriptions. Such laws are subject to change, and management should rely upon only the latest information available from government agencies or the NAB. Generally speaking, however, every member of the non-executive staff must be paid the current minimum wage, and not less than 1½-times the employee's regular rate of pay for hours worked beyond 40 hours in a workweek. Salesmen who perform or work only as salesmen are **not** covered by the overtime provision. The equal pay provisions prohibit discrimination on the basis of sex, race, or religion. When subject to the minimum wage, employees of one sex must not be paid wages at rates lower than those paid employees of the other sex for equal work on jobs requiring equal skill, effort, and responsibility which are performed under similar working conditions. An example of such jobs would include copy, traffic, bookkeeping, and production engineer.

Certain station employees are exempt from the provisions of the Fair Labor Standards Act. These are executive and supervisory employees, when certain conditions are met. When an executive or supervisor is paid at least $150 per week, and spends at least 50 percent of his time supervising the work of two or more employees, he is exempt from the provisions of the Wage and Hour laws. When an executive or supervisor is paid at least $100 per week and spends at least 80 percent of his time supervising the work of two or more employees, he is exempt. Thus, the $100-per-week program director who also pulls 21 hours weekly on the air and spends 19 hours functioning as department head and supervising the work of five other announcers, is not exempt! In this case, the PD is indeed a supervisory employee, but as he does not meet the criteria laid down by federal law, he must fill out time sheets and be paid an hourly wage just as though he were another announcer. Broadcasters must be wary of violating the Wage and Hour Laws, as to do so may result in expensive litigation. In every case, the licensee should seek advice from appropriate government agencies **before** setting up pay scales. Once management is certain of the rules, it should make every effort to see that they are followed **to the letter**. One disgruntled employee reporting to the Wage and Hour people may cost the station thousands of dollars in back pay for overtime performed.

Example:

CALLER: Mr. Jones, this is R. W. Williams at the Wage and Hour office. One of your former employees, a Mr. Dick Smith, has filed a complaint against your company. We'd like to check your payroll records, including time sheets, and we'd like to talk with some of your employees about this matter.

MANAGER: No soap, Buster. You're not getting into my records.

CALLER: Now, Mr. Jones, we'll get a court order if necessary; but one way or the other, we will see the records. It would be more pleasant for everyone involved if you'd just voluntarily open your records to us.

CALLER: (Now at the station) Mr. Jones, Smith complains that he was fired last week because he wouldn't work overtime without overtime pay. Could that allegation be true?

MANAGER: Absolutely false. The man was fired for insubordination. He can't take instruction and he's a troublemaker.

CALLER: Well, that may be true, but it's no defense for working a man overtime without extra pay.

MANAGER: As far as I know, he has not worked overtime without extra pay.

CALLER: Well, if you don't mind, we'd like to look at the time sheets he said he signed over the last year, and while we're at it we may as well look at the time sheets of the other hourly people who work here. And by the way, we'll need to talk with some of Smith's co-workers. He said they'll support his statement that he has worked a lot of overtime.

MANAGER: Maybe I'd better call my lawyer.

CALLER: Might be a good idea, Mr. Jones. We, of course, will represent Mr. Smith if this thing gets into court.

Wage and Hour agents, we will assume, inspected the station's payroll records and talked with employees. It was found that Smith, indeed, had worked overtime, that he had entered the overtime on his time sheet, but had never been paid for it. Employees with whom the Wage and Hour inspectors talked confirmed that Smith often came to the station at night to work in the production room. Smith himself said much of the overtime he worked was not claimed on his timesheet. Through these means, the inspectors found ten hourly workers, including Smith, who had worked overtime for at least one year and had never been paid for it. The overtime, for all workers amounted to 2,600 hours (5 hours per worker x 52 weeks). The Wage and Hour office ordered the station to pay each employee for 260 hours of overtime at overtime rates ranging from $4.50 to $6.00 per hour. The average of $5.25 per hour cost the station $13,650.00. This money must be paid the employees, whether they want it or not.

One broadcaster who had just paid $3,500 to two engineers developed a policy of ordering all employees out of the station at the appointed quitting time under a fear that Wage and Hour inspectors were clocking their arrival and departure times. Employees who are affected by Wage and Hour laws should be told to leave the station after work. It is possible that the station would be liable for overtime pay, even if the employee stayed late to write personal letters or engage in self-training work that in no way benefitted the station (such as practice in using a typewriter, control board, recording equipment, etc). A broadcaster once explained to a Wage and Hour inspector that to pay an employee back overtime due would "put the station out of business." "That's not our concern," said the Wage and Hour inspector. Our job is to protect the interests of the employees, and we intend to do that even if it does put you out of business." While this harshly indicts the inspectors and the laws supporting the Wage and Hour Division of the Department of Labor, the scene is not uncommon. It is pure folly for the broadcaster to try sneaking around laws governing the operation of his station. The FCC, FTC, and the Wage and Hour Division are concerned with the general public's welfare and the employee respectively, and have been known to deal unmercifully with the broadcaster when their rules are violated. Money saved through skimping or cheating simply doesn't justify the possible penalties.

Company Benefits

As competition for skilled and talented employees grows, management develops more and more fringe benefits. These may range from paid vacations and sick leave to elaborate retirement plans, stock options, and profit sharing. The larger the broadcast company, the greater the market size and competition, the broader the fringe benefits. A small station in a major market may offer nothing more than paid vacations. This also may apply to a highly successful company in a single-station market. Fringe benefits normally are offered, not because of management's compassion for labor, but for the very real reasons of competition for productive employees. An offer of $30,000 annually to a broadcast executive who is currently earning $20,000 may be refused because of the "extras" the executive earns with his present company.

Example:

OFFER:	Joe, we want to pay you a flat $30,000 a year to come over and run our station.
JOE:	Sounds good. How about paid vacations?
OFFER:	We got 'em! Two weeks every year for everybody?
JOE:	How about your retirement plan?
OFFER:	Nah! We don't need 'em. We figure the extra money we pay you now will make up for that.
JOE:	Your company went public a year ago, I understand. Do I have an option to buy stock at the original price?
OFFER:	Nah! The stock was sold over the counter and there's none left. But we don't figure you have to be a stock holder to really make some money here.
JOE:	What sort of insurance program do you have for employees!
OFFER:	We got the best. We have a group deal with a certain company and you save 25 percent under what you'd pay in premiums as an individual.
JOE:	You know, it seems you're offering me $10,000 a year more than I'm getting, but you're really not. As a matter of fact, you're offering me less over the long run.
OFFER:	Joe, they **couldn't** be giving you $10,000 a year in extras, could they?
JOE:	That, and more. For one thing, when I became an executive in the company, I was allowed to buy 5,000 shares of treasury stock for $3 a share. It was worth $5 a share on the open market when I bought it and it's worth $10 now. It should double in the years ahead, and I stand to make a lot of money on it. Furthermore, I get three weeks paid vacation, free hospitalization insurance, and a life policy that will pay my family $50,000 if I die while employed here. But, best of all, I'm in on the profit sharing plan and the retirement plan. My share of the profits goes into an investment fund and last year my statement showed I now have something like $20,000 coming to me when I want it. I didn't need the money so I left it there to be reinvested. At age 65, I'll be able to retire with a monthly income equal to 40 percent of my highest 3-year average income. For example, if I earn as much as $25,000 a year for three years, my retirement pay will be around $800 a month. This income, plus the sale of my stock and my share of the reinvested profits, will make me and my wife about as financially independent as anyone.
OFFER:	Sounds good, Joe. We don't have anything like that, although I must say I wish we did. Any openings over at your station?

287

Such a plan, of course, is used only in the largest and most successful operations. The average station, regardless of market size, has a modest, relatively inexpensive set of company benefits. These benefits usually include paid vacations, paid holidays, and a limited amount of sick leave. One plan provides one week vacation after six months, two weeks after one year, and three weeks after five years. Paid holidays may include only Christmas Day, New Year's Day, Labor Day, and Thanksgiving. Employees may be granted annually one to two weeks sick leave. That is, they would be allowed ten working days off the job without suffering loss of income. Pay would stop after two weeks and would resume only after the employee returned to work.

Fringe benefits provide a measure of security to both company and employee. The station may feel that its staff is permanent, more or less, and that it will not be faced continually with the problems of finding and training replacement personnel. The employee may feel a measure of security, knowing he won't be fired if he is sick for a day or two, that his hospitalization plan will handle the bills if he or a member of his family becomes ill, and that once a year he will receive a paid rest. Management, even those which function independently of labor unions, have developed fringe plans to not only attract competent employees, but keep them on the job. Development of the fringe plans have led in many instances to the potential employee being more interested in security than he is in challenge or the opportunity to grow. A plan that omits incentives for the individual to grow can result in a staff filled with security-minded individuals who have neither the will nor the ability to help the station grow. The union announcer, for example, may be concerned mainly with not violating a rule that will cost him his job. He may not be particularly interested in increasing station ratings. The union engineer, as another example, may not care about the quality of the station signal, so long as he can work within the jurisdiction (work area) outlined in his union agreement.

UNIONS

Modern broadcasters must deal with several unions. NABET (National Association of Broadcast Employees and Technicians) and AFTRA (American Federation of Radio and Television Artists) represent the air staff in most cases. IBEW (International Brotherhood of Electrical Workers) and CWA (Communications Workers of America) represent the engineering and technical personnel. While it is conceded that unions serve a worthwhile purpose in such industries as automotive and aerospace, where thousands of workers may be covered by a single contract, many broadcasters find them obstructive. Broadcasting is big business, but it is made up of over 5,000 small staffs that range in size from four to 40.

Many stations survive financially on the ability of certain staff members to handle several jobs, such as the announcer who operates his own board and can occasionally perform minor maintenance on studio equipment. In a station where IBEW represents the engineering staff, the union's contract with the station often prohibits any nonengineer from even touching the equipment, much less performing maintenance. Announcers represented by AFTRA operate under a similar jurisdictional clause that prohibits at times even the licensee from making on-air appearances. It is the jurisdictional provisions of most contracts that impose the greatest limitations upon broadcasters. Union contracts deal with every subject from weekly pay and overtime to paid vacations and retirement. Some contracts even specify a minimum number of employees the station may keep on the staff. This clause is particularly vexing when ratings and revenues fall and management wants to reduce overhead to adjust expenses to income.

. Broadcasters' anti-union attitudes have little to do with their overview of unions in general. Gordon McLendon, for example, many times gave editorial support to union efforts, while cringing at the thought of having one of them organize his stations. It was his contention that unions inside radio stations create program inefficiency. McLendon was a founder and developer of the Top 40 format in which the announcer or DJ operated his own board. It was the fast-paced, well-coordinated effort of the disc jockey that produced the entertaining sound of the format. But the effect is lost when one man does the voice work and another handles the console and turntables. In some IBEW stations, for example, the announcer cannot even place records on the turntables. This function must be performed by the union engineer.

A successful radio station normally has a highly efficient staff with good morale. It is a well-oiled team of air personalities, engineers, salesmen, administrative and management personnel. Staff cohesion has been known to suffer dramatically with the arrival of one or more of the unions. One gets the impression that an engineering staff, for example, ceases to function for the station and works instead for the union. Personal relationships between staff and management tend to disappear, and it is this relationship that often makes the difference betweeen an efficient staff operation and one that is mediocre.

Keeping Unions Out of the Station

The broadcaster whose air and engineering staffs have not been organized should make every effort to detect the danger signs. Some of the conditions and circumstances that invite organized labor are:

1. Salaries that are below the market standard.
2. Fringe benefits that are below market standards.
3. Incompetent individuals who feel insecure in their jobs.
4. Individuals who constantly complain about working conditions.
5. Dictatorial middle-management.
6. Union organization of staffs at competing stations.

Any one or all of these conditions may result in a station being set up overnight for a union election. And once the staff members have gone so far as to request an election be held, it usually is too late for management to make its move. It is too late to discharge the incompetent individual who feels insecure; it is too late to fire the griper, because these actions and any inducements management may wish to offer the staff to remain unorganized violate laws that uphold the union's right to organize the announcers and engineers. Management must stay in tune with staff feelings and attitudes, particularly in markets where other stations are organized.

In a classic situation, a West Coast FM operation was organized when the general manager refused to seriously consider complaints voiced by the announcing staff. The announcers came en masse to the manager's office to complain about salaries and shifts. The manager responded by throwing the operating statement into their faces and advising them that the station "can't afford the salaries you demand." "Read the P&L and weep, because the story's right there," said the manager. The staff didn't read the operating statement and didn't weep. Instead, during the manager's next agency trip to New York, they informed AFTRA of their desire to hold an election to determine whether a majority of the announcers wanted to be represented by the union. In spite of top management's pleas and admonitions that unionization would destroy staff cohesions, the announcers voted five to one in favor of union representation.

Top management was unable to step in and make amends. AFTRA, on the other hand, was absolutely free to promise pay raises, paid vacations, job security, and retirement benefits. About all management could do, at this point, was yield and hope a viable contract could be worked out.

Co-Existing With Unions

Once a union has organized the staff, management must learn to live and produce in the new environment. The manager can no longer call an announcer into his office and give him a merit raise for a job well done. Incompetents can no longer be fired on the spot. And management must deal continuously with the shop steward who brings individual staff grievances to the attention of the front office.

Example:

STEWARD: Mr. Manager (always polite and respectful initially), as IBEW representative of your engineering staff, I'm here to voice a complaint filed by Engineer Jim Jones.

MANAGER: (very politely) Please, sit down. Tell me about it.

STEWARD: It seems that yesterday one of the announcers picked up and removed to his car a 35 pound tape machine that was to be used in an interview.

MANAGER: Thirty-five pound machine you say?

STEWARD: Yes, and you know as well as I do that the jurisdictional clause of our contract specifies that only an engineer may pick up and operate a station recording machine that weighs more than 30 pounds. It's a clear violation, because, as I said, the machine in question weighed 35 pounds.

MANAGER: I'm familiar with the situation. We tried to find an engineer to remove the tape machine from the station but were unable to do so. We had two engineers on duty. One was operating the board and the other was on a lunch break. What could we have done? The announcer had several people waiting for interviews, and we had to move in a hurry.

STEWARD: Our contract clearly spells out how such situations should be handled. You should have called a man in for overtime. If none wanted the overtime, you could have called in a part-time man.

MANAGER:	But when we use part-time people, we have to guarantee them six hours minimum work! You surely wouldn't want us to pay a man $72 just to carry a 35 pound tape machine from the station to a car?
STEWARD:	Mr. Manager, I only expect you to live up to our agreement.

In another case, an IBEW engineer reminded the president of a huge broadcast group that he "was not allowed to touch the volume control on the monitor of the automation equipment." The president protested that (1) he only touched the control, and (2) the equipment wasn't even wired into the station. "It doesn't matter," replied the engineer; "it is technical equipment and it is in the station. That's all that counts."

When the station is organized by one or more of the unions that represent announcers and engineers, management has little choice but to live under the rules. These actions will be helpful:

1. Study thoroughly the agreement with the union.

2. Instruct non-union personnel to comply to the letter with every provision of the contract.

3. Meet with local union officers and establish rapport with the leadership. Friendly relations between station and union brass often may prevent a strike or other work stoppages.

4. Make every effort to maintain good rapport with staff people who are members of the union. In some cases, a vindictive union member may be deliberately incompetent and have no fear of losing his job or suffering any other penalty.

An example of item four above involved a chief engineer who habitually was late in switching from the daytime to the nighttime pattern. His negligence resulted in the station paying a fine to the FCC. The station couldn't fire the man because the union bought his story that the station automobile he was forced to use was unreliable and often broke down while he was en route to the transmitter site. Ridiculous? Yes, but true.

Once a union has organized the station, removal is all but impossible. For legitimate and understandable reasons, the six or seven announcers or engineers who initiated the action may all be gone within a year or two. But as new people are employed to replace those who leave for whatever reasons, the closed shop provisions in state labor laws force the new employee to join the union and thus help to perpetuate the situation. It doesn't matter that the new employee may not want to joint the union; the station cannot employ him unless he so agrees.

To the broadcaster, then, it is obvious that if he is to keep unions out of his station he must pay salaries that are equal to those of the competition, and he must provide equal fringe benefits. He must **listen** to staff complaints and he must act on them. Chronic complainers and incompetents should be avoided, particularly in markets where other stations have been organized. Unions have improved conditions for the working man who builds cars, airplanes, buildings, and ships. But creativity and enterprise are sorely stifled and sometimes eliminated when unions take over the operating staffs of the modern-day radio station. One broadcaster told his staff before a union election that if they joined the union they would cease to work for him; they would, instead, be working for the union. He was right, and they didn't care.

STATION POLICY BOOK

Regardless of station or staff size, management should write, publish, and distribute to staff members a policy book. Company rules and operating procedures should be plainly stated and updated from time to time as policies change. New employees should be instructed to read the book and be able to comply with its provisions. Staff efficiency and coordination inevitably are improved when a station finally decides to put its rules into written form. The policy book often can preclude such lame excuses as "Well, no one told me to do it that way," when the new employee is charged with a rules violation.

Job Descriptions

Each position on the staff, from traffic to maintenance, should be thoroughly described as to detail and scope. The required relationships between staffers should be pointed out. For example, the News Director might be responsible for the gathering and writing of news while the Program Director was responsible for the methods of delivery. There often are fine lines of jurisdiction within a staff, and these should be defined so that everyone will recognize them. If the receptionist is expected to assist the bookkeeper, sales secretary or Office Manager, everyone involved should know the extent to which she is required to help.

Company Expectations

The policy book or operating manual should also explain to employees company requirements regarding work hours, coffee breaks, attire, and working attitudes. Most staffers will obey company rules, if they understand them! If long hair, mini skirts, and mod slacks are prohibited, the policy book should so state. If management requires that desk tops be cleared at the end of the working day, this should be spelled out in the operating manual.

Company Philosophy, Goals

Some broadcasters try to make it clear to each employee exactly where the station has been and where management hopes to take it. The station's policy in regard to "good citizenship" in the community helps the new employee get started on a sound footing. Employees feel more a part of the team if they understand company goals. This information might include the company's desire to pay higher salaries, increase power, own its own office building, and its aim to promote from within when department management jobs open. The only purpose of such information, of course, is to make the employees feel secure and hopeful of better pay and greater responsibility. The receptionist who may hope for more money and ultimately a job in the continuity or traffic department certainly will perform her work more efficiently if she knows there is an opportunity for advancement. It is not uncommon for highly talented individuals to take any job available at a station, so long as there is hope for consideration when the higher paying jobs become available. When a company explains its philosophies and goals, it is almost a matter of saying, "Let's compare our hopes, dreams, and aspirations, and see if we can't work together in realizing them."

Work-Flow Charts

Each station has its own peculiar method of operation. The system at Station A in Cleveland may in no way compare with the system at Station B in Chicago. The ultimate result of the effort may be the same, but the approach route never is identical. For this reason, work-flow charts often are desirable in the policy book or operating manual. Such charts may include instructions on distribution of time orders or the procedures for the production of commercials from the time the salesman turns in copy notes to the point where the announcer puts the commercial on the air. Some employees never understand the relationship between time orders, program logs, affidavits of performance, invoices and co-op copy. In the large, highly departmentalized stations this knowledge may not be necessary. But in the small operations, the better the employee understands the total operation, the more likely he is to cooperate and coordinate his efforts with others.

Department Procedures

While it is important that the employee understand how the station as a whole operates, it is more vital that he understand and appreciate the function of his particular department. It is not uncommon, for example, for the News Director to publish the station's Newsroom Policy Book. And few stations operate without a written Sales Policy. Such departmental publications pay close attention to the minute details of the operation. They may include station requirements that the names of accident victims not be aired until the next of kin have been notified, or specify that no salesman will offer time prices not published on the rate card. An administrative policy book might require that time orders be turned in to the Manager no later than 2:00 PM for a next day start and that the deadline for copy is 3:00 PM.

The policy book, essentially, is little more than a way for management to communicate with employees. In written form, policies often are more easily understood and, therefore, more easily complied with. Management can spend valuable hours dealing with staff problems when the time could be better spent on radio's two major problems, programing and sales. Too many managers submerge themselves in non-programing and non-revenue producing problems, while ignoring problems in the two areas that spell survival or failure.

Weekly Executive Meetings

A prime means of disseminating ideas and information in an orderly manner is the weekly executive meeting. Those attending may include the General Manager, Program Director, News Director, Office Manager, Sales Manager, Chief Engineer (occasionally), Director of Public Affairs, Promotion Director (unless these duties are handled by the

PD), and the General Manager's secretary. Any day may be suitable for the meeting. One broadcaster called the gatherings on Wednesday in order to "get the frustrations of Monday out of the way" and to avoid the rush for the week-end that often occurs on Friday.

Such meetings are important particularly where the staff is large (40-50 persons) and where the station's office quarters are situated on two or three different floors of a building. These conditions make informal communication between department heads difficult and impractical. The weekly gathering in the Manager's office may solve the problem. It is essential that the Manager and his secretary prepare an agenda for the meetings so that business can be conducted in as short a time as possible.

Typical Agenda:

Current Projects

1. Mail pull on stock market promotion. May wish to increase number of promos. PD and promotion manager.
2. Telephone loop and equipment for remote from First National Bank next week. Remind Chief Engineer to balance line, as music will be originated at remote site.
3. PD on development of new program log. Explain changes.
4. Promotion Director on merchandising for Colgate accounts. See if can arrange special displays in Safeway Stores.
5. Salary increases for announcers?
6. Have Chief get quotes on new transmitter building.
7. Discuss and get ideas on Agency party next week.
8. Sales manager's ideas on production preparing spec spots. Got PD's ideas on how can best be done.
9. Work on collections. Have bookkeeping prepare up-to-date aging sheet for Sales Manager.
10. News Director's ideas on replacing the PM newscaster.

Future Projects

1. NAB meeting next month. Sales Manager and Chief Engineer attend.
2. Possibility of power increase in Fall.
3. New Rate Card. Discuss with Sales Manager.

4. Vacation schedules for summer. Use of outside help while staffers on vacation. Can assistant traffic manager handle job alone for two weeks?

5. Station participation in local Home Show in July.

6. Annual Station Picnic for the public in August.

7. Merchandising on Enco campaign in August.

8. License renewal work begins in November (License expires August 1, next year, but application for renewal must be in lawyer's office no later than April 1. Composite week should be published no later than November this year).

9. Methodist Church program due off the air July 1. Talk with everyone about best replacement.

10. Every salesman member of civic club by September 1.

In addition to the agenda prepared by the General Manager, department heads should come to the meeting prepared to ask questions and bring up new issues. While certain matters (such as the pay raise for announcers) may not be discussed with the staff, the department heads would be expected to take information gained at the meeting and pass it along to members of their departments. Such meetings not only help solve the communications problem, but they also give department heads a feeling of being in on station planning. Many operators prefer to keep staff leaders in the dark until an action is taken. Program Directors, for example, may become miffed when they learn from a secretary plans for a station promotion. "Why wasn't I briefed?" is the usual question. In a recent study of communication problems in business and industry, the most viable solution came from a top manufacturing executive. His solution to the problem was, simply: "Talk to each other!" Thus, a weekly meeting of department heads allows key members of the staff to "talk to each other!"

ASCERTAINING THE VALUE OF A RADIO STATION

Determining the value of a radio station is one of the most hazardous ventures in the industry. The seller invariably wants too much; the buyer invariably offers too little. And while there are certain rules of thumb available to the buyer-seller in setting a value, none of them is ever followed to the letter.

One rule often used by buyers, sellers, and brokers is that a station is worth one and one-half times its gross revenue. Thus, a station which billed $1,000,000 during its last fiscal or calendar year would be worth $1,500,000. Another guideline is that a station is worth ten times its net profit. A station which billed $2,000,000 during its last year of operation and showed a profit of $700,000, might, according to this guideline, be worth $7,000,000. But there are many other considerations, particularly in small and medium markets. The number one rated station in a market is not necessarily the top biller, and the lowest rated operation is not necessarily the low biller. In terms of worth, the station's frequency, power, staff, tenure in the community and reputation often mean more than its revenues.

Real Property

In many cases, the licensee leases his transmitter site, office and studio space, and the transmitting and studio electronic equipment. He, therefore, has nothing to sell except the leases. In such a case, his revenue over the last few years might be the most significant factor. His inventory of furnishings and equipment would be brief, and he would need to rely upon previous earnings records to justify a high price for the station.

One thing the student should understand. The licensee cannot sell his license. The buyer and seller enter into an agreement conditional upon the FCC's approval of the buyer's application for control of the facility. Once the buyer has met all legal, financial, and other requirements of the Commission, he is free to complete his transaction with the seller. Until Commission approval is gained, the buyer may have no control over the operation of the facility. Illegal relinquishment of control of any part of the station operation can result in a heavy fine for the seller and possible loss of license. (See Chapter VI.)

When a licensee owns all or most of the land and equipment, the potential buyer will require an inventory.

KXXX INVENTORY

Item(s)	Value
Land, 10 acres	$10,000
Transmitter equipment	35,000
Antenna equipment	25,000
Transmitter building	8,000
Studio gear	16,000
Microwave equipment	7,000
Miscellaneous technical and tools	4,000

Office furniture	3,000
Company car	1,200
Office supplies	200
Office machines	1,900
Accounts Receivable	21,000
Goodwill	50,000
Total	$182,300

In the actual inventory, the buyer may require that every item be spelled out, down to and including the serial number of each typewriter and adding machine, each microphone, the number of spare tubes on hand, and the number of reams of paper in the supply room. The inventory enumerates the station's assets. From these, the negotiators must deduct the liabilities before a final contract can be drawn. If the station has $20,000 in current payables, this amount would be deducted from the selling price, or the seller would agree to pay the debts from proceeds of the sale. If the seller still owed money on the technical or other equipment, the amount owed would be deducted from the selling price, or the seller would agree to liquidate the debt from the proceeds.

In some cases, the buyer may prefer to pass accounts receivable on to the seller as they are paid, rather than take a chance on finding some of them uncollectable. This, then, would reduce the selling price of KXXX by $21,000.

The "goodwill" factor is, of all inventory items, the most debatable. If the station has a history of losing money, the goodwill factor is probably questionable. If investigation within the community reveals that people think poorly or not at all of the station, the seller probably can be talked down on his evaluation of the station's goodwill. But if the operation has shown profits over the last few years, and if the station's image in the community is good, chances are the buyer will have to buy the goodwill.

Buying on Station Potential

Often, an experienced broadcaster will purchase a "dog" station because of its revenue potential, rather than because of its immediate assets. The country is literally dotted with radio stations which are poorly and unprofitably operated because of ignorance, ineptitude, or indifference. The professional broadcaster who finds and buys one of these may make a fortune as well as lead a highly satisfying life in the community.

Assume there are four stations in a market of 200,000 persons. The leading money-maker is a contemporary music formatted daytimer at 1080 kHz on the dial with 1,000 watts of power. The number two station is a network affiliate, fulltime, at 990 kHz with 5,000 watts day and 1,000 watts night in power. The format is network block with middle of the road music. The third station is a fulltime operation with 1,000 day and night, non-directional, at 1460 kHz. Its format is a mishmash of C&W music, Top 40 programs, gospel shows, dreary interview programs, and poorly executed news programs. The fourth station is a moderately profitable but ethnic-oriented daytime facility with 400 watts power at 1390 kHz.

A professional broadcaster who believes radio hasn't reached its potential in the market, decides to approach one of the owners with an offer. There are several considerations. First, although the daytimer is number one in the market, it is too vulnerable to attack from a well operated full-time facility. As he is interested in building the top rated station in the market, the broadcaster decides against approaching the owners of the daytimer.

The equipment at the old-line network affiliate is old and would need to be replaced almost in its entirety to execute the format he has in mind. Although the 1460 frequency and the power are desirable, he decides against making an offer because of the additional investment needed.

He decides against approaching the operators of the ethnic facility for two reasons. First, it, too, is a daytimer and would have the same vulnerability as the other daytimer. Second, the station is doing a good job in its field; it is providing an excellent service, but the potential buyer is not interested in entering this format of broadcasting.

The final decision, then, is to approach the owners of the full-time station at 990 kHz. It is non-directional, and this means fewer technical problems. Its frequency is in the middle of the dial and not far from the frequency of the number one station. This means simply that listeners have a middle-of-the dial habit, and therefore will more likely move to the 990 kHz position. If the buyer is an agressive, community-minded broadcaster, his chances of winning top position in the market are excellent.

In 1960, in Austin, Texas, KOKE was the top rated station. Because of its well-executed Top 40 format, it outranked other stations with greater power, better frequencies, and full-time licenses. Earl Fletcher, an experienced pioneer in broadcasting and an executive in a group operation that owned a sluggish, but full-time, station in Austin, made it known to the local industry that he was going after the top spot in the Austin market. Fletcher hired a Top 40 Program Director to re-staff the program department. Newsmen were employed, and news gathering equipment was purchased. A billboard and newspaper campaign was planned. After filing his plans with the FCC through his Washington attorney, he introduced the new format and was immediately successful. Within only a few weeks, the new format had taken the numbers in the market, and KOKE began searching for a new approach to serving Austin. Ultimately, it adopted a Country & Western format and began to recover.

It is virtually impossible for a daytimer to get and hold top spot in any market because it cannot develop **audience continuity**. The station goes off the air at sundown, and the listener is thus left to grope with outside signals for his type of music. The full-time station, on the other hand, can develop audience continuity; and if the format is executed imaginatively and efficiently, can hold its audience around the clock and preclude vulnerability to being taken by another station.

None of this, of course, means a daytime station cannot be operated profitably and provide a needed service. On the contrary, there are literally hundreds of profitable daytime-only operations in the U.S., stations that are held in high esteem by the community. In a single-station market, the daytimer is king. In a multi-station market, where the competition is lax, the daytimer can be top-rated. But in a competitive market where there is the eternal struggle for ratings, upon which so many advertising dollars are spent, the daytimer is easily outclassed by aggressive fulltime operations. There are hundreds of case histories where professional broadcasters have moved in and taken daytimers.

Another important consideration in evaluating a radio station is its power **potential**. A 500 watt facility may be on a frequency that would allow an increase to 5,000 watts. A thorough engineering study would determine what, if any, power increases might be effected. The student may wonder why the seller would not increase power if the potential were there. The most immediate answer, usually, is cost. Another is indifference. Only the agressive operator, the professional, has the motivation to bring a station to its full power potential. KLIF in Dallas began as a 1,000 watt day, 500 watt night facility in 1947. By 1970, its daytime power was 50,000 watts with 5,000 watts at night. The facility improvement took years and many hours of engineering studies, not to mention the hundreds of thousands of dollars in cash. The last improvement came in 1970 when McLendon built an "antenna farm" consisting of twelve towers near Rockwall, Texas, to increase night-time power from 1,000 to 5,000 watts.

There are many instances where a station is purchased and left alone. That is, the station was highly profitable when the buyer made the purchase, and he decided to leave well enough alone. Such was the case when McLendon sold KILT in Houston. The General Manager, staff, format, and facility continued under virtually the same operating policy. McLendon had done a near-perfect job in building and operating the station, and the new owners wisely left everything intact. This, however, is not usually the case. When a new owner takes over, many changes are made and, in some cases, an entirely new staff is hired. Formats are changed, new equipment is purchased, call letters are changed, and a new image is developed. Why? Simply, because, in the opinion of the new owners the "old" station cannot be turned into a financial winner.

Questions, not necessarily in this order, a buyer should ask when considering the purchase of a new radio station:

1. How much real estate is involved, and what is it worth?

2. What is the age of the present technical equipment, and is it adequate to carry out my format plans?

3. What was the station's gross revenue over the past five years?

4. What was the station's net revenue over the past five years?

5. What is the status of the station's finances? Are the payables delinquent? Are equipment payments in arrears? Are the receivables collectable?

6. Are local taxes and other statutes sufficiently liberal to permit the kind of operation I plan?

7. What contracts, such as wire service, ASCAP, BMI, SESAC, trades, barter, are in force?

8. Can the facility's power be increased? Does it need an increase to effectively compete in the market?

9. Is the station's frequency a good one? Is it in the center of the dial in the vicinity of other local stations, or is it isolated at one end or the other?

10. Is the market overpopulated with radio, TV, and FM stations, or is there still room for growth?

11. Is the station full-time or daytime only?

12. Does the station have an FM affiliate, or is there an FM channel open in the market?

13. Is the station's format really serving local needs, tastes, and desires, or will I have to completely rework the format?

14. What programing competition is present? Does the competition leave room for my format, or is one of them so badly done that I can take its audience?

15. Is the staff competent, or will I need to re-staff?

16. How do local merchants feel about the station, as is?

17. Is the market a primary one, or is the station licensed to operate in a suburb of a primary market?

If the buyer is handling negotiations himself, he will need answers to these and other related questions. If, however, a broker is used, he will get the answers and relay them. When a broker is involved, negotiations may continue for weeks or months before the principals meet face to face. The broker plays a valuable role in the buying and selling of radio stations. He usually is an experienced broadcaster and, therefore, is competent to offer good advice to the buyer or seller, whichever he represents. He brings not only his station experience to bear on the issue, but also his experience in helping to buy and sell properties.

The seller usually pays the broker's fee of from 4 to 7 percent of the selling price. In a two million dollar deal, then, the broker stands to earn from $80,000 to $114,000. Not only are the broker's expenses high, but he often spends a great deal of time travelling back and forth between his office and the seller and between the seller and the buyer. Some deals take years to consummate. When Giles Miller purchased KBUY from Dave Worley in Amarillo, the two men spent three days together in a hotel suite before either would make an offer. Worley was convinced that his asking price would be too low, and Miller was convinced his offer would be too high. So, they played the game of "you go first." This was a case of principals negotiating. There was no broker involved.

Summary

Administration is not confined to the paper work aspect of a radio station operation. It pervades every corner of every department, not only in terms of systems and procedures but in the efficient execution of policy and the management of staff members' time. Good administration is an omnipresent

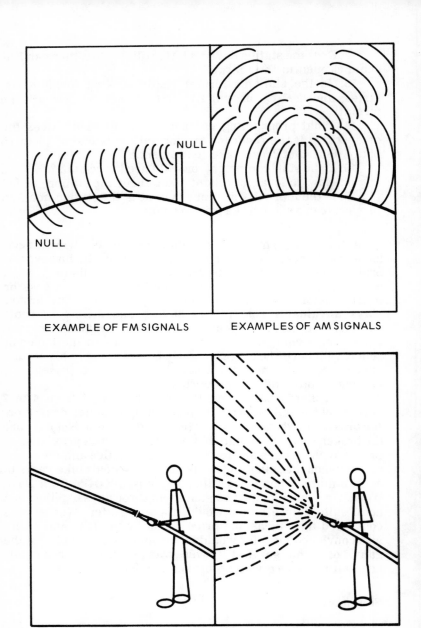

EXAMPLE OF FM SIGNALS

EXAMPLES OF AM SIGNALS

NULL

NULL

STRONG STREAM OF WATER

NOZZLE SET TO SPRAY

Fig. 25. Comparison, AM-FM Signals.

lubricant that builds staff morale and reduces friction between the varied personalities required to operate a commercial station. The administrative functions so often are taken for granted, as the city dweller takes milk, eggs, and other farm products for granted. Administration isn't noticed until it becomes low in quality or disappears altogether. Many good salesmen are incapable of management because they either don't understand the administrative processes or because they are inept at handling administrative problems. The same is true for announcers and engineers. A good administrator can usually formulate and execute viable plans and systems and is able to explain and **sell** them to subordinates. Programing and sales are the big wheels of radio. Administration is the essential but tiny cog that makes them turn smoothly.

CHAPTER 5

Technical Operations

Few professional broadcasters in sales, programing, and management are also qualified engineers. Most station personnel, in fact, don't know a diode from a coaxial cable. Fortunately, there are a great number of highly qualified technicians available to the industry as maintenance men or as consultants. While it is not important that non-engineering personnel understand technical problems, it is important that management grasps the general nature of technical operations. A dishonest engineer, for example, may run a profitable "moonlight" radio and TV repair service with the station providing the inventory of spare parts. This sort of thing, of course, is rare, **but it has happened**! In other instances, heavy capital expenditures are required to replace or add certain equipment and management should be capable of understanding at least the performance potential of the equipment in question. One of the chief reasons management stays in the dark about technical operations is that qualified engineers are unable to explain their business in lay terms. Dr. Barney McGrath, and Dr. Harold Weiss, of Southern Methodist University, co-authored a book, **Technically Speaking**, that addresses itself directly to the subject of articulating technical subjects in laymen's language. Glenn Callison, National Director of Engineering for the McLendon Corporation, made special studies to equip himself to talk with non-engineering personnel. He often was called upon to speak to meetings of McLendon managers and other non-technical groups and, in his words, "I had to develop a language that those people understood or simply admit that I had wasted my time."

Often asked the difference between AM and FM signals, Callison used the following plain language explanation:

"I like to relate AM and FM signals to water coming from a garden hose. When the nozzle is adjusted for a hard, steady stream of water, we are getting an FM signal. When the nozzle is adjusted for a fine, broad spray of water, we are getting an AM signal. Emissions from an AM station sort of flood the area, while emissions from an FM station tend to go in a straight line and do not follow the curvature of the earth as AM signals do.

"Another plain language way of comparing AM and FM emissions is to liken them to light beams. The search light mounted on a tower shoots into the distance, but skips the space immediately under the tower. The flood light, on the other hand, covers the immediate area but does not directly cover a great distance."

While management must concede that it will never be technically proficient in broadcast operations, there are certain areas in which it must delve in order to ascertain that the station is operating according to FCC specifications. These may be referred to as **Legal Requirements**, and relate primarily to the Commission's operator requirements, sign on and sign off time for daytime-only operations and change of pattern for stations that have different power and-or coverage patterns for day and night operations.

Operator Requirements

Operator Requirements are covered in Par. 73.93 of the Commission Rules. The Rules, paraphrased, are as follows:

(a) One or more radio operators holding a valid radio-telephone first-class operator license (first ticket), except as provided in (b) of this section, shall be in actual charge of the transmitting apparatus and must be on duty either at the transmitter or at the remote control point. If operation by remote control is authorized, the control and monitoring equipment must be readily accessible and clearly visible to the operator at his normal operating position.

It is not the concern of the Commission how the licensee meets the requirements outlined above, only that he does indeed meet them. The key phrase is that the transmitter or remote control equipment be readily accessible and clearly visible to the operator at his normal operating position. And the operator must be able to perform all required functions, such as (1) raise and lower power, (2) turn plate on and off, (3) check tower lights, and (4) turn stereo pilot on and off. The following illustrations define more clearly the requirement that equipment be clearly visible and accessible:

Figs. 26A and B indicate respectively the correct layout for operations with remote control authorization and those

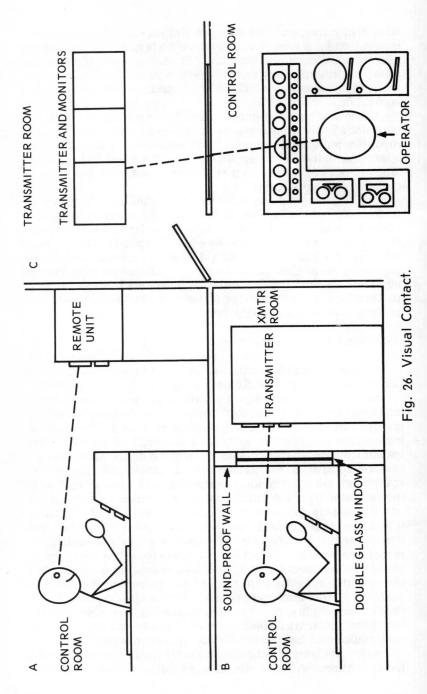

Fig. 26. Visual Contact.

308

where the operator (or combination disc jockey-operator) must take readings directly from the transmitter and monitoring equipment. Fig. 26C indicates an incorrect layout in which the announcer-operator on duty cannot see the meters on the transmitting apparatus from his **normal operating position**. In the case of Fig. 26C, the operator would have to leave his normal operating position and walk into the transmitter room to determine if the equipment is operating properly and to make the half-hourly entries on the operating log. In the early days of radio, announcers **announced** and engineers **operated**. During the early 50's when television began consuming advertising budgets and throwing radio station licensees into economic trauma, the combo man became popular. One man with announcing ability and a "first ticket" could do the work of two men. This significantly contributed to lowering staff costs, particularly in stations employing a free-form or Top-40 type format. Some stations moved to the transmitter; that is, they constructed transmitter buildings of sufficient size to accommodate not only the transmitting apparatus but also the program, sales, and administrative staffs. Stations that would have suffered economic disaster with staffs of five engineers and five announcers, for example, were able to survive through developing combo staffs. Announcers entered trade schools for several weeks of intensive training in order to acquire the first class radio telephone operator's licenses. This was done to meet Commission requirements for license, and the announcers learned little more than how to pass the Commission's examination for persons seeking the first ticket. Possession of the ticket meant a little extra money for the announcer, and considerably less expense for the licensee. For the most part, the announcers learned absolutely nothing about equipment maintenance. Some licensees waggishly warned such ticket holders they would be fired if they ever attempted to work on station equipment.

Different class stations have different operator requirements. Paragraph (b) of the section under discussion requires the following:

In cases where an AM station is authorized for non-directional operation with power not over 10,000 watts, the routine operation of the transmitter may be handled by the holder of a third class ticket that has what the Commission terms a "broadcast endorsement." It should be noted that when a third class ticket holder is permitted to "read the meters," the rule also allows second and first class ticket holders to do the same. The operator must be on duty at the transmitter or remote control point and is actually in charge of the operation of the transmitter. Except at times when the operation of the station is under control of a first ticket holder, adjustments of the transmitting equipment by the third ticket holder are limited as follows:

1. Those necessary to turn the transmitter on and off.

2. Adjustments of **external** controls that may be required to compensate for voltage fluctuations in the power supply.

3. Adjustments of **external** controls to maintain the modulation of the transmitter within the prescribed limits.

4. Adjustments of **external** controls necessary to effect routine changes in operating power which are required by the station's license.

5. Adjustments of **external** controls necessary to effect operation in accordance with a National Defense Emergency Authorization during an Emergency Action Condition.

It is the **responsibility of the licensee** to be certain that the person required to perform these tasks, as well as others, such as announcing, making program and operator log entries, is properly instructed on how to handle the above five duties when not under the immediate supervision of a first class ticket holder.

Printed step-by-step instructions should be posted for those transmitter adjustments which the lesser grade operator is authorized to make. Some chief engineers post such instructions at all times, regardless of the class operator on duty, under an assumption that FCC field engineers will upgrade reports on the station. Should the transmitting apparatus be observed to be operating in any manner inconsistent with this subchapter (b) or the current license, and the holder of a first class ticket is not available and none of the above adjustments is effective in correcting the condition of improper operation, **the station must, under the rules, be turned off immediately**.

Paragraph (c) provides additional exceptions. If the routine operation of the transmitting apparatus at an AM station with power of 10,000 watts or less with a non-directional antenna is performed by anyone with less than a first ticket, the licensee must employ a first class ticket holder as a full-time member of the station or contract in writing for the services, on a part-time basis, of one or more of such operators. The first class ticket holder (usually a skilled engineer, in this case) shall perform transmitter maintenance and shall be promptly available at all times to correct conditions of improper operations beyond the scope of authority of the lesser grade operator on duty. When such services are on a contractual part-time basis, a signed copy of the agreement must be kept in the files of the station and at the transmitter control point and shall be made available for inspection upon request by any authorized representative of the Commission. A signed copy of the agreement must also be forwarded to the Commission and to the engineer in charge of the radio district in which the station is located within three days after the agreement is signed. It is not uncommon, under this rule, for one first class maintenance engineer to function virtually full-time for several stations that operate with less than 10kw of power and are non-directional.

Paragraph (d) states that the licensed operator on duty and in charge of an AM transmitter may, at the discretion of the licensee, be employed for other duties or for the operation of another radio station or stations in accordance with the class of operator's license which he holds and the rules and regulations covering such stations—provided, however, that such duties shall in nowise interfere with the proper operation of the AM transmitter.

Paragraph (e) provides that at all standard broadcast stations a complete inspection of all transmitting equipment in use shall be made, by an operator holding a first ticket, at least once each day, five days a week, with an interval of at least twelve hours between successive inspections. In the case of directional, remote-controlled operations, inspections must be made within one hour of pattern change **seven days a week**. These inspections shall include such tests, adjustments, and repairs as may be necessary to insure operation in conformance with the provisions of the rules and the station's license.

The operator requirements for FM stations may be found in Paragraph 73.265 of the Rules and are substantially the same as those found in 73.93, with some exceptions. Third class ticket holders may operate FM stations with power up to 25,000 watts ERP. A first class ticket holder must be on duty at FM stations with power in excess of 25,000 watts, either at the transmitter or at the remote control point. When operator requirements rules are violated, **it is the licensee who is held responsible**. Sec. 303 (m) of the Communications Act provides the FCC with authority to suspend operator licenses on such grounds as transmitting obscene words or willfully interfering with other broadcast signals.

But because the licensee is vulnerable to such costly punishment when operator rules are violated, management must know and enforce the rules which, essentially, are simple. If the station has a power of 10,000 watts or less and is non-directional, the above rules apply and third class ticket holders may function as operators. A first class ticket holder may be employed part-time. If the station has a directional antenna system, regardless of power, first class ticket holders are required to be on duty at all times, either at the transmitter or remote control point, and the alternative of hiring a part-time maintenance engineer is not available to the licensee.

Operator Licensing Procedures

Procurement of Radiotelephone licenses is not particularly difficult, but may be time consuming. Any citizen with average intelligence can either attend specialty schools or digest available study aids and pass the tests. Information regarding application for an operator license, place, date and time of examinations, and fees, may be obtained from the FCC's Field Engineering Bureau in Washington, D.C.

The Commission's examination consists of the following:

Radiotelephone Third Class Operator Permit:

Element 1 - Basic law. Provisions of laws, treaties and regulations.

Element 2 - Basic Operating Practice. Operating procedures and practices generally followed or required in communicating by radiotelephone stations.

Element 9 - Basic Broadcast. Special endorsement on Third Class Operator License. Specialize elementary theory and practice in operation of AM and FM stations.

Radiotelephone Second Class Operator License:

Element 1, 2.

Element 3 - Basic Radiotelephone. Technical, legal and other matters applicable to operating radiotelephone stations other than broadcast.

Radiotelephone First Class Operator License:

Elements 1, 2, and 3.

Element 4 - Advanced Radiotelephone. Advanced technical, legal and other matters particularly applicable to operating various classes of broadcast stations.

Operating Schedules

When the Commission issues a station license, the license specifies the hours of operation. Some full-time stations are authorized to operate unlimited hours, while the other full-time operations have specified hours. Still others must adhere to the local sunup to sunset rules, while others may operate under pre-sunrise authority (73.99). At this point, the four main classes of stations should be considered:

Class I: Stations that operate on clear channels and with from 10kw to 50kw power.

Class II: Secondary station on clear channels that operate with from 250 watts to 50kw power.

Class III: Stations sharing a regional channel with several similar stations, using a power of from 500 watts to 5kw. There are 41 regional channels and more than 2,000 Class III stations.

Class IV: Stations that operate on local channels with a maximum power of 1kw day and 250 watts night. There are six local channels, each occupied by 150 or more stations.

There are only one or two Class I stations on each clear channel. These, obviously, are the most desirable facilities in the industry because of maximum power allowance and interference-free signals. Class II clear channel stations often operate with directional antenna to avoid interferring with Class I clear channel operations. Some Class II stations are authorized to operate daytime only, to avoid interfering with the big Class I stations' service areas. AM transmitter skywaves travel further at night than during the day, and for this reason certain stations are required to shut down after local sundown and remain off the air until local sunup. No such problem exists with FM stations, and all, therefore, are licensed for unlimited operations.

Under Classes II, III, and IV, there are sub-classes that specify certain day and night power or require that operators broadcast from local sunup until sundown or sign on at 6:00 AM local time and sign off at sundown. Stations that operate on a power at night that is different from their daytime power, must reduce power at night at a time and to a level specified by the FCC authorization. Failure to do so may result in a heavy fine being levied on the licensee by the FCC. Stations with directional antenna systems **plus** different day and night power must also make power reductions and pattern switching at times specified by the FCC. In many instances, power and pattern switching are required to protect Canadian or Mexican stations. Such mutual signal protection is provided for in international agreements entered into by the U.S. Government with foreign governments.

PRACTICAL RESPONSIBILITIES

As indicated, management and non-technical staff members cannot logically be responsible for the technically correct operation of the radio station. But, as a practical matter, management must ascertain that every staff member is made as aware as possible of Commission requirements and urge each to assist engineering staff members in operating the station within the legal limits.

Example:

CHIEF ENGINEER: Mr. Program Director, I've asked you several times to have your announcers hold the audio levels down. They're pushing the limiting equipment too hard, and I'm afraid we're over-modulating the transmitter. And in case you don't know it, over modulation violates 73.55 of the Commission Rules and can subject the owners to a fine.

PROGRAM DIR: I've warned them about running the gain too high, but so far it hasn't worked. I'll just fire the next man you hear doing it.

MANAGER: Oh, Chief. Wanted to ask you something. Last night at 7 o'clock I didn't notice the power change. Our nighttime pattern doesn't cover my house too well, and at 8 o'clock, the signal was still coming in loud and clear.

CHIEF ENGINEER: I know it. Sent Bill out as usual to make the power and pattern change, but he had an auto accident and didn't get there until 8 o'clock. I'll see that it doesn't happen again, and meanwhile I've reported the violation to the FCC Field Office. I'm hoping they won't fine us this time. First time it's ever happened at my station.

MANAGER: And, Chief. You know our morning man doesn't have a first ticket and therefore isn't permitted to make entries on the operating log. Your studio maintenance man is supposed to make those entries during the morning show, and I happen to know he was ill this morning. How did you handle it?

CHIEF ENGINEER:	Simple, sir. I did it my self. I'm aware that with this 50,000 watt directional station we **must** have first class ticket holders on duty. But how did you happen to be so familiar with the technical rules?
MANAGER:	I once had a Chief Engineer who took time to explain such things to me. Not technical, mind you; just such things as operator requirements where I could help control and manage.
	By the way, our daytime operation over in Theirtown is due for some equipment tests tonight. What time do you plan on being over there?
CHIEF ENGINEER:	Now, you tell me, sir. You know about engineering!
MANAGER:	Of course. Those tests must be conducted between midnight and 6 AM, local time. But if you're going over early, I'd like to fly over with you and see how the place looks.

These are typical situations where management can discuss technical matters with engineering personnel. When the conversation enters the areas of phasers, power amplifier tubes, power supplies, and stereo generators, it is time for management to put its complete trust in the engineering department. Often, management may employ consultants (third parties) to occasionally inspect stations and provide a plain language report on the conduct of the engineering and technical aspects of the operation.

BUILDING THE TECHNICAL STAFF

Small station operations often do not have technical staffs per se. Maintenance at all levels is handled by contract or part-time personnel. These may be quasi-professional engineers who work for several commercial and non-commerical stations, or they may be radio-TV repairmen who have first class licenses. In some cases, managers or other members of a staff have a maintenance capability on all except transmitting equipment. In larger operations, regardless of market size, an elaborate engineering organization is required to keep the station on the air and to meet FCC operational requirements.

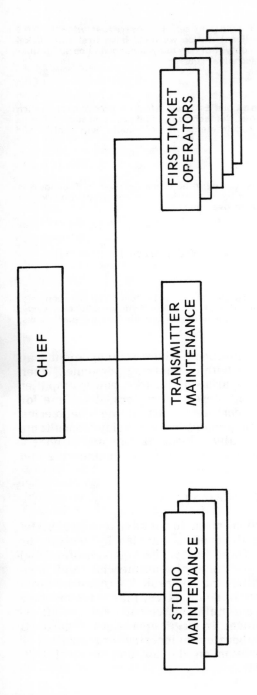

Fig. 27. Engineering Department Organization.

The Chief Engineer must be selected with care. He must have a background that includes **practical** maintenance experience, and have a valid first class ticket. He should be of a temperament that will allow him to work at odd hours and with members of the program and sales department. A degree in electrical engineering may be helpful, but absolutely is not required. Far more important than a degree is the applicant engineer's knowledge of various types of transmitters and an ability to "troubleshoot" and make repairs. Some of the best engineers in the industry have less than a college education; theirs, for the most part, is a pragmatic trade that calls for an ability to **do** rather than to theorize. Consulting engineers **theorize**. Chief Engineers execute the theories. It is safe to say that most engineering departments in U.S. radio are not highly departmentalized into transmitter and studio sections. An engineering staff of two or three persons usually performs all maintenance either as a team or on an as-available basis. A top maintenance man may finish repairing a studio console, then go directly to the transmitter and replace the final PA tube. In **most stations**, versatility is a must! In the big AM-FM-TV combines, considerable organization is required. The chart in Fig. 27 shows one organizational setup.

In AM-FM-TV combines (and there are dozens of them around the country) elaborate work rooms are constructed and equipped to handle FM and TV studio **and** transmitter maintenance, as well as AM studio maintenance. AM transmitter maintenance may be handled by the same staff, but in a work area located at the site of the AM transmitter. In some cases, stations have at least one engineer living on the AM transmitter site. This individual performs necessary maintenance, keeps the transmitter log, and often pulls an operator shift. Where possible, operators of AM-FM only operations will locate FM transmitters in the AM transmitter building and side mount the FM antenna on the AM tower. In these situations, it is possible to maintain a small maintenance crew because travel time between sites has been eliminated. One man may be able to handle studio maintenance, while another may be responsible for the transmitters. Engineering costs may be exorbitantly high unless management makes a careful study of the plant requirements. The work load may be high during a given period, while engineers may enjoy much idle time in periods when all equipment is operating troublefree. It is the idle time that becomes expensive to the operation. In most cases, it is advisable to operate with a minimum staff and have other qualified maintenance personnel on call. The rapport between engineers of competing facilities often is of such a nature that when serious trouble (such as the shorting of a plate transformer in a 50,000 watt AM transmitter) develops, technicians from several stations will converge at the trouble site. In other areas of serious trouble (such as an improperly operating phaser) consulting engineers are required to solve the problem. Some Chiefs are qualified to handle all maintenance; others simply don't have the theoretical background to build or maintain the complicated phasing equipment.

TECHNICAL PAPER WORK

The paper work relative to the technical or engineering department is extensive. Involved are:

The transmitter operating log
Daily equipment inspection and maintenance log
Quarterly tower light inspection
Monthly frequency check (optional - outside source)
Annual proof of performance
Technical interruption report (not required by FCC)

The transmitter operating log is the sticky one because entries must be made half-hourly by either the announcer-operator or by the operator on duty. In stations where combo men are used, the combo man not only keeps the program log, but also the operating log. Where combo men are not employed, the operating log is kept by a "meter reader," i.e., a man with a first, second, or third class ticket. In many cases, the meter reader is qualified only to read the meters; he is not qualified to perform maintenance.

The daily equipment inspection and maintenance log must be kept by a qualified maintenance man with a first class ticket. Combination announcer-operators usually are not qualified to handle this task. Unless otherwise specified in the license, the Commission requires that the inspection be made on all AM stations at least once each day, five days a week, with at least twelve hours between successive inspections (Par. 73.93-e).

The quarterly tower light inspection is made in accordance with Sec. 17.37 (c) and 17.38 (d) of the FCC rules. Operators conducting the inspection must describe the condition of all tower lights and associated tower lighting control devices (such as the Photoelectric cell, which automatically causes the lights to burn at sundown and turn off at sunup). The operator also observes the tower lights **daily** and enters time on and off on the daily transmitter maintenance log. In some cases, engineers incorporate the quarterly tower inspection into the daily log. Any adjustments, replacements, or repairs made on the lighting system must be noted on the maintenance log. The Federal Aviation Agency (FAA) is vitally concerned about proper tower lighting. The FAA must be notified if any tower lights are out and when they have been repaired and turned on again. The station is required to keep on hand at the transmitter site a spare stock of tower lights. The FCC will not consider an application for a construction permit (CP) until the FAA has agreed that the tower height and location will not interfere with air traffic in the area. Aeronautical section maps used by private, military, and commercial pilots pinpoint the location and height of every radio tower on the continent.

While the Commission does not require a monthly frequency check by outside sources, it does ask specific questions regarding frequency checks that make the practice feasible. For example, Paragraph 11 of FCC Form 301 (application for new broadcast station) asks:

"By what method and how often will regular checks of the calibration of the frequency monitor be repeated?"

The paragraph also asks for the date and time of the checks and the name of the agency making the check or the method used to make the check. The form then asks for the actual measurement and asks that the inspector indicate whether the reading was too high or too low. A station operating on 1190 kHz, for example, would be "within 20 Hz tolerance" if a check indicated frequency fluctuations between 1,189,980 and 1,119,020 Hz per second (PS). In FM, the tolerance is 200 Hz, up or down.

The annual proof of performance report is required of each station. To produce this report, engineers check (1) frequency response, (2) noise, and (3) distortion. "Noise" is the amount of noise generated and placed on the transmitter carrier by studio equipment, the transmitter itself, or by telephone lines. "Distortion" is a measurement of the combined audio harmonics of the audio frequency range. "Frequency Response" measurements indicate the ability of the audio and transmitting equipment to reproduce sounds faithfully. Paragraph 73.47 of FCC rules details requirements for equipment performance measurements.

The technical interruption report is an intracompany form devised by the McLendon Corporation to keep the licensee and top management abreast of equipment failures and resulting losses of program time. Under McLendon policy, any "outage" exceeding one minute must be reported in detail to the General Manager of the facility and the National Director of Engineering. Repeated outages may indicate a need for new equipment because such outages can seriously hamper audience continuity.

TECHNICAL EQUIPMENT

Technical equipment for AM stations is divided into six main categories. These are:

1. Transmitting
2. Antenna
3. Studio
4. Two-way
5. Test
6. Microwave

Transmitting devices include the transmitter, frequency monitor, modulation monitor, and limiting amplifier. Antenna devices include the antenna (tower), antenna tuning unit, ground system, transmission lines, and lighting system. Directional antenna systems include phasing components. Studio equipment consists of audio consoles, sound reproduction devices (turntables, tape machines), speakers, and microphones. When a station is authorized to operate by remote control, the remote control unit becomes a part of the studio and transmitting equipment. Technical equipment for the FM station is essentially the same, except that in FM there is no elaborate ground system for the antenna. In cases where FM operators broadcast in stereo, additional equipment, such as a stereo generator and SCA (Sub Carrier Authorization), is required. Many FM stations realize considerable income from SCA's through the programing of background music for store and office consumption. Such service usually is sold to outside contractors on a flat fee or commission plan. Two-way equipment normally is made up of a short wave base station and various mobile units employed in on-the-spot news coverage or in remote broadcasts. Most two-way units employ FM techniques, and the quality is sufficient for music as well as voice remotecasts.

Test equipment includes field strength meters, tube testers, oscilloscopes, ohmmeters, vacuum tube voltmeters and other devices for checking audio and radio frequency circuitry. Many small stations have little test equipment, relying upon contract engineers to supply such equipment when maintenance is being performed. Microwave equipment is utilized, in most cases, to replace landlines in the transmission of programing from studio to transmitter. If capital is available, considerable money can be saved in the long run by use of the microwave technique. For example, a $6,000 system would pay for itself in five years if monthly program lines cost $100 per month. Furthermore, a quality system will result in fewer outages. The student who is more than casually interested in the technical aspects of radio broadcasting is referred to **AM-FM Broadcast Station Planning Guide**, by Harry A. Etkin, and published by TAB BOOKS, Blue Ridge Summit, Pa.

AM & FM DIFFERENCES

Glenn Callison's explanation of the differences between AM and FM radio should be supported by his elaboration in more technical terms. AM means Amplitude Modulated. Amplitude, in the broadcast sense, means the extent or range of a sound. Modulation, in its simplest form, means regulated variation. Therefore, when a signal is Amplitude Modulated it is varied by the audio placed on the carrier. The carrier is the steady radio frequency impulse generated by the transmitter on the assigned frequency of the broadcast band. On an oscilloscope, the carrier is represented by a wide band across the CRT (Cathode Ray Tube). When voice, music, or other sounds are impressed on the carrier, the amplitude (size) of the carrier is varied in accordance with the audio frequency of the voice or music and is represented by waveforms on the CRT.

FM means Frequency Modulation. Frequency, in the broadcast sense, means the number of complete oscillations per second of an electromagnetic wave. While modulation of an AM station changes the size of the carrier, modulation of an FM station changes the frequency of the carrier.

All AM stations are capable of modulating from 50 to 7,500 Hz per second (HzPS). Many AM transmitters have a greater frequency range, but modulation of over 10,000 HzPS causes "splatter" and interferes with adjacent channels. FM transmitters, on the other hand, operate up to 15,000 HzPS without interfering with adjacent channels. It is this range of modulation that gives FM stations a better quality signal (this, along with an FM receiver's superior ability to detect the FM signal). As one engineer expressed it, "The FM signal

AMPLITUDE MODULATION

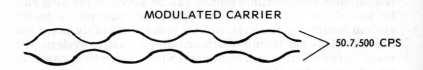

UNMODULATED CARRIER

MODULATED CARRIER

50.7,500 CPS

Fig. 28. Amplitude Modulation.

FREQUENCY MODULATION

MODULATED

UNMODULATED

30-15,000 CPS

Fig. 29. Frequency Modulation.

provides for dynamic expansion; that is to say, it has a greater range for the variation of music of all types, particularly classical music." The rationale, of course, is in the FM frequency range of from 30 to 15,000 HzPS. Sound reaching 10,000 HzPS, for example, is filtered at the top on AM stations where the "safe" frequency range is from 50 to 7,500 HzPS. When most FM stations first went on the air in the early 50's, only lush, good music, or classical music was played. It was in this area of programing that FM stations could excel. The practice was so widespread that lush, big-band instrumentals came to be known as "FM Music." There never has been music aesthetically classified as FM Music, and contemporary FM stations pretty well dissolved the notion by programing everything from Country & Western to Soul Music. Many FM stations, such as KOST in Los Angeles, became extremely profitable by establishing formats that sounded like an AM station. For years, there was an unwritten rule that FM stations would not only program "FM Music" but would also lose money. But as the AM frequency spectrum tightened and finally virtually closed, more and more operators looked to FM as a medium of total broadcast service and as a means of making money. FM stations, in many cases, were purchased or built by AM licensees as "insurance" against the day when enough FM receivers were available to make FM broadcasting profitable. Commercial FM broadcasting was authorized by the FCC to begin Jan. 1, 1941. Its growth has been tormentingly slow, but steady.

There are 100 channels in steps of 200 kHz assigned to the broadcast spectrum to FM broadcasting in the U.S. Eighty of these are commercial channels and 20 are allocated to non-commercial educational uses. In AM, there are 107 channels in steps of 10 kHz each. There are three classes of FM stations. These are:

Class A: Low powered with maximum of 3kw effective radiated power (ERP).
Class B: Maximum power of 50kw ERP.
Class C: Maximum power of 100kw ERP.

An important factor in FM broadcasting is the height of the antenna above surrounding terrain, as the FM signal follows essentially a line-of-sight course. Where advertisers look to an AM station's power and frequency to determine coverage potential, they look to the FM station's antenna height above average terrain. In AM, the tower is the antenna. In FM, the antenna is often called a radiator and is usually side-mounted on a tower.

The development of stereophonic broadcasting has been in the FM field. Reduced to its simplest terms, stereo broadcasting means a transmitter is producing dual audio signals. The term **stereophonic** is defined as a three-dimensional effect of auditory perspective. In actual practice, it means the separation of elements of music and voice to produce a greater presence for the radio listener. In stereophonic broadcasting, everything is in two's. When music is recorded in stereo, for example, two microphones may be used—one picking up brass and reeds while another picks up strings and lyrics. Properly phased, good separation is achieved in the recording. When the music reaches the turntable or tape machine, styli (needles) detect the separation and feed the impulses into **separate** left and right audio channels. The FM station equipped with a **stereo generator** thus radiates part of the music on the main channel, with the other part being radiated on a sub-carrier. At the listener level, **stereo tuners** pick up the dual signals and relay them to listeners through two speaker systems. When speakers are properly spaced, the effect is to place the listener in the orchestra. In the early 70's, engineers and scientists were working on **quadrophonics** which would require **four** separate channels.

While many broadcast engineers contend that AM stereo is feasible, little work has been done in the U.S. toward developing the theory. Kahn Research Laboratories in the late 1960's perfected a technique and put it to use at XTRA in Mexico. In the early 1970's, it still had not been approved for regular use in the U.S. The AM carrier, as with FM, has sidebands. The AM stereo technique is to place sound not only on the main carrier, but also on one of the sidebands. To pick up the signal(s), one has but to turn on two AM receivers and detune one of them to the right or left to pick up the stereo broadcast. The effect is about the same as on FM. Even if AM stereocasting is proved practical, it is unlikely that the practice will challenge FM's lead in the field.

AUTOMATION

In broadcasters' long struggle to find more economic methods of producing programing, many have successfully tried various kinds and levels of automation equipment. With some formats, automation has worked well; in others, not so well. This text will explore situations in which this specialized equipment has succeeded or failed. Most major broadcast equipment manufacturers produce automation equipment in one form or another. In most modern systems, magnetic tape machinery is employed, as opposed to some of the early systems (such as the Seaburg record player) that employed disc records. Broadcasters use automation equipment for one purpose: **to cut personnel costs.** If the equipment can accomplish this goal, and produce attractive programing, its use has been successful. If not; if programing suffers and more personnel is needed, it has failed.

Automation takes different forms. A control room that has tape cartridge equipment often is said to be partially automated. In a sense, this is true. During the days before tape machines when announcers or operators had to "cue up" commercials on disc, there was no question about the manual operation of the control room. The arrival of tape cartridges constituted such an improvement over the old method that users indeed thought automation had arrived. Equipment manufacturers such as Ampex developed remote controlled reel-to-reel equipment that allowed announcers and operators to "punch up" a taped program or spot. It was during the early 50's that such progress was being made. And with each passing NAB Convention, more automation miracles were brought to broadcasters' attention. At its inception, automation was used primarily in "good music" stations. Here, a "brain" would maintain certain program sequences that were pre-set by the operator. Reel-to-reel tape machines within an automation "package" are loaded with program features such as music, commercials, public service announcements, and news. **Simple** formats are easy to program with automation. The "brain" that has been pre-set may start a given hour of programing with a piece of instrumental music. The following functions may then be executed:

1. Commercial-Commercial
2. Public Service Announcement
3. Vocal
4. Small Group Instrumental
5. Lush, big-band instrumental
6. Novelty beat instrumental
7. Vocal
8. Commercial-Commercial
9. Public Service Announcement
10. News

This procedure would constitute a program cycle. In the following cycle, the "brain" may call upon the same tape machines to produce music, commercials, public service announcements, or news, but each such machine would produce a different sequence of material in each cycle. Once the music is programed or placed onto tape, the tasks of pre-recording other program material are relatively simple. An operator may in an hour pre-tape enough commercials and public service announcements to run the station for twenty-four hours. With the music pre-recorded on tape, some equipment manufacturers claim broadcasters may do six hours programing in thirty minutes. What broadcasters have come to call "juke boxes" may also be programed by automation. Different equipment is required, but the results are the same. The so-called Top 40 stations primarily use cartridge and carousel equipment. The music and commercials, which must be changed often, are placed on cartridge, while news, PSA's and other program matter may be placed on reel-to-reel machine.

A story is told of a New Mexico broadcaster who automated his station to the extent that the equipment would turn on his coffee pot at 5:00 AM, his bedside alarm at 5:45 AM, his transmitter at 5:55 AM, and his control room automation equipment at 6:00 AM. His task after that was to drink the coffee, sell time, write commercials, pre-record them onto the automation equipment for the next day, then return to bed. Automation has not produced such meccas, but in many cases it has fulfilled its promises. In a simple format, three announcers can do the work of six with automation. Once a working procedure is established, it becomes a matter of changing the music on the reel-to-reel equipment or in the carousel. One competent announcer may pre-record news, make music changes, keep the log, and function (if he has the proper ticket) as the operator.

Automation has extended even into the area of "meter reading." The equipment is geared to make competent checks of the transmitter every half hour. When he installed a Schaffer Package at KOST in Los Angeles, McLendon wired owner Paul Schaffer that he thought the trial run had been successful. "And during the late hours, we thought we heard the darn thing groan, "McLendon ended his telegram.

But automation has its limitations. It is almost impossible to defeat the "canned" sound, although some stations have come close. Expert programers may spend much more than thirty minutes for each six hours of airworthy material and produce a "live" overall sound. Few such programers exist and, as a result, most automated stations **sound** automated. Many automated stations have a morale problem among staff members. One station in Detroit seemed deserted to visitors.

One man occupied the complex control room; one girl occupied the general office. The manager and salesmen were on the street. Visitors felt eerie upon entering by seeing only one lone girl, working quietly at an electric typewriter.

Some automated stations use automatic program logging equipment. This equipment simply is a tape machine that records at approximately 1⅞ inches per second (IPS) the day's programing. Twenty-four hours of programing may be recorded on a 7 inch reel of ¼ inch tape. At the end of each day, the tape is boxed, labeled, and filed, the same as for a manually-kept log. At license renewal time, logs covering the composite week are, pulled, transcribed, and sent to the Commission along with the tapes themselves and the other required renewal application materials. In programing a station where autologging devices are used, programers prepare the day's tapes from work sheets that indicate the sequence in which program material will be aired.

Transcription of the tape at license renewal time may be expedited by filing the work sheet with the tape. Transcription involves determining precisely how much commercial matter, public affairs, "others" programing, and how many PSA's are run during the composite week. While transcribing the tapes is a tremendous task, many operators find it just as easy as analyzing manually kept logs.

In some cases, where stations have lost their "live" sound, programers have decided to keep the equipment, but use live announcers to give news, and time and temperature checks. Music, in these instances, is "punched up," on the equipment, along with commercials and other material. In other cases, music is programed in sets of twelve to fourteen minutes with the live announcer breaking in for commercial, PSA clusters, and news. It is not uncommon to find automation equipment in service only to provide the music "sweeps."

Automation has not reached a peak of perfection. Each year's work by electronic engineers and scientists brings innovations. Some have started coupling automation equipment to computers where everything from invoicing to billing to logging is handled by information punched into cards or recorded on magnetic tape. Such sophistication may be, as a practical matter, years away. Costs are high, and maintenance is difficult and expensive. But once these obstacles are overcome, we could see licensees conducting one-man (woman) operations. Different voices may be summoned from a stockpile much as movie makers draw various stock

327

scenes from a library. Machines would prepare commercial continuity from facts gathered by the salesmen or presented by the agency or client via telephone. It is doubtful, however, that anything will ever completely replace the warmth and grace of the live human voice on the airwaves. Machines only recreate and mimic; they cannot create.

CHAPTER 6

Reference Material for Management

Rules of the FCC are set forth in ten volumes, only two of which are of interest to the commercial broadcaster. Volume I covers Commission organization, practice and procedure, commercial radio operators, construction, marking and lighting of antenna structures, and FCC employee responsibilities and conduct. Volume III deals with radio broadcast services (Part 74), experimental, auxiliary, special broadcast, and other program distribution services.

Insofar as radio broadcasters are concerned, a key function of the Commission is the general regulation of commercial broadcasting. This regulation falls into three main phases.

"The first is the allocation of space in the radio frequency spectrum to the broadcast services and to many non-broadcast services which must also be accommodated. In view of the tremendously increased use of radio technology in recent decades, the competing demands for frequencies are among the Commission's most pressing problems. Fortunately, as technology has advanced, frequencies higher and higher in the spectrum have become usable. Apart from the frequencies used for commercial broadcasting, frequencies in other portions of the spectrum are allocated for 'broadcast auxiliary' use by remote pickup and other transmitters auxiliary to main broadcast stations.

"The second phase of regulation is the assignment of stations in each service within the allocated frequency bands, with specified location, frequency, and power. The chief consideration, though by no means the only one, is to avoid interference with other stations on the same channel (frequency) or channels adjacent in the spectrum. If his application is granted, an applicant for a new station or for changed facilities receives a construction permit (CP). Later, when the station is built and proves it is capable of operating as proposed (FCC Form 302), a license to operate is issued.

"The third phase is regulation of existing stations; inspections to see that stations are operating in accordance with Commission rules and technical provisions of their authorizations, modifying the authorizations when necessary, assigning their call letters, licensing transmitter operators, processing requests to assign the license to another party or transfer control of the licensee corporation, and processing applications for renewal of license. At renewal time, the Commission reviews the station's record to see whether it is operating in the public interest."

The third phase is of major significance to the non-technical professional broadcaster because it is in seeing that broadcasters operate **in the public interest** that the Commission travels its most uncharted and unpredictable paths. From this phase of regulation has developed The Fairness Doctrine, the new Sec. VI, The Sec. 315 Primer, and scores of other rules, directives, policies, and statutes. **Interpreting FCC Broadcast Rules & Regulations**, by the Editors of Broadcast Management and Engineering Magazine and published by TAB Books, is a reliable source of information on FCC rules for the student as well as the working broadcaster. **Broadcasting Yearbook**, updated and published annually, also is a reliable source.

Composition

The Commission is made up of five bureaus. These include the Broadcast Bureau, with which broadcasters are most concerned, and the bureaus dealing with common carriers, safety and special radio services, field engineering, and CATV. The FCC is an independent government agency and is responsible only to Congress. There are seven commissioners, appointed by the President with Senate advice and consent. The chairman of the Commission is named by the President. Each member is appointed for seven years. The Commission's first budget was $1,146,000 and it had a staff of 442 persons. Thirty-six years later, the budget had reached $21,000,000.

The Chairman presides at all meetings. He coordinates and organizes its work and represents it in legislative matters and in communications with other Government departments and agencies. If the Chairman is absent or the office is vacant, the Commission designates one of its members to act temporarily as chairman.

The Executive Director coordinates all activities of all staff units. He is directly responsible for internal administrative matters including personnel, budget planning, and implementation of the Public Information Act of 1966. He reports directly to the Commission and works under the supervision of the Chairman, assisting him in carrying out the Commission's organizational and administrative functions.

The Chief Engineer and the General Counsel advise the Commission on engineering or legal matters involved in establishing policy and implementing it. The two act in regulatory areas that exceed the responsibility of a single bureau. They also act in international communications matters. The General Counsel coordinates preparation of the Commission's legislative program and represents the Commission in the courts.

The Bureaus

Five bureaus conduct the principal operations of the Commission. The Broadcast Bureau regulates broadcast stations and related facilities. The Common Carrier Bureau regulates wire and radio communications common carriers. The Safety and Special Radio Services Bureau regulates all other radio stations, except experimental stations, including amateur stations and others engaged in communication for safety, commercial or personal purposes. These "exception" stations are regulated by the Broadcast Bureau. The Field Engineering Bureau detects violations of radio regulations, monitors radio transmissions, inspects stations, investigates complaints of radio frequency interference, and issues violation notices. The Bureau maintains field offices and monitoring stations throughout the U.S. It examines and licenses radio operators, processes applications for painting, lighting, and placement of antenna towers, and furnishes direction-finding aid for ships and aircraft in distress. The CATV Bureau develops and implements a regulatory program for community antenna television systems and community antenna relay stations.

The Secretary

Broadcasters have more contact with the Office of the Secretary than with any other single unit of the Commission. The Secretary signs the majority of the Commission's correspondence, orders, permits, licenses, and other instruments of authorization, and is custodian of the Commission's seal. He receives papers mailed to the commission and filed with it. He is responsible for the preparation and custody of permanent records of Commission actions, and for official dockets of hearing and rule making proceedings, insuring their accuracy, authenticity, and completeness. He maintains the legislative history of Commission Rules, and comprehensive library and dockets reference facilities. He is responsible for publication of documents in the Federal Register and FCC Reports, and for printing of the Commission Rules.

Hearings

The Office of Hearing Examiners, the Review Board, and the Office of Opinions and Review are responsible for decisions in hearing cases. The Hearing Examiners preside over hearing cases and issue Initial Decisions. Most Initial Decisions are subject to review by the five-member Review Board, a permanent body composed of senior Commission employees. Initial Decisions may also be reviewed by one or more Commissioners designated by the Commission. In such cases, the Board or Commissioner issues a final decision, subject to Commission review. In other cases, the Initial Decision is reviewed directly by the Commission. The Office of Opinion and Review assists and advises the Commission in the review of Initial Decisions and in drafting final decisions.

The Commission may order a hearing in a wide variety of matters. For example, when two or more parties apply for a single available radio or television facility in a city, a hearing must be held to decide which applicant will best serve the public "interest, convenience, and necessity." Sometimes, even if there is only a single applicant for the facility, there may be a hearing to determine whether basic licensing qualifications—technical or personal—have been met. There may also be hearings in other broadcast cases, as when questions are raised about the validity of a proposed license transfer. Disciplinary actions, involving revocation or suspension of station licenses, are an important hearing category. The Commission emphasizes that a hearing is not always ordered when an application is filed or some other part of the Commission's authority is invoked. Only if there is an impediment to final action, as in the filing of a mutually exclusive application, or if there is some question which cannot be resolved without further inquiry, will a hearing be scheduled. Most applications or other authorization requests are disposed of without a hearing.

THE FTC

The Federal Trade Commission's Bureau of Consumer Protection is concerned with misleading and fradulent advertising. It has the power to punish advertisers and their advertising agencies when deceptive or misleading claims or statements are made in **any** medium. Broadcasters are not subject to FTC rules and regulations. Certain federal statutes that deal with consumer protection, such as lotteries and the Truth in Lending Laws, **do** affect broadcasters, and there is evidence to indicate an informal melding of some FTC and FCC jurisdictions to protect "the public interest." In 1969, the chairmen of the FCC and the FTC and members of their staffs met to explore the possibility of conducting joint hearings on television advertising beamed at children. The January, 1971 issue of **FTC News Summary** said: "The two agency heads agree that the matter should be pursued by a joint FTC-FCC committee and that it should be discussed by each chairman with other members of both commissions."

In recent years, the FTC has urged broadcasters to cooperate with it in cleaning up misleading advertising, and the FCC has supported such requests. For example, an FTC regulation which became effective in 1969, deals with games of chance in the gasoline and food retailing businesses. The regulations are divided into two parts:

1. The **conduct** of the game.
2. The **advertising** and **promotion** of the game.

The rules provide that it constitutes an unfair and deceptive act or practice for the sponsor to:

(a) Fail to mix, distribute and disburse all game "pieces" (the slips of paper, tokens, other paraphernalia of the game) on a random basis. The sponsor of the game must also keep records so that it may demonstrate to the FTC that such distribution was random.

(b) The game must be such that it is incapable of being "broken" or solved in such a manner that winning game "pieces" can be identified or predetermined prior to their random distribution to the public.

(c) In addition, the game may not be terminated prior to the distribution of all the game pieces, regardless of the scheduled termination date. For example, if the game is scheduled to end on December 1, and all of the game pieces have not been distributed as of that date, the game must continue until all the pieces have been distributed to the public.

(d) Additional winning game pieces may not be added during the course of the game or the prize structure of the game replenished while it is in progress, i.e., more prizes cannot be "seeded" to stimulate sagging interest in the game.

All advertising copy dealing with games described above must conform to certain standards. As part of each advertisement, the copy must include all five of the following elements:

(a) The exact number of prizes in each category or denomination must be made available during the game. For example, the announcements must specifically refer to **two** automobiles, or **five** separate $1,000 prizes and not just general statements that automobiles or $1,000 prizes are to be given away—without identifying **how many** of each.

(b) The odds of winning each such prize—if the prize value is $25 or more. For example, "Each piece has one chance in one million of winning first prize, one chance in 30,000 of winning second prize, etc." If the game is to last longer than 30 days, the odds broadcast must be revised each week to reflect the number of prizes still available.

(c) The geographic area covered by the game (for example, nationwide, Chicago area, San Francisco, etc.).

(d) The total number of retail outlets participating in the game (i.e., at 200 neighborhood Shell stations).

(e) The date the game ends.

In addition, there are limitations on advertising more than one game by any food or gasoline retailer in a given area. If, for example, X gas company has been running a game for three months, it must be three months after the end of that game before the station may air copy advertising a new game to be carried by the same retail outlets. (i.e., The waiting period between games must be at least as long as the length of the earlier game.)

Both the sponsor **and** the broadcaster have the duty of complying with these requirements.

To the broadcaster, it is inconsequential that an FTC rule does not apply to him. It is enough that the Commission supports FTC efforts to clean up hanky-panky offers, promotions, and contests. To remain free of the Commission's inquiries, the broadcaster must inform himself of FTC requirements and make every reasonable effort to comply with them. If there is the slightest doubt about the legality or morality of a promotion or piece of copy, legal counsel should be obtained. It should be noted that in applications for construction permits and applications for transfer of control, the Commission pointedly asks whether the applicant is involved in any litigation regarding restraint of trade, monopolies, etc. The Commission wants licensees to remain **legally clean**; and any licensee who becomes involved in an FTC investigation may expect to be questioned either when he applies for a CP, seeks Commission approval of a license transfer, or asks that his license be renewed.

The Bureau of Consumer Protection (FTC) has urged advertising agencies to help in cleaning up fraudulent or misleading advertising. Too often, the FTC doesn't know about an advertising campaign until it is over! Therefore, its spokesmen have pleaded with ad men on Madison Avenue and elsewhere to assist. Even after the FTC is informed of a misleading advertising campaign, it takes years to get results on cease and desist orders. ONE SPOKESMAN LAMENTED: "It took us 16 years to get the 'liver' out of Carter's Little Liver Pills." In the early 70's, the FTC still was in court protesting Geritol's claim that the tonic is a cure for "tired blood."

Radio stations are not immune to FTC regulations and rules when they step across the line and engage in unfair trade practices. An example is the case of WQXY-FM in Baton Rouge, La. Without admitting guilt, the station agreed to stop using unusual promotional practices during rating periods. The practice is termed "hyping" in the broadcast industry. In the case cited, the station launched a $30,000 giveaway campaign during a period in which one of the rating companies was conducting a survey. While no competitor was identified in the **FTC News Summary** (January - 1971) that carried the story, some competitor obviously had complained to the FTC. Investigation showed that the offender not only had never conducted an audience promotion of such magnitude, but it rarely conducted an audience promotion of any kind. After the investigation was completed, the FTC accepted a consent order prohibiting WQXY-FM from using unusual promotional practices designed to temporarily increase audience size during a rating period.

As a practical matter, the effectiveness of hyping died when major advertising agencies stopped using results of a single rating in making schedule changes. Furthermore, all rating services make special note of hyping when publishing a report. And since buyers know a station's position can be improved by an extraordinary promotion, they usually decline to make a buy based on a single report. When a station can show that its ratings have improved consistently over a long period of time, (i.e., two consecutive reports) agencies usually react favorably.

335

LOCAL LAWS

There are few local laws that actually interfere with the broadcasters' day-to-day activities. But where laws affecting the station do exist they should be scrupulously obeyed. Failure to do so could result in damage to the station's image and, far worse, inspire a strike application when the station's license is next up for renewal. There invariably are city, county, and state taxes to pay on station equipment, including office furniture and machines. A Milwaukee broadcaster complained once that he couldn't do station promotional stunts, such as DJ marathons in store windows, because the state enforced a law against self-inflicted punishment. Some cities and states have strict laws prohibiting red, green, or blue lights on mobile news units. Others prohibit using mobile news station wagons as auxiliary or emergency ambulance units. The broadcaster opening up in a new area, whether he is building a new station or buying an existing one, should make contact with the local city or district attorney and acquaint himself with the local rules. Better still, he should retain the services of a local attorney who can more thoroughly check the rules for him.

A FAIRNESS DOCTRINE SUMMARY

The FCC issued The Fairness Doctrine in 1949 to explain its position on licensee handling of controversial issues of public importance. The Doctrine represented a culmination of ideas on and efforts toward development of editorial freedom for broadcasting. It reversed earlier thinking that broadcasters could not be advocates, that the private or personal opinions of the licensee could not be expressed over the airwaves, that a free radio cannot be used to advocate the causes of the licensee, and that with the limitations in frequencies inherent in the nature of radio, the public interest can not be served by a dedication of any broadcast facility to the support of partisan ends. During the so-called golden days of radio when the medium was the country's primary source of entertainment, the issue never arose. Radio entertained! Networks were formed to report political conventions and baseball games. Franklin D. Roosevelt and some of his predecessors used radio to talk to the electorate. But no broadcaster tried advocating anything.

The issue of licensee editorializing didn't develop until 1941 when The Mayflower Broadcasting Corporation filed an application for a construction permit, requesting the frequency and power of WAAB in Boston. Briefly, WAAB, starting in 1937 and continuing through most of 1938, broadcast "editorials" urging the election of various candidates for political office or supporting one side or the other in public controversies. WAAB officials freely admitted broadcasting the editorials and promised not to repeat the "offense." Mayflower's application for a CP on WAAB's frequency was denied for several reasons, but the case served to effectively halt radio editorializing for around nine years. In its decision and order resulting from the hearing, the Commission concluded:

A truly free radio cannot be used to advocate the causes of the licensee.

In August, 1944, the Commission called a hearing during its consideration of the application for renewal of license by WHKC. The hearing resulted from a petition filed in June, 1944 by the UAW-CIO alleging that the licensee was throttling free speech and therefore not operating in the public interest for the following reasons:

(a) The station had a policy not to permit the sale of time for programs which solicited memberships, discussed controversial subjects, race, religion, and politics.

(b) The station did not apply this practice uniformly; on the contrary, it applied the policy "strictly to those with whom the management of Station WHKC disagrees, including petitioners, and loosely or not at all with respect to others."

(c) The station unfairly censored scripts submitted by petitioners.

WHKC management, in essence, argued that its policy was based upon the provisions of the Code of the National Association of Broadcasters. In October, 1944, however, the station and the UAW-CIO filed a joint motion, as follows, in part:

"The record of the hearing discloses that Station WHKC in the past had pursued a policy which it believed to be in the best interest of the public and at no time did the station believe that the application of the policy was contrary to the interests of labor. The recorded testimony further discloses that at the time of the hearing the station enunciated a revised policy which it had adopted prior to the hearing which it intends to follow in the future."

The crux of the policy was as follows:

1. Applications for time to be considered only on merit.

2. With respect to public issues, the station's policy will be one of open-mindedness and impartiality.

3. WHKC will make time available for the full and free

discussion of public issues.

4. When time is refused for such discussion, reasons will be set forth in writing.

5. Station will not censor broadcast matter, except in cases where a law or Commission regulation will be violated.

6. Station will ascertain that all important sides of any public issue are aired. The petition continued. "The parties (WHKC-UAW-CIO) believe that the above statement of policy properly sets forth the duties of a licensee under the Communications Act of 1934 with respect to the availability of time for discussion of issues of public importance, the censoring of scripts by the licensees, and the maintenance of an overall program balance."

In its consideration of the joint motion, the Commission pointed out the "duty of each station licensee to be sensitive to the problems of public concern in the community and to make sufficient time available, on a nondiscriminatory basis, for full disclosure thereof, without any kind of censorship which would undertake to impose the views of the licensee upon the material to be broadcast."

Before dismissing the proceeding in June, 1945, and granting the joint motion, the Commission further stated:

> "The Commission recognizes that good program balance may not permit the sale or donation of time to all who may seek it for such purposes and that difficult problems calling for careful judgement on the part of station management may be involved in deciding among applicants for time when all cannot be accommodated. However, competent management should be able to meet such problems in the public interest and with fairness to all concerned. The fact that it places an arduous task on management should not be made a reason for evading the issue by a strict rule against the sale of time for any programs of the type mentioned."

The Scott Case developed additional thinking by the Commission and broadcasters on the subject of public affairs. On March 27, 1945, Robert Harold Scott of Palo Alto, California, filed a petition requesting that the Commission revoke the licenses of radio station KQW in San Jose, California, and of KPO and KFRC in San Francisco. The ground on which the petitioner sought to have the Commission take this action was that these stations had refused to make any time available to him, by sale or otherwise, for the broadcasting of talks on the subject of atheism, while they had permitted the use of their facilities for direct statements and arguments against atheism.

The stations argued that the broadcasting of atheistic talks would not be in the public interest. The Commission denied Scott's petition, but made, in essence, this observation:

> Stations cannot make time available for all possible points of view. But this fact cannot serve as a basis for denying time to those holding unpopular viewpoints.

The Commission thus warned licensees not to use its decision in the Scott case as precedent for future decisions involving public controversial issues.

On June 1, 1949, the Commission issued its report "In the Matter of Editorializing by Broadcast Licensees." Basically, it reversed the previous policy toward editorials brought out in the Mayflower decision. This report came to be called The Fairness Doctrine, and its interpretation by licensees led to the widespread broadcasting of editorial views on the air and affirmative efforts by licensees to involve their stations in public affairs.

The Doctrine itself deals primarily with the Commission's rationale supporting its position that radio stations should deal with public issues. The Commission's "Fairness Primer," adopted July 1, 1964, went to the heart of licensee problems of living with the Doctrine and did much to clarify the intent of the document. The FCC's stated purpose of the Primer was to "advise broadcast licensees and **members of the public** of the rights, obligations, and responsibilities of such licensees under the Commission's Fairness Doctrine, which is applicable in any case in which broadcast facilities are used for the discussion of a controversial issue of public importance."

THE FAIRNESS PRIMER

In the fourteen year period between issuance of The Fairness Doctrine and the adoption of the Fairness Primer, the Commission received hundreds of complaints that stations had violated provisions of the Doctrine. When complaints appeared legitimate and well founded, the Commission made a ruling on whether the broadcaster had acted "in good faith" or had exercised "good judgment." In adopting the Primer, the Commission drew from its files cases that seemed to cover the entire spectrum of human complaint and published them as examples of how the Doctrine should be interpreted.

Selections from Commission Rulings

Civil rights as controversial issue: In response to a Commission inquiry, a station advised the Commission, in a letter dated March 6, 1950, that it had broadcast editorial programs in support of a National Fair Employment Practices Commission on January 15-17, 1950, and that it had taken no affirmative steps to encourage and implement the presentation of points of view with respect to these matters which differed from the point of view expressed by the station.

Ruling: The establishment of a National Fair Employment Practices Commission constitutes a controversial question of public importance so as to impose upon the licensee the affirmative duty to aid and encourage the broadcast of opposing views. It is a matter of common knowledge that the establishment of a National Fair Employment Practices Commission is a subject that has been actively controverted by members of the public and by members of the Congress of the United States and that in the course of that controversy numerous differing views have been espoused. The broadcast by the station of a relatively large number of programs relating to this matter over a period of three days indicates an awareness of its importance and raises the assumption that at least one of the purposes of the broadcasts was to influence public opinion. In our report In the Matter of Editorializing by Broadcast Licensees, we stated that:

In appraising the record of a station in presenting programs concerning a controversial bill pending before the Congress of the United States, if the record disclosed that the licensee had permitted only advocates of the bill's enactment to utilize its facilities to the exclusion of its opponents, it is clear that no independent appraisal of the bill's merits by the Commission would be required to reach a determination that the licensee had misconstrued its duties and obligations as a person licensed to serve the public interest.

In light of the foregoing the conduct of the licensee was not in accord with the principles set forth in the report. (New Broadcasting Co. (WLIB), 6 R.R. 258, April 12, 1950.)

Political spot announcements: In an election an attempt was made to promote campaign contributions to the candidates of the two major parties through the use of spot announcements on broadcast stations. Certain broadcast stations raised the question whether the airing of such announcements imposed an obligation under Section 315 of the

Act and-or the Fairness Doctrine to broadcast such special announcements for all candidates running for a particular office in a given election.

Ruling: The "equal opportunities" provision of Section 315 applies only to uses by candidates and not to those speaking in behalf of or against candidates. Since the above announcements did not contemplate the appearance of a candidate, the "equal opportunities" provision of Section 315 would not be applicable. The Fairness Doctrine is, however, applicable. (Letter to Lawrence M.C. Smith, FCC 63-358, 25 R.R. 291, April 17, 1963.)

Substance of broadcast: A number of stations broadcast a program entitled "Living Should Be Fun," featuring a nutritionist giving comment and advice on diet and health. Complaint was made that the program presented only one side of controversial issues of public importance. Several licensees contended that a program dealing with the desirability of good health and nutritious diet should not be placed in the category of discussion of controversial issues.

Ruling: The Commission cannot agree that the program consisted merely of the discussion of the desirability of good health and nutritious diet. Anyone who listened to the program regularly—and station licensees have the obligation to know what is being broadcast over their facilities—should have been aware that at times controversial issues of public importance were discussed. In discussing such subjects as the fluoridation of water, the value of krebiozen in the treatment of cancer, the nutritive qualities of white bread, and the use of high potency vitamins without medical advice, the nutritionist emphasized the fact that his views were opposed to many authorities in these fields, and on occasions on the air, he invited those with opposing viewpoints to present such viewpoints on his program. A licensee who did not recognize the applicability of the Fairness Doctrine failed in the performance of his obligations to the public. (Report on "Living Should be Fun" Inquiry, 33 F.C.C. 101, 107, 23 R.R. 1599, 1606, July 18, 1962.)

Substance of broadcast: In 1957, a station broadcast a panel discussion entitled "The Little Rock Crisis" in which several public officials appeared, and whose purpose, a complainant stated, was to stress the maintenance of segregation and to express an opinion as to what the Negro wants or does not want. A request for time to present contrasting viewpoints was refused by the licensee who stated that the program was most helpful in preventing trouble by urging people to keep calm and look to their elected representatives for leadership, that it was a report by elected officials to the people, and that therefore no reply was necessary or advisable.

Ruling: If the matters discussed involved no more than urging people to remain calm, it can be urged that no question exists as to fair presentation. However, if the station permitted the use of its facilities for the presentation of one side of the controversial issue of racial integration, the station incurred an obligation to afford a reasonable opportunity for the expression of contrasting views. The fact that the proponents of one particular position were elected officials did not in any way alter the nature of the program or remove the applicability of the Fairness Doctrine. See Ruling No. 3. (Lamar Life Insurance Co., FCC 59-651, 18 R.R. 683, July 1, 1959.)

Affirmative duty to encourage: In response to various complaints alleging that a station had been "one-sided" in its presentations on controversial issues of public importance, the licensee concerned rested upon its policy of making time available, upon request, for "the other side."

Ruling: The licensee's obligations to serve the public interest cannot be met merely through the adoption of a general policy of not refusing to broadcast opposing views where a demand is made of the station for broadcast time. As the Commission pointed out in the Editorializing Report (par. 9):

If, as we believe to be the case, the public interest is best served in a democracy through the ability of the people to hear expositions of the various positions taken by responsible groups and individuals on particular topics and to choose between them, it is evident that broadcast licensees have an affirmative duty generally to encourage and implement the broadcast of all sides of controversial public issues over their facilities, over and beyond their obligation to make available on demand opportunities for the expression of opposing views. It is clear that any approximation of fairness in the presentation of any controversy will be difficult if not impossible of achievement unless the licensee pays a conscious and positive role in bringing about balanced presentations of the opposing viewpoints. (John J. Dempsey, 6 R.R. 615, August 16, 1950; Editorializing Report, par. 9.) (See also Metropolitan Bctg. Corp., Public Notice 82386, 19 R.R. 602, 604, December 29, 1959.)

Overall performance on the issue: A licensee presented a program in which views were expressed critical of the proposed nuclear weapons test ban treaty. The licensee rejected a request of an organization seeking to present views favorable to the treaty, on the ground, among others, that the contrasting viewpoint on this issue had already been presented over the station's facilities in other programing.

Ruling: The licensee's overall performance is considered in determining whether fairness has been achieved on a specific issue. Thus, where complaint is made, the licensee is afforded the opportunity to set out all the programs, irrespective of the programing format, which he has devoted to the particular controversial issue during the appropriate time period. In this case, the Commission files contained no complaints to the contrary, and therefore, if it was the licensee's good faith judgment that the public had had the opportunity fairly to hear contrasting views on the issue involved in his other programing, it appeared that the licensee's obligation pursuant to the Fairness Doctrine had been met. (Letter to Cullman Bctg. Co., Fcc 63-849, September 18, 1963; Letter of September 20, 1963, FCC 63-851, to Honorable Oren Harris.)

Unreasonable limitation; refusal to permit appeal not to vote: A station refused to sell broadcast time to the complainant who, as a spokesman for a community group, was seeking to present his point of view concerning a bond election to be held in the community; the station had sold time to an organization in favor of the bond issue. The complainant alleged that the station had broadcast editorials urging people to vote in the election and that his group's position was that because of the peculiarities in the bond election law (more than 50 percent of the electorate had to vote in the election for it to be valid), the best way to defeat the proposed measure was for people not to vote in the election. The complainant alleged, and the station admitted, that the station refused to sell him broadcast time because the licensee felt that to urge people not to vote was improper.

Ruling: Because of the peculiarities of the state election law, the sale of broadcast time to an organization favoring the bond issue, and the urging of listeners to vote, the question of whether to vote became an issue. Accordingly, by failing to broadcast views urging listeners not to vote, the licensee failed to discharge the obligations imposed upon him by the Commission's Report on Editorializing. (Letter to Radio Station WMOP, January 21, 1962 (staff ruling).)

Unreasonable limitation; insistence upon request from both parties to dispute: During the period of a labor strike which involved a matter of paramount importance to the community and to the nation at large, a union requested broadcast time to discuss the issues involved. The request was denied by the station solely because of its policy to refuse time for such discussion unless both the union and the management agree, in advance, that they would jointly request and use the station, and the management of the company involved in the strike had refused to do so.

Ruling: In view of the licensee's statement that the issue was "of paramount importance to the community..." the licensee's actions were not in accordance with the principles enunciated in the Editorializing Report, specifically that portion of par. 8, which states that:

...where the licensee has determined that the subject is of sufficient import to receive broadcast attention, it would obviously not be in the public interest for spokesmen for one of the opposing points of view to be able to exercise a veto power over the entire presentation by refusing to broadcast its position. Fairness in such circumstances might require no more than that the licensee make a reasonable representation of the particular position and if it fails in this effort, to continue to make available its facilities to the spokesmen for such position in the event that, after the original programs are broadcast, they then decide to avail themselves of a right to present their contrary opinion. (Par. 8, Report on Editorializing by Broadcast Licensees; The Evening News Ass'n (WWJ), 6 R.R. 283, April 21, 1950.)

Personal attack: A newscaster on a station, in a series of broadcasts, attacked certain county and state officials, charging them with nefarious schemes and the use of their offices for personal gain, attaching derisive epithets to their names, and analogizing their local administration with the political methods of foreign dictators. At the time of renewal of the station's license, the persons attacked urged that the station had been used for the licensee's selfish purposes and to vent his personal spite. The licensee denied the charge, and asserted that the broadcasts had a factual basis. On several occasions, the persons attacked were invited to use the station to discuss the matters in the broadcasts.

Ruling: Where a licensee expresses an opinion concerning controversial issues of public importance, he is under obligation to see that those holding opposing viewpoints are afforded a reasonable opportunity for the presentation of their views. He is under a further obligation not to present biased or one-sided news programing (viewing such programing on an overall basis) and not to use his station for his purely personal and private interest. Investigation established that the licensee did not subordinate his public interest obligations to his private interests, and that there was "a body of opinion" in the community "that such broadcasts had a factual basis."

As to the attacks, the Editorializing Report states that "...elementary considerations of fairness may dictate that time be allocated to a person or group which has been specifically attacked over the station, where otherwise no such obligation would exist..." In this case, the attacks were of a highly personal nature, impugning the character and honesty of named individuals. In such circumstances, the licensee has an affirmative duty to take all appropriate steps to see to it that the persons attacked are afforded the fullest opportunity to respond. Here, the persons attacked knew of the attacks, were generally apprised of their nature, and were aware of the opportunities afforded them to respond. Accordingly, the license was renewed. (Clayton W. Mapoles, FCC 62-501, 23 R.R. 586, May 9, 1962.)

Personal attack: For a period of five days, September 18-22, a station broadcast a series of daily editorials attacking the general manager of a national rural electric cooperative association in connection with a pending controversial issue of public importance. The manager arrived in town on September 21 for a two-day stay and, upon being informed of the editorials, on the morning of September 22d sought to obtain copies of them. About noon of the same day, the station approached the manager with an offer of an interview to respond to the statements made in the editorials. The manager stated, however, that he would not have had time to prepare adequately a reply which would require a series of broadcast. He complained to the Commission that the station had acted unfairly.

Ruling: Where, as here, a station's editorials contain a personal attack upon an individual by name, the Fairness Doctrine requires that a copy of the specific editorial or editorials shall be communicated to the person attacked either prior to or at the time of the broadcast of such editorials so that a reasonable opportunity is afforded that person to reply. This duty on the part of the station is greater where, as here, interest in the editorials was consciously built up by the station over a period of days and the time within which the person attacked would have an opportunity to reply was known to be so limited. The Commission concludes that in failing to supply copies of the editorials promptly to the manager and delaying in affording him the opportunity to reply to them, the station did not fully meet the requirements of the Commission's Fairness Doctrine. (Billings Bctg. Co., FCC 62-736. 23 R.R. 951, July 13, 1962.)

Personal attacks on, and criticism of, candidate; partisan position on campaign issues: In more than 20 broadcasts, two station commentators presented their views on the issues in the 1962 California gubernatorial campaign between Governor Brown and Mr. Nixon. The views expressed on the issues were critical of the Governor and favored Mr. Nixon, and at times involved personal attacks on individuals and groups in the gubernatorial campaign, and specifically on Governor Brown. The licensee responded that it had presented opposing viewpoints but upon examination there were two instances of broadcasts featuring Governor Brown (both of which were counterbalanced by appearances of Mr. Nixon) and two instances of broadcasts presenting viewpoints opposed to two of the issues raised by the above-noted broadcasts by the commentators. It did not appear that any of the other broadcasts cited by the station dealt with the issues raised as to the gubernatorial campaign.

Ruling: Since there were only two instances which involved the presentation of viewpoints concerning the gubernatorial campaign, opposed to the more than twenty programs of the commentators presenting their views on many different issues of the campaign for which no opportunity was afforded for the presentation of opposing viewpoints, there was not a fair opportunity for presentation of opposing viewpoints with respect to many of the issues discussed in the commentators' programs. The continuous, repetitive opportunity afforded for the expression of the commentators' viewpoints on the gubernatorial campaign, in contrast to the minimal opportunity afforded to opposing viewpoints, violated the right of the public to a fair presentation of views. Further, with respect to the personal attacks by the one commentator on individuals and groups involved in the gubernatorial campaign, the principle in Mapoles and Billings should have been followed. In the circumstances, the station should have sent a transcript of the pertinent continuity on the above programs to Governor Brown and should have offered a comparable opportunity for an appropriate spokesman to answer the broadcasts. (Times-Mirror, FCC 62-1130, 24 R.R. 404, Oct. 26, 1962; FCC 62-1109, 24 R.R. 407, Oct. 19, 1962.)

Personal attacks on, and criticism of, candidates; partisan position on campaign issues—appropriate spokesman: See facts above. The question was raised whether the candidate has the right to insist upon his own appearance, to respond to the broadcasts in question.

Ruling: Since a response by a candidate would, in turn, require that equal opportunities under Section 315 be afforded to the other legally-qualified candidates for the same office, the Fairness Doctrine requires only that the licensee afford the attacked candidate an opportunity to respond through an appropriate spokesman. The candidate should, of course, be given a substantial voice in the selection of the spokesman to respond to the attack or to the statement of support. (Times-Mirror Bctg. Co., FCC 62-1130, 24 R.R. 404, 406, Oct. 19, 1962, Oct. 26, 1962.)

Personal attacks on, and criticism of, candidate; partisan position on campaign issues: During the fall of an election year, a news commentator on a local affairs program made several critical and uncomplimentary references to the actions and public positions of various political and nonpartisan candidates for public office and of the California Democratic Clubs and demanded the resignation of an employee of the staff of the County Superintendent of Schools. In response to a request for time to respond by the local Democratic Central Committee, and after negotiations between the licensee and the complaining party, the licensee offered two five-minute segments of time on November 1 and 2, 1962, and instructed its commentator to refrain from expressing any point of view on partisan issues on November 5, or November 6, election eve and election day, respectively.

Ruling: On the facts of this case, the comments of the news commentator constituted personal attacks on candidates and others and involved the taking of a partisan position on issues involved in a race for political office. Therefore, under the ruling of the Times-Mirror case, the licensee was under an obligation to "send a transcript of the pertinent continuity in each such program to the appropriate candidates immediately and (to) offer a comparable opportunity for an appropriate spokesman to answer the broadcast." However, upon the basis of the showing, the licensee's offer of time, in response to the request, was not unreasonable under the Fairness Doctrine. (Letter to The McBride Industries, Inc., FCC 63-756, July 31, 1963.)

SECTION 315
(Communications Act of 1934)

Section 315 of the Communications Act of 1934, as amended, has been in force as long as the Act itself, but until the early 60's many broadcasters and the Commission either ignored its provisions or simply looked the other way. Some thirty years after passage of the Act, the Commission issued its Section 315 Primer in the form of a Public Notice. There had been complaints to the Commission that stations had violated the provisions of Sec. 315, but they were sparse compared to the volume of complaints received in the 60's and 70's. Even today the Act is ignored in remote or small markets because members of the general public do not know how to lodge a complaint or because they fear "calling the cops" on a broadcaster. As an illustration that the Act indeed was ignored, in the late 1950's a widely known Southern politician decided to speak on a state-wide radio network. His aides made contact with about one hundred stations to determine costs for one hour of time. In only a few cases did the politician get the published rate. Some stations charged double for political time and thumbed their noses at anyone who complained. Others, favoring the politician, provided free time. In virtually every case, rates quoted were arrived at arbitrarily. It was as though Sec. 315 didn't exist! In another case, a licensee decided he wouldn't allow a commission to advertising agencies handling politicians. His rationale was that candidates who could afford a "high powered" ad agency had an advantage over the poor candidate who couldn't pay agency retainers and fees. He did agree to "gross his local rate" for such agencies, thereby enabling them to bill their client with a commissionable figure. One agency complained to the Commission that the station was in violation of Sec. 315. The Commission agreed and through the licensee's Washington attorney suggested the station immediately send rebates to the offended agencies. Had the agency not complained, the violation would have gone unnoticed.

Crux of the Statute

"If any licensee shall permit any person who is a legally-qualified candidate for any public office to use a broadcast station, he shall afford equal opportunities to all other such candidates for that office in the use of such broadcasting stations: Provided, that such licensee shall have no power of censorship over the material broadcast under the provisions of this section. No obligation is hereby imposed upon any licensee to allow the use of its station by any such candidate. The charges made for the use of any broadcasting station for any of the purposes set forth in this section shall not exceed the charges made for comparable use of such station for other purposes. The Commission shall prescribe appropriate rules and regulations to carry out the provisions of this section. In 1959, the Act was amended to exempt from the equal time requirement appearances by candidates on newscasts, news interviews, and other news coverages." In most instances, the Act is simple to interpret. When a station allows one legally qualified candidate for office to use its facilities, it is obligated under Sec. 315 to allow every other legally qualified candidate for the same office to use its facilities (Equal Opportunity). In such cases, the broadcaster exercises no judgment; he simply obeys the clear provisions of the statute. It is equally clear under Sec. 315 that the station may not establish special political rates; it must treat the candidate or his advertising agency precisely as it would a commercial account. And while the station may not censor the material delivered personally by the candidate, it may censor material voiced by a representative of the candidate. A representative would include the radio announcer who voices the copy or the candidate's public spokesman.

The Commission's definition of a "legally qualified candidate" is:

"A legally qualified candidate means any person who has publicly announced that he is a candidate for nomination by a convention of a political party or for nomination or election in a primary, special, or general election, municipal, county, state or national, and who meets the qualifications prescribed by the applicable laws to hold office for which he is a candidate, so that he may be voted for by the electorate directly or by means of delegates or electors, and who:

(1) Has qualified for a place on the ballot or
(2) Is eligible under the applicable law to be voted for by sticker, by writing in his name on the ballot, or other method, and (a) has been duly nominated by a political party which is commonly known and regarded as such, or (b) makes a substantial showing that he is a bona fide candidate for nomination or office, as the case may be."

The 315 Primer

It is not always easy to determine when a candidate has made "use" of a facility. The Primer provides answers to more than one hundred questions dealing with this often perplexing question. A select group of those answers follows:
Q. If a legally qualified candidate secures air time but does not discuss matters directly related to his candidacy, is this a use of facilities under Sec. 315?

A. Yes. Sec. 315 does not distinguish between the uses of broadcast time by a candidate, and the licensee is not authorized to pass on requests for time by opposing candidates on the basis of the licensee's evaluation of whether the original user was or was not in aid of candidacy.

Q. Must a broadcaster give equal time to a candidate whose opponent has broadcast in some other capacity than as a candidate?
A. Yes. For example, a weekly report of a Congressman to his constituents via radio or television is a broadcast by a legally-qualified candidate for public office as soon as he becomes a candidate for re-election, and his opponent must be given "equal opportunities."

Q. If a candidate appears on a variety program for a very brief bow or statement, are his opponents entitled to "equal opportunities" on the basis of this brief appearance?
A. Yes. All appearances of a candidate, no matter how brief or perfunctory, are a "use" of a station's facilities within Sec. 315.

Q. If a candidate is afforded station time for a speech in connection with a ceremonial activity or other public service, is an opposing candidate entitled to equal utilization of the station's facilities?
A. Yes. Sec. 315 contains no exception with respect to broadcasts by a legally qualified candidate carried "in the public interest" or as a "public service." It follows that the station's broadcasts of a candidate's speech was a "use" of the facilities of the station by a legally-qualified candidate giving rise to an obligation by the station under Sec. 315 to afford "equal opportunities" to other legally-qualified candidates for the same office.

Q. Does Sec. 315 apply to broadcasts by a legally-qualified candidate where such broadcasts originate and are limited to a foreign station whose signals are received in the United States?
A. No. Sec. 315 applies only to stations licensed by the FCC.

Q. If a station owner, or a station advertiser, or a person regularly employed as a station announcer were to make appearances over a station after having qualified as a candidate for public office, would Sec. 315 apply?

A. Yes. Such appearances of a candidate are a "use" under Sec. 315.

Q. A television station employs an announcer who, "off camera" and unidentified, supplies the audio portion of required station identification announcements, public service announcements, and commercial announcements. The announcer is not authorized to make comments or statements concerning political matter, and has no control over the format or content of any program material. In the event that this employee announced his candidacy for the city council, would his opponent be entitled to equal opportunities?
A. No. The employee's appearance for the purposes of making commercial, noncommercial, and the station identification announcements would not constitute a "use" where the announcer himself was neither shown nor identified in any way.

Q. An employee of a radio station who had been for a number of years the station's news director and is responsible for preparing the news material and presenting it on regularly scheduled news programs announced his candidacy for the School Board. Prior to becoming a candidate the employee was identified on the news programs he announced, but he will not be identified during his candidacy. Would the appearance of the employee while he was a legally-qualified candidate on the particular news-type programs constitute a "use" of the station entitling the employee's opponents to "equal opportunities?"
A. Yes. In cases where the newscaster is identifed up to the date of his candidacy and prepares and broadcasts the news, including that of a local nature, the general line of rulings prior to the 1959 amendments to Sec. 315 would be applicable and such appearances would constitute a "use" of the station's facilities.

Q. When a station, as part of a newscast, uses film clips showing a legally-qualified candidate participating as one of a group in official ceremonies and the newscaster, in commenting on the ceremonies, mentions the candidate and others by name and describes their participation, has there been a "use" under Sec. 315?
A. No. Since the facts clearly showed that the candidate had in no way directly or indirectly initiated either filming or presentation of the event, and that the broadcast was nothing

more than a routine newscast by the station in the exercise of its judgment as to newsworthy events.

Q. A Philadelphia TV station had been presenting a weekly program called "Eye on Philadelphia." This program consisted of personalities being interviewed by a station representative. Three candidates for the office of Mayor of Philadelphia, representing different political parties, appeared on the program. Would a write-in candidate for Mayor be entitled to "equal opportunities?"

A. No, since it was ascertained that the appearances of the three mayoralty candidates were on a bona fide, regularly scheduled news interview program and that such appearances were determined by the station's news director on the basis of newsworthiness.

Q. Certain networks had presented over their facilities various candidates for the Democratic nomination for President on the programs, "Meet the Press," "Face the Nation," and "College News Conference." Said programs were regularly scheduled and consisted of questions being asked of prominent individuals by newsmen and others. Would a candidate for the same nomination in a State primary be entitled to "equal opportunities?"

A. No. The programs were regularly scheduled, bona fide news interviews and were of the type Congress intended to exempt from the "equal opportunities" requirement of Sec. 315.

Q. The President of the U.S. during a presidential campaign used fifteen minutes of radio and television time to address the nation with respect to an extraordinary international situation in the Middle East (the so-called Suez crisis). Would the networks carrying this address be obliged to afford "equal opportunities" to the other presidential candidates?

A. No. On the basis of the legislative history of Sec. 315 the Commission concluded that Congress did not intend to grant equal time to all presidential candidates when the President uses the air waves in reporting to the nation on an international crisis.

Q. May the station under Sec. 315 make time available to all candidates for one office and refuse all candidates for another office?

A. Yes. The "equal opportunities" requirements of Sec.

315 is limited to all legally-qualified candidates for the same office.

Q. If the station makes time available to candidates seeking the nomination of one party for a particular office, does Sec. 315 require that it make equal time available to the candidates seeking the nomination of other parties for the same office?

A. No. The Commission has held that while both primary elections or nominating conventions and general elections are comprehended within the terms of Sec. 315, the primary elections or conventions held by one party are to be considered separately from the primary elections or conventions of other parties, and therefore, insofar as Sec. 315 is concerned, "equal opportunities" need only be afforded legally qualified candidates for nomination for the same office at the party's primary or nominating convention. The station's action in this regard, however, would be governed by the public interest standards encompassed within The Fairness Doctrine.

Q. Is it necessary for a station to advise a candidate or a political party that time has been sold to other candidates?

A. No. The law does not require that this be done. If a candidate inquires, however, the facts must be given to him. It should be noted here that a station is required to keep a public record of all requests for time by or on behalf of political candidates, together with a record of the disposition and the charges made, if any, for each broadcast.

(Note: While the Commission does not require that competing candidates be notified when time is purchased, it does require that stations make an **affirmative effort** to gather and air opposing points of view when a controversial public issue is discussed on the air.)

Q. If one political candidate buys station facilities more heavily than another, is a station required to call a halt to such sales because of the resulting imbalance?

A. No. Sec. 315 requires only that all candidates be afforded equal opportunities to use the facilities of the station.

Q. Where a candidate for office in a state or local election appears on a national network program, is an opposing candidate for the same office entitled to equal facilities over stations which carried the original program and serve the area in which the election campaign is occurring?

A. Yes. Under such circumstances an opposing candidate would be entitled to equal time on such stations.

Q. If a legally-qualified candidate broadcasts libelous or slanderous remarks, is the station liable therefore?

A. In Port Huron Broadcasting Co., 12 FCC 1069, 4 R.R. 1, the Commission expressed an opinion that licensees not directly participating in the libel might be absolved from any liability they might otherwise incur under state law, because of the operation of Sec. 315, which precludes them from preventing a candidate's utterances. In a subsequent case, the Commission's ruling in the Port Huron case was, in effect, affirmed, the Supreme Court holding that since a licensee could not censor a broadcast under Sec. 315, Congress could not have intended to compel a station to broadcast libelous statements of a legally-qualified candidate and at the same time subject itself to the risk of damage suits.

Q. Does the same immunity apply in a case where the chairman of a political party's campaign committee, not himself a candidate, broadcasts a speech in support of a candidate?

A. No. Licensees are not entitled to assert the defense that they are not liable since the speeches could have been censored without violating Sec. 315. Accordingly, they were at fault in permitting such speeches to be broadcast.

Q. May a station charge premium rates for political broadcasts?

A. No. Sec. 315, as amended, provides that the charges made for the use of a station by a candidate "shall not exceed the charges made for comparable use of such stations for other purposes."

Q. When must a candidate make a request of the station for opportunities equal to those afforded his opponent?

A. Within one week of the day on which the prior use occurred.

These questions and answers attempt in no way to cover every situation that may arise. The student is advised to read the entire Primer if he desires to develop a broader understanding of the Commission's interpretation of Sec. 315. Once a fundamental grasp of the section is obtained, however, it is fairly easy to make a determination on any given situation. When there is doubt, it is advisable to discuss the matter with a communications attorney.

PROCUREMENT OF LICENSE

The Construction Permit

There essentially are two methods of obtaining a license for a radio station. The most common method is acquisition through purchase or other means an existing facility. The other method is to find a vacant channel or frequency and **build one.** The following dialogue between two non-owners illustrates how some stations are conceived:

JONES: Bill, I talked with a consulting engineer last week, and he said he thinks there's a daytime frequency available in Ourtown.

SMITH: Joe, can't believe it. Must be an FM. I know a guy who tried several years ago to find a new frequency here and he failed.

JONES: But the picture changes. A lot of times when a station changes its power, it also has to change its directional array. And when the array is changed, there's always the chance that a channel will become available in one market or another.

SMITH: Okay. Let's assume your consulting engineer has located a frequency. What do you want to do about it?

JONES: Well, here's what I had in mind. Between the two of us we've had about 20 years experience in all phases of radio. I'm strong in sales and you're backgrounded in programing. I believe we could put together a soul station in this market and really make it go. Blacks represent 30 percent of the population here and their patronage is tremendously important to local and national advertisers. Plus, I think we could provide tremendous public service to the Black community with a station that concentrates on problems of this minority group.

355

SMITH:	I'm game, if we can come up with enough capital on our own—without having to borrow too much.

JONES:	I figure my net worth at about $50,000. It would mean selling my stock and re-financing my house, but I feel strongly about the possibilities of the Soul format here. I feel especially strong about my owning a chunk of it.

SMITH:	My net worth is about the same, and I'd have to mortgage my home. How much do you think we'd need?

JONES:	Well, let's put our costs on paper. I think we can get the consulting engineer to give us a free ride on the frequency find; he's an old friend, and he'll make money handling the engineering part of the application for us.

SMITH:	So...let's get it on paper.

Estimated CP Costs

Engineering Fees	$1,000.00
Legal Fees	1,000.00
Antenna Site	(lease)
Offices-Studios	(lease)
Antenna System (Installed)	8,000.00
Transmitting Equipment	12,000.00
Studio Equipment	6,000.00
Office Equipment	1,000.00
Other Engineering	3,000.00

JONES:	Okay, We've already spent $32,000.00, and I think that'll handle a little daytimer at 1580 kHz in this market. But the Commission wants to know that we have enough money to operate for about a year without getting into financial trouble. Two of us can't do everything, so we'll have to hire people. And we've got other overhead, such as power, telephone, music licensing fees, office supplies, not to mention the leases for land and studio-office quarters.

SMITH: Okay. Let's look at the people first. They're always the biggest expense.

Proposed Staff

Smith, programing		$700.00 month
Jones, sales		700.00 month

Proposed Staff

Name	Position	Monthly Salary
Smith	Program Director	$700.00
Jones	Sales Manager	700.00
-----	Office Girl	400.00
-----	Anncr A	500.00
-----	Anncr B	500.00
-----	Anncr C	500.00
-----	Contract Engineer	200.00
-----	Salesman A	500.00 (draw)
-----	Salesman B	500.00 (draw)
Total estimated payroll		$4,500.00

JONES: That looks close. I may be able to work with two announcers after we get organized, and you may find that you can handle enough of the sales to use only one other guy. But the girl we **gotta** have for logs and billing. Now, let's look at some other expenses.

Other Expenses

Item	Monthly Cost
Telephones	$150.00
Power	125.00
Land Rental	300.00
Office-Studio Rental	200.00
Office Supplies	50.00
Wire Service	300.00
Music & production expendables	25.00
Engineering	75.00
Land lines (Studio to Xmtr.)	25.00
Local Taxes	50.00
All other taxes (Payroll incl.)	300.00
Total estimated other	$1,600.00

SMITH: Okay. Let's put our total together.

Estimated First Year Costs

Construction	$32,000.00
Operating (12 months)	73,200.00

SMITH:	Boy! That's a lot of money! Do you think we can swing it?

JONES:	I sure do, and here's how. It'll be close for the first year, but after that we should make a buck or two. By refinancing our homes, by selling other assets and turning them into cash, we can raise $50,000. That'll take care of construction costs and leave us $18,000 in the bank. Our operating costs are about $6,100 a month, measured against **net sales**. I say **net** because we haven't figured in the cost of agency local salesman or national rep commissions or the music licensing fees. The $18,000 will carry us, then, for three months with **no** sales and **no** collections. I think if we get a letter of credit from the bank for another $36,000, the Commission will consider that we can make it. With a letter of credit, we don't have to borrow the money unless we need it and, frankly, I don't think we will. I know I can generate about $10,000 a month in gross sales, and that should net out to about $8,000. If I'm anywhere near correct in this estimate, we'll make some sort of profit in the first year.

SMITH:	Well, grab Form 301 and let's get going!

The partners now must decide to apply for the CP as partners, or to form a corporation to make the application. Once they decide they may be able to swing it, they must re-contact the consulting engineer, retain a Washington attorney, and go to work completing the FCC's Form 301. The form requires information about the citizenship and character of the applicants, as well as their financial, technical and other qualifications, plus details about the transmitting apparatus to be used, antenna and studio locations, and the service (programing) proposed. An extensive survey to determine community problems must be conducted, and the applicants will have to show how they propose to help solve such problems. Applicants are required to show their financial ability to operate for one year after construction of the station. Triplicate copies of the application are required. Applicants for new stations, license renewals, or major changes in facilities, must give local public notice of such intent. The notice is published in the local newspaper under specific instructions from the FCC. The public notice affords interested persons an opportunity to comment on the application to the Commission. All broadcast applications are reported twice by the FCC. Receipt of the application is acknowledged first, and again when the application is formally accepted for filing. An application is not formally acted upon until at least thirty days after the Commission gives notice of its acceptance. In many cases, Broadcast Bureau staff members may require clarification of dozens of answers given in reply to questions in the application form. Once the applicant gets past the inevitable questions, and if no one has posed valid objections to the applicant's qualifications to operate the station, it becomes a matter of waiting. However, until the Construction Permit is actually granted, it is not prudent to make any unconditional agreements for land, office, and studio facilities or equipment. Any agreement made prior to receipt of the CP should be conditioned upon FCC approval of the application. Once the station has been constructed and call letters have been granted, the applicant then files Form 302 for the actual license to operate the station. The applicant must begin construction of the station within sixty days after the CP is issued, and construction must be completed within six months thereafter. If these deadlines cannot be met, the permittee must request and receive extensions from the Commission. Authority for program tests will not be granted until the CP holder applies for a license (Form 302). Program test authority may be requested in the application for license or it may be requested separately. A station license and program test authority are issued if no new cause or circumstance has come to the attention of the Commission that would make operation of the station contrary to the public interest or to Commission Rules.

LICENSE RENEWAL

Of all the contact a licensee has with the FCC, his application for license renewal is among the most significant and frequent. The normal period of license is three years for AM, FM, and TV stations. Under some circumstances, the Commission may elect to renew the licenses for a shorter period. This part will deal primarily with Sections IV-A and VI of Form 303, used by the licensee to apply for a renewal of his license. The form contains four sections, ownership data (I), engineering data (II), program service (IV-A), and equal opportunity employment program (VI). The application must be filed ninety days prior to the expiration date of the license sought to be renewed. In instances where the licensee uses a communications attorney, the attorney usually requires a thirty-day study and preparation period, so the licensee should have basic renewal materials in Washington 120 days prior to expiration of the current license.

In this exercise, assume the license expires August 1. The application must reach the attorney's office by April 1, and the Commission's Office in Washington by May 1. During the third quarter of the preceding year, the Commission will announce its composite week for those stations whose licenses are up for renewal next August. The composite week reads as follows:

Sunday	November 12	(last year)
Monday	December 13	(last year)
Tuesday	January 28	(current year)
Wednesday	February 18	(current year)
Thursday	April 21	(current year)
Friday	June 16	(current year)
Saturday	July 23	(current year)

Upon receipt of the composite week, the licensee and-or his representatives should begin work. The following procedures are recommended:

Pull the program logs covering the days of the composite week and prepare an analysis. For accuracy, two persons should handle the project. One of them should read and analyze the log, while the other records his findings. The worksheet, prepared at the station, may be as follows:

RADIO STATION KXXX

Day & Date _____
Hours-Minutes On _____

Hour	News	Public Affairs	PSA's	Other	Comm. Mins
12-1A					
1-2A					
2-3A					
3-4A					

A worksheet should be prepared for each day of the composite week. Once the analysis begins, it should be completed as soon as possible, because it represents only a small part of the overall project. The following dialogue indicates the analysis procedure:

ANALYST: Okay, Sally. Let's go with Sunday, November 12. We'll start with the midnight-to-1:00 AM hour. Not much there, but we have to cover every minute of the broadcast week.

SALLY: I'm ready.

ANALYST: Okay. News, 3½ minutes. No Public Affairs.

Four PSA's. No Other, and no commercials.

SALLY: Didn't we have news on the half-hour?

ANALYST: Oh, yes, Thanks. Add one minute of news to the 12:00-1:00 hour.

In the noon-to-1:00 PM hour. News 3¼ and 1. Public Affairs, five, PSA's, two. Other, 15 minutes. Commercial Minutes, 15½. And by the way, under Public Affairs, enter another minute; we ran an editorial during that hour.

In the analysis, every commercial minute of every hour must be counted, **by the hour**! In the previous application for license renewal, the applicant proposed to run no more than eighteen commercial minutes per hour, for example, and in the past programing part of Section IV-A the Commission requires the applicant to specify the amount of commercial minutes programed and wants an explanation if **any** hour of the week contained more than eighteen minutes.

The previous application proposed a certain amount of News, Public Affairs, Others, and PSA's and the Commission now wants to know if the licensee lived up to his promises.

The analysis continues until every page of every log has been thoroughly studied. Once the study has yielded its figures, the second phase of the analysis begins. The following table is helpful:

Performed

	Hrs.	Min.	Pct		Hrs	Min	Pct
News	10	31	6.3		10	30	6.3
PA	6	50	4.1		6	51	4.1
0	2	34	1.5		2	34	1.5
PSA's	265				267		

Commercial

A. Up to and including 10 minutes........................68
B. Over 10 and up to and including 14 minutes...........50
C. Over 14 and up to and including 18 minutes...........50
D. Over 18 minutes.......................................--

In the programing part of the worksheet, the analyst has translated the hours and minutes into minutes. Thus, 10 hours and 31 minutes of news amounts to 631 minutes of news matter broadcast during the composite week. By dividing 10,080 minutes (the number of minutes in a 168 hour broadcast week) into 631, the 6.3 percentage figure is derived. The same procedure is used in making the computations for Public Affairs and Other type programing.

In the Commercial part of the worksheet, the analyst has counted each commercial in each of the 168 hours of the composite week. In no case did he find that the station had broadcast over eighteen commercial minutes per hour. Had he found one or several hours in which the self-imposed limit of eighteen minutes had been exceeded, he would have had to explain the overage. Licensees often will provide some leeway, by explaining in the application that the proposed limit of 18 (or 15 or 12) commercial minutes will be exceeded only during political campaigns when the demand for time may be extraordinary. One such station stated it would, during political campaigns, allow up to 21 minutes of commercial time, with the three minute overage being political. The Commission granted the license. Such practice is common among AM and FM stations.

While the analyst is working on the program logs, the Engineering Department should be alerted to begin thinking about the engineering data for Section II. Section I will be completed by the General Manager, the Chief Engineer, and the head of the Bookkeeping Department. The General Manager, the analyst, and the Program Director will complete Section IV-A while the General Manager and the Office Manager will complete Section VI. With an April 1 deadline for getting the completed information to the Washington attorney, work should begin in earnest no later than mid-January.

The **single most important project** in an application for license renewal is the licensee's ascertainment of community problems and the programing he proposes to help solve them. The survey of community needs is made (1) through interviews with community leaders and (2) through interviews with members of the general public. While the Commission does not specify precisely how many persons must be interviewed, most Washington attorneys, through their familiarity with Commission staff members, can give the applicant an educated guess that probably will be acceptable. In a market of one million, 100 community leaders and 300 members of the general public should be interviewed. Licensees are permitted to employ outside survey firms to handle general public studies, but they **themselves or top executives** must perform the community leader surveys. Many communication attorneys warn licensees that the Commission is more interested in the conduct of the community problem study than in any other single part of the application for renewal.

The survey and its results should be set up in three parts to answer the three questions contained in Part I of Sec. IV-A. The questions are:

A. State in Exhibit No. _____ the methods used by the applicant to ascertain the needs and interest of the public served by the station. Such information shall include (1) identification of representative groups, interests and organizations which were consulted and (2) the major communities or areas which applicant principally undertakes to serve.

B. Describe in Exhibit No. _____ the significant needs and interests of the public which the applicant believes his station will serve during the coming license period, including those with respect to national and international matters.

C. List in Exhibit No. _____ typical and illustrative programs or program series (excluding Entertainment and News) that applicant plans to broadcast during the coming license period to meet those needs and interests.

To answer Question A, the licensee must establish a plan of action to interview different people from every different walk of life in the area of service. The Exhibit might read:

> Applicant principally serves the City of Dallas and Dallas County, including the cities of Richardson, Garland, Grand Prairie, and Farmers Branch. Fifteen percent of the population is black; five percent is Mexican-American, and the remainder is white. Approximately 50 percent of the population is engaged in retailing; 20 percent in manufacturing (light industry); and 30 percent in sales, services, and government.

Methods applicant used to determine the needs and interests of the public included the following:

1. Survey of 100 business leaders
2. Survey of 300 members of the general public in age, race, and sex categories described for this area by the U.S. Census Bureau.
3. KXXX advisory board, composed of 50 community leaders
4. KXXX's continuing public survey

Community leaders included:

1. John Jones, president, local NAACP
2. James W. Vincent, manager, Chamber of Commerce
3. A. D. Adams, president, Local Council of Churches
4. Alex Sanchez, president, Mexican-American Society
5. Mrs. Mary Jones, president, Women's Liberation Movement
6. Theo. W. Adamson, president, Adamson Manufacturing Co.
7. Samuel G. Grace, president, Local UAW No. 2468

The exhibit should continue until every person interviewed has been named and identified by the part he plays as a community leader. Then, the applicant may wish to name the persons on his Advisory Board, and identify each of them. He may describe an annual survey which members of the Advisory Board are asked to complete, or describe a dinner meeting attended by members of the Board during which community problems were discussed. Essentially, the applicant, through this exhibit, tells the Commission **how he found out about community problems**.

To answer Question B, the licensee must describe the problems uncovered in the survey. The following format may be helpful:

PROBLEMS OF OURTOWN COMMUNITY

KXXX interviewed 100 community leaders and 300 members of the general public. The problems, listed in order of their awareness factor among interviewees, are as follows:

Problem	Community Leader Mention	General Public Mentions
Illegal Drug Traffic	40	100
Public Sanitation	30	50
Public Housing	10	35
Public Transportation	5	35
Law Enforcement	5	20
Pollution	4	15
Employment	3	15
Discrimination	2	15
Educational Facilities	1	15

In general, applicant learned that the illegal drug traffic in Ourtown is still the most serious problem, as it was three years ago. Members of black organizations appeared to be more concerned with law enforcement and employment than with discrimination and education. The general public, for the most part, identified and gave about the same priorities to problems as community leaders did.

In this exhibit, the applicant explained to the Commission that he did indeed **identify many important community problems**.

To answer Question C, the licensee must explain how he plans to help solve the problems uncovered in the survey. The following format may be useful:

Applicant proposes to use his facilities in every way possible consistent with balanced programing to aid in developing solutions to the problems outlined in the previous exhibit. The problems and KXXX's proposed method of aiding are:

Problem	Method of Aid
Illegal Drug Traffic	Public Service Announcements Editorials
Public Sanitation	Telephone Talk Show, Editorials
Public Housing	Editorials
Law Enforcement	Public Service Announcements, Telephone Talk Show, Editorials
Discrimination	Editorials
Educational Facilities	Round-Table discussion Telephone Talk Show

In this exhibit, the applicant describes to the Commission what he proposes to do to **help solve community problems**. The Commission is mainly interested in knowing how the facilities of the applicant will be used in the development of solutions to local problems. There is little if any interest in what the applicant and his staff will do **off the air** in contributing to problem solutions. Outside activities are important in that they indicate that management and staff are keeping abreast of problems, but the Commission wants to know how **the station** will be used in improving life in the community. The Commission does not expect the station to **solve** problems, but to **contribute** to their solutions through programs that instruct, inform, and in general improve communications among members of the community.

GENERAL PUBLIC SURVEY

Date:

Name: (Not absolutely necessary)

Address: (At least town)

Race:

Sex:

Age: (Circle one)

   12-15; 16-18; 19-21; 22-30; 31-40; 41-50; over 50

1. Identify one or two of the most significant problems or needs of your community:

2. How can our station help meet those needs?

_____

                                                      Interviewer

Fig. 30. General Public Survey Form.

A COMMUNITY LEADER SURVEY FORM

Name   : _____

Address: _____

City   : _____ Phone: _____

Age   : _____ Sex: _____ Ethnic Origin: _____

Organizations, Affiliations, (Basis for Selection): _____

_____

_____

Interview Conducted: ( ) In Person   ( ) By Phone   Interviewer: _____

Date: _____ Time: _____ Place: _____

1. With regard to your participation and experience within the groups you
   represent, what community problems are most significant, and how can these
   best be resolved?

2. What are the other problems, needs, and interests of your community, and
   how can these best be resolved or served?

3. Do you have any suggestions as to how radio can be more relevant and effective?

Fig. 31. Community Leader Survey Form.

It is almost impossible to include too much information in the first three exhibits to Part I of Sec. IV-A. The information in every case should reflect **precisely** what actually occurred. The applicant should include no information that he cannot support with documents. He must not include fictitious interviews; he **cannot** dream up any part of the exhibits because they are subject to close scrutiny by the Commission Staff and he could be denied a renewal because he falsified information.

Part II of Sec. IV-A deals with past programing. The information developed through the log analysis will be used to complete answers in Part II. Part III requires that applicant describe the programing he proposes to broadcast during the coming period of license. Again, he notes the amount of News, Public Affairs, and Other programing he intends to carry; how he plans to make time available for the discussion of public issues and how he plans to select subjects and participants, and how his programing will contribute to the overall diversity of program services available in the area or communities to be served.

Part IV may be completed also from information gained through the log analysis. This is Past Commercial Practices. The applicant describes the commercial load of the station during the composite week, and explains all cases where he exceeded his commercial limit. In Part V, the Commission asks the applicant to describe his proposed commercial practices during the upcoming license period. In some cases, the applicant may wish to change the commercial limitation from 18 to 20 minutes, or from 18 to 15 minutes, though few operators will ever propose fewer minutes, since the Commission has no quarrel with licensees who run fewer commercials than proposed. And no operator should attempt to increase an 18-minute limit without advice from counsel.

Part VI deals with general station policies and procedures, such as who makes day-to-day programing decisions, how the licensee keeps himself and staff informed of requirements of the Communications Act and Commission Rules, and the number of full-time and part-time employees. This section simply requires a recitation of facts, and complete candor is required. Part VII is a certification and catch-all part that enables the applicant to submit additional information that will support his application. If the applicant believes his answers to the other questions sufficiently qualify him for a renewal of the license, he may choose to ignore the question. On the other hand, he may have future program plans that he wishes to reveal to the Commission; or he may have broadcast considerable public service material that was not or could not properly be included in other exhibits. In either case, the exhibit would be included in Part VII.

Section VI is the newest part of Form 303; it deals with the applicant's equal employment opportunity program. Essentially, the Commission in Section VI wants to know what the applicant has done to (1) assure nondiscrimination in recruiting, (2) assure nondiscrimination in selecting in hiring, (3) assure nondiscriminatory placement and promotion, and (4) assure nondiscrimination in other areas of employment practices. The following exhibit proved to be acceptable as an answer to Part I of the Section:

KXXX Renewal
Exhibit No. EEOP-1

STATION KXXX'S EQUAL EMPLOYMENT OP-PORTUNITY PROGRAM

Part I

1. To assure nondiscrimination in recruiting.

a. Station KXXX has posted in its employment office a notice informing employees and applicants of their equal employment rights and their right to notify the Equal Employment Opportunity Commission, 1800 G. Street NW, Washington, D.C., 20201. (A copy of the notice is attached to this exhibit.)

b. Station KXXX's application for employment bears the stamp:

"Discrimination because of race, color, religion, national origin, or sex, is prohibited. Applicants may notify the Federal Communications Commission or other appropriate agency if they believe they have been discriminated against." The application, at the bottom of the page, asks applicants to:

"Exclude any organization, the name or character of which indicates the race, color, creed, or national origin of its members." (A copy of the application is attached to this exhibit.)

c. Station KXXX has not advertised for applicants in media which have significant circulation among minority-group people in the recruiting area. However, the applicant did run in Broadcasting Magazine an advertisement aimed specifically at members of the black race. (A copy of this ad is attached to this exhibit.)

d. On June 26, Station KXXX sent a letter to many colleges and universities in the area. A copy of the letter sent to Smith

College, a predominately Negro college, is attached to this exhibit. A response from one of the Universities is also attached.

e. Station KXXX has made significant contact with minority and human relations organizations, leaders and spokesmen to encourage referral of qualified minority applicants. A letter similar to the one sent to Smith College was sent to such minority and human relations organizations. A letter from the Equal Employment Opportunity Commission, in response to the KXXX letter is attached. Also attached is a list of the persons and-or organizations receiving the letter. A letter from the General Manager of Station KXXX, to the URBAN LEAGUE, also is attached. KXXX's office manager maintains contact with the Community Action Center, which occasionally supplies KXXX with qualified applicants from minority groups.

f. Present employees are encouraged to refer minority applicants.

g. Varied recruiting sources are notified that qualified minority members are being sought for consideration whenever Station KXXX hires.

2. To assure nondiscrimination in selection and hiring.

a. The attached "Policy Statement," letter and interpretative from KXXX's Washington Law Firm was duplicated and copies given to all department heads.

b. Not applicable, as Station KXXX has no union employees.

c. Station KXXX avoids using selection techniques or tests which have the effect of discriminating against a minority group.

3. To assure nondiscriminatory placement and promotion.

a. (See statement of policy referred to in 2a above.)

b. (See statement of policy referred to in 2a above, Paragraph 6, and letter from Mr. _____ to Mr. _____ .) The employee identified as Jane Smith was originally trained as a Key Punch Operator, given raises in pay, and was later promoted to the position of Billing Clerk, and subsequently received other pay increases. She is a member of a minority group and left only in March, after suffering chronic illness.

In another case, Miss Judy Jones, member of a minority group, was trained as Station KXXX's Director of Community Participation. She left on her own accord to accept employment in Florida.

c. Not applicable as Station KXXX has no union employees.

370

4. To assure nondiscrimination in other areas of employment practices.

a. Department Heads at Station KXXX and the General Manager of Station KXXX do, from time to time, examine rates of pay and fringe benefits for present employees, and adjust any inequities found.

b. All qualified employees are notified when there is an opportunity to perform overtime work.

Further, the Commission requires the following:

"Submit a report as Exhibit No. _____ indicating the manner in which the specific practices undertaken pursuant to the station's equal opportunity program have been applied and the effect of these practices upon the applications for employment, hiring and promotions of minority group members."

In this exhibit, the applicant describes the results of the equal employment opportunity program under which he has been operating. The following statement may suffice:

KXXX during the current license period employed four blacks and 2 Mexican-Americans. The blacks occupy positions in sales, programing, news, and one is Director of Community Relations. Each has received regular pay raises during the last two years. The two men in programing and news have received a fair share of available extra duty that resulted in overtime pay. One of the Mexican-Americans is Sales Manager and the other is Head Bookkeeper. The Bookkeeper was employed as a result of KXXX running a classified ad in the local Spanish language newspaper, **El Toro**. The black newsman was employed as a result of an ad run in a local black-oriented newspaper.

Part III of Sec. VI asks whether any complaints have been filed against the station alleging discrimination in employment practices. If none has been filed, the applicant so states. If complaints have been filed, the applicant must explain the disposition or current status of the matter.

During the forty-five days before the application for license renewal is due to be filed with the Commission, the applicant must advise the public of his intention of seeking a renewal of his license. The public notice, under Sec. 1.580 of the Commission's Rules, must be published at least twice a week for two consecutive weeks within the three week period immediately after the application has been tendered for filing, or within the three week period after the Commission officially accepts the application for filing. Under Sec. 1.578 of the Commission Rules, the notice must be broadcast at least once daily on four days of any single week starting not more than 45 days prior to the due date for filing the renewal application. The notice reads as follows:

Pursuant to the provisions of the Communications Act of 1934, as amended, notice is hereby given that (name of licensee), licensee of (class of station) broadcast station (call letters, city and state) is required to file with the FCC, no later than (a date 90 days prior to the expiration date), an application for renewal of its license to operate station (call letters), on (frequency or channel). The officers, directors and owners of 10 percent or more of the stock are____(names)____. Members of the public who desire to bring to the Commission's attention facts concerning the operation of the station should write to the FCC, Washington, D.C., 20554, not later than (a date 30 days after the above required filing date). Letters should set out in detail the specific facts which the writer wishes the Commission to consider in passing on the application. A copy of the license renewal application and related material will, upon filing with the Commission, be available for public inspection at____(address)____ between the hours of_____ and _____. (Regular business hours)

Within seven days of the last day of publication or broadcast of the notice, the applicant must file certified copies of the material setting forth the dates and times broadcast and the dates and name of the newspaper in which the notice was published. Any member of the public wishing to protest the application has 30 days to act after the Commission officially accepts the application for filing. There are many exceptions to these guidelines, and the Rules should be studied or legal counsel obtained before any effort is made to deal directly with the Commission. Applications that do not comply precisely with FCC requirement will be returned.

While this section doesn't take the student step-by-step through completion of Form 303, it should provide a good grasp of what is involved. The day of the licensee easing through a renewal application disappeared years ago. The Commission wants and gets hard-fact answers, or the applicant can expect at least a hearing or at most a denial of his application. The applicant should use supporting documentation wherever possible in the exhibits. Such documents may include copies of all editorials run in the last year, resumes of public service campaigns, thank you letters from recipients of public service time, any citations or awards earned for outstanding public service, clippings of newspaper stories about the station's community involvement. One broadcaster humorously remarked that the Commission has stopped reading the applications, so voluminous have they become, and started simply weighing them against a secret poundage requirement.

Sales and Transfers

The student who becomes adept at completing FCC Forms 303 (renewal application) and 301 (application for a construction permit) will have no trouble completing forms relating to sales and transfers. Requests for permission to sell a station or transfer control of a station are made on FCC Forms 314, 315, or 316. Regardless of the form used, the Commission seeks full disclosure of the facts of the transaction. Form 316 is the "short form" used where there is, for example, a corporate reorganization which involves no substantial change in the beneficial ownership of the station. The Commission reserves the right to require refiling of the application on the longer forms if in its judgment the short form does not apply to the assignment or transfer when approval is sought.

When an individual wishes to sell his station, he and the buyer must coordinate efforts in completing Form 314. The seller completes:

Part I. Sec. I—Reasons for desiring to sell, description of the facility, original purchase price, copy of the sales contract, up to date balance sheet, and other administrative detail.

Part II, Sec. IV-A—Past programing.

Part IV, Sec. IV-A—Past commercial practices.

Part VII—General matters and final certification.

With these requirements, the Commission simply is asking whether the licensee has lived up to his promises. The buyer completes:

Part II, Sec. I—Reasons for desiring license, balance sheet, and other administrative data.

Sec. II—Legal qualifications.

Sec. III—Financial qualifications.

Part I, Sec. IV-A—Ascertainment of community needs.

Part III, Sec. IV-A—Proposed programing.

Part V—Sec. IV-A—Proposed commercial practices.

Part VI, Sec. IV-A—General station policies and procedures.

Part VIII—General matters and final certification.

The Commission, in this instance, wants full disclosure on the individual or corporation desiring the license along with statements concerning the buyer's plans for meeting community needs, tastes and desires. It is necessary that the buyer conduct a survey of community leaders and the general public on a scale described in the license renewal section of this chapter. The fact that the current licensee may have conducted a similar survey only a few weeks or months earlier is of no concern to the Commission. A new survey indicating the buyer's knowledge of problems in the community must be conducted.

The buyer also must complete Sec. VI which deals with his equal employment opportunities program (see license renewal section).

Sale of stations held less than three years are subject to hearing except in case of death, hardship, or other mitigating circumstances beyond the licensee's control. Furthermore, public notice similar to that outlined in the license renewal section must be given in order that interested parties may object if they desire.

CRITICAL GUIDELINES AND RULES

Payola

The record companies' practice of "sweetening the DJ pot" came to light in the late 1950's and resulted in amendments to the Communications Act that prevent air personnel from virtually **all** associations with record manufacturers, distributors, and retailers. Payola, as the practice came to be known, simply is bribery and is a federal crime. Essentially, it meant disc jockeys would accept money or gifts in exchange for playing a record on the air. When the practice flourished, money was often stashed inside boxes of records delivered to the DJ's home. Other bribes came in the form of expensive record players, automobiles, household furnishings, and sums of cash reportedly in excess of $50,000. Payola is the acceptance of money, goods, or services as inducement to playing records or presenting other programing or announcements which would not otherwise be presented, or for playing records more often than they would otherwise be played. Payola can easily result from outside activities involving recording artists and recording companies of which the following are illustrative:

a. An announcer accepts money, food, payment on his car, transportation money, or any similar benefits in return for an understanding, express or implied, that he will play records over the radio station.

b. An announcer makes a recording for a company for a fee and royalties, with the understanding, express or implied, that the record will be played over the radio station.

d. An announcer participates in a show or dance at which recording artists appear. The artists agree to accept no fee, or less than they would ordinarily be paid, with the understanding, express or implied, that their records will be played over the radio station.

Plugola

Plugola is the making of a commercial announcement or references over a radio station, for something in which the announcer is personally interested, without reporting the recordings to management and without their being logged as commercial matter (CM). Examples of "plugola" are:

a. An announcer makes a recording with the understanding, express or implied, that he will push the record on the radio station. This is payola. Plugola develops when the announcer, on his own initiative, makes unusual "promos" for the record in an effort to increase his own royalties or to insure the popularity of the record so that he will be called upon to make other records in the future.

b. An announcer participates in outside activities, such as dances or shows. He makes announcements for those shows over the air, without telling management and without logging them as commercial matter, in order to increase his income at the shows or insure their success so that he will be called upon for other shows.

Announcer Affidavits

Many licensees require the filing of affidavits by all air personnel that they are not involved in payola schemes. This file of affidavits should be reviewed periodically to make certain that all program personnel, including program directors, announcers, disc jockeys, news directors, and part-time air personnel, are covered. The statements should be notarized. Good policy warns air personnel to be especially careful during the Christmas season about accepting gifts (except nominal ones costing under $10.00) from any record distributor, advertising agency, or other business concern.

RADIO STATION:_____

DATE:_____ NAME:_____

1. List on reverse side hereof the name of all corporations, companies, firms, governmental organizations, research organizations and educational or other institution in which you are serving as employee, officer, member, owner, trustee, director, expert, adviser, or consultant, with or without compensation.

2. Name all corporations, companies, firms, or other business enterprises in which you have any financial interest through the ownership of stock, stock options, bonds, securities, or other arrangements.

3. Do you now or have you ever personally, or on behalf of the station, accepted money or other consideration from anyone, other than the station, for broadcasting any information?

4. Describe the method of payment for services. (Use additional pages if needed.)

It is recognized that all attachments consitute an integral part of this response.

Signature:_____

Title:_____

Subscribed and sworn to before me this_____day of____ _____,

_____
Notary Public

My Commission expires:_____.

Fig. 32. Announcer Affidavit (1).

RADIO STATION:_____

DATE_____ NAME:_____

1. Do you now or have you ever personally, or on behalf of the station, accepted money or other consideration from anyone, including persons in the record or music publishing field, for playing records or broadcasting any other information?

2. To what extent do you engage or have any business interest in shows, dances, hops or outside business activities? (Explain on back of this page)

3. Describe the method of payment for services. (Use additional pages if needed).

4. Do you have an interest in or connection with record companies, retail record stores or music publishing companies? If the answer is in the affirmative, please list all such companies or stores detailing your interests in such ventures.

5. Have you ever required recording artists to appear at functions without pay (or at a rate lower than the artist would ordinarily command), with the implication that if they did not so appear, their records would not be played on the air?

It is recognized that all attachments constitute an integral part of this response.

Signature:_____

Title:_____

Subscribed and sworn to before me this_____day of_____,

_____
Notary Public

My Commission expires:_____

Fig. 33. Announcer Affidavit (2).

Any manager in doubt about a gift being "nominal" should contact the group's Washington attorney.

One policy states:

1. Since the Commission has indicated that it is important for each licensee to maintain continual supervision in order to prevent payola practices at his station, managers should make sure that new "payola" affidavits are executed by all station employees who have anything to do with programing, and that such affidavits are executed by station employees on a frequent and continuing basis.

2. If management becomes suspicious of the existence of payola practices, contact the Washington attorney immediately. Do not reject as unfounded any suspicion of payola which may come to management's attention, regardless of the source, without discussing it with the Washington attorney.

3. Management should require each station employee (who has anything to do with programing) to submit, in writing, a completed questionnaire which sets forth any and all **past** (last 6 months), **present,** and **future** outside employment or business interest, whether regular or sporadic. A new questionnaire should be completed at least every six months, in order that station management be continuously apprised of any possible conflict of interest which its employees may have. If the completed questionnaire should raise a question of conflict of interest with respect to any employee, contact the Washington attorney.

Double Billing

Double Billing is a practice whereby the station enters into a conspiracy to defraud. Section 73.124 of the Commission Rules specifically prohibits the practice. The section reads as follows:

"No licensee of a standard broadcast station shall knowingly issue to any local, regional or national advertiser, advertising agency, station representative, manufacturer, distributor, jobber, or any other party, any bill, invoice, affidavit or other document which contains false information concerning the amount actually charged by the licensee for the broadcast advertising for which such bill, invoice or affidavit or other document is issued, or which misrepresents the nature, content, or quality of such advertising. Licensees shall exercise reasonable diligence to see that their agents and employees do not issue any documents which would violate this section if issued by the licensee."

There are several methods of "double billing" that the student should be aware of:

1. Appliance retailer makes arrangements with distributor (jobber) to pay 50 percent of a radio advertising campaign. Retailer then makes arrangements with station to bill him "double" the actual amount of the advertising invoice. Double invoice is then submitted to distributor who reimburses retailer what the distributor thinks is half the cost of the campaign when the distributor, in fact, is paying the entire amount. Another device in this connection is to maintain the "card rate" on the phony invoice, but bill the retailer for twice the number of spots run.

2. In the heyday of double billing, some stations would bill the retailer on the national rate when actually the local rate was being charged.

3. Unscrupulous salesmen have stolen invoices from the station and entered into a conspiracy with a local retailer to collect co-op money from a distributor when no advertising was run! (The licensee may protect himself from this scheme by numbering invoices and requiring the accounting department to account for each number.)

Forfeitures (fines)

The 1960 amendment to the Communications Act of 1934 (PL 86-752) permits the FCC to levy fines on licensees for "willful and repeated" violations of the Commissions' Rules or of the Act. Commission Rules, adopted early in 1961, are contained in Section 10.503. The Commission is enpowered to recover $1,000 for each day during which an offense (rule violation) occurs. No fine, however, may exceed $10,000.

Since passage of the 1960 amendment, the Commission has exercised its new power more and more each year. In 1964, for example, the FCC issued "notices of apparent liability" to thirteen stations. Thirty-eight stations received such notices in 1965, and the figure rose to 78 in 1966. Some of the more common reasons behind the "notices of apparent liability" are:

1. Operating without a properly licensed operator

2. Violation of logging requirements

3. Failure to broadcast identification of the sponsors of sponsored programs or announcements

4. Failure to file ownership or financial reports

5. Broadcast of lottery information

6. Excessive deviation from assigned frequency.

7. Failure to give proper station identification

8. Unauthorized transfer of control

9. Failure to maintain tower lights.

10. Broadcasting with excessive power

11. Rebroadcast of programs of another station without obtaining authority of the originating station

12. Rigged contests

13. Failure to change from "day"to "night" pattern at proper time

There are at least three criteria by which the Commission determines the size of the fine to be levied against the offending station. These are (1) the past broadcast record of the licensee, including the number of prior offenses, (2) the financial condition of the station, and (3) the importance of the station in its market. (Source: Interpreting FCC Broadcast Rules & Regulations, Vol. 2, by the editors of BM-E Magazine, published by TAB BOOKS.)

In mid-1966, the FCC decided to issue a forfeiture schedule for those licensees who were late in filing renewal applications. The Commission requires that applications for licensee renewals be at the Commission office ninety days prior to expiration of the current license. The forfeiture schedule calls for a $25.00 fine for the first through the fifteenth day of delinquency, $100.00 for the sixteenth through the sixtieth day, and $200.00 for the sixty-first through the ninetieth day. Section 0.218 of the Commission's rules authorizes the Broadcast Bureau to issue notices of apparent liability in amounts not in excess of $250.00 under Section 503 (b) of the Communications Act. Prior to this delegation of authority, each forfeiture was reviewed by the Commissioners. Licensees fined under Commission rules are entitled to appeal the decision in a federal district court.

Duopoly

The Commission's rule on duopoly decrees that one licensee may not have two similar facilities serving basically the same area. This means two AM's, two FM's, etc. In AM, a duopoly is said to exist if there is common ownership of two stations whose 1 mv-m (micromillivolt) contours overlap (73.183). In FM, the rule is the same. In TV, there may not be an overlap of the Grade B contours. No licensee may own more than 7 AM's, 7 FM's, and 7 TV's. At least two of the TV facilities must be in UHF.

Sponsor Identification

Section 317 (a) (1) of the Communications Act requires that the true identity of program sponsors be revealed. The section reads:

"All matter broadcast by any radio station for which any money, service or other valuable consideration is directly or indirectly paid, or promised to or changed or accepted by, the station so broadcasting, from any person, shall, at the time the same is so broadcast, be announced as paid for or furnished, as the case may be, by such persons. **Provided**, that service or other consideration shall not include any service or property furnished without charge or at a nominal charge for use on, or in connection with, a broadcast unless it is so furnished in consideration for an identification in a broadcast of any person, product, service, trademark, or brand name beyond an identification which is reasonably related to the use of such service or property on the broadcast."

In the case of commercials, an announcement must state the sponsor's corporate or trade name, or the name of the sponsor's product, when it is clear that the mention of the name of the product constitutes a sponsorship identification. The rules do not apply to **individuals** who sponsor want ads or classified ads. They do apply to business enterprises sponsoring such ads.

Paragraph 73.119 of Commission R&R spells out in considerable detail the licensee's obligations with reference to sponsor identification. Clearly, the Commission intends that no deception be practiced over the air waves. The problem usually lies not with the commercial advertiser, but with the sponsors of public affairs and political programing. Some stations use the political time contract, which specifies the names and organizations of sponsors, on public affairs as well as political programs and announcements.

Teasers

Anytime material is aired that relates to a paid schedule, the sponsor must be identified. This rule killed the old station and advertiser practice of running **teasers**, e.g., provocative one-liners that alluded to an upcoming event. For example, "Friday will be a big day in your life, because a big event is scheduled for that day." If the teaser referred to the grand opening of a new furniture store, it violated the Act and Commission R&R, because the name of the furniture store was not included. The station sales manager may have agreed to give the teasers to the advertiser as a bonus for purchasing a schedule of announcements. But because the bonus teaser campaign is directly related to a paid campaign, sponsor identification must be made. Newspapers run teasers regularly and legally, but radio stations may not do so.

Libel and Slander

There has always been some confusion, particularly on the part of lay people, about the differences between libel and slander. Libel has been thought of as something **written**, while slander was regarded as something **spoken**. Most states, however, classify broadcast matter among those subject to the libel laws. Many broadcasters have been faced with a charged of libel or slander. It is possible to purchase insurance for protection against libel suits. News personnel and editorial writers are the most vulnerable, as they are the staffers assigned to report, interpret, and comment on news events.

If a statement made over a radio station is to be proved libelous, it must be established that the statement was untruthful and was calculated to damage an identifiable person's reputation. The person so injured need not be necessarily identified by name; he may also be identified by description. Proof that the truth was spoken is the best defense against a libel suit. However, the truth may be a poor defense if the injured party can prove maliciousness.

License Revocations

There is nothing **permanent** about a broadcaster's license to operate a radio station. The Commission has the authority to revoke the license or deny its renewal. Such action doesn't usually have the same effect as being arrested by a policeman, but the results can be as traumatic. Paragraph 1.89 of the Rules provide generally that any licensee who appears to have violated any provision of the Communications Act or of Commission Rules shall be served with a written notice calling the facts to his attention and requesting a statement concerning the matter. The licensee is expected to file a written reply to the notice of violation within ten days of receipt, stating what has been done to correct the situation complained of and the action that has been taken to prevent its recurrence. The problem lies not necessarily in receiving a notice of violation, which happens to licensees frequently. Expensive litigation develops when the licensee **ignores** such notices, or lies to the Commission about how the problem was solved or action taken to prevent recurrence. As traffic cops learn to spot habitual speeders, Commission inspectors keep their eyes on repeat violaters of FCC Rules and the Communications Act. After several violations of a similar nature, the licensee may have to "show cause" why his license should not be revoked. Repeated violations often become significant issues at license renewal time, or when an operator attempts to purchase another facility or expand an existing one. The licensee may get away with a few violations, so long as they are of a different nature. He may even get away with two or three violations of a similar nature, but ultimately **he will receive** the "show cause" order or he will be ordered into a hearing at the time his application for license renewal is received.

Revocation and-or cease and desist proceedings are outlined in Paragraphs 1.91 and 1.92 of the Rules.

While the Commission has failed to renew many licenses over the years, one of the most prominent involved the Charlie Walker Case. The Commission **denied** WDKD's application for license renewal, and the disc jockey involved was found guilty of violating Section 1464 of the Criminal Code. The Commission's decision was upheld by the Court of Appeals and the Supreme Court refused to review the case.

The questions in the case were:

1. Did licensee misrepresent facts or lack candor in representing facts to the Commission?

2. Did applicant maintain adequate control and supervision over program material during the period of his most recent license renewal?

3. Did licensee, particularly during the period Janualy 1 - April 30, 1961, permit material to be broadcast that was coarse, vulgar, suggestive, and susceptible of indecent double meaning?

4. Has the programing of licensee's station met the needs of the population served during the station's most recent license renewal period?

The case is prime evidence that the Commission **can** and **will** force the licensee to reply to complaints, not only from FCC inspectors, but also from listeners. If the reply is not satisfactory or does not resolve the problem as the Commission sees it, the licensee is subject to having his license revoked or having it denied when it next is up for renewal.

REPORTS TO BE FILED WITH THE FCC

In the Commission's effort to keep abreast of how the licensee is operating the radio station, certain periodic reports are required. These include:

1. Annual Financial Report
2. Political Reports
3. Ownership Reports
4. Annual Employment Report
5. Copies of Network Contracts
6. Copies of Brokerage Contracts
7. Mortgages and Loan Agreements, copies of
8. Management Contracts, copies of
9. Copies of Part-time Engineer Agreements
10. Annual Proof of Performance

Considerable other material is required to be filed with the Commission, and most of this relates to CP applications and applications for license renewals. Paragraphs 1.611, 1.615, and

1.613 of the Commission Rules specify the documents that must be on file at FCC offices in Washington.

Financial Report—Must be filed annually, on or before April 1, on FCC Form 324.

Ownership Report—Must be filed with license renewal applications on FCC Form 323. An important exception is that a supplemental Ownership Report must be filed within 30 days after any change occurs in the information required by the report from that previously reported.

Political Report—Must be filed no later than November 30 following receipt of FCC Form 302 which is mailed to all licensees during primary and general election campaign years. The report must include all information regarding appearances on the station by candidates and-or their supporters. All appearances, except newscasts, must be included, whether or not exempt from Sec. 315.

Annual Employment Report—Must be filed annually on or before May 31 on FCC Form 395. Stations with five or fewer full-time employees need not file this report.

Network Contracts—Agreements made with national, regional, or special networks must be filed with the Commission immediately after such agreements are consummated.

Brokerage Contracts—When agreements are made to sell time to an individual or organization for re-sale, the agreement must immediately be filed with the Commission.

Mortgages and Loan Agreements—Any such agreement that restricts the licensee's freedom of operation, such as those affecting voting rights, must be filed with the Commission.

Management Contracts—Agreements that call for an individual to share profits **and** losses must be filed with the Commission.

Part-time Engineer Contracts—Must be filed with nearest FCC Field office as well as with FCC offices in Washington.

Proof of Performance—Required annually under Part 3, Sections 3.47 and 3.254 of Commission R&R.

The perhaps oversimplification of the above requirements should not delude the student into a lethargic attitude toward the requirements. Failure to file documents in a complete and timely manner can result in heavy forfeitures, hearings, renewal applications denied, or license revocation. With regard to the **Ownership Report**, when control of a licensee corporation changes, prior Commission approval must be obtained. There are exceptions, contained in Paragraph 1.613, but generally when corporation officers even suspect that a stock transaction will transfer control of the station from one person or group to another person or group, **prior Commission approval must be obtained**. One of the more common causes of Commission forfeitures is **unauthorized transfer of control**. To avoid such fines, legal advice usually is absolutely essential, preferably from a communications attorney or law firm.

PENAL PROVISIONS

Sec. 501 of the Communications Act reads as follows:

"Any person who willfully and knowingly does or causes or suffers to be done any act, matter, or thing, in this Act prohibited or declared to be unlawful, or who willfully or knowingly omits or fails to do any act, matter, or thing in this Act required to be done, or willfully and knowingly causes or suffers such omission or failure, shall, upon conviction thereof, be punished for such offense, for which no penalty (other than a forfeiture) is provided in this Act, by a fine of not more than $10,000 or by imprisonment for a term not exceeding one year, or both; except that any person, having been once convicted of an offense punishable under this section, who is subsequently convicted of violating any provision of this Act punishable under this section, shall be punished by a fine of not more than $10,000 or by imprisonment for a term not exceeding two years, or both."

Section 502 states:

"Any person who willfully and knowingly violates any rule, regulation, or condition made or imposed by the Commission under authority of this Act, or any rule, regulation, restriction, or condition made or imposed by any international radio or wire communications treaty or convention, or regulations annexed thereto, to which the United States is or may hereafter become a party, shall, in addition to any other penalties provided by law, be punished, upon conviction thereof, by a fine of not more than $500 for each and every day during which such offense occurs.''

Conclusion

A colleague commented that the work deals so extensively with the hardships and regulations of radio broadcasting that it may tend to discourage students from entering the industry. The broadcast field is involved and difficult; and this text is intended to provide students with the underpinnings necessary for survival and success. Contrary to the impression left by the rash of rules, regulations, guidelines, raised eyebrows, do's and don'ts, broadcasting is a deeply satisfying and rewarding profession. The business is crammed with genius, industry, and progress. Its people indeed **are different** from those of other fields. They live in fishbowls and like it, thrive on it! Broadcast **employees** know and do single tasks within a station. Broadcast **professionals** know the whole story and seek continually to update and improve themselves, much as doctors, lawyers, architects, and engineers. A general practitioner in the medical field isn't really a professional if he can't mend everything from a ruptured appendix to a skin rash. And a broadcaster isn't really professional unless he can perform every job from DJ to salesman to General Manager. The field grows and beckons to the imaginative, the innovative, and the energetic. Broadcasting offers much and extracts an awesome toll from those who seek high pay and short hours. It can be a way of life for the student who wants to become a professional and no life at all for the individual looking for easy pickings.

Glossary

ADI   Area of Dominant Influence

AQH   Average Quarter Hour

ARB   American Research Bureau

ASCAP   American Society of Composers, Artists, and Performers

Account   Advertiser

Account Switching   Swapping of accounts within a sales force

Actuality   News report from the scene

Adjacencies   Commercial time immediately before or after a program.

Affidavit of Performance   Station's guarantee that time ran as invoiced.

Affirmative Action   Action taken on station initiative

Agency Trip   Management visit to major market agencies

Aging Sheet   Condition of receivables, from current to 90 days and over

Air Check   Recording of portion of radio show

Applicant   Anyone applying to FCC for anything

Audience Demographics   Breakdown of audience by sex and age

Audience Survey   Study of radio listening in given area

Avails   Commercial time available on station

BMI   Broadcast Music, Inc.

BRI   Brand Rating Index

Barter   Trade or sale of time for resale

Bed   Instrumental portion of singing jingle and-or background music in commercial

Billboarding   Frequent promotion of upcoming or running event

Billing, Gross   Commissionable billing figure

Billing, Net   Non-commissionable billing figure

Block   In programing, where different shows are "blocked out" on log

Bonus Spot   Free commercial matter given in connection with paid schedule

Buy   When account or agency "buys" time on station

Buying by the Numbers   When time buyer buys strictly on results of surveys

CP   Construction Permit

CPM   Cost per Thousand persons reached

C&W   Country & Western

Call-In When account or agency calls station for sales service

Call Letters FCC designations for station identification

Canned Prerecorded

Carbon Mike Microphone that gives effect of telephone recording

Card Rate Card

Cart Endless tape cartridge

Cassette Reel-to-Reel cartridge

Citation FCC's language heading up complaint against licensee

City Grade Signal Interference-free broadcast signal

Client Used interchangeably with "account"

Cold Call Sales call made without appointment

Combo Man Announcer who also keeps operating log

Commercial Bed Background music for commercial

Community Survey Study of community needs

Contemporary Format Format using pop (Rock'n Roll) music

Contingency Budget Money held in reserve by client or agency for special promotions or rate increases

Console Control Board (mixer)

Contour Lines Mathematical estimates of station geographic coverage

Control Room Usually, main or primary source of station programing

Control Sheet Form used in traffic to insure accuracy in making up program log

Co-op Money from manufacturer on distributor providing part-payment for time purchased by retailer

Coverage Map Map indicating by contour lines a station's geographic coverage

Cue A signal given by one person to another that he's "on the air." Also the positioning of a stylus on a record at a point where the record may be started without "wowing" or dead air

Cume Survey term used to mean unduplicated audience

Cut-Ins Material, such as mobile news report, inserted in basic program

DJ Disc Jockey

Daypart Survey term meaning 6a-10a, 10a-3p, 3p-7p, 7p-12 midnight

Daytimer Station authorized to operate during daylight hours only

Deal Usually indicates rate-cutting action with specific account

Discrepancy Sheet Sheet attached to back of program log on which DJ makes notes regarding equipment failure and program material missed

Dog Station Poor facility, low ratings, low billing

Drive Time Morning and afternoon period when listeners are driving to and from work. Exact time varies from market to market

Duopoly When licensee operates two like stations whose signals overlap

ERP Effective Radiated Power

ET Electrical Transcription (archaic word for recording)

Earned Rates Rates earned from volume purchases

Ethnic Format Format aimed at specific ethnic group, such as Negro, German, Spanish

Frequency Discount Discount on rates given for volume purchases

GRP Gross Rating Points

Gain Volume given to console output

Gimmick Unorthodox promotion

Group Group of stations under common ownership

HUR Survey term meaning Homes Using Radio

Hiatus When advertisers break schedule with intention of returning to air at specific time

Hit Sheet List of currently popular records

House Account Handled by management, usually, with no sales commission paid

Hypoing Action taken by station to increase audience during survey period

IBEW International Brotherhood of Electrical Workers

IPS Inches Per Second

Impact Schedule Large number of announcements used in short period of time

Inspector, C&C Inspector from Complaints & Compliance Division of FCC who usually visits station as a result of a complaint

Inspector, Field FCC employee who conducts routine inspection of station's technical performance

Intro Matter used to introduce a program

Jingle Musical material, usually associated with commercials

License Instrument of authorization, related either to a station or an individual

Market Term used to describe station's sales area

Media Multiples of radio stations, television station, newspapers

Merchandising Extra service provided by station to client

Middle Management Program Directors, News Directors, Sales Managers

Monitor Recorded or written report on station programing

Moonlighting Employees who have jobs outside regular job

MOR Music Middle-of-the-road, usually a type of music that is neither contemporary nor old

Multi-Station Market Market which is served by more than one local station

Music Policy Written policy stating methods used to select station music

NAB National Association of Broadcasters

Network A group of stations linked together to broadcast common programing

Non-Directional Technical term indicating that station uses single antenna and is not required to protect other stations on same frequency except in terms of power output

Off-the-Card Selling by rates not published

One-Card System Station that uses one rate card for both national and local accounts

Open Rate Station's highest one minute rate

Outage Technical term meaning "off the air"

Outro Matter used to end program

PA Public Affairs

PI Per Inquiry Advertising

PS Public Service

PSA Public Service Announcement

PUR Survey term meaning Persons Using Radio

Package Plan Sales plan in which advertiser is offered a fixed spot program (ROS, TAP)

Permitee Holder of a Construction Permit

Pirating Stealing employees from competitive stations

Pitch Sales presentation

Playlist List specifying music to be played by announcer

Pot Volume control on console

Projection Sheet Chart in which advertising schedules and contracts are plotted to indicate future revenues

Promo Announcement promoting upcoming station event

Promotion, Sales Promotion designed to make money

Promotion, Station Promotion designed to build audience

Protected Account List List of advertisers-agencies assigned to specific salesman

RAB Radio Advertising Bureau

ROS Run Of Schedule

R&B Rhythm and Blues

Rating Survey figure indicating percentage of total market reached by given station

Reach Number of different persons "reached" by a station in a week

Remote Program originating outside the station

Rep Usually refers to a station's national sales representative

SCA Sub-Carrier Authorization

SESAC Society of European Singers, Artists, and Composers

SMSA Standard Metropolitan Statistical Area

SRDS Standard Rate and Data Service

Sales Aid Material used by salesman, such as surveys, to aid in presenting station to advertiser

Segue Unbroken phasing of one piece of program material into another

Service Area Station's primary listening area

Shelf Talker Sales term meaning printed point of sale sign

Short Flights Schedule of announcements run in short period of time in "flights" or stages

Short Rate Earned rate paid by advertiser who fails to fulfill contract

Simulcast Usually refers to program carried by commonly owned AM & FM stations

Sold Out When commercial matter count has reached amount specified in application for license

Soul Format Refers to black oriented programing

Spec Spot Spot prepared on a speculative basis

Station Broker Person or firm that assists in buying and selling broadcast stations

Strike Application Application filed on top of another application for license renewal or a construction permit

Success Story Letter from advertiser whose schedule on station produced good results

Switch Pitch Sales effort to move an account from one station to another

TAP Total Audience Plan

Tape Insert Usually an actuality inserted in a newscast

Target Advertiser's specific market

Ticket Operator or engineer license

Trade Mailing Letters to specific advertiser's group of retailers

Trade Out Exchange of time for merchandise

Trafficking Purchasing, upgrading, and immediate resale of a station

Woodshed To rehearse copy before airing or recording

Index

A

B

C